Intervening in Children's Lives

Intervening in Children's Lives

An Ecological, Family-Centered Approach
to Mental Health Care

Thomas J. Dishion and Elizabeth A. Stormshak

American Psychological Association • Washington, DC

Published by
American Psychological Association
750 First Street, NE
Washington, DC 20002
www.apa.org

To order
APA Order Department
P.O. Box 92984
Washington, DC 20090-2984
Tel: (800) 374-2721
Direct: (202) 336-5510
Fax: (202) 336-5502
TDD/TTY: (202) 336-6123
Online: www.apa.org/books/
E-mail: order@apa.org

In the U.K., Europe, Africa, and the Middle East, copies may be ordered from
American Psychological Association
3 Henrietta Street
Covent Garden, London
WC2E 8LU England

Typeset in Goudy by World Composition Services, Inc., Sterling, VA

Printer: Book-Mart Press, Inc., North Bergen, NJ
Cover Designer: Naylor Design, Washington, DC
Technical/Production Editor: Pamela McElroy

Library of Congress Cataloging-in-Publication Data

Dishion, Thomas J., 1954-
    Intervening in children's lives : an ecological, family-centered approach to mental health care / by Thomas J. Dishion and Elizabeth A. Stormshak.—1st ed.
        p. cm.
    Includes bibliographical references and index.
    ISBN-13: 978-1-59147-428-9
    ISBN-10: 1-59147-428-0
    1. Child mental health services. 2. Family psychotherapy. 3. Children—Mental health. I. Stormshak, Elizabeth A. II. Title.
    RJ111.D57 2006
    618.92'89—dc22   2005037872

British Library Cataloguing-in-Publication Data
A CIP record is available from the British Library.

Printed in the United States of America
First Edition

We dedicate this volume to Joan McCord for her inspiration as a behavioral science intellectual and for her honesty and integrity in conducting research on the effectiveness of interventions for youth.

IMPORTANT NOTICE

This book is intended to present a clinical model for working with children, adolescents, and their families. All case illustrations are fictional, and any similarity to actual persons or situations is coincidental and unintended by the authors. Because ethical, clinical, and legal issues are highly fact-specific, the book's guidance is not meant to be a substitute for obtaining relevant consultation prior to making decisions regarding particular circumstances. It is important for readers to understand that the views expressed in this book are those of the authors and not necessarily those of the American Psychological Association (APA), the APA Ethics Committee, or any other APA group. They do not create APA standards or guidelines. Any discussion herein by the authors concerning ethics should not be understood or relied on as an official interpretation of the APA Ethics Code. Only the APA Ethics Committee can issue authoritative interpretations of the Code.

CONTENTS

Acknowledgments ix

Chapter 1.   Child and Family Intervention From an
              Ecological Perspective: Introduction 3

I. Conceptual Overview 13

Chapter 2.   The Ecology of Development and Change 15

Chapter 3.   Family and Peer Social Interaction 31

Chapter 4.   The Ecological Family Intervention and
              Therapy Model 49

II. The Family Check-Up 69

Chapter 5.   Initial Contacts That Establish a Collaborative Set 71

Chapter 6.   Ecological Assessment 91

Chapter 7.   Mobilizing Change With the Family Check-Up 109

III. Intervention Strategies 123

Chapter 8.   Brief Parenting Interventions 125

Chapter 9.   Interventions With Children and Adolescents 141

Chapter 10.   Family Management Therapy 163

Chapter 11.   Parent Intervention Groups 183

Chapter 12.   Child and Adolescent Intervention Groups 201

IV. Professional and Ethical Considerations **217**

Chapter 13.　The Ecology of the Child and Family Therapist 219

Chapter 14.　Ethical and Professional Standards in Child
and Family Interventions 241

References 265

Author Index 297

Subject Index 305

About the Authors 319

ACKNOWLEDGMENTS

The work in this volume emerged from 10 years of collaboration between the two authors. During that time we had the unusual opportunity of linking two doctoral training programs, one in counseling and the other in clinical psychology. Each program was based in a separate college at the University of Oregon—one in the College of Education and the latter in the College of Arts and Sciences. The leadership at the University of Oregon made it possible for both programs to simultaneously offer the same child and family practicum, advanced clinical training for doctoral students. Coordinating the two yearlong doctoral training seminars allowed us to articulate the ecological approach described in this volume as a general, empirically supported child and family intervention strategy and to refine this model with ongoing feedback from families and therapists. For this opportunity we appreciate the leadership support provided by Robert Mauro in the Department of Psychology and Benedict McWhirter and Ellen McWhirter in the Department of Counseling Psychology, all at the University of Oregon. Also, we appreciate the support of Thomas Dyke, acting vice president of Research and Graduate Studies at the University of Oregon in 1999, who supported the founding of the Child and Family Center in 2000 and the creation of a family university-based clinic located within the community. Without the leadership and support of these individuals, we would not have had the opportunity to collaboratively think about and discuss how diverse, empirically supported intervention paradigms could be integrated to improve mental health services for children and families.

We want to acknowledge the many doctoral students in counseling, clinical, and school psychology at the University of Oregon, with whom we have had the rewarding opportunity to learn and work.

We appreciate the remarkable contributions of our colleagues at the Child and Family Center, specifically Alison Boyd-Ball, Bernadette Bullock, Arin Connell, and Kate Kavanagh, as well as other colleagues in the Oregon community, including Tony Biglan, Marion Forgatch, Carol Metzler, and Jerry Patterson. All have participated in numerous informal seminars during which many of the ideas and strategies presented in this volume were discussed and enriched, and all have served as valuable sources of inspiration for our own work.

We appreciate the careful editorial support provided by Cheryl Mikkola in preparation of this work.

Finally, we must acknowledge the continuous financial support provided by the National Institute of Drug Abuse (NIDA), which since 1988 has played a tremendous role in making this work possible. The peer-reviewed funding system of the National Institutes of Health is without a doubt the foundation of the innovations in intervention science observed during the past 50 years. We especially appreciate the NIDA Division of Epidemiology, Services, and Prevention Research. In the early 1990s NIDA supported a shift toward support for family-centered intervention and prevention strategies, and this shift directly led to the approach outlined in this book. Specifically, we thank Aria Crump, Elizabeth Robertson, and Zili Sloboda for their leadership and guidance in the process of seeking and obtaining support for research.

Intervening in
Children's Lives

1

CHILD AND FAMILY INTERVENTION FROM AN ECOLOGICAL PERSPECTIVE: INTRODUCTION

This volume describes an ecological approach to child and family intervention designed to improve the effectiveness and efficiency of both treatment and prevention services. The approach is uniquely suited to the needs of children and adolescents presenting with mental health difficulties in which problem behavior is a core component. This chapter provides an overview and rationale for the ecological approach as it applies to the unique needs and contexts of children and adolescents.

THE NEED FOR A NEW MODEL

Interventions for children and adolescents are often derived from adult clinical models, emphasizing change at the individual level (Kazdin, 1995). Yet adult-derived models may not be adequate for three major reasons. First, adult clinical models tend to underemphasize developmental variation: The intervention strategy used for a 20-year-old would also be used for a 50-year-old. In contrast, understanding developmental norms and the developmental status of a child or adolescent is critical to being an effective child- and family-focused clinician. There is significant developmental change from childhood through adolescence, which has implications for the viability of

3

intervention strategies. Therefore, effective interventions for children and families must be developmentally sensitive and appropriate. Second, child and adolescent mental health issues are embedded within family relationships and amplified by peer and sibling relationships. Interventions that do not address these dynamics, especially those within the parent–child relationship, are less likely to be effective and long-lasting (Kazdin, 2002). Last, children and adolescents are most often referred by their parents, who tend to have primary concerns about problem behavior. Problem behavior may be as simple as not cooperating with parents, or as complicated and emotional as stealing, lying, staying out all night, or purging. Furthermore, children and parents often disagree about the core problem to be addressed in treatment, which leads to confusion about who is the target of the treatment (Hawley & Weisz, 2003). The central role of problem behavior for the majority of referred children and adolescents suggests the need to mobilize and support caregiver strategies for behavior management, in addition to other potential intervention strategies.

Because a vast majority of children who require mental health services present with behavior problems and emotional distress (depression, anxiety, etc.), an overarching framework is needed to guide the selection of interventions addressing the child in context. In an ecological view of children with problem behavior and emotional distress, these symptoms are seen as being influenced by the child's daily interactions with caregivers, siblings, peers, and teachers (e.g., Dishion, 2000; Granic & Lamey, 2002; Wright, Zakriski, & Drinkwater, 1999). Daily interactions with significant others and motivation to change are influenced by community dynamics and resources (Barker, 1960). An ecological approach to child and family intervention requires attention to the features of the environment as well as to the child to reduce and eliminate problem behavior and emotional distress. An ecological approach considers the environment as a system (Bronfenbrenner, 1979, 1989), and, therefore, interventions often involve the coordination of multiple environments (e.g., home–school, divorced parents, family–peer). Inspired by the emphasis on integrating interventions that potentially target individual children, families, and multiple systems affecting children, we developed an ecological approach to family intervention and treatment, called EcoFIT.

FEATURES OF THE EcoFIT MODEL

The EcoFIT model is an empirically based, assessment-driven, family-centered intervention. It can be delivered in mental health clinics or community settings such as schools. The model has six unique features that set it apart from other child and family intervention models.

Empirically Based

The EcoFIT intervention is based on an empirical model of child and adolescent psychopathology in general and behavior problems in particular (e.g., Dishion & Patterson, 2006; Patterson, Reid, & Dishion, 1992). An empirical model involves the integration of two scientific literatures: one on empirically supported interventions and another on basic research on the development of psychopathology in children and adolescents (Achenbach, 1982; Cicchetti, 1993; Sroufe & Rutter, 1984). Intervention science researchers benefit from understanding the causes of problem behavior and mental health difficulties and from knowing which interventions are likely to prevent or reduce mental health problems. Developmental models have been applied to understanding childhood trauma and childhood psychosis (e.g., Pynoos, Steinberg, & Wraith, 1995; Volkmar, Becker, King, & McGlashan, 1995). Furthermore, longitudinal data on the developmental dynamics and ecological circumstances correlated with severe child mental health problems are critical to the design of effective prevention and treatment programs (P. A. Fisher & Stormshak, 2000).

Empirical models of the development of child and adolescent mental health problems benefit from knowledge of interventions that are effective in reducing problem behavior and emotional distress. In fact, intervention trials can be seen as a test of a developmental model of childhood disorder (Dishion & Patterson, 1999; Forgatch, 1991). Although the establishment of empirically supported interventions for children and families is a relatively recent development, general principles can be derived to guide intervention decisions. Integrating the empirical literature on scientifically supported interventions with the literature on ineffective or harmful interventions for children and adolescents results in the following two conclusions (see Figure 1.1). First, interventions that mobilize adult caregivers, support skillful behavior management practices, and promote youth self-regulation tend to produce positive effects on reducing behavior problems and emotional distress (e.g., anxiety and depression; Kazdin & Weisz, 2003). Interventions that aggregate youth without the appropriate level of supervision and structure or attempt to scare youth out of misbehavior are less effective or, in some conditions, iatrogenic (Dishion & Dodge, 2005).

There is an important synergism between research on the causes of psychopathology and the literature on intervention effectiveness (Cicchetti & Toth, 1992; Dishion & Patterson, 1999). As discussed in this volume, etiological models have a very practical function. For example, longitudinal studies on the etiology of problem behavior repeatedly indicate that parenting practices in general, and family management in particular, are highly correlated with the extent of child and adolescent problem behavior (e.g., Loeber & Dishion, 1983). As discussed earlier, interventions that support family

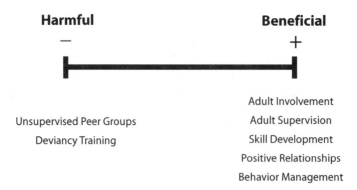

Potentially

Harmful   **Beneficial**

Unsupervised Peer Groups	Adult Involvement
Deviancy Training	Adult Supervision
	Skill Development
	Positive Relationships
	Behavior Management

Figure 1.1. A broad overview of intervention outcome literature on child and adolescent problem behavior.

management practices tend to both prevent and effectively treat child and adolescent problem behavior (Spoth, Kavanagh, & Dishion, 2002). Therefore, both intervention outcome and developmental literatures support the idea that family management is central to a model guiding an ecological intervention with children and families.

Family-Centered

Thus, in an ecological approach, child and family interventions are family centered. As much as possible, interventions with children and adolescents attempt to engage caregivers to lead the change process. Although interventions may target multiple systems such as schools and families, we assume that change will be more enduring if caregivers are successfully engaged in the process of attempting to change their own interactions with the child, and if they are made more aware of their child's behavioral and emotional needs. Empirical support for this family-centered approach to child and adolescent interventions is substantial. There is also strong support in the literature for family-centered strategies that incorporate effective child and adolescent mental health treatments (e.g., Borduin & Henggeler, 1990; Dishion & Patterson, 1992; Eddy & Chamberlain, 2000; Henggeler, Schoenwald, Borduin, Rowland, & Cunningham, 1998; Kazdin, 2003; Liddle, 1999; Patterson, 1974; Sanders, 1999; Szapocznik & Kurtines, 1993; Webster-Stratton, 1990) and prevention programs (e.g., Brody, McBride Murry, Kim, & Brown, 2002; Bugental et al., 2002; Conduct Problems Prevention Research Group, 2002; Forgatch & DeGarmo, 1999; Hawkins et al., 1992; Kumpfer, Molgaard, & Spoth, 1996; O'Donnell, Hawkins,

Catalano, Abbott, & Day, 1995; Olds et al., 1997; Spoth et al., 1998; Staton et al., 2004).

Although the majority of research on family-centered interventions has focused on disruptive behavior problems, a growing body of literature shows that family-centered approaches to treatment are effective with a wide range of mental health problems across development. Family-centered interventions have proven to be instrumental in improving adjustment among young adults with a history of schizophrenia. Efforts to improve the family management practices of caregivers of adults with a history of schizophrenia have reduced the amount of expressed emotion (critical, negative emotional dynamics) that is associated with increased likelihood of psychotic relapse (Falloon et al., 1985). Family-based approaches are also effective and central to the treatment of eating disorders in adolescent females (e.g., Robin, 2003). Furthermore, recent years have seen a trend toward a parent focus for interventions with children who present with emotional distress, such as anxiety and depression (Barmish & Kendall, 2005). Although the findings are promising, there remains a need to better understand the unique dynamics of parent–child interactions that undermine children's emotional adjustment and to specifically address these issues in prevention and treatment programs.

Family-centered interventions have undergone a critical shift in the past 20 years, from a treatment model that is delivered to clients in clinic settings to an intervention model involving proactive recruitment of parents to engage in interventions in community settings such as schools (Stormshak, Dishion, Light, & Yasui, 2005). The proactive approach was designed specifically to increase the potential public health impact of child and family interventions. If an intervention is designed in settings such as public schools, then service delivery systems that effectively engage children and families most at risk could potentially improve the mental health of a larger group of children (Biglan & Taylor, 2000). The approach described in this volume is potentially applicable to implementation within several service settings, including preschools, welfare family service settings (Shaw, Dishion, Supplee, Gardner, & Arnds, in press), and public school settings (Dishion & Kavanagh, 2003).

At times, in work with adolescents, it is difficult if not impossible to identify a caregiver with whom to work. Parents of adolescents are less likely than parents of younger children to engage in treatment and prevention services (Dishion & Patterson, 1993). Yet even under these circumstances, a family-centered approach is viable and, in fact, essential (Szapozcnik & Williams, 2000). An ecological approach addresses caregiver motivation to engage in interventions (Szapocznik et al., 1988), emphasizes brief, strategic interventions that involve caregivers, and presses to incorporate family issues into individual work with children and adolescents.

Assessment-Driven

An ecological approach to intervention is also assessment driven. Approaches to child and family intervention are usually eclectic, which means that the therapist decides, on the basis of clinical judgment, what intervention to use with a specific client. The selection is often made on the basis of the therapist's training and preferences as well as the perceived needs of the client. In the real world of service delivery, with limited resources, the needs of the client are often assessed on the basis of self-reports from the caregiver and the child. Thus, initial, unstructured clinical interviews are an important source of information underlying decision making (Othmer & Othmer, 1994).

In an ecological approach, however, intervention decisions are made on the basis of a comprehensive, objective, and psychological assessment of the child, family, and other relevant environments. As we discuss later, direct observations of family interaction are essential to assessments. An ecological assessment can complement clinical impressions and increase the reliability and validity of the case conceptualization that underlies clinical judgment and, therefore, the design of an effective intervention.

Social Interactions Addressed

Another feature of an ecological approach to intervention is its emphasis on addressing social interactions of children and adolescents with families and peers. Family systems theorists focus on changing unconscious parent–child interaction patterns to improve children's behavior problems and emotional well-being (Haley, 1971; Minuchin & Fishman, 1981; Watzlawick, Weakland, & Fisch, 1974). Developmental science has made tremendous progress during the past 30 years in identifying and measuring more precisely the functional dynamics of family and peer relationships that amplify psychopathology in children and adolescents (Dishion & Patterson, 2006). In particular, coercive parent–child interactions are related to antisocial behavior (e.g., Patterson, Reid, & Dishion, 1992) and targeting these interactions reduces problem behavior (Dishion, Patterson, & Kavanagh, 1992; Forgatch, 1991; Forgatch & DeGarmo, 2002). In addition, a process of deviancy training among peers covaries with increases in problem behavior in children (Snyder et al., 2005) and adolescents (Dishion, Nelson, & Yasui, 2005) and is prognostic of failed interventions that aggregate peers at high risk (Dishion, Poulin, & Burraston, 2001). Recent work examined the role of family interactions and adolescent depression, with the aim of targeting these family interactions in interventions to reduce adolescent depression (Connell & Dishion, 2006; Sheeber, Hyman, & Davis, 2001). From an ecological perspective, individual adjustment is embedded within relationship dynamics, and so interventions to improve mental health must necessarily assess and motivate change in these social interactions to improve both problem behavior and emotional adjustment.

Motivation to Change Addressed

Another area that the EcoFIT model explicitly addresses is motivation to change. A common problem in child and family intervention is lack of engagement of parents of adolescents. Research during the past 15 years indicates that a key ingredient of effective interventions is to explicitly address motivation to change (Prochaska & Norcross, 1999). It is now assumed that identifying a change technology (e.g., behavior modification, cognitive therapy) is necessary but not sufficient for an effective intervention strategy (Patterson, 1985). Miller and colleagues (W. R. Miller & Rollnick, 2002) have developed a systematic approach, called *motivational interviewing*, to address motivation to change. A key component of motivational interviewing is to give clients feedback on their assessments in a supportive, nonconfrontational fashion. We adapted this strategy when designing the Family Check-Up, an intervention to engage caregivers in relevant intervention services (Dishion & Kavanagh, 2003). As we discuss later in this volume, the Family Check-Up is central to an ecological approach to child and family interventions. Assessments are critical for addressing client motivation to change within an ecological approach.

Suitable Within a Health Maintenance Framework

Finally, an ecological approach works within a health maintenance framework (Stormshak & Dishion, 2002). This feature of the EcoFIT model is a radical departure from conventional approaches to child and adult clinical and counseling psychology. Empirically supported interventions are designed to treat mental health disorders as if a permanent cure were possible. However, if an interaction between biological and environmental factors in mental health is assumed (Rutter, Dunn, & Simonoff, 1997), some individuals are more vulnerable to environmental stress than others, as seen in both initial manifestations of disorder and recurrence (Monroe & Harkness, 2005). In light of the variation in vulnerability to environmental stress, periodic assessments and interventions are needed to prevent, treat, or reduce harm associated with problem behavior and emotional distress. In this sense, a health maintenance model for mental health intervention is more consistent with a dental plan than with a medical model of intervention.

For children and adolescents, transitions are salient environmental stress points (Sameroff, 1981). Two types of transitions are particularly salient to the mental health of children and adolescents. The first type includes transitions associated with biological maturation. For example, toddlers learn to walk, early childhood is associated with an increased need for independence, and in adolescence, pubertal changes are associated with an increased interest in peers (Peterson, Silbereisin, & Sorenson, 1996).

Biological maturation can directly affect problem behavior and emotional distress and, indirectly, family and peer relationships. This first type of transition also includes changes in context. A major change in context for children is attending school, which often begins in early childhood. Transitions occur at school entry, middle school, and high school. Successful adjustment to these transitions is associated with positive outcomes for youth.

A second major transition type involves divorce and remarriage. More than 50% of all children experience divorce, and a large percentage of them will be exposed to new adult caregivers or stepparents. These transitions are both opportunities and stress points and are crucial times for assessment and intervention within an ecological approach. Children who do not handle stress well (e.g., those who have poor self-regulation) are particularly vulnerable to these transitions but are also most responsive to environmental interventions. Thus, the intervention model outlined in this volume would ideally be available as both a periodic preventive check-up and a more intensive intervention. In our prevention research, we offer the Family Check-Up every year, with a menu of intervention options that follow, depending on the results of the assessment, the caregiver's resources and motivation, and available community resources.

WHAT FOLLOWS

This volume is written for three groups of readers. First, it is aimed at graduate students and professionals in training. We have the pleasure and privilege of supporting the training of graduate students in school, clinical, and counseling psychology programs in child and family intervention using the model outlined in this volume. The second group of readers we hope to reach are practitioners who work with children and adolescents, who may find useful information in this volume that will encourage innovation in their clinical contexts. Child and family therapists within the United States are often overworked and underpaid. We suspect that the call for an even broader framework for conducting interventions with children and families will be met with some skepticism, because some aspects of the intervention model are not supported by current systems of reimbursement. For example, it is rare that the comprehensive psychosocial assessment and feedback session required for a Family Check-Up would be paid for in current insurance and public reimbursement systems within the United States. We are aware of the disjunction between the EcoFIT model and current service delivery systems. Our hope is that future cost-effectiveness research will test the ideas presented in this volume and inform the design of mental health service delivery systems that benefit children and families but are also economically feasible. We have found that as few as 6 hours of intervention following the EcoFIT model has a moderately large effect on reducing substance use among the youth at highest risk over a 4-year period (Dishion, Kavanagh, Schneiger, Nelson, & Kaufman, 2002; Nelson & Dishion, 2004). Thus, addressing motivation and having an empirically supported intervention framework may actually reduce the costs associated within intervention. Finally, this volume is intended for individuals in leadership positions who have the political mandate to affect, through design and funding, the mental health service delivery systems in the United States and internationally. The approach described here is ultimately a set of principles that can be adapted to fit the cultural and economic realities of diverse communities and service delivery systems.

In this sense, the approach we outline is a work in progress. Interventions are often offered as the final solution to a mental health problem. The ecological framework in general, and the EcoFIT model in particular, offer the advantage of providing a set of tools for the systematic design and execution of mental health services for children and families. They also provide a road map for innovation of future interventions that are even more effective and efficient. This pragmatic emphasis on model building is the key to progress in applying science to improve the mental health of children and adolescents (Dishion & Patterson, 1999). Clinicians, families, basic scientists, intervention scientists, and policymakers are partners in setting the research agenda and targeting areas for future study that will increase intervention effectiveness. What we offer in this volume is not a school of therapy but rather a systematic approach to innovation and change.

This volume has four major parts. The first part provides a conceptual overview of what is known about the developmental factors that underlie child and adolescent problem behavior and emotional adjustment and how this knowledge informs the design and implementation of interventions. Clinicians who work with children and adolescents need to know the literature on etiology and development so they can sensitively and effectively adjust intervention strategies, as well as provide sound advice to parents and caregivers. It is clear that some gaps exist in the scientific literature, but they are being filled. We attempt to provide the big picture of what we know while avoiding tedious details of the expansive literature. Much of what we know about environmental factors concerns child and adolescent problem behavior, with less focus on anxiety, depression, and more severe mental health problems such as bipolar disorder and early-onset schizophrenia. However, the little research that has been conducted in those areas suggests that the family-centered focus such as that used in the EcoFIT strategy is effective in increasing remission in schizophrenia (Falloon et al., 1985). The overview of the EcoFIT approach in chapter 4 (this volume) clarifies that our approach is complementary to the psychopharmacological strategies for reducing mental health problems in children and adolescents.

The second part of this volume provides the details of the three phases of the Family Check-Up, including the initial contact, the assessment session, and the feedback session. This material outlines a family-centered intervention strategy for children ranging from age 2 through ages 17 and 18. We use this approach in our outpatient clinical services offered at the Child and Family Center at the University of Oregon. We find the approach generally useful for all client referral problems typically seen in an outpatient clinical setting, with the exclusion perhaps of families in acute crises when immediate, more direct interventions may be necessary.

The third part of this volume provides details on the specific intervention strategies that follow the Family Check-Up—the intervention menu of the EcoFIT model. In our outpatient work with children and families, we use a combination of approaches. For example, with an adolescent with depression who is self-destructive and engaged in problem behavior, we typically focus on family management therapy with the parents and integrate this work with interventions aimed at the adolescent's self-regulation, using a cognitive–behavioral approach. For families in which the referral problems are less severe or the child is younger (less than 6 years old), we may provide brief family-centered parenting interventions. Decisions about what interventions best fit the needs of a child and family are based on a broad ecological assessment.

In the fourth part, we address the context of the clinician. Two major concerns require attention and are particularly relevant to child and family clinicians. The first is the professional context within which a clinician works. Emerging literature suggests that the quality of the intervention delivery system is directly linked to the level of benefit a child and family derive from an intervention (Forgatch, Patterson, & DeGarmo, 2005). Maintaining high levels of service quality, however, requires team support, accountability, feedback, and training for clinicians. These issues are discussed in some detail in chapter 13 (this volume).

The second major concern are the unique ethical dilemmas in child and family interventions that challenge our conventional system for ethical decision making. We hope chapter 14 (this volume) offers some guiding principles for ethical decision making in child and family interventions and, more important, stimulates future discussion and dialectic about the ethics of intervening in the lives of children and families in community settings.

I

CONCEPTUAL OVERVIEW

2

THE ECOLOGY OF
DEVELOPMENT AND CHANGE

In an ecological approach, interventions are based on an empirical model of the development of psychopathology in children and adolescents. Model building, in fact, gives rise to innovative intervention studies, and the results stimulate developmental and basic research that further refine an understanding of etiological mechanisms (Dishion & Patterson, 1999; Forgatch, 1991; Patterson, Reid, & Dishion, 1992). Although several empirically supported interventions are clearly ecological (e.g., Chamberlain & Moore, 1998; Felner & Felner, 1989; Henggeler, Schoenwald, Borduin, Rowland, & Cunningham, 1998; Kelly, 1988; McWhirter, Gragg, Hayashino, Torres, & Kaufman, 2001), fewer are explicitly guided by a model. This chapter provides an overview of the empirical model that informs the intervention strategy outlined in this volume.

The developmental psychopathology literature clearly has strengths and weaknesses with respect to providing a database from which a model can be derived. In particular, there is a surplus of longitudinal studies on the development of problem behavior in children and adolescents, whereas studies on emotional distress and other forms of psychopathology are few. The reason for this discrepancy is obvious: Disruptive behavior is more noticeable and problematic for schools, parents, and communities. As a result, the science of child and adolescent problem behavior is better developed, as of this writing, than that of anxiety and depression. We assume that the next 10 years of research will improve the empirical foundation for the design of even more effective intervention and prevention strategies for a wider array of mental health concerns.

Although the state of the science is imperfect, enough is known about child development and mental health to suggest a recent radical shift in current intervention practice. Children and adolescents live in systems of relationships (Bronfenbrenner, 1979, 1989) that reduce or amplify adjustment problems. Children with genetic liabilities for mental health disorders (psychosis, bipolar disorder, attention-deficit/hyperactivity disorder) are especially vulnerable to pathogenic family, peer, and teacher relationships. Therefore, nearly all child and adolescent clients will benefit from interventions in the family or school setting. From this perspective, psychopathology is not within the child but rather is the child's maladaptation to a set of relationship experiences; this maladaptation may in part be determined by his or her own genetic characteristics (e.g., emotional reactivity, activity level, attention level, and extent of self-regulation). Thus a child's problem-behavior escalation when caregivers set limits may be understood as both a functional response to a disrupted family and a predisposition to overreact.

The point at which a particular behavioral or emotional pattern reaches a threshold warranting a diagnosis of psychopathology is in part a function of culture and the reporting agents (e.g., child, parent, teacher; Harkness & Super, 1990). From an epidemiological perspective, much of what can be defined as psychopathology may go undetected by the child or caregiving adults (Offord, 1989; Walker-Barnes, 2003). The reality is that adults are the primary agents for defining whether behavior or experiences are deemed abnormal and worthy of attention and remediation. In this sense, an ecological perspective is useful for considering the dynamics of defining psychopathology as well as the realities of service delivery for children and families across cultural contexts. For example, consider the case of an impoverished, single-parent family with a hyperactive 5-year-old.

> Jerome was an African American 5-year-old boy in a low-income day-care school that had a full-time social worker. Jerome was referred to inpatient psychiatry because of severe hyperactivity and because his mother was deemed violent and potentially abusive. Jerome's behavior problems escalated over a period of 6 months. During this time, he was being seen by the day-care social worker, who conducted weekly play therapy sessions. His single mom brought him to the therapy sessions and patiently waited with her three other children in the waiting room. Allegations of abuse were made against the mother because of her use of physical discipline. However, parent training was not offered. In a court hearing designed by the social work team to remove Jerome from his mother's care, Jerome's mother tried to strike the social worker. It was for this behavior she was deemed violent and unfit to parent Jerome. Her perspective was that the members of the social work team, all

European Americans, were racist and negatively biased toward her and her family. After 20 days of psychiatric inpatient treatment and evaluation of Jerome, a decision was made to remove him from the home and place him in foster care.

This case example illustrates the principle just outlined. Although Jerome most likely had a liability of hyperactivity, the context of his life complicated and exacerbated his difficulties. The result was that a combination of clinician concern, cultural ethnocentricity and misunderstanding, and the lack of an ecological approach to intervention (which would include perhaps medication and parent training) rendered a manageable mental health issue into a more serious mental health problem. Although we do not know Jerome's long-term outcome, it is easy to imagine the effect that low-quality foster care might have on a difficult-to-manage 5-year-old. In this sense, we propose that attention to cultural variation, the effect of contextual factors on considerations such as parenting, and knowledge of effective and ineffective intervention strategies for specific mental health issues should be inherent in clinical training.

The ecological perspective is not a theory; it is a heuristic framework. Figure 2.1 provides a basic summary of what is known about the ecology

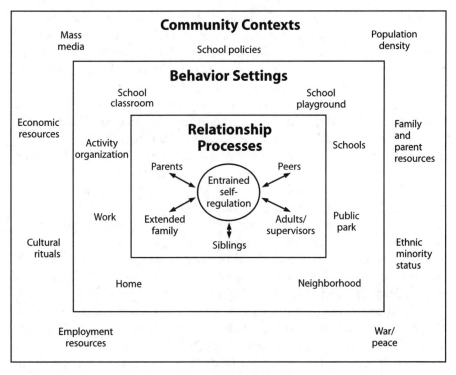

Figure 2.1. An ecological perspective on development.

of development of children and adolescents and is based on Bronfenbrenner's elegant conceptual organization (Bronfenbrenner, 1979, 1986, 1989; Bronfenbrenner & Ceci, 1994). The central idea is that children and adolescents are interacting and developing in multiple settings and relationships. Each level of influence is potentially powerful in shaping the development trajectory of the child. Moreover, interactions across relationships can define a system that is uniquely powerful in contributing to child and adolescent mental health outcomes. For example, there is a dynamic interplay between parents' reduced monitoring in adolescence and the youth's association with deviant peers (Dishion, Nelson, & Bullock, 2004). In fact, an interaction between parent reductions in family management during adolescence (i.e., a longitudinal slope score) and the youth's movement toward, and involvement with, deviant friends predicted very high levels of antisocial behavior in young adulthood. Known as *premature autonomy*, this development can be understood only by looking at both the peer and the family environment as two linked relationship systems (i.e., a mesosystem; Bronfenbrenner, 1989).

The ecological framework depicted in Figure 2.1 reflects two issues. First, biologic (brain, genetics, endocrine, temperament) and environmental influences are explicitly integrated (Bronfenbrenner & Ceci, 1994; Rutter, Dunn, & Simonoff, 1997). It has become increasingly clear that enduring traits that have a genetic or biological basis in children interact with socialization processes to render both positive and negative outcomes. Because it is difficult to disentangle unique aspects of behavior that are biological from those that are social in origin, we refer to enduring child characteristics that influence psychopathology as *entrained biosocial traits* (Dishion & Patterson, 2006). Entrained biosocial traits include facets such as attention, callousness, negative affect, hostile attribution bias, responsiveness to reward, the ability to inhibit, and sensitivity to punishment (Crick & Dodge, 1994; Kolb & Robinson, 2003; Posner et al., 2000; Rothbart & Posner, 2006). The term *entrainment* is used to describe the role of environments in structuring neural pathways that have implications for automatic, overlearned behavior patterns (Lewis, 2000). For example, avoidance, anger, response to reward, and inattention are child characteristics that are potentiated through thousands of interactions and routines within the family and within the context of a community and culture.

The second issue is that the ecological framework is not very useful as a practical guide for intervention activity. It is a truism that the social world is complex and that to truly understand a child's behavior, it would be helpful to follow a child across all settings and carefully observe all of his or her interactions (Rutter, Maughan, Mortimore, Ouston, & Smith, 1979). From a clinical perspective, doing this is not possible or practical. Thus, clinicians need a conceptual model to organize the structure of the child's world in a way that fits the data and is conceptually useful for the interventionist. To accomplish this ecological framework, we must step back from the specificity of the scientific literature and provide a broader perspective on child and adolescent psychopathology and the environmental factors that cause or amplify behaviors and experiences.

CHILD AND ADOLESCENT PSYCHOPATHOLOGY: KEY DIMENSIONS

A common thread among most conceptualizations of child and adolescent psychopathology is the notion of internalizing and externalizing disorders (Achenbach, 1982, 1992). These broad dimensions of children's adjustment are based on myriad factor analytic studies of adult (parent, teacher) and child reports of mental health symptoms. The conceptualization of internalizing disorders and externalizing disorders is derived from a psychodynamic view of psychopathology. Individuals may either turn psychic distress inward (i.e., internalize) or direct it outward toward others (i.e., externalize). We prefer the less inferential terms *emotional distress* and *social maladaptation* in lieu of internalizing and externalizing disorders, respectively. Emotional distress refers to psychological discomfort (e.g., depression, anxiety, and somatic complaints). Considerable evidence, including several factor analytic studies with children (King, Ollendick, & Gullone, 1991) and adults (Watson & Clark, 1984; Watson, Clark, & Tellegen, 1988), supports viewing emotional distress as a general construct. Social maladaptation refers to a set of behaviors that undermine children's adjustment at home, such as aggression and delinquency clusters. Behaviors considered socially maladaptive differ for children and adolescents. In early childhood, the most salient behavioral trouble sign is aggression (Dodge, 1991; Dodge, Lochman, Harnish, Bates, & Pettit, 1997; Poulin & Boivin, 2000; Tremblay, 2000; Vitaro, Brendgen, & Tremblay, 2002). For most children, this behavior begins to ebb gradually through early adolescence. In middle childhood, more proactive forms of antisocial behavior, such as lying, stealing, and bullying (usually in groups), begin to take shape. Around early adolescence, some youth engage in substance use (usually tobacco and alcohol first) and other clandestine antisocial behaviors that are often illegal and conducted in the company of peers (Dishion, Capaldi, Spracklen, & Li, 1995). Finally, by middle to late adolescence, some may begin to demonstrate more serious forms of conduct disturbance and sexual precocity (Capaldi, Crosby, & Stoolmiller, 1996) and face serious legal difficulties and community sanctions (Loeber & Dishion, 1983).

It is surprising that work on examining the developmental path of children's emotional distress has been less systematic than the work on problem behaviors. Early emotional difficulties begin with separation distress, night terrors, and simple phobias. Just as with aggression and noncompliance, these emotional difficulties are often resolved by middle childhood. However, in middle childhood simple phobias, including phobias related to attending school, may still be present. Also, depression can be experienced in childhood, especially in boys. In early to middle adolescence, a tendency toward shyness can reach the level of social phobia, which may interfere with a child's ability to form friendships and cope in the world of peers and may undermine school adjustment. In addition, pervasive mood disorders emerge in adolescence, showing a shift in prevalence, with girls experiencing more depression than do boys—a difference that continues through adulthood. Issues of emotion regulation are certainly serious in their own right, as they potentially lead to suicide and other forms of tragic self-destruction.

The vast majority of the clinical referrals for children and adolescents are for behavioral problems (Kazdin, 1993; Patterson, Dishion, & Chamberlain, 1993). Research by Stanger et al. (1999) revealed that social maladaptation, in contrast to emotional distress, shows the most stability from childhood to adolescence and from adolescence to young adulthood. Several investigators reported that children and adolescents who are socially maladapted and emotionally distressed (i.e., comorbid) experience the highest risk for family dynamics (Granic & Lamey, 2002) and peer difficulties (Dishion, 2000). Youth who are comorbid are generally more at risk in childhood and adolescence on a variety of outcomes (Capaldi, 1992).

Contextual Sensitivity

From an ecological perspective, children's social maladaptation and emotional distress are not necessarily traits that are consistent across settings. In fact, in our intervention approach, we investigate the variation in the settings and the perceptions of important participants in the child's life. We have used data to investigate the setting specificity of social maladaptation and emotional distress. In a sample of 214 young adolescents at high risk (male and female; Dishion & Kavanagh, 2003), we collected teacher and parent reports of psychopathology from the Child Behavior Checklist (CBCL), using the cross-informant, multiaxial system developed by Achenbach (1992). Social maladaptation is defined by two scale factors referred to as Aggressive and Delinquency. Emotional distress is defined by three scale scores: Withdrawn, Somatic Complaints, and Anxious/Depressed.

These data can be thought about in two ways. First, these two dimensions reflect traits of the child that are relatively consistent at home and at school. Young adolescents who have behavior problems tend to exhibit them in most situations. In a similar way, children who are emotionally distressed are consistently so at home and school. If this conceptualization of psychopathology is accurate, a confirmatory factor analysis should reveal

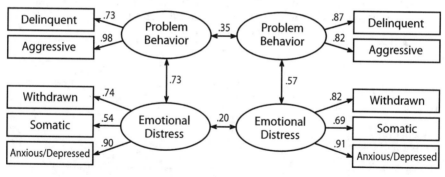

$\chi^2_{(24)} = 35.9, p = .056$
GFI = .97, NFI = .969, CFI = .989

Figure 2.2. A confirmatory factor analysis of an ecological model of child and adolescent psychopathology. CFI = confirmatory fit index; GFI = goodness-of-fit index; NFI = normed fit index.

that a two-factor (Social Maladaptation and Emotional Distress) model would best fit the data, allowing the two factors to correlate. We tested such a model and found that the fit was not good ($\chi^2 = 486.7$, $df = 34$).

In the second way of thinking about the data, using the ecological conceptualization of psychopathology, four factors would be more representative. The four factors are (a) Social Maladaptation at Home, (b) Social Maladaptation at School, (c) Emotional Distress at Home, and (d) Emotional Distress at School. This model is a substantially better fit than the two-factor model ($\chi^2 = 35.9$, $df = 24$). The results of this model are summarized in Figure 2.2.

The correlations among the constructs are especially interesting. Note that the correlation between social maladaptation and emotional distress, as reported by the mother, was .72. Thus, if a mother reported behavior problems, she also perceived the young adolescent as depressed and anxious. In contrast, the correlation between teachers and mothers on social maladaptation was low ($r = .35$): They agreed less than half of the time on the child's level of behavior problems across home and school. The correlation between mothers and teachers on emotional distress was lower yet, indicating that a teacher's perception of a child as anxious or depressed was only modestly related to a mother's perception, and was often dissimilar.

These data clearly indicate that a child's behavior varies significantly across home and school contexts; this finding is especially important in light of the fact that adults are the primary referral source for mental health services. Moreover, children's behavior at school is influenced by peers and

TABLE 2.1
Co-occurrence Matrix for Clinically Significant Parent and Teacher Child Behavior Checklist Ratings on Externalizing and Internalizing Adjustment Problems

| | Internalizing | | | | |
Externalizing	Normal	Parent only	Teacher only	Parent and teacher	Total
Normal	42	12	7	5	66
Parent only	13	33	3	17	66
Teacher only	9	0	6	2	17
Parent and teacher	16	19	9	21	65
Total	80	64	25	45	214

teachers. For example, highly aggressive peers in the classroom can create a climate at school in which problem behavior is supported and popular; this leads to higher levels of problem behavior in youth as well as higher rates of peer acceptance in this context (Snyder et al., 2005; Stormshak et al., 1999; Warren, Schoppelrey, Moberg, & McDonald, 2005). The clinical message is that, at a minimum, assessments of child adjustment should include multiple informants across home and school before an intervention is designed. Understanding the conditions and functions of the child's behavior and emotion may be half the work in designing an effective intervention. Simply talking to the child or parent about his or her perceptions may not provide a complete picture.

In that vein, it is important to know whether the child's behavior and emotions are consistent across settings (Bem & Funder, 1978; Loeber & Dishion, 1984). With the data from our sample (also in Figure 2.2), we considered the prevalence of children who were deemed above the clinical cutoff on the Achenbach CBCL using a t score of 62 on the externalizing and internalizing dimensions. These data are summarized in Table 2.1. How many of the youth showed a trait for clinically significant problem behavior and emotional distress? Note that 45 of the 214 children were seen by both teachers and parents as being in emotional distress, about half the number who were perceived as distressed by either group independently. Also, the subset of youth who were perceived as socially maladapted by both parents and teachers numbered less than half the total ($n = 65$) seen as maladapted by either group independently. The most important clinical group, common to clinical practice, is youth who are rated high in problem behavior and emotional distress by both parents and teachers. These adolescents with comorbidity are at extremely high risk for deviant peer dynamics, family dysfunction, and long-term adjustment risk. For example, by age 16, youth in this group had an average of eight sexual partners in a year (Dishion, 2000).

In this volume, we do not emphasize the use of diagnostic classifications as the primary assessment strategy. Politics aside, the main reason is that diagnostic information for children and adolescents at this time is of limited usefulness in the design and execution of interventions. Second, diagnostic classifications are insensitive to context. For example, in light of a relatively low correlation between child and parent report of symptoms, it is often the practice to combine the two reports to create a diagnosis.

Achenbach and others (Achenbach, 1992; Patterson et al., 1992) emphasized the importance of using multiple reporting agents when conducting assessments across both home and school. We recommend that such assessments form the foundation of an ecological approach to child and family intervention. To formulate realistic intervention strategies, clinicians need to know whether a child or adolescent is perceived as having a behavior problem both at home and at school or in only one of these settings. Cross-setting consistency also happens to suggest higher risk for continuity and more difficulties in the home (Loeber & Dishion, 1984). The risk is even higher for youth with anxiety and depression, because these difficulties are less likely to be consistent across settings. Study of cross-setting consistency in depression and anxiety as an indicator of severity has been less systematic. In our analyses, in the absence of social maladaptation, cross-setting consistency in emotion dysregulation did not independently predict adjustment outcomes (Dishion, 2000).

Middle to late adolescence is when individuals can develop serious difficulties in thought processes and mood regulation, such as psychoses (e.g., thought disorder, hallucinations) and bipolar disorder (mood swings with the presence of mania). Although these disorders rarely occur in early childhood, preadolescent children unfortunately are often diagnosed as having bipolar disorder and given medication for it. Medication is often thought of as a diagnostic tool, but psychologists and psychiatrists have known for some time that psychopharmacologic medications can improve the behavior and mood of anyone, regardless of whether that person is disordered (Rappaport, Hopkins, Hall, Belleza, & Silverman, 1978).

Several factors are strongly driven by biological processes related to birth trauma or genetic inheritance, including schizophrenia, autism, Asperger's syndrome, and mental retardation. Although these disorders are biologically driven, their effect is also modulated by relationship systems. For example, the daily life of an adolescent with mental retardation will be dramatically affected by his or her level of social maladaptation. Because social maladaptation plays such a critical role in determining long-term outcomes for children and adolescents, we offer a developmental model that summarizes longitudinal and intervention research from the early 1930s through the present.

A FAMILY-CENTERED MODEL

Using the family structure as a means of organizing the ecology of influences on child and adolescent adjustment is helpful for simplifying the ecological perspective and rendering it useful for the design of effective interventions. The list of behavior settings relevant to the mental health of children is finite. Children grow up in families and in neighborhoods, and they attend public schools that are organized within political communities. Each level of social aggregation has its own systemic dynamic. Families, however, often provide structure to children's overall ecology. Parents select schools, churches, neighborhoods, organized activities, and work settings that are conducive to their conception of family and child rearing. Teachers, counselors, and other professionals, in contrast, come and go in children's lives.

For this reason several of the most promising intervention practices emphasize and focus on parents and caregiving environments (e.g., Henggeler et al., 1998; Minuchin, Rosman, & Baker, 1978; Patterson, Reid, Jones, & Conger, 1975). Thus, we propose that in working with children and adolescents, interventions are most effective when they are organized to address the caregiving system. Interventions with children and adolescents that ignore the caregiving system risk, in the long run, iatrogenic effects or negative side effects (e.g., Dishion, McCord, & Poulin, 1999; Kelly, 1988).

A traditional strength of psychology is the study of the individual. An ecological emphasis, however, demands a new level of sophistication in psychological theory, research, and clinical practice. From a theoretical point of view, we need to expand our emphasis to consider relationship systems. In addition, our notion of temporal effects is expanded to consider development across the life span. Figure 2.3 provides an overview of a family-centered perspective on the ecology of child and adolescent development.

Each stage in the life span has its own unique potential for change and formulates a basis for subsequent adaptation. The work of Olds and colleagues (Kitzman et al., 1997; Olds et al., 1997) revealed the relevance of an ecologically sensitive intervention with young mothers (pre- and postnatal) to long-term adjustment.

Early childhood is a time of sensitivity within the caregiving relationship. Many young children are now involved in preschool and child-care settings, and the quality of preschool and day care is linked to children's social development (NICHD Early Child Care Research Network, 2002). Careful, collaborative support interventions with parents whose children are in early childhood result in short- and long-term benefits in the social behavior of those children (Webster-Stratton, 1990). Such interventions can be delivered cost effectively in day-care centers for low-income families with observed benefits to the child's behavior (Gross et al., 2003). Brief,

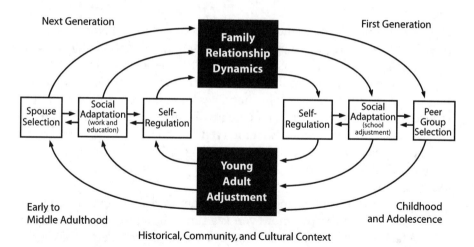

Figure 2.3. A life span view of development in context.

cost-effective parenting interventions can also be offered in the context of welfare agencies such as Women, Infants, and Children (WIC). Shaw et al. (in press) found that random assignment to the Family Check-Up among high-risk families involved in WIC resulted in improved parent involvement and reduced problem behavior during early childhood.

Schools are increasingly important in providing a foundation for social development and well-being in children (Kellam, 1990). The vast majority of children in the United States attend school up to age 13 or 14. Moreover, schools serve as convenient meeting places for deviant peer groups (Dishion, Duncan, Eddy, Fagot, & Fetrow, 1994; Kellam, 1990; Rutter, 1985). Attending to the school environment, as well as family dynamics, may be necessary to effect comprehensive change in the behavior of children at high risk (Patterson, 1974). In an ecological model, it is critical to embed family interventions within influential social contexts (Biglan, 1995). Preventive intervention programs must "consider schools as potential sites for service delivery, as well as potential objects of intervention activity" (Trickett & Birman, 1989, p. 361). Several interventions, designed to be delivered in the schools, have been shown to be empirically effective in improving child problem behavior. Perhaps the most comprehensive model-driven intervention is the Fast Track program for addressing the needs of children at very high risk (antisocial at home and school; Conduct Problems Prevention Research Group, 2002).

Enhancing communication and cooperation between parents and school staff can drastically improve parents' potential for monitoring, limit setting, and supporting academic progress (Gottfredson, Gottfredson, & Hybl, 1993; Reid, 1993). Simply increasing specific information to parents about their child's attendance, homework, and class behavior results in improved monitoring and support for at-risk children's academic and social success (Blechman, Taylor, & Schrader, 1981; Heller & Fantuzzo, 1993). Creating a family resource room in a middle school environment and actively targeting parenting practices also improves parental monitoring as well as reduces substance use and deviant peer involvement (Dishion & Kavanagh, 2003). The general principle is that interventions that target either parenting or school dynamics, or both, are the most promising as a prevention strategy (Kellam, Rebok, Ialongo, & Mayer, 1994; Patterson, 1974; Reid & Eddy, 1997).

Peers are relevant to social development and well-being throughout development. Adolescence, however, is a time when the influence of peers is amplified as young people create a social niche (Cairns, Perrin, & Cairns, 1985; Dishion et al., 1999). Establishing a peer group has many long-term implications, one of which is selecting a partner. This choice is highly significant to adult adjustment and the nature of young adults as future parents. Inattention to peer influences in the design or execution of an intervention can undermine otherwise effective interventions and, in some situations, result in increases in problem behavior (Dishion & Dodge, 2005; Gifford-Smith, Dodge, Dishion, & McCord, 2005).

The model in Figure 2.3 suggests a cyclical socialization process that accounts for continuity across generations. Child and adolescent emotion regulation, social adaptation, and peer group selection are basically seen as mutually embedded within family relationship dynamics. From a clinical perspective, one would hypothesize that interventions that address family relationship dynamics would have beneficial effects on these dimensions of child and adolescent adjustment. One would also presume that positive outcomes in these three domains of functioning bode well for the individual's adjustment as a young adult. In this model, young adult adjustment is defined by emotion regulation, social adaptation (work and education), and spouse or partner selection.

Adjustment in these domains is hypothesized to have an impact on the viability and well-being of the family and on relationship dynamics of the next generation. In clinical work with adolescents, it is easy to lose track of the family and school context and to focus on individually oriented change strategies. For example, providing an intervention for the depression affect of a precocious adolescent girl, while ignoring her family and peer group and other problem behavior, could be a major miscalculation. Following is a case in point.

Cosmic was a 16-year-old European American girl raised by her highly educated but underemployed mother. She was seen at an outpatient clinic because of her mother's concerns about her increasing tendency to sit in her room wearing earphones, her falling grades in high school, and her failure to communicate with her family members (mother and brother). Cosmic was often high on marijuana, and she had developed a habit of stealing and lying, in part to acquire funds to support her drug use and time with peers. Cosmic was an unhappy, depressed person. The clinician approached Cosmic's condition with an empirically supported intervention for depression, derived from an adult model of depression. When conceptualizing the case, however, the clinician did not consider Cosmic's family situation or her problem behavior. Although Cosmic connected with the clinician well, she tended to manipulate both her mother and the clinician and was eventually arrested for stealing a stranger's credit cards. She claimed to her therapist that she had found the cards and planned to return them soon. Although her depression was improving, her problem behavior seemed to be on the rise.

For some adolescents, an adult model of depression and its treatment may fit very well. However, we suspect that those who present with problem behavior and for whom family dynamics are relevant would benefit from a family-centered approach that includes coordination with school staff. In this sense, Cosmic would have benefited from a more comprehensive assessment, leading to a broader case conceptualization and the coordination of interventions for both problem behavior and depression.

Cultural and community factors must be considered as well. In Cosmic's case, her highly educated mother most likely holds a set of attitudes and expectations about mental health issues and parenting. For example, she may see Cosmic as an adult, or the two may function more like siblings than a parent–child dyad. If so, changing her parenting practices to address some of Cosmic's issues would not occur to her. In a similar way, a well-matched therapist, working from the same model, might also be inclined to approach Cosmic's issues from an individual perspective, rather than as an outcome of a system that not only was depressing her but also supported her problem behavior. Yet Cosmic's problem behavior is unlikely to spontaneously remit and will potentially undermine her successful transition to adulthood with respect to school completion, partner selection, and parenting the next generation (see Figure 2.3). Thus a careful assessment and a more comprehensive case conceptualization, according to the ecological approach outlined in this volume, may have resulted in a somewhat different intervention that emphasized both Cosmic's self-regulation of her emotional distress and the management and reduction of her problem behavior.

Heterotypic comorbidity is the term used to describe the condition of a child or adolescent who shows problem behavior and is emotionally distressed. However, another consideration that must be made when considering a youth's symptoms is context: Do they occur only at home or only at school, or do they occur in both settings (Dishion, 2000; Dishion & Patterson, 1993; Loeber & Dishion, 1984; Patterson et al., 1992)? Figure 2.1 suggests that in addition to disruption across domains (i.e., home and school), there are more severe disruptions in the environment, and the long-term consequences are more severe. In adolescence, a major factor to consider is how the child, who is both problematic and emotionally distressed, interacts with peers. Granic and Dishion (2003) found a tendency of such youth to get stuck in deviant talk and for that tendency to predict long-term future problems with both drugs and authority figures. Dishion (2000) found that youth with comorbidity at home and school showed patterns of high-risk sexual behavior and substance abuse 3 years later.

For example, a child or adolescent with difficulties in self-regulation, who is otherwise doing well in school and is not associated with a deviant peer group, is clearly less at risk than a child who is both emotionally distressed and socially maladjusted. In this respect, as indicated by the bidirectional arrows between domains, there would be an interaction effect of disruption in both domains on long-term outcomes. For children and adolescents, these long-term adjustment problems are primarily realized and enacted within the context of the early- to late-adolescent peer group (Dishion, Poulin, & Medici Skaggs, 2000; Patterson, Dishion, & Yoerger, 2000).

Contextual and cultural factors are highly relevant to the life span perspective summarized in Figure 2.3. As we proposed in a more theoretical discussion of socialization and adolescence, most cultural communities automatically self-organize around the family as a unit of socialization and around community activities that support a similar view of child rearing (Granic & Dishion, 2003). Successful outcomes for children and adolescents are exponentially increased when settings involving children are organized around the task of socialization. In this sense, historical dynamics interface with cultural patterns. Such socialization systems are quite enduring, although eventually they may be disrupted by outside efforts to modernize, westernize, commercialize, or otherwise colonize (Duran & Duran, 1995).

A family-centered approach to understanding the development and design of interventions has several advantages. First, parents are the adults most likely to be able to address the school and home contextual influences that can undermine child and adolescent behavior and emotional adjustment. Parents can even influence peer groups in childhood and adolescence (Chilcoate, Anthony, & Dishion, 1995; Dishion, Nelson, & Kavanagh, 2003; Fletcher, Darling, & Steinberg, 1995; Pettit, Bates, Dodge, & Meece, 1999). Second, cross-generation transmission of mental health problems can be effectively prevented or effected. Third, it is reasonable to assume that the entire family, including the siblings, benefits from successful family interventions (Arnold, Levine, & Patterson, 1975). Fourth, as we show later in this volume, family-centered interventions can be delivered cost effectively if they focus primarily on the interactive dynamics within which both problem behavior and mental health problems of children and adolescents are embedded. The next chapter focuses exclusively on relationship dynamics and their measurement, as they are crucial for the design of effective interventions.

SUMMARY

This chapter provides an introduction and overview of the ecological framework for child and adolescent intervention science. The ecological framework proposes a context-sensitive approach to thinking about child and adolescent competence and mental health on a continuum, with a primary emphasis on family and school environments. We have promoted a family-centered perspective as an organizing focus for studying development and for the design of effective mental health interventions. The implications of the ecological perspective are threefold. Interventions should (a) be both contextually sensitive and mindful of a life span developmental focus; (b) consider the role of parents in organizing school and, ultimately, peer environments; and (c) consider child and adolescent adjustments across domains in evaluating long-term prognosis and in designing interventions. The next chapter highlights the central role of relational dynamics in families and peers in understanding the etiology and course of child and adolescent mental problems and in designing effective intervention strategies.

3

FAMILY AND PEER
SOCIAL INTERACTION

One of the central themes of an ecological perspective is that development and change occur in the context of adult caregiving (parent and teacher) and peer relationships (friends and siblings). Teacher relationships are also important to the long-term development of children. It has been shown that the key social interaction patterns that support both normative and psychopathological development in children and adolescents are based on overlearned patterns of behavior of which the participants have limited awareness (Patterson & Reid, 1984). For example, parent reports of family interaction patterns correlate only modestly with observed interaction patterns (Patterson, Reid, & Dishion, 1992). This common lack of awareness presents a challenge to the clinician, because it is often difficult to motivate change in these problematic interpersonal relationship patterns. For this reason, it is especially important that clinicians are knowledgeable about the key social interaction patterns of interest for understanding and changing child and adolescent problem behavior and emotional distress. These patterns of interaction are the focus of this chapter.

OVERVIEW

There is agreement that characteristics of the child may elicit specific parent and peer reactions and social interactions. However, there is also considerable evidence that social interactions with parents and peers potentially amplify child traits to levels of clinical concern. A difficult toddler can elicit negative affect and parenting practices, which feed into escalating cycles of conflict, which, in turn, increase the child's problem behavior (Olson, Bates, & Bayles, 1990; Patterson, 1982; Patterson & Cobb, 1971; Stoolmiller, 2001). Antisocial boys develop friendships that support their antisocial tendencies, which escalate into more serious behaviors such as violent crime (Dishion, Eddy, Haas, Li, & Spracklen, 1997). Anxious girls may develop friendships that support their unrealistic expectations about body image, which, in turn, lead to eating disorders (Crandall, 1988; French, Story, Downes, Resnick, & Blum, 1995). Similar to systems theorists, we assume that child and adolescent psychopathology (emotional distress and social maladaptation) serves a complex interpersonal function through which it can be transformed, amplified, or maintained. The power of relationships in maintaining emotional and behavior patterns is most noteworthy when an individual changes a significant aspect of his or her relationship network.

Types of Relationships

It is helpful to step back and consider the network of relevant relationships from childhood through adolescence. Interventions often focus only on the family. Until recently (e.g., Henggeler, Schoenwald, Borduin, Rowland, & Cunningham, 1998), peer interactions had been largely ignored, and the monitoring of interactions between children and teachers was relegated to other professionals such as school psychologists or counselors. In many families, particularly ethnically diverse families, relationships with extended family members may also be significant to a child's development. Reflection on the kinds of relationships in the child's interpersonal life provides a basis for considering optimal approaches to assessing relationship processes relevant to emotional distress and problem behavior.

Figure 3.1, derived from the ideas of interpersonal (e.g., Clark & Reis, 1988) and social development (Oden, Herzberger, Mangione, & Wheeler, 1984) theorists, provides an overview of an ecological perspective on relationships. The idea is relatively simple: Relationships can be categorized relative to how they fall on three dimensions. The first dimension is interdependency. Highly interdependent relationships share a collective fate. Spouses are unlike friends in that one member can affect the future of the other. A parent losing his or her job can affect the economic well-being of the family, thereby affecting the climate and resources of the children.

Relationships also vary as to closeness. One way of thinking about closeness is to consider the level of emotional charge the relationship provides. Signs of a high level of emotional charge are feelings of attachment

		Equal (Intimacy)		Hierarchical (Intimacy)	
		Close	**Distant**	**Close**	**Distant**
Interdependence	**Shared**	Spouse	Coworker Team member	Parent–child	Teachers Supervisors Extended family
	Separate	Friends	Peers Acquaintances	Older siblings Therapists Mentor	Past teachers Past supervisors

Figure 3.1. An ecological conceptualization of close relationships.

or missing someone if not seen for a week or more. For example, compare the emotional connection of friends versus peers, or spouses versus coworkers. Of course, the configuration of those emotional connections can change; for example, when a marriage is distressed, individuals may prefer coworkers to spouses, or when a family is distressed, individuals may prefer teachers to parents.

Finally, inherent to many relationships is the concept of a hierarchy. Adults are in a leadership role with children. Parent–child relationships that feel like sibling or peer relationships are often problematic at some stage in development, typically adolescence, when concerns for safety and health often demand that caregivers step in, set limits, and restructure adolescent lives. If the caregiver is not in a leadership role, these interventions can be difficult for an adolescent to accept.

Figure 3.1 suggests that much of our work in studying whether social and emotional dispositions can be generalized is probably ill conceived. For example, given the different demands of friendships compared with those of parent–child relationships, one would not expect that observed interactions would correlate across the two relationship contexts. In our work with the Oregon Youth Study boys, in fact, we found very little correlation in the parent–child and friend–child interactions, even though both were observed in a laboratory setting for the same amount of time and guided by similar task instructions (Dishion, Andrews, & Crosby, 1995). The only behavior that correlated across friendships and parent interactions was the boys' tendency to laugh during the interactions. When we observed children (first and fifth grade) on the playground and in the lab interacting with parents, the correlation between coercive behaviors observed in each setting was similarly negligible ($r = .19$; Dishion, Duncan, Eddy, Fagot, & Fetrow, 1994).

The lack of correlation across relationships underscores the need for an ecological perspective. It is often unrealistic to assume generalization in changes within both a parent–child relationship and a friendship relationship. There is a sense, however, that the parent–child relationship is central to the change process. For example, coercive exchanges with a child can discourage parents from setting limits and, with adolescents, from monitoring and structuring access to deviant peers (Patterson et al., 1992), leading to a state of premature autonomy (Dishion, Poulin, & Medici Skaggs, 2000). Recent research by Snyder and colleagues (Snyder et al., 2005) suggests that peers at school who are as young as 5 to 6 years can amplify antisocial traits, which, in turn, feed back to disrupt parent–child interaction vis-à-vis the changed behavior of the child at home. If change at home and school is required, interventions in both settings will likely need coordination (Dishion & Kavanagh, 2003; Patterson, 1974).

This lack of correlation between behaviors across relationships does not mean that some dynamics in relationships are stable and consistent. For example, coercive exchanges in families disrupt marriages (Gottman, 1991; Gottman & Levenson, 1986; Margolin & Wampold, 1981) and parent–child relationships (Patterson, 1982). In relationships that are highly interdependent, there is a tendency toward coercive interactions. Therefore, one would expect a higher level of agreement between teacher–child and parent–child interactions. However, as noted in the previous chapter, we observed only modest correlation ($r = .35$) in teacher- and parent-reported problem behavior. The relatively low correlation on behavior ratings suggests that patterns of interpersonal behavior may vary dramatically with different partners. In fact, an important individual difference factor is the level of rigidity of a pattern of behavior across settings. Dishion (2000) examined young adolescents who were distressed and maladapted both at home and at school and found marked tendencies to be more engaged in deviant interactions with their friends and to show extreme levels of psychopathology when followed for 3 years into middle adolescence.

Family and Peer Dynamics

Figure 3.2 provides an overview of the evidence linking family and peer interaction dynamics with emotional distress and social maladaptation from early childhood through adolescence. The most studied family dynamic of all is the coercion process as it relates to children's social maladaptation. This work, the body of which has been summarized recently by Snyder, Reid, and Patterson (2003), is relevant to understanding the etiology of antisocial behavior and for linking interventions to change (Martinez & Forgatch, 2001). The idea is relatively simple in concept, although difficult to detect without careful observation. Coercion is about pain control. Children basically learn to turn off parental demands by engaging in aversive and avoidant behaviors. If a parent makes a request for change, the young child

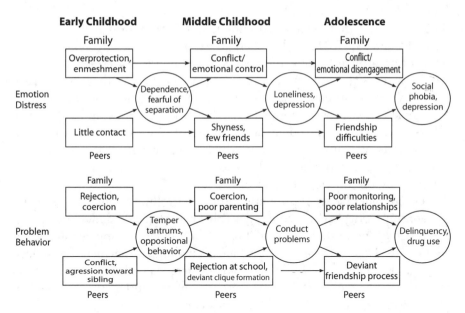

Figure 3.2. Relationship processes and the emergence, amplification, and transformation for two prototypical trajectories.

whines or complains, and the parent eventually gives up. In a market, the child has a temper tantrum, and the parent gives in to the child's demands to avoid embarrassment. The parent becomes worn down by a surly, uncooperative adolescent and eventually discontinues monitoring and supervision. To detect the coercion process, the clinician must devise a situation in which the parent tries to change the behavior of the child. For young children, we use a toy cleanup task. For adolescents, we have the parent discuss a recent limit-setting situation and family problem. Coercive interactions and dynamics have been linked to oppositional behavior in young children (Gardner & Griffin, 1989; Shaw et al., 1998; Snyder, Edwards, McGraw, Kilgore, & Holton, 1994) and antisocial behavior in middle childhood (Patterson, 1982; Patterson et al., 1992) and adolescence (Dishion & Andrews, 1995; Forgatch, 1984; Hops, Sherman, & Biglan, 1990).

Parental monitoring can also be directly observed. We recently found that coder impressions of parental monitoring revealed the worn down hypothesis described earlier. We followed the Oregon Youth Study boys from middle childhood through adolescence, coding their interactions with parents biannually, including global ratings of monitoring. We found that the parents of the boys initiating antisocial behavior in middle childhood through adolescence were those who had dramatically decreased their monitoring and engagement in early to middle adolescence (Dishion, Nelson, & Kavanagh, 2003). Thus, one problem in working with adolescents and their families is that even when clinicians structure a discussion, parents may have already disengaged to such an extent that they are avoidant and nonconfrontational, so that the coercion dynamic is not present.

Less research has been done on the family dynamics that covary with clinically significant emotional distress (anxiety and depression) in children and adolescents. Most noteworthy is the work by Hops and colleagues (Hops et al., 1987) that builds on the concept of escape conditioning. In observations of marital couples in which one partner is depressed, they found that depression functioned to turn off marital conflict and aggressive reactions by the other partner (Hops et al., 1990). From this perspective, depression could be seen as functional for controlling conflict in intimate relationships. Sheeber and colleagues (Sheeber, Hops, Andrews, Alpert, & Davis, 1998) found that this model applied to understanding depression in adolescents. Depressive and negative affects in families in which the adolescent was depressed increased support and decreased conflict. It is interesting to note that longer duration of depressive affect during the videotaped interaction was diagnostic of adolescent depression.

We know that the emotional distress of the parent and child are linked, but we know less about the dynamics of those linkages. Ge and colleagues followed adolescents in two-parent European American families over time and found that adolescents' and parents' emotional distress (anxiety and depression) was mutually influential (Ge, Conger, & Elder, 1996). Many of the children we see clinically, as discussed in the previous chapter, are experiencing both clinically significant emotional distress and social maladaptation. Granic and Lamey (2002) considered the interaction dynamics of boys who were classified as externalizing and comorbid (both externalizing and internalizing), and their mothers. They were working from a dynamic systems perspective and thus introduced a perturbation to a parent–child problem-solving discussion: They knocked on the door of the room in which the parent and child were interacting and asked them to wrap up the discussion. It was the family's response to this perturbation that differentiated the youth with comorbidity from the externalizing-only youth. The families with comorbidity escalated their conflict under pressure, whereas the externalizing-only disengaged. Data such as these suggest that emotional distress serves as an amplifying mechanism in family and peer dynamics related to the development of psychopathology.

Most clinicians do not consider the role of peers in the etiology and course of emotional distress and social maladaptation. However, we think this is unwise. As shown in Figure 3.2, peer dynamics are related to both the emergence and the maintenance of emotional distress and problem behavior. For problem behavior, we find that a youngster's affiliation with antisocial peers is the single best predictor of antisocial behavior from first grade (Dishion et al., 1994) through late adolescence (Dishion & Owen, 2002; Dishion et al., 1997). As early as preschool, casual observation of playground interactions will reveal children clustering and playing in groups, with aggressive children mutually selecting one another as playmates (Snyder, West, Stockemer, Givens, & Almquist-Parks, 1996). As we suggest in this volume, one critical component of family management is guiding the selection of peer groups and monitoring peer dynamics.

The search for dynamics that explain the influence of peers on social and emotional development led to the analysis of deviancy training (Dishion, Andrews, & Crosby, 1995; Dishion, Bullock, & Granic, 2002; Dishion, Spracklen, Andrews, & Patterson, 1996; Dishion et al., 1997). Because friendships do not involve *fate control* (i.e., control over one's future), we think the major influence pattern is positive reinforcement. A peer can influence development in two ways. The first is by association. Agreeing to be a friend may function as a strong reinforcement for a set of behaviors and values. There has been little research on selection effects, but we presume they occur as soon as children are placed in ecologies with large groups of peers who are disconnected from family relationships. It is worth noting that as early as preschool, the time children spend with peers equals the time they spend with parents (Ellis, Rogoff, & Cromer, 1981).

The deviancy training process is simple in concept but difficult to detect for youth and parents. When bad companions shape deviance, they do so by selectively attending to deviant talk and ignoring or punishing prosocial talk. As in all conversations, there is a tendency to move to topics of mutual interest or to discontinue the discussion. When two people are friends, it is presumed that the mutual interests have been established and that they have a well-practiced repertoire of discussions that define their relationships. We found that in dyads headed for more serious social maladaptation, the duration of the adolescents' deviant talk sessions was longer and they were more likely to elicit positive affective reactions than were adolescents who were at less long-term risk. It is worth noting that the deviant friendship process was easily detectable within 25 minutes of videotaped interaction with a best friend. We recently found that the more polished the youth was at the deviancy training process, the higher the likelihood that his or her antisocial behavior would persist into adulthood (Dishion, Nelson, Winter, & Bullock, 2004). As discussed earlier, some youth initiate their deviancy-training careers as early as first grade and are able to find other children as willing audiences. Deviancy training initiated by children as young as 5 to 6 years old predicts growth in antisocial behavior during the next 2 years (Snyder et al., 2005).

Two factors seem to account for a child's tendency to connect with peers who support and reinforce antisocial behavior. One is that early-onset antisocial behavior usually represents a prolonged developmental tendency to use antisocial behavior as a way to connect with other children, as revealed in work by Snyder and colleagues (Snyder et al., 2005). The second is that some parents tend to engage in antisocial behaviors and endorse antisocial attitudes. This deviant subculture is naturally adopted by children and carried over to the world of peers. We found that fathers with a history of adult arrests, substance use, and antisocial attitudes, who endorsed antisocial behavior at home tended to have sons who engaged in deviancy training with a selected friend during videotaped observation sessions. This effect was found even when the boys' childhood antisocial behavior and the families' parenting practices were controlled for (Dishion, Owen, & Bullock, 2004).

The deviancy training is particularly relevant to clinicians, intervention program managers, and policymakers. We found that cognitive–behavioral interventions focused on the development of self-regulation.

Siblings are clearly important to social and emotional development. Sibling dynamics can be coercive or high in deviancy training. Sibling coercive dynamics and relationships are linked to antisocial behavior (Bullock, Bank, & Burraston, 2002; Patterson, Dishion, & Bank, 1984; Stormshak, Bellanti, Bierman, & Conduct Problems Prevention Research Group, 1996; Stormshak, Comeau, & Shepard, 2004). In addition, siblings can collude to undermine parental authority (Bullock & Dishion, 2002) and engage in deviancy training to facilitate problem behavior in adolescence. Sibling deviance, in fact, can be as powerful as friendships in terms of its association with adolescent problem behavior (Stormshak et al., 2004).

Peer dynamics related to emotional distress have been less studied. Peer rejection is certainly a covariate of depressed mood (Boivin, Poulin, & Vitaro, 1994; Patterson & Stoolmiller, 1991). It appears that one effect of depression is to amplify the child's perceptions of peer difficulties (Brendgen, Vitaro, Turgeon, & Poulin, 2002). The confounding difficulty is that depression in children and adolescents rarely occurs in the absence of other family experiences or social maladaptation. Thus, children with comorbidity (Capaldi & Patterson, 1991) show more severe forms of peer difficulties and peer deviance. In our observation assessment, we found that male and female adolescents with comorbidity engaged in more intense forms of deviancy training, were more involved in the deviant peer group, and had much poorer outcomes with respect to social maladaptation and future sexual behavior than were adolescents without comorbidity (Dishion, 2000).

In summary, Figure 3.1 provides an approximate empirical map of the types of peer, sibling, and family dynamics that are linked to both emotional distress and social maladaptation in children and adolescents. We assume that significant clinical change occurs only if these functional relationship patterns change as well.

Three Cautionary Notes

The relationship perspective does not imply that interaction processes are the primary cause of psychopathology. Certainly depression, conduct problems, anxiety, attention and activity problems, and thought disorders have biological underpinnings. However, behaviors, thoughts, and emotions transform as a function of the interpersonal context. For example, excessive worrying can draw caregivers and partners into a web of dependency, which ultimately exacerbates the individual's basic pattern. Overcoming worrying and phobia requires an active pattern of coping, including a willingness to withstand the discomfort of exposure and desensitization with little support (Zinbarg, 1990). However, it would be unfair to say that family and friends of an individual who is anxious or acting out are to blame for the individual's emotional distress or problem behavior. Actions and reactions of family and friends, however, can inadvertently worsen or maintain the problem.

The second cautionary note is that individuals are rarely aware of the dynamics of interpersonal relationships (Patterson, 1982; Patterson et al., 1992). Relationship processes are largely learned patterns that transpire without much thought, similar to driving a car, running, or playing a musical instrument (Dishion, French, & Patterson, 1995; Patterson & Reid, 1984). Although individuals certainly have preferences when picking a friend or partner, the momentary actions and reactions are rarely tracked and exceedingly difficult to change. It is not surprising that children do not track the functional dynamics of their family environments, and parents are barely one step ahead.

It often requires extensive professional training to attend to and respond mindfully to one's own relationship transactions. Subtle changes in responding within a relationship can often lead to rather large changes in the emotional experience, the ability to self-regulate, or the probability of unpleasant conflict.

It is unlikely that children and adolescents intentionally manipulate parents, relatives, and friends with their troubled behavior and emotions. It is more likely these interaction patterns are experienced as providing a sense of immediate control or relief of discomfort. For example, a depressed adolescent is probably unaware of how his or her depressive behavior transforms family conflict into support. In the short run, these shifts feel good; in the long run, depression and dependence become difficult to change for all those involved (Sheeber et al., 1998). In a similar way, careful observational work by Patterson and colleagues (Patterson, 1977; Patterson & Cobb, 1971, 1973) revealed that simply removing the antecedents to children's problem behavior significantly reduced the reoccurring conflict cycles, which are referred to as *coercion*. Also, reducing aversive reactions to conflict reduces the tendency to escalate (Snyder et al., 1994).

It is a ubiquitous human experience to be caught in relationship processes that are less than healthy. We compassionately understand that these processes take on a life of their own. In a very real sense, relationship patterns are entrained. Time and structure are often needed to change a problematic pattern, even when identified by the participants. Homeostasis is the rule rather than the exception.

The third cautionary note is that contexts can disrupt or enhance relationship processes. Sudden changes in leadership, resources, or contingencies can dramatically affect a network of relationships in a relatively predictable form. Structural family therapy is based on this principle. Barker's (1968) classic example of the covariation between staff size and attitudes toward work and absenteeism is relevant here. Elder et al.'s work relating the onset of the Great Depression to changes in irritable family interactions is also relevant to this discussion (Elder, Van Nguyen, & Caspi, 1985). Sometimes changes in context are introduced by professionals. For example, we found that aggregating children at high risk into groups was associated with escalation in young adolescent problem behavior as a function of incidental deviant-training interactions within the intervention groups (Dishion, McCord, & Poulin, 1999; Poulin, Dishion, & Burraston, 2001). The major point is that human relationships change as a function of context, and simply changing contexts may suffice to change a cascade of interaction processes considered problematic for a child or adolescent.

Because most people are not accurately tracking the minutiae of the moment-by-moment exchanges in significant relationships, it becomes necessary to conduct direct observations. State-of-the-art developmental and intervention research and clinical practice incorporate direct observations of social interaction. However, several issues must be considered when microsocial exchanges in relationships that are relevant to various areas of psychology are measured (Patterson, 1984).

MEASUREMENT ISSUES AND METHODOLOGY

Studying close relationships requires direct observation. Initial research at the Oregon Social Learning Center involved observers who visited family homes and coded family interaction live (Reid, 1978). Observers visited families up to five or six times to collect a baseline of behavior before initiating an intervention. Baselines were necessary to establish (with some confidence) the relative occurrence of specific parent–child interactions, such as the rate of compliance to parent commands or the tendency for the parent–child interaction to escalate when in conflict. Even for distressed families, repeated observations are needed to derive a reliable estimate of many of these variables, especially those describing negative interactions.

TABLE 3.1
Family Interaction Task

Family management construct	Early childhood	Middle childhood	Adolescence
Relationship quality	Child-directed play Separation and reunion	Planning activity Family celebration	Planning activity Family celebration
Behavior management	Cleanup task	Problem solving Monitoring Limit setting	Problem solving Monitoring Limit setting

Many investigators have recently moved to structured tasks to elicit the behaviors of interest. These studies began with the early observations of marital interactions (Birchler, Weiss, & Vincent, 1975). In the process of structuring interactions to understand close relationships, a principle emerged: It was imperative to use real situations. For example, Birchler et al. (1975) were able to differentiate distressed couples from nondistressed couples when they discussed real problems within their relationships. However, the two types of couples were undifferentiated when they discussed hypothetical issues or interacted with a stranger.

The accepted rationale for this finding is that negative emotion disrupts interactions in close relationships (Forgatch, 1989; Patterson, 1982). Real situations make it difficult to mask or avoid the problematic reactions that disrupt one's best intentions to get along with a partner or family member. Therefore, most studies of close relationships structure interactions that involve real issues within the family or relationship. However, it is essential to adapt family interaction tasks to the developmental level of the child. We propose the grid in Table 3.1 as a summary of the interaction tasks relevant for clinical family assessment at each age.

Each task has specific instructions that are memorized by the assessment staff. A time limit is provided for each task, and when the time is up the family is instructed to proceed to the next interaction. The structure is useful because it provides a sense of how various families respond in each situation. Diversity is better understood when flexible ways of responding to structure are studied—much like understanding how children approach complex cognitive tasks in the context of a structured assessment of intellectual abilities.

One of the major concerns in observational assessment is cultural diversity. We are only beginning to understand the variability in the organization and process of relationships across cultural groups. Therefore, within any intervention group, it is imperative to include members of diverse cultural groups and for clinicians to undergo diversity training. For example, the way families respond to a structured family assessment may vary as a function of minority status. The demand characteristics associated with diverse cultural groups are different. Minority members being studied by a primarily European American research group may respond differently than European American families, who may intrinsically trust the research process and promises of confidentiality.

When direct observation of family interaction is discussed, concerns about reactivity are usually raised. *Reactivity* refers to the possibility that people change when they know they are being observed. It would be hard to argue against that assertion. How does reactivity affect the validity of our research and clinical assessments? The little work that has been done suggests that the more distressed a relationship is, the less important reactivity probably is. Most families of children showing clinically significant emotional distress and social maladaptation at home and school can be safely assumed to be distressed and, thus, are unable to completely control family dynamics once the task is initiated. It is difficult for people to fake positive responses when interacting with someone who is upsetting them (Johnson & Bolstad, 1975).

For example, using observational coding methods, we examined the interactions of clinic-referred and comparison families during a family intake interview. Most clinicians conduct an open-ended, clinical interview with families when first providing mental health services. When these intake interviews (consisting of 1 hour of observation) were coded and compared with those of nonclinical families, different patterns of family interaction and distress emerged, including negative affect and family dynamics that are detrimental to child development (Stormshak, Speltz, DeKlyen, & Greenberg, 1997). Jacob and colleagues (Jacob, Tennenbaum, Seilhamer, Bargiel, & Sharon, 1994) examined distressed and nondistressed families and came to similar conclusions. To the extent that we want to measure positive parenting or relationship practices, however, reactivity may be an issue. Although regulating negative emotion in close relationships seems to be central to adjustment, it is also true that positive relationship behaviors that are sensitive to context may be missed in our observational protocols. In this sense, our methodology of direct observations may disrupt sensitive, positive interpersonal processes that hold relationships together. Or perhaps some of the positive aspects of relationships unfold over longer periods and require different coding and rating procedures, or different methods of data collection. For example, D. R. Peterson (1979) found interesting patterns of both positive and negative marriage interactions using a diary method. Pettit and Bates (1989) used a social-events approach to coding family interaction from the transcripts provided by live narratives.

Dimensionality

Two dimensions of social interaction are currently particularly relevant to understanding developmental trajectories and change dynamics. The first is what we call *coding of interpersonal process*, which refers to coding systems that describe features of the behavior such as physical and verbal interactions and the interpersonal valence of the behavior. Observations of process describe the basic descriptive dynamics within a relationship such as the amount of talking, nonverbal gestures, affect quality, commands, and physical interaction. The second dimension of human interaction that is relevant to development and change is the organization of semantic content in relationship exchanges. Developmental research reveals that topic convergence is relevant to the formation of new relationships (e.g., Dishion, Andrews, & Crosby, 1995; Gottman, 1980) and, therefore, is potentially powerful in shaping and maintaining verbal schemas within which development and change are embedded (Hayes, 1987; Skinner, 1945). Linguistic capabilities enable the establishment of an *as if* reality (i.e., stimulus equivalence) that has the power to affect future behavior, appraisal of life circumstances, and sense of emotional well-being. Human beings are the only species, for example, that commit suicide (Hayes, 1992). It is assumed that the study of the verbal schema organizing the relationships and behavior of individuals provides insights into acts (e.g., suicide, murder) that seem incomprehensible from a utilitarian perspective.

Measuring Process

Describing the relationship processes is by no means simple. A system for coding interactions is necessary. Training is required for coders to reliably use the coding system (Reid, 1978, 1982). The system provides a description of how the family interacts, in a way that could not be captured by using global reports. Most often, topographical coding systems are designed with a special purpose in mind. For example, in the early studies of aggression, Patterson and colleagues (Patterson, Chamberlain, & Reid, 1982; Patterson, Littman, & Bricker, 1967) designed a system for observing children interacting on the playground, describing the escape conditioning process that would later define the coercion model. Relatively recent is the design of all-purpose coding systems that attempt to define the universe of social interaction (and occurrence of behaviors) within a prespecified grid. This approach was first used with the Family Process Code (Dishion, Gardner, Patterson, Reid, & Thibodeaux, 1983), then revised into the Interpersonal Process Code (Rusby, Estes, & Dishion, 1990).

TABLE 3.2
Relationship Process Code

	Positive	Neutral	Negative
Verbal	Positive verbal	Proactive structure	Negative verbal
Nonverbal	Compliant	Solitary	Noncompliant
Physical	Physical affection	Physical interaction	Physical aggression

Examining relationships more closely, we recently designed the Relationship Process Code (see Table 3.2; Jabson & Dishion, 2005), an omnibus coding system potentially used for coding the relationship process across a variety of situations and contexts. The Relationship Process Code can be used to study friendships, sibling interactions, parent–child relationships, and peer interactions in playground settings. In comparison to other coding systems, the code shown in Table 3.2 offers a parsimonious and cost-effective strategy for describing social interaction patterns. Salience is a critical concern in coding interaction. Certain behaviors do not occur much and therefore are difficult to reliably measure. Other behaviors are simply difficult to code because they rely on high levels of inference by coders. For example, is an interaction considered teaching when it becomes a statement of meaningless platitudes? Teaching in close relationships rarely takes a direct form and often occurs as a function of adults structuring a discussion or situation to provide instruction, such as in scaffolding (Rogoff, 1994).

The coding system shown in Table 3.2 is accompanied by a manual (Jabson & Dishion, 2005) with detailed descriptions of definitions for each category. We used time-sampling or event-duration coding in the collection of data. Time-sampling strategies, which involve recording the occurrence of various codes within a specified time interval, are by far the easiest in terms of coder training. Event-duration coding has the advantage of providing information about the sequencing and duration of behavior within a relationship. These indices provide a more detailed description of the process of exchange.

Several interesting scores can be derived from the Relationship Process Code. The first score is the frequency and duration of specific clusters such as Positive Engagement, Negative Engagement, Talk, Structuring, and Directives. O'Leary (2000) examined the effect of a brief family intervention on the parent–child interactions in preschool children at high risk finding increases in structuring as a function of having received a motivational feedback session. Structuring (e.g., providing clear limits and consequences) is considered a parenting skill in contrast to directives, which increase the likelihood of a coercive interchange. In addition to frequency and duration of behavior clusters, conditional z scores can be computed. Sequential scores index the structure of the interaction (Patterson, 1982). For example, *negative reciprocity* can be defined as the likelihood of a family member responding in like manner to a negative interaction. However, the various complex issues surrounding the formulation of z scores are beyond the scope of this chapter (Bakeman & Gottman, 1986; Bakeman & Quera, 1995; Gottman & Roy, 1990).

In our intervention and developmental research with families, we complement the microsocial coding of family interaction with macroratings of family management (Dishion, Hogansen, & Winter, 2000). For families of young adolescents, we trained coders to view videotapes of families with young adolescents and systematically rate the skills that are targeted in our intervention program, including encouragement, limit setting, monitoring, norm setting, problem solving, and relationship quality. We viewed high- and low-risk families in a culturally diverse metropolitan area and found that the overall family management score differentiates successful families from high-risk families (Dishion & Bullock, 2002).

Verbal Schemas

Close relationships generate a unique worldview that could be described as a verbal schema. Attitudes and beliefs are heavily influenced by a network of close relationships. It is not by chance that, regardless of the situation, more than 70% of family and peer interactions are coded simply as *talk* (Dishion, Andrews, & Crosby, 1995; Patterson et al., 1992). In therapeutic interactions, friendships, romantic relationships, and parent–child interactions, a lot of energy goes into sharing information and influencing our interaction partners. This process can be captured by systematically coding the topics of the verbal behavior, mostly by viewing videotaped interactions.

A major concern in coding verbal conversational topics is the power of context in defining meaning within social interaction. This construct is referred to as the pragmatics of communication. For example, winking after a statement suggests that the statement should not be taken literally. To deal with the complexity of coding content reliably, clinicians have to simplify the focus. For example, in our studies of deviant peer influences, we coded rule breaking and normative talk as the two potential topics. In studies of conversations with friends, we defined two reaction codes, pause and laugh. The goal was to understand how conversation topics served to organize, and be organized by, reactions of the listener. This goal followed from Skinner's early thesis (Skinner, 1945) that to understand verbal behavior, one needs to study the reactions of the listener.

This simple approach to coding the verbal schema of adolescent friendship interactions revealed a process we call *deviancy training*. The idea is simple: In some friendship interactions, positive reactions are elicited primarily in the context of deviant talk. Thus deviance becomes what Gottman

(1983) referred to as a *common ground activity*. Applying a matching law model to the observation data, we found that the rate of deviant talk matched the relative rate of reinforcement. Moreover, deviancy training predicted subsequent adolescent escalations in substance use (Dishion, Capaldi, et al., 1995), delinquency (Dishion, Spracklen, et al., 1996), and violent behavior (Dishion et al., 1997). Patterson, Dishion, and Yoerger (2000) found that after controlling for various risk factors, deviancy training predicted multiple forms of young adult problem behavior. Finally, we recently reported findings suggesting that hostile attitudes toward women expressed by adolescent boys among their friends uniquely predicted observed aggression with a female partner 5 years later (Capaldi, Dishion, Stoolmiller, & Yoerger, 2001). We used a similar code to examine the sibling relationships of youth at high risk and found that deviancy training in the context of siblings predicted the escalation of substance use over 3 years (Stormshak et al., 2004).

We do not know to what extent close relationships influence the establishment of verbal schemas at different points in development. We suspect that adolescence is a sensitive period for friendship influence in that such relationships are central for selecting intimate mates (Dishion, Poulin, & Medici Skaggs, 2000). It is possible that the early phases of new relationships represent an opportunity for influence and change, perhaps in the context of relocating or other social transitions, which result in establishing new social networks. It is thought that individuals can reorganize attitudes and behaviors to fit within a social network and, similarly, seek out a social niche that best fits their belief systems (Scarr & McCartney, 1983). Humans are very sensitive to selecting the companionship of others who are likely to respond positively to their interpersonal repertoire. Perhaps this process explains the rather paradoxical pattern of adults repeating the selection of intimate partners who abuse or emotionally denigrate them.

Figure 3.3 provides an example of a strategy for studying the norm validation process in close relationships. Note that topics are generally categorized as either deviant or normative, and the response as facilitating, neutral, or discouraging. It is also possible to use the affective codes in Figure 3.3 to code responses to verbal topics. When adolescent friendships are studied, a relatively high rate of both deviant and normative topics is observed. In contrast, when families and couples are studied, a relatively low rate of deviant topics is observed. In fact, interestingly enough, our studies are indicating that interdependent relationships do not often engage in deviancy training.

The Norm Validation Code in Figure 3.3 is most likely useful for studying peer relationships across contexts and developmental phases (Piehler & Dishion, in press). We suspect that affective responses to topics in close relationships are less influential in changing attitudes. The major

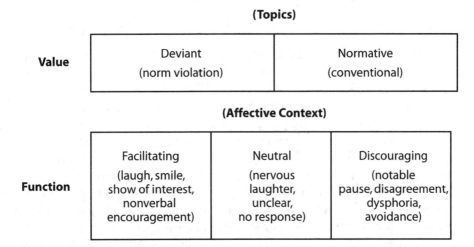

(Topics)

Value	Deviant (norm violation)	Normative (conventional)

(Affective Context)

Function	Facilitating (laugh, smile, show of interest, nonverbal encouragement)	Neutral (nervous laughter, unclear, no response)	Discouraging (notable pause, disagreement, dysphoria, avoidance)

Figure 3.3. Norm validation code.

influence strategy in close relationships seems to be escape conditioning (Patterson, 1982; Patterson et al., 1992); that is, verbal behavior that reduces conflict and ends unpleasantness in a close relationship is more likely to increase in the future. For example, talking about drinking may increase conflict in a marriage. Therefore, avoiding these discussions and reducing drinking would be reinforced by virtue of reducing the tension and conflict in the close relationship. Thus it is hypothesized that escape avoidance is the influence process in interdependent relationships, and positive reinforcement is the influence process in peer relationships.

The majority of research on the role of close relationships in shaping attitudes and beliefs has focused on understanding, and intervening with, problem behavior, primarily in adolescence. An interesting extension would be to understand how peer and family relationships might influence the course of those behaviors and attitudes associated with depression, eating disorders, and anxiety disorders. A cognitive–behavioral approach assumes that these difficulties result from errors in thinking. However, very little developmental research focuses on the social origins of these cognitive biases. Perhaps depressive topics elicit support in close relationships and inadvertently reinforce a negative, depressive worldview. In a similar way, relationships that reinforce unrealistic expectations about social interactions, academic performance, or weight concerns elicit a verbal schema conducive to social phobia, generalized anxiety, or eating concerns. This is a promising area for future research. Table 3.2 could be modified for each specific problem, with topics tailored to each research problem. The central concept is that the affective climate of the relationship would be organized around specific kinds of verbal information.

SUMMARY

The ecological framework emphasizes the importance of understanding and addressing social interactions within caregiving and peer relationships in assessment and interventions. Although children and adolescents may elicit maladaptive social interactions with caregivers and peers, the evidence is clear that interventions that address those social interactions affect long-term outcomes in children and adolescents (e.g., Dishion, Patterson, & Kavanagh, 1992; Forgatch, 1991; Forgatch & DeGarmo, 2002). One of the most important innovations in child and family intervention research is the use of direct observations in the study of change (Patterson, Reid, & Maerov, 1978). Of particular importance to child and adolescent problem behavior are caregiving relationships that are coercive (problem behavior is negatively reinforced) and peer relationships that involve deviancy training (problem behavior is positively reinforced). We suggest that direct observations of caregiving and peer relationships are the optimal assessment strategy; children and parents are not reliable reporters of the dynamics of their own relationships. In the next chapter, we provide an overview of our intervention model, which discusses the role of assessment in addressing clients' motivations to change and their corresponding awareness of the factors that interfere with their child or adolescent's mental health.

4

THE ECOLOGICAL FAMILY INTERVENTION AND THERAPY MODEL

In this chapter we provide an overview of our ecological family intervention and therapy, which we refer to as the EcoFIT model. This intervention model explicitly integrates the process of defining intervention targets (i.e., family management, child self-regulation, peers) with principles of behavior change. It is not enough to know what to change, but clinicians also need to know how to change behavior. In other words, they must go beyond technology and consider the dynamics of guiding a change process in children and families (Patterson, 1985). Chapters 5 to 12 (this volume) provide the details of each component of the intervention. The approach outlined in this manual is an adaptation of a social learning approach to parent training, family therapy, and couples therapy.

BACKGROUND OF EcoFIT

The major source of influence on this work is the intervention model developed at the Oregon Social Learning Center (OSLC) and referred to as Parent Management Training, Oregon model (Forgatch, Patterson, & DeGarmo, 2005). The OSLC approach (Patterson, Reid, & Dishion, 1992) emphasizes supporting change in social interaction patterns in families to reduce problem behavior in children. This particular intervention model has a strong empirical foundation (e.g., Reid, Patterson, & Snyder, 2002) and is consistent with a broad range of intervention strategies that have demonstrated effectiveness (Kazdin, 2002; Patterson, Dishion, & Chamberlain, 1993).

Unique Aspects of the Approach

The intervention approach described herein, however, has three additional emphases that are unique in comparison to a social learning approach to family treatment (Stormshak & Dishion, 2002). First, in the EcoFIT approach, we tailor our interventions with children and families to fit their current family circumstances. Interventions that are tailored and responsive to the clients' needs have been called *adaptive* (Collins, Murphy, & Bierman, 2004). In this approach, interventions are tailored to fit the child and family's mental health needs on the basis of results of the Family Check-Up (FCU). Some families may be involved in interventions that target only positive reinforcement, especially if limit setting, monitoring, and communication are parenting strengths. Moreover, we may tailor our approach to limit setting with families, depending on the number of parents in the family, the physical context of the living situation, and the sociocultural background of the family. In this sense, the EcoFIT approach proposes a menu of empirically supported interventions with diverse venues of service delivery. Offering an intervention menu and diverse service delivery options promotes parent engagement and motivation (Dishion & Kavanagh, 2003; W. R. Miller & Rollnick, 2002). Selection of an intervention strategy is based on the assessment results and the motivation and circumstances of the child and family.

A second difference in the EcoFIT approach is that we support periodic, and sometimes brief, interventions during times of developmental and contextual transition. For example, the early childhood years can be thought of as an extended transition period when the child's rapid development of cognitive (e.g., problem solving), motor (e.g., walking and running), and language skills demand change in parenting strategies and family ecology. The optimal service settings for an EcoFIT approach are those that offer continual contact with a child and family over a specific period of development—in other words, continuity in mental health services to families over a long period. Our approach is most akin to a health maintenance model of mental health service delivery, and least like a medical disease model of intervention. In fact, we propose that six to eight sessions can lead to relatively large effect sizes if delivered skillfully and strategically over 2 to 3 years.

A third difference is that we actively address motivation to change at all stages of the intervention process. The FCU provides an assessment and addresses parents' motivations to change (W. R. Miller & Rollnick, 2002). During the intervention, we address motivation at several stages of the change process. For example, when delivering this intervention, we rely heavily on the work of OSLC to address issues of resistance to change. In addition, we provide brief, motivational support for families to support persistence and maintenance of change.

Three Types of Sensitivity

Our approach to child and family intervention is ecologically sensitive in that we are aware of the importance of considering the family's needs with respect to a variety of social and community resources. For example, in middle childhood and adolescence, it is essential to interface interventions and assessments of children and families with relevant staff in school environments. In early childhood, we actively link family intervention services to social services that support the health and education of young children, including preschool programs such as Early Head Start and Head Start.

Cultural sensitivity emerges as an inherent strength of the intervention's ecological perspective. The EcoFIT model addresses both cultural and regional contexts by incorporating the specific needs of African American, European American, American Indian, and Latino low-income families who live in northwestern suburban, eastern urban, and southeastern rural communities. The EcoFIT design incorporates the distinct aspects of the client's culture as a part of the treatment approach. For example, parent consultants provide home-visit sessions in Spanish to Latino families and are trained to be aware of the specific cultural aspects of family life and child rearing in African American and Latino homes as well as sensitive to regional and population density issues. Moreover, because the intervention is built around the family's identified needs and goals, cultural and personal perspectives of the family become central to the intervention.

Finally, sensitivity to child and family ecology mandates that clinicians focus on parents and caregivers as central to strategies that promote child and adolescent mental health. This emphasis is consonant with systems therapies that strive to support, build, and differentiate parents as the executive system in managing and maintaining change and stability. The systems perspective is also strategic, as is our approach (e.g., Haley, 1971; Minuchin & Fishman, 1981; Szapocznik & Kurtines, 1989). However, the approach described in this volume is different from strategic family therapy in that the intervention foci are based on an ecological family assessment and are collaboratively derived with the parent. As such, a critical piece of effective service delivery is case conceptualization (Dishion & Kavanagh, 2003; Stormshak & Dishion, 2002). Principles and objectives that guide our strategic approach to case conceptualization are as follows: (a) Reduce the risk of immediate harm to the child and family; (b) change social interaction patterns known to maintain or exacerbate mental health problems; (c) fit interventions within the family ecology; and (d) support existing parenting and family strengths.

Addressing Change

As we discussed earlier, there is considerable empirical support for targeting families and parenting practices in the effort to address nearly all clinical issues involving children and adolescents. There are two major hurdles to making change in families. First, as discussed in chapter 3 (this volume), many of the daily interaction patterns between caregivers and children are automatic, which often means that the participants are not cognitively tracking their own behavior as it relates to their perception of the problem. Even when coercive interactions are understood intellectually, that knowledge is difficult to apply toward changing one's own relationships to eliminate the coercive component. Second, even when there is insight and understanding about the need to change, there can also be substantial resistance to change. Specific therapist behaviors can either facilitate the change process or elicit more resistance to change from caregivers and other family members (Patterson, 1985; Patterson & Forgatch, 1985). The key feature of our approach to child and family intervention is that we attend to motivational issues at all phases of the change cycle, with respect to client and therapist interactions within the change process.

To address these two barriers to change, we use structured, cost-effective assessments to initiate and maintain the change process. Assessments not only reveal the potential targets of change but also are a tool for eliciting motivation to change and for developing collaborative working relationships between the client and therapist (W. R. Miller, 2002; Sanders & Lawton, 1993). Clients benefit from assessments as a source of motivation and engagement. Also, therapists can use assessments to help conceptualize cases, prioritize intervention targets, and develop a collaborative set. This approach to child and family therapy is referred to as AIM to emphasize that *assessment*, *intervention*, and *motivation* are inextricably linked. Several features of an ecological perspective on development and change warrant repetition. One is the issue of the agents in the change process. We prioritize engaging families and specifically targeting parenting practices as a necessary but insufficient condition for meaningful clinical change. In chapter 1 (this volume), we presented an empirically based perspective on the developmental factors associated with social adaptation and emotional regulation throughout the life cycle. The implication of this perspective is that in early childhood, much of the intervention focus should be on supporting a family system and parenting practices. In middle childhood, the focus necessarily expands to the child's social adaptation in the school setting, involving consultations and assessments in school. Finally, in adolescence, attention to the broader ecology of the young person's life, including sensitivity to the evolving peer context and community risks that may exacerbate problems for youth, becomes increasingly important.

Thus, interventions that target only the child and ignore parenting practices or that are delivered in peer groups may be unwise, or worse, iatrogenic (Dishion, McCord, & Poulin, 1999; Poulin & Boivin, 2000). Several carefully developed interventions directly address intrapersonal dynamics related to aggression (Lochman, Burch, Curry, & Lampron, 1984; Lochman, Lampron, Burch, & Curry, 1985), conduct disorder (Kazdin, Siegel, & Bass, 1992), anxiety (Dadds, Spence, Holland, Barrett, & Lacrens, 1997), and depression (Lewinsohn & Clarke, 1990). We propose that such interventions would have more enduring benefits and be more cost-effective if they addressed parenting and contextual factors as well. The next stage of our intervention trials should clarify this issue.

Second, interventions with children should address comorbidity, specifically dimensions of problem behavior and emotional distress. One of the central problems in linking intervention research with the design of mental health service delivery systems is that the psychopathology addressed in most clinics is different from what is observed in government-funded intervention trials. Most of the children and adolescents seen in services do not fit neatly within the *Diagnostic and Statistical Manual of Mental Disorders* (4th ed.; American Psychiatric Association, 1994) system and would be screened out of a traditional research trial targeting only one type of disorder. As we discussed in chapters 2 and 3 (this volume), the comorbidity of depression and problem behavior is significant in this population and co-occurs with additional risk behavior (e.g., cutting, drug use).

Finally, a distinguishing feature of the AIM clinical model is its health maintenance emphasis (Stormshak & Dishion, 2002). That is, we do not expect that a mental health treatment, especially when delivered to an individual, will cure a mental health problem as if it were a disease. Rather, we assume that periodic interventions will be necessary to support the maintenance of an ecology that supports child and adolescent social adaptation and emotion regulation. We suggest that it is more productive to compare mental health interventions for children and families with dental interventions (Kazdin, 1993; Loeber, Dishion, & Patterson, 1984). In dental work, it is assumed that periodic check-ups; the client's dental hygiene, diet, and preventive practices (e.g., fluoride); and assessment-based interventions (e.g., X-rays, gum assessments) are necessary to maintain dental health.

In the EcoFIT model, we provide a yearly FCU as a basis for promoting mental health and preventing difficulties across development. This intervention can be delivered with relatively few resources. For example, in one study, we found that an average of six intervention contacts spread over 2 to 3 years prevented early-onset substance use for identified young adolescents at high risk and their families (Dishion, Kavanagh, et al., 2002). In fact, the families at highest risk were the most likely to engage in the FCU and to effectively reduce the risk for their youngster during the ensuing 4 years (Connell, Dishion, & Deater-Deckard, in press). We have observed more recently that the youth and families who engaged in the FCU intervention showed 6-year reductions in the use of marijuana, alcohol, and tobacco, compared with a similar set of randomly assigned families (Connell, Dishion, & Kavanagh, 2005). These adolescents at high risk were also less likely to be involved in deviant peer groups, had fewer and less-severe arrests, and engaged in fewer antisocial behaviors (Connell, Dishion, Yasui, & Kavanagh, in press). Again, these long-lasting effects with the youth at highest risk were supported by an average of six sessions over 3 years.

Entrained Self-Regulation

An interesting point is worth making at this juncture. Genetic propensities and temperamental substrates conducive to social and emotional difficulties are probably an indicator that environmental interventions are critical for the prevention and maintenance of mental health. In addition, traumatic experiences can permanently place a child within a developmental trajectory that is at high risk for serious mental health problems. From a diathesis–stress perspective (Dishion & Patterson, 2006; Rende & Plomin, 1992), some children and adolescents may, by nature or developmental history, be more sensitive and vulnerable to pathogenic environments. Several findings in the intervention literature reveal that youth at high risk are more likely to respond positively to ecologically based interventions (e.g., Connell et al., in press; Eddy, Reid, Stoolmiller, & Fetrow, 2003; Ialongo, Poduska, Werthamer, & Kellam, 2001; Kellam, Ling, Merisca, Brown, & Ialongo, 1998).

For this reason we have developed the concept of *entrained self-regulation* to capture the heightened vulnerability or resilience of some children to problematic environments and relationships, as well as their responsiveness to interventions (Dishion & Patterson, 2006). Although designed for children and adolescents, the concept could also be applied to parents who are engaged in the change process. Like the work of Sanders (1999), the EcoFIT model is designed from a self-regulatory framework, in that motivation to change is integral to case conceptualization and the manner in which we work with children and families.

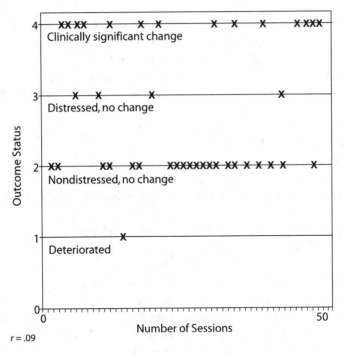

Figure 4.1. Outcome status for each child on the Family Process Code Negative Engagement Scale (parent to target child).

Measuring Outcomes

We think that the integration of motivational and ecological issues in child and family interventions will help solve old paradoxes of the behavior therapy outcome research. For instance, our research on the therapy process has not found ample justification for expecting dose–response relations in interventions that deliver standard packages that are not based on assessments. We found that the families making clinically significant change in parenting groups did so within the first 5 sessions of a 12-session curriculum. Clinically significant change seemed to occur rapidly and was not associated with learning the specific skills targeted in the cognitive–behavioral curriculum or the completion of homework assignments (Dishion & Kavanagh, 2003).

This pattern seems to also be true for individual behavior family therapy. In a careful analysis of 70 clinical cases treated in parent management training, Weber (1998) did not find a link between the number of sessions a family completed and statistically reliable, clinically significant change (see Figure 4.1). In the Weber study, children ages 6 to 12 were recruited and retained if they were in the clinically significant distress range on parent-reported problem behavior as well as direct observation on child–parent interactions in the home. Clinically significant and statistically reliable change was defined with the criteria developed by Jacobsen and Truax (1991). Clients who show clinically significant change are those who were in the clinical range before treatment and who improved to such an extent that they were reliably within the nondistressed range following treatment. This result is certainly what we hope for in a clinical outcome study. On occasion, however, children and families may remain within the clinical range yet make substantial improvements nevertheless. Reliable change addresses this positive outcome. Both clinically significant and reliable change are highly relevant to the question of how much therapy is needed to improve families' lives.

Weber (1998) analyzed both indices of change on the parent and teacher versions of the Child Behavior Checklist as well as the Negative Engagement Score from the Family Process Code (Dishion & Andrews, 1995; Dishion, Gardner, Patterson, Reid, & Thibodeaux, 1983). For the Child Behavior Checklist, Achenbach and colleagues (Achenbach, 1992; Achenbach, McConaughy, & Howell, 1987) provided norms to determine the normal and distressed range of those scores. For the Family Process Code, Weber used the norms for Negative Engagement from the 206 boys in the Oregon Youth Study (Patterson et al., 1992). Figure 4.1 provides an overview of the percentage of children who improved clinically on the Negative Engagement home observation score as a function of the number of sessions with a therapist. Figure 4.1 suggests that about 30% of the families made clinically significant reductions in 4 to 15 sessions, and 60% required more than 15 sessions to make that change. It is clear that there was absolutely no relation between clinically significant change on observed behavior and the number of sessions.

It is possible that dosage of behavior family therapy is related to the magnitude of change, and not necessarily to whether the change is clinically significant. Some families may be marginally in the distressed range before therapy, making movement into the normative range relatively easily. Other families may be extremely distressed and, therefore, moving them to a range typical of normal families is time consuming and labor intensive. Thus, one should look at statistically reliable change, which is basically a t score reflecting the difference between the termination and baseline scores, divided by the standard error of measurement (Jacobsen & Truax, 1991). Figure 4.2 provides a summary of the relation between the number of sessions and reliable reductions in negative engagement as observed within the family at home using the Family Process Code. This analysis was repeated for parent and teacher reports for both clinical and reliable change, with the general conclusion that there was no relation between the number of sessions and a family's change during behavior family therapy.

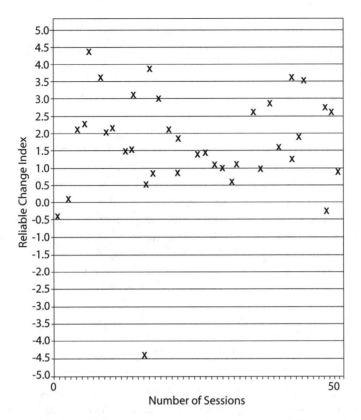

Figure 4.2. Reliable change index value for each child on the Family Process Code Negative Engagement Scale (parent to target child). r = .20.

These findings were consistent with the conclusions we drew when examining factors that predicted change in another sample of families engaging in parent management training (Dishion & Patterson, 1992). In this study, we examined a variety of predictors of statistical and clinically significant change, including the number of sessions. The only predictor of change was the child's age when entering treatment. Older children (ages 6–12) were modestly more likely to drop out of therapy. Indeed, the past 20 years of work examining behavior family therapy clearly shows that it is effective in reducing problem behavior in children; it is perhaps the most effective strategy known (Kazdin & Weisz, 1998). However, the process in which change is initiated and maintained when interacting with a therapist is not clearly understood. There are many untested assumptions about how to work with families and the types of judgments clinicians need to make when working with families in supporting healthy change (Kazdin, 2000). Perhaps this ignorance results from a lack of research on change, as articulated by

Kazdin (1999): "We have hundreds and hundreds of therapy studies that focus on treatment effects but precious few that attempt to explain and test why these effects occur" (p. 541).

Summary of Main Points

In summary, the ecological approach to supporting family change and mental health services is consistent with this paradigm: (a) Check-ups are often necessary, especially for families in transition or individuals who are developmentally vulnerable; (b) services are assessment driven rather than theory driven; (c) there is a menu of possible intervention services that are empirically derived and volitional; (d) many aspects of mental health depend on hygienic practices, and therefore are motivationally based; (e) several interrelated dimensions of mental health are systemically connected in a family and, often, there is not a clear point of demarcation for when individuals are sick or well; and (f) the change process essentially promotes mental health, rather than treats psychopathology.

THE ECOLOGY OF CHANGE

A major insight into clinical and counseling psychology during the past 15 years is the work linking naturalistic change with change as a function of intervention. In studying change in addictive behavior, Prochaska and colleagues (Prochaska, Velicer, Guadagnoli, & Rossi, 1991) discovered that a large proportion of the population changed their own addictive behaviors without seeking professional help. This finding led these investigators to posit individual differences in motivation to change. By way of extension, Prochaska et al. (1991) attacked the old problem of schools of therapy, introducing the transtheoretical approach. The idea is that diverse therapeutic schools are focusing on different parts of the same phenomenon and that these forms of therapy could be integrated within a more comprehensive framework (Prochaska, 1993; Prochaska & DiClemente, 1982, 1986).

The transtheoretical model well serves the ecological emphasis we propose. Not only can developmental processes be studied at multiple levels, but interventions that address individual, relationship, and contextual systematic change can also be developed. The key is realizing that motivation does not reside in the individual but is an interaction between the agent and the environment in which the change is taking place. This understanding implies that clinical and counseling skills are in fact critical to either promoting—or dampening—motivation to change. In the classic process research on behavior family therapy, we find that therapist interactions with parents were instrumental for promoting change (Patterson, 1985; Patterson

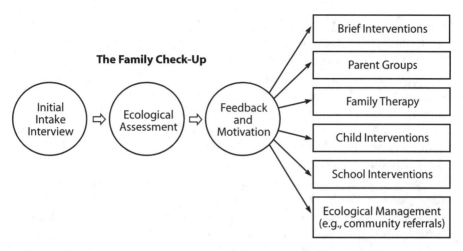

Figure 4.3. An ecological service delivery system for children and families.

& Chamberlain, 1994; Patterson & Forgatch, 1985). Miller adapted these ideas to consider therapeutic interactions, showing that the counselor's approach to interacting with his or her client can enhance motivation to change problematic drinking practices. This line of research led to the development of motivational interviewing and the Drinker's Check-Up (Brown & Miller, 1993; W. R. Miller, 2002; W. R. Miller & Rollnick, 2002; W. R. Miller & Sovereign, 1989).

Thus a critical feature of a mental health intervention is to explicitly address motivation to change. The assessment-based feedback session is designed to target the client's stage of change. In this section, we outline other features of a service delivery system for working with children and families. The service delivery system presumes that interventions for children and families should (a) be guided by a developmental model of child and adolescent maladaptive behavior and emotional maladjustment; (b) attend to the functional dynamics of key relationships; and (c) address motivation to change in parents, children, and larger social systems. The ecological intervention system is summarized in Figure 4.3. Each intervention module is described in detail in this volume. It is presumed that as our intervention science progresses, there will be an increase in the menu of intervention options described in Figure 4.3 and that such an increase in our empirically based, clinical armamentarium will improve the mental health services of children and families and public health in general (Biglan, 1995; Biglan & Taylor, 2000).

Establishing a collaborative set at the time of the initial contact with a client is the first step of the change process. The second step is a carefully conducted, ecologically relevant assessment. The third step is to provide to the change agents motivational feedback that is solution focused. We refer to the first three steps of the change process as the FCU.

The FCU is the foundation of the change process. On the basis of a carefully conducted assessment, a collaborative set is established between the family and the therapist with respect to the menu of possible relevant interventions. The menu is empirically based, evolving as the field matures and becoming more pragmatic in the business of supporting family change. Family mental health, like dental hygiene, does not depend solely on the therapist–client interaction but is in part a function of the community ecology—with each community having a unique profile of barriers to, and resources for, family living. Clinical interventions are embedded within community contexts and should explicitly link to these service delivery systems.

The goal of support for family mental health is to promote the well-being of all individuals and to reduce problem behavior. As discussed, these two aims are interrelated empirically and conceptually. A variety of intervention options are promising for promoting change. In our work with adolescents and their families, we provide a range of interventions (see Figure 4.3). The selection of interventions is a joint enterprise between the parent and the therapist, as informed by a comprehensive assessment, and is conditional on the resources within the intervention setting and the community.

OVERVIEW OF EcoFIT

EcoFIT is an adaptive, tailored approach to intervening with children and families. The general features are summarized below.

Structuring Support

As discussed previously, the different family management constructs we target are highly intercorrelated and mutually embedded. Figure 4.4 summarizes the four basic sets of parenting skills, adapted from the conceptualization offered by Dishion and McMahon (1998). The three domains of practice include monitoring, behavior management, and relationship building. Although parent–child relationships are fundamental to behavior management and monitoring, they are often the last area of focus when clinicians support change in highly disrupted families. However, for families that require minimal intervention, relationship skills are the first area of focus for effective, brief interventions.

The level of regulation in a family must be considered when the point of entry into the change process is being determined. Structural family

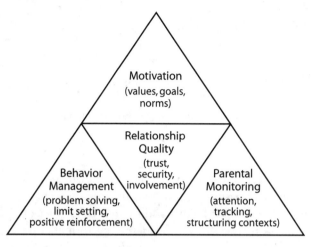

Figure 4.4. A general perspective on family process.

therapists have aptly emphasized the need for an executive system within a family structure (Haley, 1971; Minuchin, 1974). On occasion, a child will dominate the change process in the family. For example, the family will not attend therapy because the child refuses or the caregivers are anxious about confronting the child. Consider the following case scenario.

> Ted was a 13-year-old boy living with his 50-year-old mother. He was the youngest of four children, but his older brothers and sisters had long since left the house. His mom had remarried when he was 7 years old, but recently divorced his stepfather with whom he was very close. Ted had been his mother's main source of social support for the past 5 years. His grades in middle school had dropped, he had quit sports, and he had started spending time with some older peers in the neighborhood. He was not pleased with the idea of therapy and had generally come to feel contempt for his mother's desire to be closer to him, which she expressed clearly to the therapist during the course of the FCU. Following the feedback session, Ted announced he was not participating in clinical services. At this point, the therapists consulted with his mother to continue her own work on parenting. Eventually Ted became interested in participating in some of the sessions.

The initial step in the change process is to identify the executive system within a family and determine the extent to which the caregivers are able to regulate daily living and the change process. There is no single definition of a family, but typically adults and elders provide a leadership structure. If they are able to organize themselves around the FCU, chances are leadership and regulation are sufficient to initiate a change process.

There is an implicit hierarchy among the parenting practices shown in Figure 4.5. For highly regulated families with reasonable levels of monitoring

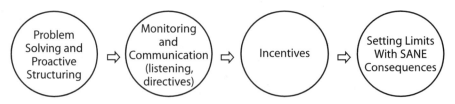

Figure 4.5. Hierarchical sequence of family-centered interventions.

and behavior management skills, we would begin by focusing on relationship building. At the most basic level, minor clinical issues can be addressed by collaborative problem solving with adult caregivers. For example, a parent concerned about a recent drop in academic performance by an otherwise well adjusted young adolescent may benefit from therapist guidance and problem solving, which might include changing study times, reducing activities that compete for time with responsibilities, or recalibrating parent expectations. For clinical issues that are primarily relationship oriented, communication skills and practices may require attention. For example, a recent remarriage, divorce, or other family change may attenuate communication practices, leading to disrupted parenting practices (Patterson, 1983). Simple attention to communication skills (e.g., listening, neutral problem statements, conflict negotiation) may considerably benefit the child and family (Forgatch & Patterson, 1989).

These brief interventions, which we discuss in more detail in chapter 8 (this volume), can be codetermined with a parent following an assessment. Highly skilled and regulated families can still have difficulties, especially within the domain of happiness and well-being. Caregivers who spend their days in complex social situations in a leadership role may fail miserably to communicate with their own partners or children. Emotion disrupts people's best efforts to solve problems in their families and leads to communication styles that induce guilt, rigidity, and depression. For example, Barber (1996) studied and documented the relation between a parent's use of psychological control and adolescent depression. The relation is especially strong when it is based on the adolescent's self-report, and less so when it is measured with direct observation. The idea is that parents who attempt to control the thoughts and feelings of their children by using mind reading, guilt induction, and other tactics can undermine their child's happiness.

Highly regulated families can experience difficulties during the children's adolescence because of the influence of a peer group. As many psychologists have demonstrated, the peer group can dramatically affect the course of socialization (Dishion, Capaldi, et al., 1995; Dishion et al., 1999; Elliott, Huizinga, & Ageton, 1985; Harris, 1998). Early-maturing girls can suddenly become interested in older, more deviant males and thereby be catapulted into a context with a high density of contact with negative peer influences (Magnusson, Stattin, & Allen, 1985). Peer influences can undermine family harmony and challenge communication, parenting, and problem-solving practices that would suffice under less stressful conditions.

In addition, couples with distressed relationships most likely have difficulty parenting as a team and presenting a united front throughout their children's lives. In this case, basic communication and relationship-building skills would enhance the capacity of the marital dyad to parent. Moreover, reducing marital conflict and improving marital satisfaction goes a long way toward solving behavior-management problems and improving the family relationships (Patterson, 1982; Patterson et al., 1992; G. C. Roberts, Block, & Block, 1984).

When behavior management is weak, we begin with the caregiver establishing awareness of the child's behavior and considering the extent to which the child spends time in environments that are disruptive to socialization. Family life is complex and emotional, and we can help families by considering the best focus for their change efforts. For example, caregivers may label the toddler as defiant, the child as emotionally disturbed, and an adolescent as delinquent. A functional emphasis combined with a developmental perspective can help caregivers focus on the key events as well as their own role in the problem. The FCU should be a motivational tool to get the caregiver to focus on the interactions that surround the problem behavior or other conflictual family events. We recommend an initial focus on how caregivers make requests and their response to the child's cooperation (Dishion & Kavanagh, 2003; Dishion & Patterson, 1996). Other foci include the details of the homework routine, school and peer relationships, and children's daily moods.

It is recommended that a positive approach be taken with behavior management, beginning with the caregiver's supporting positive behavior. We advocate a *realistic* approach to parenting that is *under* the parent's control and *measurable* over time. We call this the RUM principle of positive support (Dishion & Kavanagh, 2003). Thus, we might have caregivers keep track of cooperation with their requests and target one per day for a child who is highly uncooperative. In doing so, goals are set in consideration of the developmental level of the child and his or her behavioral competence. When one is supporting positive social behavior, it is essential to build success. It is also important for rewards to be contingent and fit within the ecology and community of the family. For example, one powerful way of rewarding a child for accomplishments is to tell others about his or her positive behavior at a family gathering or to have an elder notice and comment on the positive behavior. Most of the traditional parenting practices of indigenous people, in fact, were carefully designed over thousands of years to create and re-create the cultural community of a tribe. Many of these skills and practices unfortunately were lost in the process of colonization by the European world during the past 500 years (Duran & Duran, 1995). Whiting and Whiting (1975) noted that higher rates of prosocial behavior are characteristic of nonindustrialized communities that emphasize child involvement in the work of the tribe. Positive strategies for improving children's behaviors are optimal when integrated within the cultural community of the family.

Many behavior management problems can be solved by simply increasing the awareness of, and incentives for, positive behavior. However, when behavior is potentially dangerous or unhealthy, limits may need to be set. Limit setting can often be difficult for families, especially for those in which the parent–child relationship is more like that of siblings, characterized as positive but permissive. Often, parents with permissive close relationships with their children experience some difficulty setting limits for adolescents, when the foundation for being parental is not established. In working with parents of all age groups, we use the SANE guidelines for limit setting: (a) *Small* consequences are superior to large, punishing consequences; (b) *avoid* punishing parents with consequences that are burdensome; (c) *never* abuse children or adolescents; and (d) *effective* consequences are those used consistently. At times, parents or other community adults need to set limits on problem behavior, which may lead to giving consequences for misbehavior. The SANE guidelines provide a framework for parents selecting appropriate consequences when needed (Dishion & Patterson, 1996).

When families are in distress because of a child's problem behavior, we complete the change process with building family relationships. It is clear that if behavior management and monitoring issues are not addressed, all efforts to build a positive parent–child relationship are likely to be undermined. A positive relationship evaporates when a parent is embarrassed in a public place by his or her child's problem behavior, or called to the school repeatedly, or confronted by a neighbor because of the child's stealing or lying. Thus, when families seek help, behavior management skills are likely needed. However, it is also likely (although currently untested) that positive changes will be maintained into the next developmental stages if efforts are made to promote positive relationships within the family. Skills emphasized when building family relationships are communication skills (listening, respectful requests, clear requests), parent–child recreation and play, and family activities.

Many structured, empirically tested, and well articulated approaches to parent training are available and are highly recommended as guides for working with families of all ages. As of this writing, only the Adolescent Transitions Program (Dishion & Kavanagh, 2003) provides the detailed linkage between assessment, the FCU, and a menu of intervention options for supporting family change. In our individual work with adolescents and their families, we use a curriculum designed for parent family management groups as a resource.

MANAGING CLIENT MOTIVATION

Behavior change often requires therapists to push through a client's resistance to change. The paradox of change is such that despite best intentions, clients may sometimes sour at the prospect of actually behaving differently in close relationships (Patterson, 1985). A model-driven intervention strategy often involves identifying change targets—such as parenting practices—that elicit resistance to change. Passively or reactively responding to a client's resistance to change is not in the client's best interest. The dental metaphor is apt here, in that people expect the dentist to inform them when they engage in practices that undermine their dental hygiene. However, behavior in close relationships is much more sensitive, and perhaps more difficult to change, because of the power of interpersonal dynamics. The therapist, therefore, must be highly skilled in building a positive relationship with his or her clients and in managing resistance to change. Techniques and skills useful for managing resistance are discussed in detail in chapters 10 and 11.

For several reasons, in our approach to child and family interventions we propose working with both children and parents. It is often the case that aggressive children engage in coercive interactions with parents, peers, and other adults. Their behavior reduces noxious events in their lives (Patterson, 1982; Patterson et al., 1992). Moreover, the caregiver's depressed mood may be related to parenting skills, such as backing off when trying to provide guidance to a coercive youngster or perhaps failing to recognize positive behaviors and engage in relationship-building interactions. This pattern of coercion, parent depression, and eventually parent rejection seems to set the stage for early-onset antisocial behavior (Shaw, Gilliom, Ingoldsby, & Nagin, 2003). Thus, the clinical picture is complex and fits within a systems perspective of change.

We often assign two therapists to work with families, one with the youth and the other with the parent. The therapeutic team attempts to address the bilateral trait within the family system that underlies the family's clinical presentation (i.e., the parent and child system). When working with the parent, we are collaborative and noncoercive. We provide honest support for change and assist the caregiver in changing parenting patterns. We do not manipulate or shape the parent to act as we would wish; we work with his or her conscious efforts to change and respect his or her leadership in the family.

Our work with youngsters supports the parent in a leadership role. The nature of the role is, of course, negotiated with respect to the developmental status of the family members, their culture, and other community characteristics. We often focus on enhancing skills in the youngster that promote parent leadership and well-being in the family. In addition, we may serve as an advocate for the child, ensuring that abusive interactions (emotional, physical, and sexual) are prevented or stopped. When there are unfair practices in the family, we often work with family on problem-solving and communication skills, especially with the adolescent. At times, it is helpful just to work on developing a supportive relationship with a youngster, to communicate benevolence and support for the youth during a family transition or therapeutic change process.

Within an ecological approach to working with families, the assessment drives our case conceptualization and overall team strategy for meeting with the parent and child. We work occasionally together—as in family therapy— and occasionally apart. If engagement in family therapy is enhanced by meeting in the family's home, we conduct home sessions, following the work of Henggeler and colleagues (Henggeler, Schoenwald, Borduin, Rowland, & Cunningham, 1998). We are flexible and responsive to the child and family's ecological and interpersonal context, but our focus is derived from systematic assessment and an explicit process of motivation building and collaboration with parents.

It is important to note from the onset the notion of therapeutic responsibility. Beginning therapists often take responsibility for the change process. Doing so is both a professional and a personal mistake. We can only set up the conditions for the change process; we cannot control the magnitude of change or the clients' willingness to change. In fact, we have to let go to create a therapeutic context for lasting, realistic change. This statement is consistent with an outcome-oriented approach to supporting change. An AIM service delivery approach provides a continual record of client-centered outcomes. This level of therapist accountability actually enhances the therapist's ability to emotionally let go. When a therapist has done everything possible to promote change with a given set of resources, it's possible to feel satisfied with one's work, even with families who are engaged in high levels of daily stress.

SUMMARY

In this chapter, we provide an overview of the ecological approach to child and family interventions, which includes a hierarchical strategy for addressing clinical issues with children and families. The ambiguity of the ecological framework is resolved by the use of a multifocused assessment that guides intervention activity. We emphasize the importance of addressing motivation and knowledge of empirically validated behavior-change processes as the active ingredients of effective service delivery. We propose that families be engaged as a system and that adults be supported in the leadership role in the child's development and the change process.

II

THE FAMILY CHECK-UP

5

INITIAL CONTACTS THAT ESTABLISH
A COLLABORATIVE SET

This chapter discusses strategies for establishing, during the initial clinical contacts, a collaborative and helpful relationship with children and families. In this discussion, we cover how to maximize engagement and avoid common pitfalls in the beginning stages of work with a family. We focus on the process leading to a shared understanding of the change process, a family relationship perspective, and methods for motivating family engagement.

NONSPECIFIC FACTORS

We have suspected for some time that much of the change we see in clients is influenced by nonspecific therapist effects. Systematic research by Wampold (2001) revealed that 12% of the variation in clinical outcomes in the treatment of adult depression was attributable to therapist effects. About 1% of the variance, in contrast, resulted from the therapeutic philosophy. It is thus ironic that clinical and counseling psychologists persist in emphasizing schools of therapy. A decade or more of research on therapist nonspecific effects is clearly needed to make sense of the specific dynamics and processes that account for these nonspecific effects. After years of experience working with families and supervising new therapists,

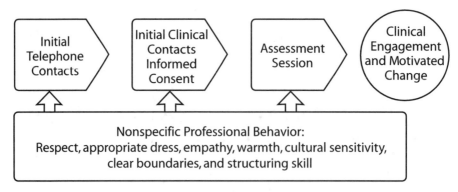

Figure 5.1. Overview of steps toward meaningful clinical engagement and change.

we hypothesize that the therapist behaviors listed in Figure 5.1 are critical for promoting client engagement during the course of clinical intervention, beginning with the first contact.

Perusal of these factors does not yield any startling revelations. Much of the research on nonspecific factors was confirmed in the early work of Carl Rogers (1940, 1957), especially his studies on warmth, empathy, and respect (unconditional positive regard) in the therapeutic process. Clients are quite sensitive to verbal and nonverbal signs of disrespect, disagreement, lack of understanding, or contempt by helping professionals. Often, clients do not assertively counter the signs of disrespect; they simply will not show up for the next session or return telephone calls and will likely decline future services. However, warm positive regard may be sufficient to engage adults in therapy, but it is rarely enough to engage families. Positive regard is also essential in establishing a professional, helping relationship, presenting oneself with the confidence necessary to establish appropriate boundaries, and structuring interactions so that clients feel that the helping process is professionally guided and safe. For example, too much client self-disclosure in the initial contact may lead to a feeling of vulnerability, embarrassment, or violation. The therapist must sensitively regulate the interpersonal closeness, especially in the initial contacts.

Depending on the clinical setting and the client (whether child or parent), an initial contact can occur in a variety of settings and circum- stances. For example, contacts can occur in the family's home, a principal's office, the juvenile court, a divorce attorney's office, a mental health clinic, or, more commonly, on the telephone. Regardless of the setting, these initial contacts set the stage for prompting dynamics of the change process such as self-appraisal, motivation, and confidence in therapeutic services. It is usually during the initial contacts that families read therapists for attitudes or values that may be counter to their self-interest.

Clinical Logistics

In many situations, initial interactions occur with parents by telephone. These seemingly trivial contacts are actually a critical step in establishing the collaborative relationship. Caregivers may begin by blaming the teenager (labeling him or her hyperactive, traumatized, depressed, bipolar, or ADHD [attention-deficit/hyperactivity disorder]) or others (e.g., spouse, ex-spouse) for the problem. The stories and blame are part of the experience of interpersonal distress but carry many traps that can serve as barriers to self-appraisal and change. The initial contact should be friendly, respectful, and optimistic but also concrete with respect to the concerns of the parent, the urgency and risk of the situation, and scheduling the first meeting. In focus groups with parents about the Family Check-Up and related services, the major concern parents cited was the prospect of being judged. Across geographic and ethnic contexts, parents did not want to participate in services that would lead to negative judgments about their parenting practices or about themselves as people. Thus, initial contacts with parents are most effective when a supportive, nonjudgmental process is communicated both explicitly and implicitly.

The function of the initial contact is to gain understanding of the family situation with respect to its engagement in a family-centered service. During the first intake call, it is important to determine who serves in a caregiving role, sibling issues, family members' schedules, and family members' willingness to participate. Questions and discussions should focus specifically on involvement of family members, especially fathers or other caregivers who may not see themselves as central to child-rearing issues. Therapists can ask something like this: "Would Jerome be interested in talking with us about this issue?"

Caregivers may not understand the need to bring in partners or other family members (e.g., a grandmother or an aunt). Until recently, parents often were confused by their own involvement in adolescents' therapy. It may be helpful to structure questions so that they broaden the issue to include other caregivers. Consider the following:

> From what you've said, it sounds like a good time to take some action. Who else in your family shares your concern about this situation?

The telephone contact is the initial step in the change process. As such, therapists may unwittingly engage or collude with an existing dynamic that could undermine the potential for healthy family change. A mother who excludes a father because of his work schedule may unintentionally be fulfilling a script in which she alone is responsible for parenting issues. The father's lack of engagement could also be a major part of the problem—his work becomes a convenient excuse to disengage from his marriage and family. However, the mother's involvement in therapy without her partner may be the first step in extricating herself and her children from an abusive relationship. Of course, a decision not to include the father in the initial contact is often just what it seems—a scheduling issue.

The initial contact is not meant to determine which of these scenarios apply. Extended discussions of the parents' story about the problem should be deferred to an initial in-person interview. The focus of the initial contact is to accurately represent the family-centered approach to service delivery and to respect the parents' initial judgments about how the collaboration should start. The therapist should also assume that the constellation of participants will change over time. For example, a family with joint custody may eventually involve the second parent, because usually coordination and discussion are required to address the behavior of a child who experiences the child-rearing routines of two houses.

If appropriate, the next step is to schedule an intake and send out a Family Intake Questionnaire (FIQ). Ninety minutes should be enough time to give an overview of the services of the clinic, to address confidentiality, to review informed consent, to complete an intake form, and to conduct the initial contact. Some families may take longer or have difficulty scheduling that much time.

The FIQ has three versions: Early Childhood, Middle Childhood, and Adolescent. The FIQ provides preliminary information about marital status, household constitution and caregiving structure, problem behavior in the target child and siblings, developmental issues, friendships, stress level, family strengths, past trauma and present contextual disrupters, use of mental health services, and positive activities.

The FIQ also includes a summary of the results of the intake, which provides an excellent opportunity to present the preliminary case conceptualization. It is especially important to have caregivers determine the behaviors in the questionnaire they consider to be a problem and would like help with. Chamberlain and Reid (1987) found that such targeted problem behaviors are most likely to change when using the Parent Daily Report as a measure of clinical outcome.

Parents commonly lose or forget to complete the FIQ prior to the intake interview. If time allows, having them complete the questionnaire immediately before the first meeting will help circumvent this possibility. The therapist should allow time to look over their answers and to make notes about issues requiring clarification or those that need to be discussed further.

Channeling

In the initial contact, the therapist's work is to channel individual points of view into a family relationship perspective, which is a neutral

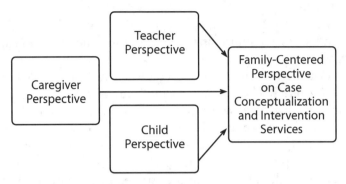

Figure 5.2. Channeling perspectives within an ecological approach.

statement about the family's current situation that is acceptable and conducive to change for the entire family. A classic scenario is that of a teenager who wants more freedom and a parent who is upset by problem behavior such as going to parties, potential substance use, and disengagement from school. A family relationship perspective might be phrased as follows:

> Okay, from everything I've heard from you and Jerome, it would be helpful for this family to find a way to talk about and agree on the expectations for Jerome for the rest of the school year. Let's find a way for you to deal with this issue without fighting.

This statement facilitates collaboration of all family members and, at the same time, provides an opportunity for moving the discussion forward and for potentially building motivation to have assessment and feedback sessions. The family relationship perspective is the first step in turning the problem into a solution, as shown in Figure 5.2. In this way, the past, present, and future are linked by a pragmatic goal: Where does the family go from here?

Note that in Figure 5.2, we include teachers in the initial contact phase. For children 6 years and older, schools are often a critical setting for defining both social adaptation and emotional adjustment. Establishing collaborative relationships with teachers and other helping professionals is as important as it is challenging at times. A high level of clinical and professional skill is required to understand the teacher or professional perspective and story line, without suggesting overidentification with either the parent or child.

As we discuss in the next chapter, school assessments are included within our protocol. Because we often rely on teachers to collect these assessments, our initial contacts are critical for generating interest and cooperation with the assessments. Even when there is no apparent difficulty in school, the child's relationship with peers, anxiety, or social withdrawal may be of interest. Thus a well-placed telephone call or visit to the school after receiving parental consent and approval may be critical in establishing a collaborative set for future assessment and for eliciting movement and motivation.

It is also essential to meet and connect with the child's perspective on family difficulties. The ultimate goal is to understand every family member's point of view to ensure fairness and compassion for all members. However, initial contacts may be limited to only one or two individuals within the family. To channel the perspective of various members into a family relationship perspective, it is necessary to clinically engage both the parent and the child. Next, we discuss strategies to facilitate interactions we found to be useful for engagement.

THE INITIAL INTERVIEW WITH PARENTS

In a discussion of clinical contacts, it is helpful to differentiate between process and content. The process refers to the interpersonal dynamics and strategies used to get at the content. The content refers to the specific information of clinical interest. Content and process are intimately intertwined: Without a good process, not much content is likely to be generated, and too much content can undermine the process. It is interesting to note that if clients feel a therapist is too process oriented and "doesn't have a clue" about the presenting problem or situational dynamics, they could lose confidence. Thus, without content, even therapists with the most skilled process cannot maintain a meaningful clinical relationship. We summarize the content goals and provide suggested clinical strategies (process) in Figure 5.3. Note that the goals of the initial contact with parents are relatively straightforward, although some comment is required.

For example, topics such as developmental and medical histories require more or less detail depending on the nature of the presenting problem.

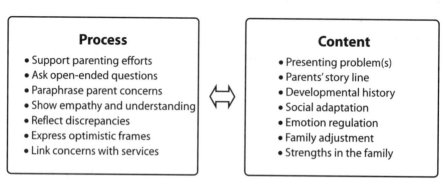

Figure 5.3. Process strategies and content goals of the initial clinical contact with parents.

Going through 4 hours of developmental history may not be productive for a 9-year-old oppositional girl who is being referred with a recently remarried, blended family. At the very beginning, judgment is required about the level of depth for any given area. Sullivan (1953) described the initial contact as a reconnaissance mission: Therapists get a broad perspective on the child and family to help focus future assessment and clinical activity. If developmental issues are suspected, then we suggest, at a very minimum, administering a structured assessment of the child's achievement of developmental milestones.

We prefer to conduct the initial meeting as a semistructured interview. The FIQ allows the therapist to focus on key areas of concern that are relevant to the family's current situation. For example, a history of domestic violence raises unique clinical concerns that should be addressed initially when working with a parent. The therapist needs to be aware of restraining orders and other procedures developed to protect a child or parent from future violence or abuse. The therapist is in a better position to establish a solid collaboration with a parent if issues such as these can be addressed during the initial contacts. Hearing about a history of child abuse as the client is walking out the door at the end of an initial interview indicates that a solid collaborative relationship has yet to be established.

We discourage reviewing the FIQ in detail in the company of parents or children. Too much attention to a form or questionnaire when meeting with a parent or child disrupts the process of listening, reflecting, and understanding his or her perspective vis-à-vis motivation to change and the family relationship perspective (W. R. Miller & Rollnick, 1991).

The therapist should typically begin with initial questions that can structure the course of the discussion. One example could be the following:

> Tell me in your own words about your concerns for Lupé and your family.

To get more detail about a possible safety issue, the therapist might ask an open-ended question such as this one:

> I see that you had a restraining order for your ex-husband. How is that situation now?

Questions such as these not only provide direction and structure, but also allow the parent to bring the therapist into the present circumstance of his or her life.

Under ideal circumstances, we have two therapists meet with the child and parent simultaneously. (It is quite helpful if the clinic has child care available for younger children.) They meet with the family together to discuss the logistics of the intake interview, then separate for about 40 minutes, with the child and the parent each spending time alone with their own therapist. The family reconvenes at the end of the initial contact, and the parents' therapist summarizes the parents' decision about the next step. At that time, the child's therapist may wish to summarize the child's interests in the family change process.

The priority from a family-centered perspective is to meet with the parent. If there is only one therapist, he or she should meet with the parent first, then with the child (for children 6 years or older). An alternative is to schedule one meeting with the parent and a second with the child and parent together. Discussions about the child's problem behavior, emotional distress, divorced partners, and so forth, must be minimized in the presence of children and adolescents. Families often terminate the therapy because the child refuses to attend. Thus it is important to establish a strong collaborative relationship initially with the parent to reduce the vulnerability of dropout resulting from the child's resistance to change.

Differences in level of concern, availability, trust in mental health services, family dynamics, and other factors may limit which adults participate in the initial interview. Willingness to adjust and reconsider one's original formulation of the family is critical at times. Consider the following example and see how the definition of the family changed over time, during the course of the initial contacts:

> Dennis is a single father with two boys, both diagnosed with Asperger's syndrome. He is unemployed but receives disability. He is also overwhelmed with parenting and managing the demands of various social service agencies. On the basis of the telephone report and initial interview, it becomes clear that the boys need daily structure and a routine that ensures they get to school on time and that they complete their homework.

This example illustrates the importance of understanding that child problem behavior comes in all forms. These boys, although difficult to manage in the family home, were not drug-involved or delinquent. The diagnostic label of Asperger's, although not technically accurate, mobilized intervention resources for the family. However, the Asperger's label also distracted professionals from the functional dynamics driving the problem behavior. Despite all the services, the boys were falling rapidly behind in basic academic survival skills.

In the telephone conversation and in the initial interview, the therapist might have fallen into the same pattern as did other helping professionals. Despite his good intentions, Dennis did not communicate clearly and was unable to implement a parenting plan. The natural tendency for some therapists is to set up a system in which the father's role is less central. However, this therapeutic trap never works in the long run, because chronically overloaded social service workers, volunteers, and others who help with household routines always move on with their lives, leaving the family in an even weaker position to manage their children and their lives.

It is fortunate that this family's therapist took a broader view and actively solicited more information about the absent mother and discovered that she periodically became depressed and, during these episodes, often left the household. She returned when the depression subsided. During her 2- to 3-month absences, it was not unusual for the father to seek help from low-cost services in the community, usually family counselors with limited training.

After the therapist talked with the mother and father separately, the family agreed to participate in the family assessment as a unit. The assessment revealed hidden strengths that would not have been seen otherwise. The therapist gradually worked on improving the partnership of the mother and father and, eventually, the family was reconstituted. The therapist focused on supporting them in developing better strategies for coping with the dynamics of their lives as well as making better use of the services available. This case illustrates the importance of exploring assumptions and options at the initial stages of contact. Also in this case, proper attention to the absentee mother as a resource empowered reorganization within the family and an adjustment of the services that were previously experienced as ineffective.

The initial interview with the parent should rely on basic strategies in motivational interviewing (W. R. Miller & Rollnick, 1991), with respect to understanding the parents' motivational climate. Consistent with Prochaska and DiClemente's (1982, 1986) empirically based conceptualization, family members might be thought of as being in the precontemplation or contemplation stage during the intake interview. Rarely do we as clinicians interact with a parent who is ready to take action or who is in the maintenance-of-change stage. If families are in crisis, however, they may well be in the action stage, but only relative to handling the crisis. They may not see how patterns of family mismanagement and disruption placed them in a state of crisis. In light of their understanding of dynamics leading to crises, it is often important to handle the crisis first. Consider this situation:

> Ebony was a 21-year-old spirit trapped in a 14-year-old's body. She and her older sister (age 16, no longer attending high school) spent most of their free time at an apartment belonging to a group of young men known for partying and some drug sales. Ebony's European American father and African American mother had no influence on her. If they set limits on Ebony, she left and did not return for 3 or 4 days. A Family Check-Up was not feasible until the family stabilized. The therapist worked only with the parents (Ebony would not attend an intake session) to develop plans for Ebony for the summer. When she returned, the parents and Ebony were more closely aligned and a Family Check-Up and family therapy were pursued.

When families are in crisis, support is needed to manage the turmoil before long-term support for change can be provided. Empirically successful approaches to working with children and families demonstrate that with highly disorganized, chaotic families, home visits and crisis management are the best means for improving family functioning and reducing child problem behavior (Henggeler, Schoenwald, Bourduin, Rowland, & Cunningham, 1998; Olds et al., 1997; Olds, Hill, Robinson, Song, & Little, 2000).

In statistical terms, the more prevalent clinical scenario is one in which at least one parent is in the contemplation phase of the behavior-change cycle. We therefore offer some basic interviewing strategies that specifically address the emotional issues of seeking help for parenting. These strategies are seen as complementing the motivational interviewing that accompanies any initial clinical contact.

1. Support effort. It is easy to identify parenting deficits when working clinically with children and families. It takes more skill to recognize parenting strengths and efforts. It is a rare parent who has not spent hours worrying about his or her children and felt guilty about errors of commission or omission. A critical skill in engaging parents is to find and support their parenting efforts. Parents need to know that the clinician understands that they have been trying. At a minimum, the fact that they show up to an intake interview and complete a questionnaire requires effort and courage. Therapists can show support with a statement similar to this one:

> It's clear to me that even though you're getting upset with Ebony, the fact that you're here shows you're doing everything you can to keep her safe and in the family.

2. Paraphrase parent concerns. Again, understanding the parents' primary concern is the basic work of the intake interview. Parents will respond to a therapist who shows understanding, and this link can go a long way toward mitigating any mistakes or breeches in the emerging therapeutic relationship. Here is an example of paraphrasing:

> Oh, I'm sorry. I see what you're saying. It's not that you want to change John's personality. You're worried that if he's this impulsive now, when it comes time to drive, he'll do something crazy and hurt himself or someone else.

3. Show empathy and understanding. All family difficulties have a history and ecology. All the factors that are related to a clinical concern may never be fully apparent in working with children and families. It is tempting for a therapist to get lost in contextual details and thereby lose an opportunity to engage the parent. Thus, sticking with the big picture and staying close to the larger, emotionally driven issues is essential. Following is an example of empathy:

> Some divorces can be quite difficult, and the effects on the family last a long time. How would you describe yours, in terms of effects on parenting?

Beginning clinicians often get caught in details of dates, sequences, and specifics of a family's past. These can be confusing and irrelevant to the primary concerns of the parent. Details regarding contextual factors should be queried only when clearly relevant to the emotional and behavioral dynamics of the here and now. When asked about contextual factors during the initial contacts with parents, parents often provide abundant detail that detracts from the flow of the initial interview. This is a time for the therapist to assume leadership and redirect parents to more relevant discussion, as in the following example:

> I know this situation was complicated, and there are a lot of details. We may come back to it later. Right now I'm interested in getting the big picture about how your family is working. Tell me more about how you see these experiences affecting Ebony.

In this way the therapist guides the parent to focus on how contextual factors, especially the concerns that drove the parent to seek clinical services, are affecting the present. The therapist can search for the functional dynamics linking the past with the present by saying something like this:

> This is important information. It seems that when you started working evenings, Jeremy's behavior became more extreme, and he started refusing to go to bed. Do you think this had anything to do with him missing you or wanting to spend time with you before he went to bed?

4. Reflect discrepancies. This strategy is central to motivational interviewing. When talking to parents, therapists commonly hear conflicting and competing emotions. These discrepancies are the grist of the motivational mill. If the therapist listens carefully and reflects these discrepancies during the initial interview, he or she can scaffold the parents' process of working through what is the most important first step for family change. Here is a possible scenario:

> It seems as if it's a little unclear to you whether your problems with Ebony are disrupting your marriage or if your disagreements about parenting are what's creating the problems.

5. Link concerns to assessment. By the end of the initial contact, it is critical that the parents have a clear sense of how the services offered genuinely address their concerns. At the end of the initial contact, if an assessment of the family's interaction process or the child's school behavior is appropriate, it will be evident and obvious to both the parent and the therapist. The therapist might say,

> In light of what we said, it might be helpful to take a close look at how the family communicates and deals with conflict, so you can get a handle on what to do now.

6. *Frame the situation optimistically.* Turning a child's problem behavior into a positive prognostic sign is a useful way to engage both parents and children in the change process (Robins, Alexander, Newell, & Turner, 1996). This high-level therapeutic skill requires practice and sensitivity. Because family behavior is complex, however, it is likely that even unpleasant behavior has unintended positive implications for family change. The therapist can redirect the perception this way:

> I've seen this before in other stepparent families. Even though John seems negative with you, he also does a lot to keep you engaged in his life. Some teenagers wouldn't tell you so much; they would be sneaky.

7. *Normalize problems.* A common strategy for supporting parents is to normalize their struggles and concerns. Doing so is an excellent way of providing support, as there is no greater relief than to know that others in the world often share the same issues and struggles. However, normalizing does not always build engagement and motivation to change, and therefore should be used carefully. Here is an example of a good balance:

> A lot of parents experience more conflict with their kids during adolescence. In this sense, your experiences aren't unusual. But the swearing and pushing between mom and daughter is a clear sign that things are getting out of control in your family.

It is noteworthy that many families will have sought help previously and have experienced some successes and failures (or perhaps even treatment traumas). These past treatment experiences will undoubtedly leave them with baggage with respect to their engagement in services and openness to self-appraisal and the change process. About half of young adolescents with arrest histories have been involved in some form of mental health treatment (Stouthamer-Loeber, Loeber, van Kammen, & Zhang, 1995). When school professionals are included in this count, the percentage is likely much higher. The therapist must address previous professional experiences, paying special attention to the individual family members' current motivational stance. These experiences, if left unattended, can serve as disruptive ghosts to the change process. If discussed, these experiences can form a basis for better understanding. We discuss this issue in more detail when addressing issues of working with families during the change process.

INITIAL INTERVIEWS WITH CHILDREN

Conducting initial interviews with children varies rather dramatically from child to child. The major issue is the age of the child. We discuss specific strategies for these initial contacts for children and adolescents.

Developmental Issues

Parents often will not return to receive clinical services if children have negative experiences at a clinic or with a therapist. Thus, the first goal is to develop some level of rapport with children. The strategies of engagement in the initial interview vary according to the developmental level of the child. However, for both very young children and adolescents, the therapist follows the child's lead in beginning the "getting to know you" process. A frequent mistake is to start out being too clinical—asking the child about his or her problem behavior or asking personal questions that may be emotionally overwhelming.

As in interviews with parents, it is important to distinguish between the process and the content of the child intake sessions. Figure 5.3 provides a summary of both factors for children ages 2 to 11. This developmental span is clearly very broad, requiring considerable adjustment to the goals and dynamics of the initial interview. For example, it is questionable whether a 2-year-old child can be separated from a parent for any significant length of time. We often conduct initial interviews with the parent in the home, with a child therapist allocated to play with the child.

Young Children

It is important to be familiar with the normative skills, interests, and abilities of children. Time spent around children at all ages provides the experiential base for being an effective child clinician. With young children, it is vitally important to be prepared with activities, toys, and settings that will be interesting, engaging, and developmentally appropriate for the child. With respect to the goals (i.e., the content) of initial clinical contacts with young children, the younger the child, the less ambitious the goal for content. The primary goal is developing rapport and trust and establishing the clinic or oneself (the therapist) as a pleasant experience.

Therapists have long doubted the reliability of child report for children younger than adolescent age. However, work by Measelle, Ablow, Cowan, and Cowan (1998) revealed that careful attention to the structure of the questions and the process of interviewing can render reliable and valid child-report data as early as age 3. These researchers used a procedure they refer to as the Berkeley Puppet Interview, which requires extensive training and certification to administer. This procedure uses two puppets (Iggy and Ziggy), much like what Susan Harter used in her innovative measure of children's self-esteem (Harter, 1990, 1992). Children are asked questions about their family and their social–emotional competence, and these questions are anchored by the puppets, which represent opposite viewpoints. Children then pick which puppet is more like them.

Such an interview can be constructed to fit the clinical needs of a child and family. However, in setting up the puppet interview, therapists must ensure sensitivity to the context of interviewing for the child. For example, children being seen in a clinic may be anxious about how the answers to their questions are going to be used.

An essential feature of a constructive initial contact within a clinic environment is for the therapist to be skilled in behavior management. Children who are stressed or traumatized or show attention deficit or behavior problems may be quite difficult to manage. This information is important to know before the child comes to the clinic. Brief activities that are within the child's capacity and are reinforced with tangible incentives are an excellent way to elicit cooperative child behavior. One of the primary goals with young children is to teach them how to interact with adults outside the home and to comply with reasonable adult guidance. For guidelines on behavior management with young children, see Dishion and Patterson (1996).

Adolescents

Some people assume that to engage an adolescent, it is necessary to be like one. Adolescents, however, are acutely sensitive to adult presentations of a false self in an attempt to gain affection. It is important for the therapist to be him- or herself and work hard to understand the uniqueness of the young adult's personality, strengths, and perspective on the family. It is impossible to generalize a set of concerns or interests of a child, but some unique features of their developmental status in the family and community can be addressed to promote engagement.

Respecting Space and Privacy

A young person needs plenty of room to cooperate with the initial contact process and to discuss sensitive issues related to the family. The teenager is often distrustful of mental health professionals and the therapy process, which makes it imperative that the therapist's initial gestures and interactions communicate respect for privacy. The therapist should plan ahead for what the adolescent can do if he or she decides not to participate as well as communicate that the pressure is off.

Okay, fair enough. Sounds like you weren't too happy about coming here today, and you aren't sure if you even want to talk to me.

Normalizing Experiences

This tool may be important in working with adolescents, who are often concerned with being normal. By referring to experiences with other adolescent clients, the therapist can get to a place that opens doors for talking about feelings and experiences:

> I know of a lot of young people who aren't always happy when their parents remarry, even though everyone else seems to think it should be a happy occasion. Can you imagine feeling like that?

This statement provides a possible bridge to having a frank discussion about a child's obviously negative reaction to a recent stepparent marriage. If the client says either "That makes no sense" or "That makes a lot of sense," it opens doors for further discussion.

Advocating Adolescent's Interests

Early on, it is important for the therapist to articulate the nature of his or her relationship with a child. The therapist is an adult who is going to use all of his or her knowledge and skills to help this child get along in a world of adults. This outcome may mean having fewer negative experiences at school, reducing the fighting at home with parents, improving the fairness of household rules, or keeping the child out of harm's way. Here is one way to make this clear:

> It sounds like things get out of control in your house when you and your parents disagree. One way we might work together is to figure out ways you can ask for things without it turning into a fight.

The therapist should be careful not to oversell his or her advocacy and inadvertently collude with a child to engage in behavior that puts a child at risk on a variety of dimensions. This script finds a good balance:

> I see why you want to be with your boyfriend all the time. On the other hand, I know that any parent who really cares about his or her kids is going to have problems with that. Can you see your mom's point of view at all? What are some of the things she might worry about?

In this dialogue, the therapist demonstrates an understanding of the child's reference point without betraying the parents' perspective or unintentionally colluding with the adolescent against the parent. Collusive communications such as these can further alienate young people from their delicately perilous protective shield of a family.

Linking Interests With Services

Just as he or she does with the parent, the therapist can show children the connection between their concerns and the assessment and intervention that follows:

> One of the services we provide is looking carefully at how family members communicate. We then use that information to help them get along better. It seems that most of us don't always understand why we act the way we do in family life, and it helps to have someone else look more closely.

Creating Optimistic Reframes

Young people come to therapy with the idea that they are the problem and that the therapy is about fixing them. The implication is that their behavior is hurting the family. This implicit understanding feels bad and is not conducive to discussing family issues, because the expectation is that all roads are connected to their bad behavior. But research by Robins et al. (1996) found that the effect of positive reframes on the child's behavior was most strongly related to the child's engagement in therapy. Here are two examples of reframes:

> This may sound funny, but I'm starting to see that you might be helping your parents by distracting them from other worries. You might not even see this.

> I can see that you and your dad fight a lot about chores. On the other hand, I'm impressed with your work skills, especially when you work for other people. Maybe it's the arguments that interfere with you helping more around the house.

Keeping It Brief, Starting Slow

Many therapists err on the side of being too friendly, too intrusive, or both, with children; these approaches may lead to the child's resistance to being involved in family therapy. They need opportunities to disengage, and the intake session should be brief, unless otherwise indicated. One rule of thumb is a maximum of 30 minutes per session until age 15 or 16. To engage the child, the therapist can say something like,

> Okay, we're not going to meet for very long today. I just want to make sure I get a chance to hear your point of view so I can understand what you would like to see happen in the family.

Engaging children in intervention services that are believed to be in the child's best interest is much like the old idiom, "You can lead a horse to water but you can't force it to drink." To engage children, a therapist needs to respect their initial posture in therapy but also continue to look for opportunities to support their motivation to improve their family situation. Respecting the parents' leadership roles while also advocating for the interests of the child provides a solid foundation for eventual engagement. Sensitivity to the implied dynamics of the therapeutic situation is needed. It may be difficult to establish a therapeutic alliance with a child when the situation is loaded. For example, a parent who brings a child to discuss the parent's recent marriage to a young male, with a therapist who is a young male, may encounter some initial resistance.

The Next Step

One of the advantages of direct clinical contact with families is that direct observations of the child and family (and perhaps the school system) can be synthesized to yield a set of hypotheses about a variety of dimensions of the family system. These direct observations are invaluable for formulating a case conceptualization (as discussed in chap. 7, this volume) and designing an assessment that tests the hypotheses. Figure 5.4 provides a summary of the key elements of family functioning, from which a clinical impression can be derived using the initial contacts. A strong collaborative, cotherapy relationship helps build a synergistic synthesis.

From the initial contacts, therapists can often surmise the leadership structure of the family, the emotional climate, communication (and lack thereof), sibling dynamics, and how emotional boundaries are defined and maintained. Often such clinical discussions revolve around the child and

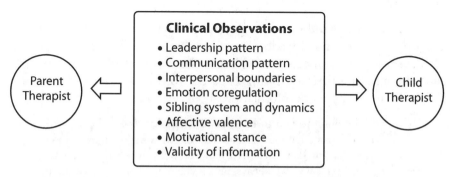

Figure 5.4. The synergism of child and parent therapist observations.

family psychopathology. However, this type of discussion is less useful than one about current issues because those issues define the family's strengths. Every family, as such, has strengths from which to build, and the skillful child and family clinician can identify these as a starting point for establishing a working relationship.

As shown in Figure 5.2, it is necessary to engage key family participants in building a family relationship perspective that works for all involved. Once this perspective is established, it is important to sell the family on the need for assessment before they move forward on their own or with the help of professional services. Most families (and professionals) do not see the value of sound psychological assessment in their personal lives.

If there is an opportunity to meet with the child and parents, the therapist should spend a brief time with them as a group before the end of the initial contact. The therapist then takes the lead on summarizing what has been learned and what is recommended as the next step. The therapist also promotes the family's investment in the assessment and feedback sessions, as shown in the following example:

> From our talk today, it seems like the family agrees that the conflict has gotten out of control, especially concerning Ebony's time away from home and her school situation. I share the concern that, in the long run, the situation is really going to hurt Ebony.
>
> What I would recommend is that the family participate in the Family Check-Up. This involves two more meetings, the first of which is a careful assessment of how Ebony and the family are doing. It gives us a chance to see how things unfold in your home. We will also assess how Ebony is doing at school in a variety of situations.
>
> Then we will study all this information and sit down with all of you and give you feedback. Many families never have an opportunity to take a careful look at their situation before making critical life decisions. We offer you that service, and we'll also help you make sense of it in our feedback meetings. Does this sound like it will be a useful service for you?

It is important to leave enough time to discuss concerns or questions about the assessment and feedback sessions that will follow. Most families, by this stage of the process, are willing to be involved in the assessment, partly because the therapist has pointed out to the parents how they can benefit from getting more information about an issue:

> It would be helpful to you to have more detail about how Ebony gets along with other students at school. You might want to take a closer look at how you work together to handle Ebony when she becomes challenging. That's why we always have a videotaped family assessment task before we start working with a family.

This process links the family's concerns with the assessment services to follow. By and large, it is easy to convince parents and children that more information can help them solve a problem they are experiencing.

SUMMARY

This chapter discusses a variety of strategies to use in the initial contacts with a family. These contacts set the stage for a family's potential to change as they work with therapists or, in the future, other helping professionals.

The task of the initial contacts is to form a bridge from a past problem to a future solution. The therapist and family accomplish this task by exploring parent and child family appraisals and finding a frame of reference that prioritizes improving the family management and communication processes. The frame of reference should persuade the family that a careful assessment could help determine the next step. In ideal circumstances, both parents and teenagers will be curious and interested in getting feedback on the family assessment.

6

ECOLOGICAL ASSESSMENT

The greatest contribution of applied psychology to the behavioral sciences is the development of valid and reliable measurement strategies. Major advances in assessment practices have been made in the areas of understanding personnel selection (Cronbach & Glesar, 1965), individual differences in personality (Nunnally, 1978; Wiggins, 1973), cognitive functioning (Lezak, 1995; Weschler, 1974), and behavior development (Mash & Terdal, 1997). Also, standardized assessment batteries and the skills to use these tools differentiate licensed clinical, counseling, and school psychologists from counselors, social workers, and other practitioners. In this chapter, we discuss a framework for assessment of child and family problems within the ecological model.

The key to understanding where to target interventions lies in a valid and thorough assessment of the problem. In light of the importance of measurement to model building (Dishion & Patterson, 1999; Meehl, 1978) and clinical decision making (Dawes, 1994; Meehl, 1978), it is surprising that more effort has not been made in developing measurement procedures that link to interventions. The power of linking theory, measurement, and intervention practices can be seen in the work of Gordon Paul (Paul & Menditto, 1992) in the area of schizophrenia.

There are two basic strategies for developing a clinically relevant assessment battery. The most common is a deficit model. After an initial interview with a client (either by phone or in person), the clinician formulates hypotheses about deficit areas of functioning. The clinician uses assessments designed to isolate and identify hypothesized deficits, tailoring the assessment strategy to each client. This deficit model is often used in pediatric psychology and neuropsychology (e.g., Lezak, 1995). An alternative assessment model makes use of a standardized assessment battery. Standardized assessments provide a broad perspective on individual functioning across a variety of domains. Each assessment strategy has strengths and weaknesses. The deficit model provides more detail with respect to psychopathology, whereas the standardized model provides a comprehensive profile of strengths and weaknesses, is developmental, and can be used to assess a broad range of potential problems.

In our approach to assessment, a comprehensive assessment forms the foundation for decision making and case conceptualization. This comprehensive assessment provides information about clients' areas of strength and weakness as well as gives a direction for intervention targets. Following the comprehensive assessment, there may be reason to further assess specific areas of problematic functioning. This case history illustrates the point:

> Tandem was a 13-year-old boy in a two-parent family and had a history of few behavior problems at home or school. His older brother was a junior in high school, earning nearly a 4.0 in college prep classes. In the seventh grade, Tandem's grades began to deteriorate and became worse in the eighth grade. At the same time, he began spending time with a group of youths who were using drugs. As would be expected, other problem behaviors, such as missing class, tobacco use, and belligerence with teachers, emerged. His parents were confused by the recent turn of events. After a comprehensive assessment was completed, there was an agreement to pursue a more in-depth assessment of his neuropsychological functioning. Because academic achievement was a valued goal in this family, Tandem's trouble with learning could have potentially provoked sequelae such as low motivation, peer group problems, and problem behavior. A careful neuropsychological assessment indeed revealed a receptive auditory processing difficulty that was particularly challenging in a public middle school environment that depends on oral communication in large groups. Remedial educational programming resulted in improved academic achievement and decreased problem behavior.

In a clinical setting, acquiring a comprehensive assessment can provide the clinician with an overview of a child and family's strengths and weaknesses. On the basis of an initial interview, other measures can be incorporated to provide more depth to the assessment. For example, it would be useful to include an inventory of traumatic experiences and posttraumatic stress for a child, parent, or adolescent with whom the clinician suspects a history of trauma. In a similar manner, cognitive and neuropsychological

TABLE 6.1
An Overview of Assessment Domains

	Infancy (0–14 months)	Early childhood (15 months–5 years)	Childhood (6–12 years)	Adolescence (13–19 years)
Biological frontier	• motor	• language	• cognition	• pubertal/ hormonal
Ecological adaptation	• mother • siblings	• caregivers • peers	• teachers • peers	• intimate partners
Microsocial process	• regulation/ sychronicity	• security/trust • coercion/ cooperation	• academic engagement • peer play	• deviant/ conventional peer process • intimacy negotiation
Psycho-pathology	• dysregulation	• oppositional behavior • self-control (toiletting) • separation anxiety	• attention • conduct problems • depression • withdrawal/ shyness	• delinquency • substance use • depression/ anxiety • mood dysregulation • sexual promiscuity • thought disorder/ schizophrenia

assessments may be useful when a clinician hypothesizes that attention, memory, or cognitive processing is clinically relevant for a particular family member.

One of the difficulties in making assessments is deriving the set of constructs to be measured within a comprehensive measurement strategy. A nomological network describes the set of constructs deemed relevant within an assessment procedure (Cronbach & Meehl, 1955). For example, in our intervention program for adolescent problem behavior, we assess emotional distress (i.e., internalizing), maladaptation (i.e., externalizing), academic competence, deviant peer relationships, peer relationships, and family management and context. This nomological network emerged from years of research on the development of problem behavior (Dishion, French, & Patterson, 1995; Patterson, Reid, & Dishion, 1992). Child and family clinical psychology, fortunately, has a limited range of constructs to target. Table 6.1 provides an overview of the network of construct domains relevant from infancy through adolescence.

The ecological perspective is helpful for organizing a systematic approach to providing clinical services, designing assessment batteries, and studying development from infancy through adolescence. Biological maturation certainly provides the foundation for children's social and emotional development. Each developmental phase (grossly oversimplified in Table 6.1) is represented by a frontier of change. Infants go from being completely immobile following birth to walking and often running by around 14 to 15 months. In early childhood, an explosion of language gives rise to the cognitive advancements in childhood, continuing through adolescence. In adolescence, a rapid change accompanies puberty, which emerges on average at age 13 for girls and 15 for boys. The principle of hierarchical integration is relevant; developmental change is integrated within the next stage, carrying forth the accomplishments of earlier years.

Hierarchical integration describes other domains of development as well. For example, there is a sense that early relationships with mothers form a basis for relationships with other caregivers, siblings, and peers and form the foundation for adult intimate relationships (Dishion & Patterson, 2006). The principle of hierarchical integration, however, does not suggest great stability in all forms of behavior and emotions. Perhaps behavior and emotions change form, and thus understanding and measuring the changes in form is the key function of a developmental science (Patterson, 1993). Stability across behavior setting, as we discuss, is modest at best, and often absent. In fact, stability across settings may reflect the severity of psychopathology and the underlying relationship processes (Dishion, 2000; Loeber & Dishion, 1984).

An ecological perspective provides a useful linkage between the macro- and microsocial perspectives on development (Dishion, Hogansen, & Winter, 2000). Evolutionary views of development emphasize the role of biological change in explaining critical periods in development, whereas microsocial views emphasize the role of contingencies in relationship processes in development (Dishion, French, & Patterson, 1995; Patterson & Reid, 1984; Patterson et al., 1992).

The emphasis and salience of relationship processes change with development, and these changes are mostly embedded with biological changes in the developing individual. For example, infants are neurologically sensitive to facial and movement synchronization. Toddlers exploring the environment may be especially sensitive to cues of instability and insecurity in the caregiver system. Patterns of cooperation and coercion develop in response to caregiver efforts to set limits and control behavior for safety and socialization. These patterns of interactions with caregivers become less salient in childhood, when school adaptation and play with peers become more interesting to children (Dishion, 1990; Kellam, 1990). Finally, in adolescence, establishing friendship networks forms the basis for a long-term developmental trajectory (e.g., college, work, substance use) as well as linkages to intimate partners (Dishion, Poulin, & Medici Skaggs, 2000). These themes carry forward well through the adult years, perhaps to be supplanted only by parenthood and caregiving for one's own offspring.

From this perspective, the form and function of psychopathology are embedded within these layers of biology and ecology. Individual differences in psychopathology will naturally have biological, emotional, and social underpinnings. What is perhaps controversial, however, is the perspective that contextual and biological influences are transformed into psychopathology through developmentally relevant relationship processes.

Advances are beginning to clarify the mechanisms and processes that link brain and biological change with patterns we see in key relationships through development. For instance, attention and emotion regulation will likely emerge as clinically relevant constructs in the near future, on the basis of pioneering research in developmental psychology (Eisenberg, Carlo, Murphy, & Van Court, 1995; Kochanska, 1993; Rothbart & Bates, 1998). Children with poor self-regulation may be especially vulnerable to caregiver or peer negativity. Some data suggest that interventions may improve self-control and reduce problem behavior (Kazdin, Siegel, & Bass, 1992; Lochman, Lampron, Burch, & Curry, 1984; Patterson, Dishion, & Chamberlain, 1993). From an ecological perspective, however, improving attention control will be difficult in chaotic and emotionally volatile family relationships.

Table 6.1 provides a map intended to help clinicians target their assessments. Neglecting major contexts (e.g., school, peers) may lead to misguided or poorly specified interventions. A model-building approach to clinical psychology opens the possibility of refining the nomological network on the basis of iterations of studies suggesting new constructs relevant to social adaptation and well-being in children and families.

METHOD VERSUS TRAIT

Once we know what to measure, the question becomes, What do our measurements provide? It is generally agreed that measurements of behavior yield method and trait variance (Campbell & Fiske, 1959) in addition to random (i.e., unsystematic) error. Method variance can describe any aspect of the measurement, from the reporting agent to the data collection method (ratings, interviews, direct observations). When a parent is asked to complete a form that describes his or her daughter's behavior, at least two sets of data result: his or her style of reporting or unique vantage point and his or her daughter's behavioral tendencies. Only the latter information is typically of interest in our attempts to get an objective account of the child's mental health.

Of late, however, we have come to understand in science and practice that there is no objective account. Instead, there are behavior, subjective experiences of behaving, and other's perceptions of behavior. All of these factors must be considered in the change process—there is no simple way out.

Thinking ecologically, we learn to take into account the perception of the reporter (i.e., the method) relative to the child's characteristics or tendencies. Most clinicians seldom measure the child's behavior in more than one setting because of inconvenience or cost of the interventionist's time. But in our clinical work at the Child and Family Center, we assess children's behavior at home and at school, at a minimum. In addition, we collect direct-observation data in the home or at school. These observations are the most objective measures of family functioning. These indices provide a basis for disentangling the issue of perceptions and behavior in our efforts to provide help to a distressed family.

Assessing Traits

As discussed in chapter 2 (this volume), there is little evidence that children's social maladaptation (oppositional defiant disorder, compulsive disorder, and attention-deficit/hyperactivity disorder [ADHD]) and emotional distress display as traits that are consistent across settings. Thus, it is critical to assess both from the perspective of the child, parent, and teacher. Many clinicians are not paid for conducting careful assessments such as these.

As a culture, we think of psychopathology in children and adults as a trait, assuming that some aspect of the disorder is apparent in a variety of settings and across time. For example, we treat children with ADHD with the conceptualization that ADHD is a trait that occurs across settings and relationships. This way of thinking is inconsistent with an ecological perspective, which suggests that many behaviors are context specific. If psychology operated from a model in which we conceptualized most mental health problems as setting-specific, we would have a completely different orientation to providing treatment. If children's mental health issues were largely setting-specific, it would seem logical to provide interventions in those settings targeted as concerns rather than treat the individual child, which would be more consistent with an ecological perspective.

Assumptions about measurement originally articulated by Campbell and Fiske (1959) can be readily tested with structural equation modeling, as originally articulated by Dwyer (1983). The idea is simple, but the computations are relatively complex: Patterns of correlation within a complex set of data can be tested with respect to a theoretical model. A chi-square goodness-of-fit test yields an overall index of model adequacy, with the low chi-square meaning that the model fits the data. The differences in the data generated by the model and the actual observed data are relatively minor. This tool is handy for testing hypotheses about measurement assumptions, especially because two competing models can be compared and systematically tested to determine which is the superior model (i.e., which provides the most parsimonious account of the variation within a data set).

The study of child psychopathology is organized around the concept that children experience two broad types of psychopathology: internalizing and externalizing disorders (Achenbach, 1982). As discussed in chapter 2 (this volume), these tendencies, which presumably reflect intrapersonal coping styles, would be expected to show some degree of stability across settings. From a pragmatic view, the assumption is that parents and teachers, who are typically the adults who refer children for treatment, would agree on whether a child is externalized or internalized.

To examine this assumption further, we looked at teacher and parent reports of these two symptom clusters and tested models of fit using 220 youth at high risk involved in the Adolescent Transitions Program (ATP) study. In general, the factor loading of the Delinquent and Aggressive subscales on the externalizing latent construct was high and statistically reliable, consistent with the massive amount of research conducted on this instrument. The Withdrawn, Somatic, Anxious, and Depressed subscales were significant on the internalizing construct. What is most interesting, however, is that the correlations between teacher and parent reports were generally quite low: .20 and .35 for externalizing and internalizing disorders, respectively. This finding is consistent with other factor analytic research on this instrument. However, the correlation between externalizing and internalizing within parent reports was .72, and within teacher reports, .57. Comorbidity of these symptom clusters is clearly the rule rather than the exception, and cross-setting stability is relatively rare. As comorbidity of problem behaviors increases, so do cross-setting stability and risk (Stormshak et al., 1998). The model shown in Table 6.1 is superior to a model that poses a general externalizing and internalizing construct that is relatively consistent across home and school.

These findings are consistent with the ecological perspective, suggesting that to be effective, clinical assessment and subsequent interventions require setting-specific assessments and interventions. It is also hypothesized that the source of the covariation between internalizing and externalizing behavior comes from (a) response biases in parents and teachers that may be clinically relevant and (b) the integral connection between social adaptation and children's sense of well-being. Conflict and trouble in the family or at school would understandably lead to emotional distress in that setting.

Consistent with this perspective, externalizing disorder is referred to as *problem behavior* and internalizing disorder referred to as *emotional distress*. These labels are less inferential and remind the reader that these clinical concerns are often setting-specific and influenced by a variety of factors, including the adult perceptions of adjustment.

Parenting Traits

The field of child and family psychology is converging on the issue of supporting parenting practices during interventions (Patterson et al., 1993). We have conducted a similar analysis on parenting traits to better understand the issues in assessing parenting practices. Using structural equation modeling, we performed a multitrait, multimethod analysis of the parenting practices of the ATP participants (Dishion, Burraston, & Li, 2002). We studied the relation between measurement method and five parenting constructs: Limit Setting, Monitoring, Positive Reinforcement, Problem Solving, and Relationship Quality.

Each construct was measured by parent, child, and staff report. We conceptualized the reporting agent as the major method of interest. Thus, our multiagent, multimethod analysis included five trait constructs (parenting practices) and three method constructs (reporting agents). We relied on global ratings of parenting practices because the majority of developmental and clinical studies focus on a global report measure of parenting.

The structural equation model resulting from these analyses is summarized in Figure 6.1. Neither a pure method nor a trait model fit the data (see Table 6.2).

The correlation among the latent parenting constructs was quite high. In fact, the correlation between limit setting and monitoring was 1.0, which means that when all statistical factors were taken into account, parental limit setting and monitoring were impossible to differentiate by global ratings. Other parenting constructs were simply highly correlated. For example, the correlation between positive reinforcement and relationship quality was .70. These findings suggest that even the constructs that represent very different theoretical perspectives are difficult to differentiate under the scrutiny of careful measurement. This may explain why clinicians from different theoretical views are able to achieve similar results. Because systematic research comparing the advantages of family therapy techniques is in its infancy, it may be premature to conclude that all family-centered approaches are equivalent.

Neither a pure parenting trait model nor a reporting agent model fit the data well. For the pattern of correlation within these data to be understood, it is necessary to consider both sources of variation. In fact, the reporting agent accounted for about 50% of the variation. This high percentage suggests the need for careful consideration of the perspective of each reporting agent as a significant factor in scores describing children or families.

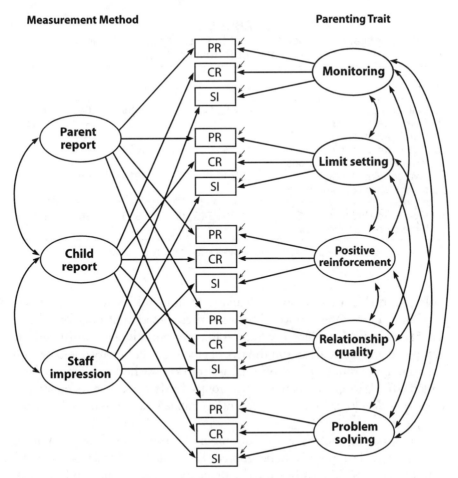

Figure 6.1. A multimethod trait approach to measuring families.

CULTURAL RELATIVITY

A major frontier in clinical and developmental psychology is the conceptualization and measurement of constructs across cultures (Wing Sue, Bingham, Porche, & Vasquez, 1999). When psychologists build models for the development of problem behavior in children and adolescents, it is critical that they examine the viability of their constructs across cultures. There are two stochastic parameters of interest: mean level analysis and structural analyses.

Mean level analysis determines the average level of a behavior across cultural groups. For example, it answers questions such as, Is there more or less substance use in European American or African American youth? In

TABLE 6.2
Summary of Goodness-of-Fit Indexes for the Multitrait and
Method Model of Parenting Practices

Model	χ^2	df	TLI NNFI	CFI	Proper
1. Trait only	417.924	80	.536	.646	No
2. Five correlated traits; correlated method errors	84.408	50	.937	.970	Yes
3. Five correlated traits; three uncorrelated methods	132.556	65	.905	.914	Yes
4. Five correlated traits; parent, child correlated methods	120.459	64	.919	.951	Yes
5. Five correlated traits; three correlated methods	102.745	62	.940	.964	No

Note. CFI = comparative fit index; NNFI = nonnormed fit index; TLI = Tucker-Lewis index.

isolation, this analysis is not particularly meaningful because of the many confounds in the Western world between these broad indicators for culture. There obviously is significant variation in parenting strategies within ethnic groups. Aggregate analyses run the risk of glossing over heterogeneity within these groups (Trimble, 1990). We also want to know whether the structure of a model holds when compared across groups. Little work that systematically compares developmental or intervention models across groups has been completed.

Diversity in models across cultural groups suggests richness in human adaptation that simply cannot be ignored. The ecological framework provides a means for systematically studying diversity across culture and context. The search for variability is unlikely to lead to a problem of infinite regress. A finite set of contexts, within which families reside, is assumed, and patterns of human adaptation can be identified within these limited sets of circumstances. Broad themes can be surmised that are particularly relevant to understanding adaptation within cultural groups. A historical analysis provides major clues. For example, the history of oppression and genocide associated with the experiences of American Indian and African American families within the United States cannot be ignored when studying the development of problem behavior and emotional distress as well as designing a service delivery system.

Consider the impact of U.S. policies designed to systematically disrupt indigenous socialization practices in American Indian communities by removing young children from their homes and sending them to boarding schools. Other injustices include terminating the status of tribes and repeated efforts to separate people from tribal lands. Although many of these governmental policies have been discontinued, there is historical continuity between the past and present. With respect to intervention science and practice, the historical context is relevant to future efforts to provide support in diverse communities.

Researchers often neglect the conceptualization and measurement of constructs, such as stigmatization, a sense of oppression, and historical trauma, that may be particularly relevant to the individual lives and experiences of minority members (Duran & Duran, 1995). Their interaction with mental health programs is limited. Families lack trust in governmental agencies that conduct assessments and evaluations. Most treatment programs and assessment practices are designed from a European cultural paradigm, at a minimum, and are disrespectful of indigenous practices and often explicitly discourage traditional practices and cultural values. This historical dynamic affects everyone by introducing often implicit biases and attributions in professionals and clients alike.

The central point is that families living within a history of oppression, stigmatization, and poverty are likely to hold unique perspectives on mental health and to have developed unique patterns of socialization and organization that are ecologically more viable. This point was particularly obvious in our direct observation analysis of successful European American and African American families at high risk.

Dishion and Bullock (2002) studied the viability of five constructs of family management. The videotaped observations were conducted in each family's home, with structured tasks designed to elicit positive reinforcement, limit setting, parental monitoring, setting norms for abstinence, problem solving, and relationship quality. The constructs were derived primarily from our research on European American boys (Patterson et al., 1992), and the sample included both boys and girls. The means for the groups are provided in Table 6.3, along with the tests for statistical differences. Note that most of the univariate analyses of variance showed statistically reliable interactions between ethnicity and risk (5 out of 7), which suggests that our understanding of the familial processes that differentiate risk from success vary significantly by whether the child is African American or European American.

The findings suggest the existence of mean level differences among groups. However, differences in mean level suggest only that parenting styles vary by cultural group. For example, see the research on limit setting reported by Deater-Deckard and Dodge (1997). In these studies, as well as in others, the data suggest that assertive limit setting in African American families is associated with positive outcomes, whereas democratic limit setting in European American families is associated with positive child outcomes. These findings are based primarily on child self-report but suggest an interesting possibility: Specific parenting practices are perceived differently within different cultural groups and are, therefore, differentially effective. If this is

TABLE 6.3
Mean Differences in Subscale and Total Scores From the Family
Assessment Task for Normative and High-Risk Youth

Observed	Normative (N = 120) M (SD)	High-risk (N = 70) M (SD)	Univariate effects
Relationship quality	6.72 (1.20)	6.42 (1.47)	R × E × G
Positive reinforcement	4.24 (1.29)	4.48 (1.62)	R × E
Monitoring	6.13 (1.03)	5.71 (1.14)	R × E
Limit setting	5.94 (1.46)	5.94 (1.46)	R × E
Problem solving	5.88 (1.62)	5.39 (1.56)	R × E
Family drug-use norms	6.28 (1.01)	5.65 (1.45)	R
Family management	6.48 (0.93)	6.10 (0.98)	R

Note. E = ethnicity main effect; R × E = risk by ethnicity interaction; R × E × G = risk by ethnicity by gender interaction.

true, then mean levels of limit setting would be expected to vary across the groups at high risk and successful groups in African American and European American families. Stormshak, Bierman, McMahon, Lengua, and the Conduct Problems Prevention Research Group (2000) found similar results in their study examining parenting practices as predictors of early child behavior problems. Punitive parenting and physical aggression in the context of parenting were associated with problem behavior for European American children but were unrelated to problem behavior for African American children.

Consider the box plots in Figure 6.2, where this pattern does seem to hold. African American and European American children at high risk are not differentiated on observation ratings of limit setting, whereas the normative youth are. In the latter group, normative African American youth are perceived as lower on limit setting than are normative European American youth. In fact, successful African American youth showed lower limit setting than did African American youth at high risk.

We speculated that the sources of the risk by ethnicity interaction are twofold (Dishion & Bullock, 2002): (a) Successful families might approach limit-setting situations more assertively, and the style of limit setting is not captured in the macroratings (if this statement is true, macroratings are not culturally sensitive); and (b) coders completing the macroratings are generally of European American descent and may have been less sensitive to cultural differences in limit setting and may have inadvertently scored parents lower on limit setting because of displays of negative affect.

When rating data on minority children and families are collected, it is extremely important to factor in cultural bias in the raters, including well-meaning professionals. Kavanagh, Burraston, Dishion, and Schneiger

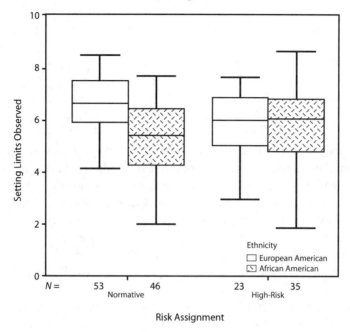

Setting Limits

Figure 6.2. Cultural variation in limit setting.

(2000) examined the patterns of risk identification based on teacher ratings for middle school boys and girls within a public school setting. Teachers completed a brief screening inventory that involved identifying risk on 10 behavioral dimensions known to predict future problem behavior among young adolescents. We also had data on the socioeconomic status of the child, peer nominations of antisocial behavior, self-reported antisocial behavior, and school records of discipline contacts.

As expected, boys received higher ratings of risk than did girls, but these differences were eliminated when the youths' actual behavior was controlled for, as reported by the youth and peers. The same was not true for ethnicity—that is, we found higher teacher ratings of risk for African American students compared with European American students, even after controlling for self-report, peer report, and school records. These data suggest that there are ethnic biases in teacher ratings of risk and that screening inventories relying on teacher global ratings may inadvertently target an overabundance of minority youth. When screening inventories are linked to preventive interventions, we think that the teacher bias could further alienate minority families from participation and engagement in school activities.

CLINICAL ASSESSMENT

A major problem in clinical work with children and families is the drawing of clinically relevant inferences about needs and focus. Clinicians are notoriously poor at making such judgments from unstructured clinical interviews with individuals and, one suspects, with children (Dawes, 1994). We have already explained that caregivers and teachers, for example, often have divergent views of the behavior and needs of any child or adolescent. Neither the parent nor the teacher should be considered as invalid reporters, because their perspective may actually be part of the ecology of the child's life. The clinician obtains insight through the investigative effort to distinguish method from trait in conducting a comprehensive assessment. In a similar way, the state of the art is such that many of the clinician's measurements may be blind to cultural diversity and, therefore, he or she will be insensitive to experiences of minority children. The bias is clinically relevant because it reflects both the daily experience of the child and the historical context of the family with whom the clinician wishes to establish a collaborative relationship.

Assessments, therefore, can be used to improve one's clinical perspective and subsequent decisions. Although uncontroversial as a general statement, it is odd that most empirically based interventions, with the notable exception of Paul and Menditto (1992), do not provide an assessment protocol that assists in decision making at all phases of the intervention process. We have recently developed a comprehensive assessment battery for adolescents and families in the ATP (Dishion & Kavanagh, 2003). It is argued that solid assessment practices provide a more accurate snapshot of the child and family ecology and, as we point out in this volume, an excellent basis for developing a collaborative set and motivation to change in the family.

CASE CONCEPTUALIZATION

In conclusion, it is argued that science can help the clinician make real-world decisions that are helpful to clients' lives. If there is one practice that would improve the standards of mental health care for children and families, it would be the use of a comprehensive assessment strategy for decision making (Dawes, 1994). A model-based framework for assessment ensures assessment of experiences that are relevant to the development of child and adolescent psychopathology, even though the clients may not see such experiences as particularly relevant to their worries and concerns. For example, ignoring the peer dynamics in an assessment of a 12-year-old boy referred for stealing and smoking is professionally neglectful, regardless of the interesting interaction patterns of the parents and family. In a similar way, not accessing the subjective experiences of a single mother who finds it difficult to set limits on her 15-year-old son perhaps neglects her daily experience of distress and dissociation when dealing with men, secondary to experiences of abuse. Finally, not being mindful of the cultural context of a family, vis-à-vis biases, the family's reaction to assessment, or one's own value structure, is likely to lead to poor clinical decisions.

Many clinicians who value their own expertise and skill in working with families, for example, find doing a school assessment too expensive and cumbersome. Teachers are often reluctant to complete questionnaires, and conducting a school observation may seem like a waste of time. From an ecological perspective, both structured and unstructured assessments are needed to provide an accurate case conceptualization. Consider the following two clinical examples that exemplify this issue and illustrate common presenting problems at any child and family clinic:

> *Example 1:* John is a 7-year-old boy referred for disruptive behavior at home and at school. His parents report that he has always been hard to manage, was a difficult infant and toddler, and has had trouble accepting limits since he was age 3. At school, the teacher reports that John has a range of problems, including attention problems, aggression with peers, and noncompliance. John's mother reports a history of depression for herself, and his parents report marital problems because of John's behavior.
>
> *Example 2:* Peter is a 7-year-old boy referred for disruptive behavior at home and at school. His parents report that he has always been hard to manage, was a difficult infant and toddler, and has had trouble accepting limits since he was age 3. At school, the teacher reports no problems and says Peter is a very compliant and easy-tempered child with lots of positive attributes. Peter's mother reports a history of depression for herself, and the couple reports marital problems because of Peter's behavior.

Although the problem behavior at home is the same in both of these examples, the problems at school are clearly very different. This one difference leads to two entirely different targets. In the first example, the problem is long term and cross-situational. John's parents need support in parenting him, tools for managing this type of problem behavior, and home-to-school planning to coordinate the services across contexts. In contrast, Peter's parents would probably benefit from marital counseling, adult depression work, and family management strategies that would help them parent Peter as a marital team.

A comprehensive strategy for measurement provides a basis for clinical decisions. It is imperative, however, that clinicians consider these complex data with other data in formulating a clinical picture. Meehl (1973) and

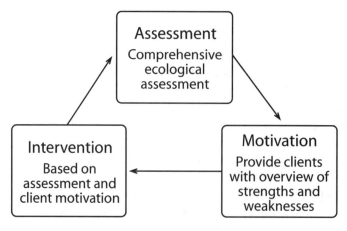

Figure 6.3. The AIM (assessment, intervention, motivation) model for linking assessment with interventions.

others have discussed strategies for improving the cognitive activity of the clinician. The many pitfalls in decision making and judgment (e.g., Tversky & Kahneman, 1974) can be circumvented if services are provided by clinical teams that have weekly case conferences. When working extensively with children and families from minority cultural groups, the clinical team must represent the community, so that biases in the professional team can be constructively identified, objectified, and incorporated into the case conceptualization. Most important, the stance that the expert clinician makes the judgment and decides, unilaterally, the nature and course of treatment is likely to lead to resistance, dropout, and poor motivation in clients. Figure 6.3 summarizes the interrelation between *assessment, intervention,* and *motivation* within the context of an overall strategy, or the AIM service delivery model. In the AIM model, conceptualization and intervention are an ongoing process, which begins with a comprehensive ecological assessment.

Each of these steps and accompanying assessment strategies are discussed throughout this volume. The first step is to conduct an assessment and consult with a clinical team. Second is to share the assessment findings with the caregiver and, when appropriate, the child (see chap. 4, this volume). This collaborative discussion often leads to a change in perspective for both the clinician and the client. A variety of factors are needed to understand the ecology of a clinical scenario. The client's level of insight is particularly important to case formulation. When assessment results reveal a marriage in distress, it is important to note how a couple responds to this information and the level of their sense of hope for, and commitment to, improving the relationship. Third, the assessments are used to serve the best interests of the clients with every effort made to communicate this sentiment. A comprehensive assessment allows the realistic discussion of strengths and weaknesses which are both important in addressing the caregivers' and child's concern. Finally, assessments are used to motivate change. Most of us engage in inappropriate behavior and feel bad for a long time before committing to change. Assessment findings can be used to support realistic motivation to change. Finally, the client's response to mutually agreed on intervention strategies is often an assessment itself. A parent may finally conclude that his drug use is a major barrier to his effort to improve his family and to his efforts to prevent his son from pursuing the same path. We have developed assessments that allow an ongoing picture of the ebb and flow of behaviors, feelings, and symptoms of children and families identified as concerns at the beginning of treatment. These assessments provide the basis for changing an intervention tactic, addressing issues of motivation, supporting motivation, and deciding on termination. Before we move on to the topic of intervention, however, it is necessary to consider in some detail the advantages and challenges of assessing relationships such as parent–child relationships, friendship interactions, peer interactions, intimate relationships, and, finally, therapist–client relationships.

SUMMARY

This chapter provides an overview of an ecological assessment strategy. We recommend that when clinicians define an intervention practice, they use an ecological framework to sample domains of influence for children and families. Models for the development of problem behavior or well-being also narrow the focus of assessment. Using multiple reporting agents and methods is critical to formulating an assessment picture. Method bias is not merely noise, but relevant to case conceptualization. Bias in reporting may come from adjustment of the reporting agent, unique demands in school versus home, or cultural biases. The ecological framework acknowledges that the diversity of parenting styles within contexts and groups needs exploration in developmental science and clinical practice. Finally, assessments, intervention teams, and a collaborative relationship with clients are offered as resources for improving case conceptualization. The AIM service delivery model summarizes the strategy of linking assessment, intervention, and motivation.

7

MOBILIZING CHANGE WITH THE FAMILY CHECK-UP

In this chapter, we review the feedback session in the Family Check-Up (FCU) and discuss motivating and engaging parents in treatment. The intervention referred to as the FCU culminates in the feedback session (Dishion & Kavanagh, 2003). The feedback session builds on information and sentiments from the initial contact and assessment. As such, the FCU can be seen as both a brief intervention and a bridge to the use of other intervention resources. The three-session FCU is appropriate for all parents, regardless of demographic characteristics or severity of clinical problems. Parents with normal concerns about adolescent behavior can benefit, as can those in need of more intensive support or behavior change. Thus, the FCU is ideal for a variety of service settings, ranging from preventive interventions (Dishion & Kavanagh, 2003) to clinical treatment in outpatient and residential settings. We see the FCU as the doorway into a range of empirically supported intervention services, including brief interventions, individual family therapy, parent groups, marital therapy, and community referrals (see Figure 7.1).

MOTIVATIONAL INTERVIEWING

Parenting practices and family interactions are overlearned behaviors that many parents have practiced during the course of a lifetime. Despite

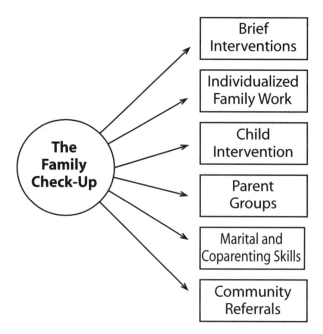

Figure 7.1. The Family Check-Up: A brief intervention with linked services.

the pain and suffering attributable to avoidance of difficulties or coercion dynamics, it is difficult for individuals to change how they behave within their family. Most adults who return to their family of origin for visits have experienced their own adolescent behavior under these circumstances. To protect against the daily onslaught of guilt, sense of failure, and discouragement, parents often tell themselves a story about the origins of their family difficulties. It is often the case that someone else is to blame or, alternatively, they blame themselves into immobilization (e.g., with thoughts or beliefs such as "I am an awful parent"). Assessment data can be a useful tool for altering destructive appraisals into a constructive frame for change.

A therapist's main tool for change is reframing, which is essentially providing the client with an alternative perspective. For example, Robins and colleagues (Robins, Alexander, Newell, & Turner, 1996) document benefits from one family's first therapy session when the therapist effectively reframed the adolescent's troublesome behavior.

Although reframing is critical to the change process, current approaches to therapy do not provide many guidelines for this process. Some say this is where the art of therapy enters. The therapist is left to his or her own innovation to finesse these cognitive interchanges. However, an inept reframe can increase resistance to change and therapy (Patterson & Forgatch, 1985). Therapists become particularly good at reframes when they

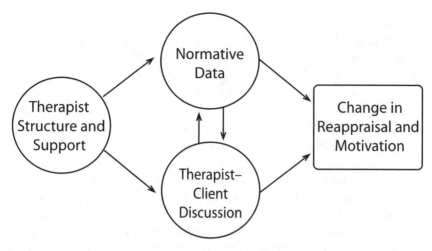

Figure 7.2. The role of assessment in addressing motivation.

encounter many clients with similar issues, such as adolescents with eating disorders, delinquency problems, or oppositional behavior. Reframing becomes a function of practice, with more seasoned clinicians developing a history of understanding the presentation of common problems. Because many therapists who work with children and families do not have extensive experience to draw from, usable tools are still needed for all practitioners.

A comprehensive ecological assessment reduces the mystery of the therapist's reframe by providing a database and time for considering carefully how the clinician can approach a family. As shown in Figure 7.2, therapists have used assessment data to structure interactions that result in a parent's reappraisal of his or her own behavior, his or her child's adjustment, and the family situation. Within the context of the motivational interviewing framework, normative data elicit discrepancies that can then be handled skillfully to support a reappraisal that is constructive to change. Developmental science directs the therapist to the processes that require attention; clinical science guides the process of change in reaching those targets.

The structure of the FCU allows the therapist to slow down the initial interactions with a family and to use data to improve clinical decision making in the interest of the family. It's as if the actions of the family are frozen before they begin the therapeutic process. Both the family and the therapists are provided with a forum to collaborate on a shared perspective on the upcoming change process.

The best label for this approach to the change dynamic is *transtheoretical* (Prochaska & DiClemente, 1982). The transtheoretical view is essentially one that is anchored in the science of the change process. Prochaska and

DiClemente (1982) found that more than 90% of smokers who quit did so without the aid of a therapist or behavior-change program. Careful examination of the process suggested stages of change. When individuals make significant changes in behavior, they often go through various emotionally oriented stages that may vary in length from weeks to years. The first stage is contemplation: The individual begins to reflect on whether change is necessary. In the second stage, action is taken to make a change. Parents may decide that they need to keep track of their son more carefully and have a family meeting to discuss strategies for better communication regarding his whereabouts. Once action is taken to make a life change, it is always necessary to maintain the change. This stage can be the most difficult part of the behavior-change process and, if unsuccessful, perhaps the most discouraging. When an attempt at behavior change fails, the sense of discouragement may lead to a redefinition of goals, including a decision that change is not possible or worth the effort. Failure at behavior change may result in parents blaming their child for being unchangeable or blaming themselves for not being capable, which deepens the perceived intractability of the problem. Many parents of adolescents may have cycled through several efforts to change and have well-founded discouragement.

Motivational interviewing was designed as an intervention technique to trigger the behavior-change process by focusing on motivation to change (W. R. Miller & Rollnick, 1991). Drawing from a broad base of research, W. R. Miller and colleagues (Brown & Miller, 1993; Miller, 1987, 1989; Miller & Sovereign, 1989) designed a set of procedures that provides parents with a basis for better decision making regarding the need for change. Motivational intervention incorporates a set of five behavior-change principles, encapsulated in a model we have designated as FRAMES.

F refers to providing parents with data-based *feedback* about their behavior and the implications of their behavior for the future. R stands for communicating to the client their *responsibility* for the behavior-change process. A reflects the need for sound *advice* from an expert about where the efforts should be focused or how to take realistic steps to promote success in the behavior-change process. M stands for a *menu* of behavior-change options provided to the parents rather than a single behavior-change option such as family therapy or inpatient drug abuse treatment. (Taking an active role in deciding on an optimal behavior-change strategy is self-motivating.) E refers to the need to express *empathy* for the parents' situation. A classic finding in psychotherapy is the need for acceptance, support, and empathy in the behavior-change process (Rogers, 1957). Therapists must cultivate understanding and compassion for a variety of circumstantial and cultural experiences presented by parents who are considering healthy changes. Finally, the S in FRAMES means that parents should leave the motivational interview with a sense of *self-efficacy*. One of the best ways to promote self-

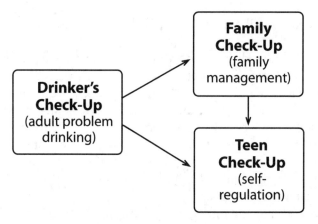

Figure 7.3. Innovations in motivational interviewing.

efficacy is to collaborate with parents in selecting behavior-change goals that are realistic, measurable, and under their control.

The FRAMES model provides the basis for the FCU. The three-session intervention includes an intake interview, a thorough assessment, and a feedback session with the parents, and possibly, with the children or adolescents. The FCU was designed to (a) target parents' motivation to maintain current parenting practices that are important for young adolescent adjustment, (b) reduce interactions that are likely to undermine the parent–child relationship or exacerbate behavior problems, and (c) increase parenting behaviors that promote adjustment and competence.

We more recently added to the FCU the Teen Check-Up (Dishion & Kavanagh, 2003). Adolescents (ages 13–17) benefit from engaging in a motivational feedback session. Families with adolescents often drop out of treatment, and according to our experience one of the major reasons is teen disenchantment with the treatment process. The Teen Check-Up addresses that problem. Figure 7.3 provides a historical overview of the development of the FCU and the Teen Check-Up. These two interventions were inspired by W. R. Miller and colleagues' work on the Drinker's Check-Up (Miller & Sovereign, 1989).

A HISTORICAL OVERVIEW

The task of the feedback session is to tailor information so that it changes an adult's perspective about his or her parenting. This task may often involve presenting information that is unsettling or difficult to hear. It is not helpful if the therapist colludes with the client not to take a realistic look at him- or herself and his or her family. The work of the feedback session is to balance information with understanding and to establish conditions for change.

Much of the work in conducting an effective feedback occurs away from the family, before the parent ever arrives for the feedback session. In his or her office, the therapist studies videotapes, scores measures, and prepares feedback in an understandable format. The family observation task provides information about key parenting behaviors. We have also used the expressed emotion task as a method for getting at a client's thoughts and feelings (i.e., narratives) about him- or herself within the family. Therefore, it is important for the family therapist to carefully view, as well as rate, the videotaped family interactions.

When working with one or more therapists, we present complex cases at a weekly meeting (after scoring the data and studying the videotape) to get professional input regarding the best approach to take for each family. In chapter 13 (this volume), we discuss setting up confidential peer supervision meetings that are therapeutically productive. We now turn to discussing the elements of a pragmatic case conceptualization and the feedback process itself.

Case Conceptualization

Five elements provide the organizing principles for case conceptualization: (a) the centrality of parenting to the child's success and well-being, (b) being based on data from observations and the assessment, (c) harm reduction, (d) tailoring feedback, and (e) supporting motivation to change. Within these elements, parenting is central to the long-term effort to promote success and well-being in young children and adolescents. See Exhibit 7.1 for a summary of these principles of case conceptualization.

Key measures of child social adaptation and emotional well-being are available with norms. For example, the Child Behavior Checklist is a valid and reliable measure and includes options for teacher, parent, and child reports in addition to direct observation. The norms for the Child and Family Center version of the home observation task for normative and clinical families can be downloaded from the Child and Family Center Web

---

EXHIBIT 7.1
Principles of Case Conceptualization

- Prioritize parenting.
- Be data oriented.
- Reduce harm.
- Tailor feedback.
- Support motivation.

---

site (http://cfc.uoregon.edu). As discussed in the previous chapter about ecological assessment, clinicians can select a comprehensive assessment battery of their own, with norms useful for deriving feedback.

When feedback is given to parents, the central theme should be that their parenting practices are central to clinical outcomes and essential for engagement in potential support services (e.g., parent groups, family therapy). Marital problems, family transitions, health issues, and more can be discussed in terms of their effect on parenting practices and family communication processes.

In thinking about the interventions for problem behavior in middle childhood and adolescence, the therapist needs to keep in mind the catalytic role of peers. Our research has consistently shown the centrality of parental monitoring in moderating the effects of peers. In this respect, focusing on family factors that serve as a barrier to parental involvement and monitoring will be of long-term value in limiting the potential negative influence of peers. Of course, there are interdependencies in families. A strong relationship, positive limit-setting practices, encouragement, and problem solving all strengthen monitoring. In the feedback process, the therapist needs to pay attention to all family management skills, especially those that are areas of strength, because doing so both builds motivation and reinforces protective factors for the child.

The second principle guiding case conceptualization is harm reduction. When families are distressed and abusive or their assessment data indicate several areas of difficulty, it is important to adopt a harm reduction perspective. Some time is required to consider the optimal next-step advice that will control damage that is secondary to pathological processes, such as divorce-related conflict, parental drug abuse, a death in the family, a runaway child, or physical or sexual abuse. When serious problems such as these occur, the feedback process focuses on the necessary step to reduce future harm to the child, parent, or other family members. Goals such as improving parenting practices or the child's behavior are put aside in favor of creating a safe, stable family environment. For instance, in the event of severe conflict creating potential for an adolescent to run away, harm reduction focuses on making the changes necessary to keep the family together. When severe school difficulties occur, the focus may be on keeping a student at high risk from being expelled.

Tailoring the feedback to the individual family is the third element of case conceptualization. Our discussion has already covered the importance of identifying larger contextual family issues that counterindicate the parents' ability to respond to specific detailed feedback. Likewise, a family could have many more risk factors than protective factors and, in light of the goal of promoting motivation and optimism about change, feedback can be provided in stages. For instance, the peer domain could be discussed and other domains saved until the family works through peer issues. Another possible situation is that parents are limited in their ability to process information. A way to maximize success and understanding is to give small portions of feedback over time. Even if all the individual feedback can be given in one meeting, the way in which it is given depends on the family situation.

The fourth element of case conceptualization and feedback is supporting motivation. Parents should leave the feedback interview feeling motivated to continue with their strengths and empowered to address their needs. During the case conceptualization process, an important goal is identifying current strengths in the parenting system. Similar to our suggested praise-to-correction ratio (Dishion & Kavanagh, 2003), a 4:1 ratio of strengths (protective factors) to concerns (risk factors) should be the goal. Even in the most difficult family circumstances, parental follow-through with the FCU process can be emphasized as a positive indication of concern for their child and commitment to change.

Therapists should complete the feedback forms when examining the assessment results within each of the broad domains: family influences, peer influences, child competencies, and problem behavior. The number of entries on these sheets should be based on the therapist's case conceptualization and the ratio of protective to risk factors. It may be helpful for the therapist to first assess the strengths within each domain, then to enter into the areas of concern, keeping a ratio of four positive feedback points to one area of concern. In formulating a strategy for giving feedback, the therapist can think about the four or five (maximum) major points he or she wants the parents to recall from the feedback session. These can also be enumerated on the Child Well-Being Profile.

The Feedback Session

The feedback session can be divided into four phases (see Exhibit 7.2). The first phase is an opportunity for parents to discuss their own self-assessment, based on their experiences in the assessment process. The second phase is clarification and support. When parents discuss their self-assessment, this is an opportunity to (a) appreciate their approach to behavior change,

EXHIBIT 7.2
Feedback Session

- Client self-assessment
- Support and clarification
- Assessment feedback
- Exploration of intervention options

(b) assess their level of insight, (c) learn more about the dynamics of the family, and (d) discover issues not covered in the assessment. The third phase focuses on summarizing feedback to families, based on the information they provide. In the final phase, the therapist and the parents work collaboratively to develop a menu of options for improving family life and promoting the success of the child. The entire feedback session is best thought of as the beginning of a work in progress, and the final outcome will reflect a parent-guided process of interaction with the therapist.

PHASES OF FEEDBACK SESSION

Providing feedback to clients in a way that motivates positive change is a delicate process. To ensure the success of this therapist–client dynamic interchange, we suggest the following phases.

Self-Assessment

The feedback process begins with the therapist saying something such as this:

> Many parents feel they've learned something about their family after going through the assessment. Did you learn anything new about your family, especially anything that might be related to your concerns about Roman?

The majority of families bring up at least one key issue for which the therapist intended to provide feedback. Parents often perceive this question as a request to self-disclose deficits in parenting. The therapist's response can help reframe this perception from a deficit to a goal. How the parents respond allows the therapist to gauge their approach to behavior change. For example, the parents might say the following:

> We learned that we get caught up in arguing no matter what we talk about.

This comment is enough to go on and is the parent's first step toward making family changes. If a parent notices the arguing, chances are the therapist was already planning on giving him or her feedback on that issue. The parent will be receptive to feedback about the arguing and, in fact, his or her insight into the family's difficulties can be supported.

In contrast, a parent who blames his or her communication problems on another family member presents a somewhat different motivational stance:

> Yeah, you can see why we never get anywhere. I've told John a thousand times that if he flunks high school, he'll never get a job. He thinks he knows everything!

This mom's view was not changed by the assessment session, nor did she see her lecturing and nattering as remotely related to the problem. It is best for the therapist to know this at the outset rather than after recommending several meetings focused on communication, which no one in the family is motivated to attend.

Support and Clarification

The therapist now begins the support and clarification process. He or she might proceed as follows (for a one-parent family):

> So, you've targeted arguing as something that interferes with good relations. I saw that, too, when I watched your family discussion. We see arguing a lot in families with children this age. You're right, it often feels like the problems get worse when you talk about them and the arguing gets out of control. The positive side of arguing is that it indicates your family cares about how issues get solved.

Feedback

The support and clarification phase can be a brief transition into feedback, accomplishing two goals: supporting the parent's activity in the meeting and supporting self-assessment efforts. With this information, the therapist can clarify misconceptions about the feedback process or the goals of the meeting. The following could be a possible transition:

> The arguing problem is solvable, and we'll see how the other information you gave guides us to some ideas.
>
> Children go through a lot of changes as they move into adolescence. Other families find it useful to have the opportunity for this checkup. Maybe you can think of this as getting blood pressure or temperature reports for different areas of Roman's life.
>
> You have a picture of how Roman is doing right now. You also know what you're doing that supports positive adjustment, which may help you sort the behaviors you want to be concerned about from those that are just part of adolescence. We'll be looking for two things: what's protecting Roman against risk and what may be putting him at risk for serious behavior problems, including substance use. You probably noticed that we asked a lot of questions about Roman's behavior and your family's current situation and style of getting along.
>
> I also gathered some information from Roman's teacher about his peer relations and behavior at school. This information will give us a good understanding of how Roman is doing right now.
>
> First, we'll start with what you and the teacher reported about Roman's behavior. . . .

The feedback phase is relatively straightforward. However, this is a substantial amount of information for the parent to receive all at once. The therapist and parent should be sitting next to each other to allow for mutual examination of the assessment results and to reduce the potentially confrontational nature of receiving feedback. Also, it is best for the therapist to have only one copy of the feedback forms so that he or she can emphasize feedback points strategically. For example, when problems are severe, it is helpful to summarize the findings from several measures into one point. Pointing to parent and teacher Child Behavior Checklist scores, the therapist can say something such as the following:

> As you can see, there's generally good agreement between you and the teacher that Roman's behavior and adjustment are a problem right now, in terms of both how he's affected by and how he's affecting others.

This statement draws the parent's attention to the larger issue of adjustment, as opposed to going over each individual scale, which can be punishing when the child's scores are all in the at-risk or needs-improvement range. Many parents will be overwhelmed by the mere process of receiving feedback on issues as personal as being a parent. It is necessary to show respect for the parents' perspective and to explain that the assessment results should be considered in the context of the family's cultural and environmental situation. The therapist can stop at strategic points and simply ask questions such as those that follow:

> Does this information fit with how you've been seeing the problem? When we talked before, you focused on your difficulties with Roman at home, but we didn't talk as much about school. Do you know much about the kinds of friends he hangs out with at school? Does this surprise you?

The therapist ought not to assume an understanding. Showing respect and selecting questions that reveal information will help in the design of a menu of change options. A therapist should be sure to continually monitor the parent's affect and reaction to information and take time to support, validate, and put the parent at ease. For example, the therapist can say the following:

> I've just given you a lot of information. Are you having any thoughts or reactions you want to bring up?

A contextual issue that often arises in two-parent families is marital problems. When this element is revealed, often divergent levels of satisfaction are expressed, which is usually not a surprise to the couple. However, some couples may not have discussed their marriage in some time. This very sensitive situation requires attention. Ignoring the marital problem could be ignoring the source of family difficulty and have long-term negative effects on a young adolescent's positive adjustment by contributing to an atmosphere of poor communication. Therefore, it is absolutely necessary to be direct, but sensitive:

> I want to draw your attention to how each of you report your satisfaction with your marriage, because there was some disagreement there. Marian, you reported that at this time you're really satisfied with how things are going and John reports being pretty unhappy with the way things are. Is this new information, or have you talked about this before?

It is difficult to know beforehand how couples will respond, but it is extremely rare when serious dissatisfaction by one member of a couple has gone completely unnoticed by the other. If it has, the information could be upsetting and arouse emotion. It is important to acknowledge and support the couple around this issue. But it is also important not to turn the feedback meeting into a marital session because the goal is to build momentum toward a menu of change options for the well-being of the child. Of course, for this couple, marital therapy would be one such option within the menu.

The therapist should review the entire feedback process and reflect on the parents' reactions, ideas, and perceptions. The therapist then communicates the importance of collaboration and emphasizes that he or she is there to share his or her expertise in children and family therapy. This process establishes the foundation for the next step, which is developing a menu of intervention activities.

Menu of Change Options

Consistent with the FRAMES model for motivational interviewing, parents are more likely to consider change when they have a choice of intervention options. The menu is derived in collaboration with the parent. Two options are needed on all menus. One is "No resources needed." Any additional comments are best worded in positive terms, such as "Continue spending time with Nina, checking in on her homework" or "Wait one term to determine if the program she's in is working."

The other essential option is to schedule a follow-up feedback session with the youth. This session is useful for generating other menu options, directing the youth toward change, and sharing the family assessment results in a motivational format. This option should be directed by the parents. In families in which things are going well, a joint feedback session may be suggested to the parents as good validation for all the positive things the parents and child are doing. Unlike the typical problem-focused family meetings with therapists, the joint feedback session has proven to be a positive family experience.

Menu items include the range of interventions within a clinical setting that therapists have been trained to implement (see Figure 7.2). In building a viable menu, knowledge of school and community resources is needed. Identifying services that are family centered is especially helpful. Again, the resources with which a therapist should have expertise are those that support family management and reduce barriers to good parenting. For instance, if there is difficulty monitoring a child's daily behavior at school, a home–school communication system (telephone calls) would be an option on the menu. One possible script follows:

> Okay, an area we identified as a concern for you, which also showed up as a problem in the assessment, is Nina's work and behavior at school. One option many parents find helpful is our home telephone calls. This involves a daily or weekly telephone call to you to give you specific information about Nina's assignments, homework completion, and her behavior at school.
>
> To prepare for these calls, we should meet twice to develop an incentive to make this system work for you at home. Does that sound like an option you might want to consider? You don't have to decide now; we can just add it to the list.

A useful tool for developing a menu of intervention options is a writing board; both the therapist and the parent can list and erase options as the discussion proceeds. The therapist's role is first to model brainstorming for generating options, and then, in the final stages of the feedback session, to promote discussion of the pros and cons of each option.

After the list of menu options has been generated, the therapist might ask the parent to select one or more for consideration:

> That's a good list we came up with. More ideas may come to you in the next week. If you wish, give me a call to see if there's a way I can help. Do you have an idea right now of what you'd like to try?

At times, when the parents' concerns are rather serious and when there are two parents in the family, they may wish to consider and decide on the options privately. Such a process should be encouraged. However, it is important to set a time to call and find out what the parents have decided. It may also be possible to schedule another meeting to proceed with the next step. We encourage feedback sessions with the adolescent if there is interest. Consider the following example:

> We didn't include Roman in this meeting because I find it's most helpful to families if I meet with parents first, then talk with the child. How would you prefer to discuss these results with Roman? You can do this yourself, we can discuss them with him together, or I can talk with him individually.

In this way, the parent continues to be supported in the leadership role, and open communication and support for the adolescent are demonstrated. A variety of strategies are available, depending on the circumstances of the case, the interest of the adolescent, and clinical conceptualization. The minimal level of feedback involves sharing the results of the family discussion. More intensive levels would involve a motivational interview for the adolescent, using the assessment to build motivation to change. The Student Self-Check (similar to the Parent Self-Check) has been created to be part of the assessment battery and can be used as a central piece of the therapist's discussion.

Therapists should finalize the FCU with a formal written report. Dishion and Kavanagh (2003) provided guidelines for writing an FCU report that is structured to support the parents' efforts to seek services for their family.

SUMMARY

The stages-of-change model and motivational interviewing were used in the design of the FCU, in general, and in the feedback session, in particular. The primary goal is using data, expert advice, empathy, and a realistic menu of change options to support the parents' decision-making process regarding the need to change.

Case conceptualization is the first step in providing feedback, which occurs before the parent arrives at the session. The feedback process is divided into four phases that include an opportunity for the parents to self-assess and for the therapist to support and clarify the parent's self-assessment and original behavior-change goals. In the third phase, the therapist goes over the assessment results collaboratively with parents and, in the final phase, the therapist and the family develop a behavior-change menu.

The next part of this volume provides a more detailed discussion of the major intervention strategies that would comprise interventions within the menu that focus on addressing family management.

III

INTERVENTION STRATEGIES

8

BRIEF PARENTING INTERVENTIONS

When an ecological model is used to conceptualize, assess, and intervene in child problem behavior, it is easy to lack focus and to develop too many goals and targets for intervention with families. The proposed treatment can be overwhelming and time consuming. It is not surprising that, under these circumstances, 40% to 60% of families drop out or leave treatment prematurely (Kazdin, 1996). In this chapter, we discuss parenting interventions for families and youth that are both brief and effective.

For many families, a long-term approach to the management of child problem behavior and family stressors is warranted. Many chronic mental health problems require a maintenance approach to mental health treatment that includes regular contact with mental health professionals over a long period. These lifelong problems, such as conduct disorder, are best addressed with a multifocused, contextual, long-term treatment model (Kazdin, 1990).

Despite this recommendation, the long-term approach to treatment presents problems. First, this approach is no longer supported by American society through insurance reimbursements or Medicare. Third-party reimbursement policies have necessitated a shift from a long-term to a short-term therapy model. Second, many families cannot commit to long-term goals because of various personal and contextual circumstances, including poverty, mobility, or job instability, to name a few. For example, poverty is associated with several other risk factors that may affect a family's ability to engage in treatment. The lack of social support, transportation, quality child care, and time and energy to commit to treatment because of work schedules are prime examples. A long-term approach may not be feasible for all families and may be overwhelming for many families. In addition, very few providers can commit to a long-term approach themselves, which, for the family, means a transfer to different therapists and clinics and results in a short-term plan for each new location of service.

Another consideration is that some family problems and mental health issues can be dealt with more effectively and efficiently in a short-term model than in a long-term model. Even within a complex presentation of risk and problem behavior, we can identify short-term goals and brief solutions to problems that benefit both children and parents and may motivate families for further treatment if indicated.

There are several ways to define a brief intervention. It can range from one session to several sessions of goal-focused therapy. Brief interventions are focused on only one or a few main family problems or parenting strategies. Brief interventions may include a comprehensive assessment or an assessment of only one problem in a particular context (e.g., school or home). They may also include interventions at home or in the community. In addition to short-term behavioral goals, brief interventions may have a goal of simply engaging families in treatment or motivating parents to seek services and begin a process of change. We discuss all of these modes of intervention in this chapter.

PARENTING PRACTICES TO TARGET

To the best of our knowledge, interventions that benefit children and adolescents are likely to be ineffective unless they address and change parenting practices. Six parenting practices are particularly important to the lives of children and may be conducive to a brief therapy approach with families and are discussed in the next sections.

Communication Effectiveness

Communication involves appropriately getting and maintaining the attention of young children when giving directions and suggestions, listening to young children and understanding their unique perspective, and communicating clearly to collaborate with other adults who may share caregiving responsibility. For parents with adolescents, communication includes listening to their child and clearly outlining expectations and consequences for behavior. Making effective requests is the fundamental communication skill needed in effective behavior management. The components of this skill are listed in Exhibit 8.1.

Proactive Structuring

This practice involves the parents' attentive and planful management of both the child and his or her environment to minimize behavior problems and to optimize emotional well-being for the child, parents, and other family members. Examples include simplifying the number of transitions a child experiences, proactively warning the child of transitions, and providing reasonable alternatives to child and parent activities. For adolescents, examples include seeking out positive extracurricular activities, working collaboratively with the school to ensure the optimal placement of the child, and structuring free-time activities. The basic components of interventions that emphasize proactive structuring are summarized in Exhibit 8.2.

Restructuring a child's environment can be an effective stand-alone intervention that is brief and changes the environment in such as way as to decrease other problem behaviors. A thorough assessment of the ecology of the problem can give the therapist important information related to the context of the problem and, possibly, some simple solutions. Consider the following case history:

> Jennifer was a 3-year-old girl who lived with her mother and stepfather and, at times, with her biological father who lived next door. Jennifer attended day care all day while her parents worked, and she was picked up around 5:00 p.m. each day by one of the parents. She spent 4 nights a week at her mother's house and 3 nights a week at her father's house,

depending on a random schedule that was contingent on work schedules and other parent commitments. Jennifer was having problems at school and was acting out aggressively toward other children, her mother, and her father. The parents in the family system meant well, with each wanting to maximize their time with Jennifer. A simple, brief intervention that included a consistent weekly schedule with each parent, a clear schedule for pickups at day care, and no random transitions or disruptions was effective in reducing Jennifer's problems in less than a month.

Relationship Building

The major foundation of social interactions in general, and of effective behavior management in particular, is establishing and maintaining a positive interpersonal relationship. Parenting behaviors such as consistency, fairness, kindness, thoughtfulness, follow-through with promises, humor, playfulness, and expression of love and affection are central to forming such a foundation. In early childhood, this approach includes appropriate play strategies and time set aside to be with the child. A key strategy for building relationships with adolescents involves spending positive time with the youth doing mutually enjoyable activities.

Monitoring

Parent attention to and tracking of the behavior, whereabouts, and safety of a child is referred to as *monitoring*. Some monitoring is facilitated by proactive structuring and relationship building. For example, parents who enjoy spending time and doing activities with young children are likely to be aware of their child's behavior and safety. Thus, examples of parent behaviors that involve monitoring are keeping a toddler within eye contact or under the supervision of a responsible caregiver, checking the safety of physical settings that involve children, and ensuring that a situation, activity, or setting is likely to occupy a child for a specific period. In addition, accurately tracking a child's behavior in interaction with others (e.g., play with peers and siblings and compliance with adults) to facilitate socialization is part of parental monitoring. For adolescent children, parental monitoring is critical and, when absent, is associated with a variety of risk behaviors (Dishion, Kavanagh, Schneiger, Nelson, & Kaufman, 2002; Kerr & Stattin, 2000). Monitoring adolescents involves tracking their behavior and peer interactions, as well as knowing where they are at all times. It may also involve communicating effectively with other parents to develop safe places for one's child and his or her peers to socialize after school or during free time.

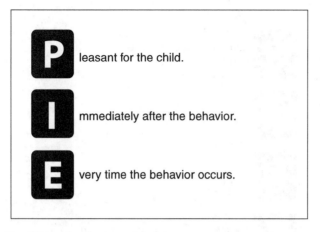

Figure 8.1. The PIE recipe for incentives.

P leasant for the child.

I mmediately after the behavior.

E very time the behavior occurs.

Positive Reinforcement

This essential and underused parenting practice involves the contingent positive reaction to a child's demonstration of a new skill, positive behavior, or clear effort. Contingent positive reactions may include a tangible reward such as a sticker (for young children), an affectionate hug, praise, or a preferred treat or activity. In adolescence, positive reinforcement may involve rewards for good grades or good behavior at school. Positive reinforcement is different from encouragement in that it is contingent and follows the behavior. Encouragement is a prompt for motivating the child's positive behavior and effort. Several important principles are involved in positive reinforcement, and they can be simply expressed by the PIE recipe: Promote the *pleasant* to the child, *immediately*, *every* time the positive behavior occurs (see Figure 8.1). The reward should be pleasant for the child and should motivate the child to continue the positive behavior. The reward should also be administered immediately following the event, not later in the day or week. And last, the reward should occur every time the behavior is observed.

Limit Setting

This parenting practice is important to children's socialization and the development of self-control. It involves the parent's contingent reaction to misbehavior by using a specific directive or applying a reasonable nonpunitive consequence that is fair and consistent. We propose the SANE

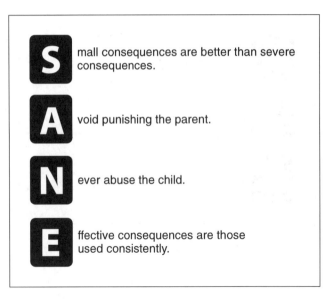

Figure 8.2. SANE limit setting guidelines.

guidelines for limit setting, which are described in detail in Dishion and Patterson (2005). In short, effective limit setting involves *small* consequences to the child, *avoids* punishing the parent by using burdensome consequences, *never* abuses the child, and is *effectively* consistent (see Figure 8.2). In early and middle childhood, the use of a time-out is an optimal technique for parents to use, because it is nonviolent and can be used frequently without harm to the child. Avoidance of limit setting, or laissez-faire parenting, may undermine children's social adaptation by promoting the development of habitual forms of misbehavior (coercion) and the child's failure to develop self-regulatory skills (i.e., inhibiting behavior). Limit setting should be approached in the context of other parenting practices and introduced only when it is clear that a parent can be effective in promoting positive child behavior through other means, especially the use of positive reinforcement. Figure 8.3 provides an overview of the joint use of positive reinforcement and time-outs in managing children's behavior.

Importance of These Practices

All of the skills listed thus far are conducive to a brief intervention approach to working with families and children. Each skill helps form the foundation for parenting effectively, and the lack of these skills in the family management system is likely related to a variety of problem behavior as

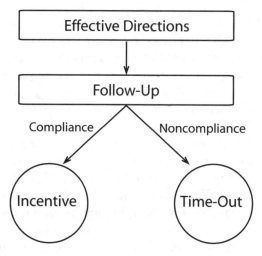

Figure 8.3. Time-out.

well as contextual stressors. Hence, the focus on any one of these skills in a brief intervention will likely change the family system in multiple ways.

BRIEF FAMILY INTERVENTION MODEL

A brief family intervention may last from three to six sessions and involve several steps. The following case example illustrates each of the steps:

> Julie was referred to the clinic by her social worker to work on parenting skills with her two male children, ages 13 and 14. The primary referral was related to her 14-year-old boy, Adam, who was engaging in various problem behaviors, including angry outbursts at home, yelling at his mother, using physical violence to threaten the family, and lying about his behavior with peers. Adam had recently been picked up by police for shoplifting alcohol at a local convenience store with his peers. The family had a variety of contextual stressors, including maternal depression, paternal substance use, job instability, inconsistent caregivers in the home, random visitation from an abusive biological father, homelessness in the past, and financial stress. Julie planned to move for a new job within the next 6 months and wanted to focus on some brief solutions to their current problems.

Assessment-Driven Foci and Goals

An ecological assessment and feedback conducted in the context of the Family Check-Up forms the foundation for change in brief parenting interventions. As discussed in chapters 5 and 6 (this volume), the Family

Check-Up model flows from a comprehensive ecological assessment that includes multirater and multimethod approaches to assessment. Norm-referenced measurement is used to give feedback to parents on strengths and risk factors. A menu of service delivery is developed collaboratively with the parents, and specific goals for treatment are targeted. This assessment procedure typically takes three or four sessions and forms the foundation for the continued delivery of services.

Research on the Family Check-Up suggests that this assessment can serve as a stand-alone, brief intervention with families. In several separate research studies conducted by our team (Dishion, Kavanagh, et al., 2002; O'Leary, 1999; Rao, 1998; Shaw, Dishion, Supplee, Gardner, & Arnds, in press) we have shown that intervention families who received the Family Check-Up assessment, including the feedback session for parents, significantly increased parenting skill behavior over a matched comparison group. These results held for both adolescents and young children.

Define a Collaborative Set of Intervention Goals

For many families, the Family Check-Up serves as an intervention in itself by focusing families on their strengths, identifying risk areas, and reformulating the situation in a way that allows parents to problem-solve on their own. In a brief therapy model, families may choose during the feedback session to focus on one or two specific problems. These problems may require further assessment and information gathering, followed by a structured response and intervention. The success of the intervention depends on identifying key issues that may affect other aspects of the family ecology, rather than on identifying problems that seem to be occurring in isolation from the rest of the system. For example, Adam's angry outbursts may be related to a variety of other problems in the household (e.g., maternal depression, substance use). Targeting these outbursts may alleviate some of the additional problems, without necessitating a focus on these problems directly. Research has shown that targeting the child's behavior problems with a parenting-skills approach can alleviate both depression and anxiety in mothers (Connell, Sanders, & Markie-Dadds, 1997).

Identify and Narrow Goals

Part of the collaboration with parents involves narrowing the goals and specifying intended outcomes. Doing so is a challenge for many families, especially those who have multiple problems, contextual risks, and stressors. Small and realistic goals are critical for success. Goals should also fall within normative developmental expectations for the child. Let's return to our earlier example. When Adam has his angry outbursts, the entire family is affected. In addition, multiple interactions within the family and outside the family (e.g., a bad day at school, negative interactions with siblings) lead up to these outbursts. Without attention to these issues, the angry outbursts will likely persist. Hence, Adam's plan should not focus just on these outbursts but should identify the antecedents that predict these outbursts and target them specifically. Also, realistic expectations for Adam's behavior goals should take into consideration that a reduction from three outbursts per day to one is more realistic than having no outbursts at all. A time frame for decreasing the outbursts should be developed and mapped onto the family's lifestyle—reducing the angry outbursts over the course of a month is more realistic than trying to accomplish the goal in a single week.

Goals should be narrow and specified in behavioral terms. After Julie was interviewed and began tracking Adam's behavior, we discovered that angry outbursts involved a variety of specific behaviors, including punching the wall, hitting siblings, and yelling at his mother. Breaking down these behaviors was a useful first step in planning an intervention.

Conduct a More Thorough Assessment

A problem-focused assessment is critical to developing the appropriate solutions. This assessment can be done through both a clinical interview and tracking of the behavior by the parents and, if warranted, the child. Basic behavioral theory, including the ABC model of change, can be used to identify points of target: The *antecedent* inventory includes all events leading up to the problem behavior, such as a bad day at school, sibling rivalry, parenting behavior, and stressors. The outbursts are then tracked in the context of these other antecedents. *Behavioral* theory involves the identification of smaller, concrete behaviors (e.g., punching the wall) that can be used to plan an intervention. The *consequences,* including the child's, parents', and family's response to the outbursts, are also tracked. One week of tracking the target behavior will give the family and the therapist ample information to help develop solutions. Consider the following example:

> Julie and Adam tracked the angry outbursts for 1 week. Julie noticed that Adam was more likely to engage in these outbursts if he was hungry (before mealtime). She also noticed that if he had complained about his day at school, he was more likely to have an outburst. Finally, she noticed that her own mood triggered outbursts. Some days she responded by ignoring, and other days she yelled at Adam. Adam also tracked the behavior. He noticed that when his mom did not listen to him, he felt very angry. He also noticed that his brother's behavior triggered his anger.
>
> Julie and Adam developed the following brief intervention goals: (a) Reduce his angry outbursts, including the target behaviors of

punching walls, hitting family members, and yelling at his mother, to once per week and (b) increase appropriate responses to frustration in the home, including going to his room, playing on computer, and going for a walk.

Identify Possible Solutions

There are always several different solutions to a problem, some parent-focused and some child-focused, but not all of them work in any given situation. At this phase in brief therapy, it is common for the parents to become discouraged. Each solution requires a focused attempt on the part of caregivers to implement it. And many solutions are not effective, thus requiring the generation of alternative solutions. It is important in a brief therapy model to make parents aware up front that the first solutions they try may fail. Making changes in a system of response requires a focused effort on the part of families, a willingness to be discouraged and fail, and a generation of alternative solutions to the problem if necessary.

One possible solution for Julie and Adam involved targeting the wall-punching behavior directly. A behavioral plan was developed that rewarded Adam with a free movie rental on nights that he chose not to punch the wall in the context of an angry outburst. Adam's plan was to use time-out in his room instead of wall punching. This plan was partly successful: Adam was not able to go to his room during these outbursts because he was too fired up, but Julie did administer the reward for no wall punching, which seemed to decrease the behavior.

Evaluate Outcomes and Generate Alternative Solutions

It is important to evaluate the outcomes of the plan and generate possible solutions. In this example, Adam's part of the plan was not successful, and so further solutions and coping strategies for Adam's plan were developed. Some of these were proactive and included talking with his mother about his day when he returned home, rather than waiting to explode during a later conflict.

Summarize and Terminate

It is also important in a brief therapy model to summarize achievements and behavior-change challenges during termination. Many families may feel that a brief therapy approach has solved the main problem, and thus they are finished with treatment and ready to terminate. For other families, termination seems premature because they are still dealing with other significant problems. In this case, a focus on their current success and the model for this success can be useful and can help caregivers continue with changes outside of therapy.

Motivate Families to Seek Further Services

One goal of a brief intervention may be to identify strengths and weaknesses for parents and to motivate parents to seek further services. Many parents are resistant to the idea of mental health services, yet they have exhausted their own resources in trying to fix the problem. A brief, strength-based approach to family problems can create motivation for parents by informing them of the positive aspects of, as well as the risks associated with, their current situation. Parents can leave the intervention with a sense of accomplishment and a clear picture of where they would like to make changes in the future.

GROUP FORMATS AND SCHOOL-BASED INTERVENTIONS

The brief parenting intervention model can be used in other approaches, including group therapies and school-based approaches. We discuss each of them in turn.

Group Approaches to Brief Therapy

Group treatments can be used to effectively address a wide range of parenting and family issues across development, including simple issues such as normative transitions and larger issues such as substance use and problem behavior. The typical format for group approaches involves a lecture or presentation, discussion, and group activity, although some role-play and individualized exercises have also been successfully implemented. The group format is probably the most common form of parenting service in communities, generally embedded in schools, day-care settings, and workplace environments. It is also the most attractive format for parents and is associated with higher rates of participation and attendance than are traditional parenting groups. We embedded a group lecture series into a family intervention delivered in rural Head Start centers. We found that home visits were the most popular and well-received intervention, followed by the lecture series and parenting groups: 43% of families in our intervention group attended at least one lecture and only 33% attended a parenting group (Stormshak, Kaminski, & Goodman, 2002). Despite the promise of such approaches, very few research studies have examined the efficacy of these interventions at changing parenting or child behavior.

Brief parenting interventions can also be used to motivate parents who may need additional services to self-assess and seek out those services. A brief intervention can be used as a motivational tool, informing parents of problems and possible solutions that may be available to them in the community. We recently examined the efficacy of a brief group parenting intervention to support parents of adolescents. We invited families of middle-school youth to participate in a brief, one-session intervention focused on enhancing parenting skills for adolescents. This intervention, called Parenting in the Teenage Years (Dishion, Kavanagh, & Christianson, 1995), was administered to 81 randomly assigned families over the course of 3 months. The intervention families received the one-session intervention, including a pre- and postassessment of child behavior and parenting skills. The control families received only the pre- and postassessment. We found that this one-session intervention increased parents' motivation to change their parenting and parenting involvement, as did the videotaped, direct observations with their adolescent. Those who received the intervention showed more positive interactions with their adolescent than did the comparison group (Lim, Stormshak, & Dishion, 2005). The results of this research suggest that brief group interventions can be effective at motivating parents to change or seek additional services as well as to change specific parenting behavior.

Embedding Brief Family-Based Interventions Into Schools

In light of the extent of developmental research linking parenting and family management to the development of problem behavior, one might question the usefulness of integrating such a time-intensive intervention into a school system. However, not all family interventions necessitate intensive family therapy or even parent training groups. Simple interventions (e.g., increasing parental involvement in learning and school) can significantly reduce risk behaviors as well as academic achievement. Parents who work collaboratively with the school have more successful youth. For example, parents play a crucial role in promoting early academic success through parent–school involvement, stimulating cognitive growth at home, and promoting values consistent with academic achievement (Greenwood & Hickman, 1991; McMahon, Slough, & Conduct Problems Prevention Research Group, 1996). Early parental involvement in reading and learning increases academic achievement and early literacy skills 5 years later (Senechal & LeFevre, 2002). Parental involvement in school from ages 5 to 17 enhances school performance (Stevenson & Baker, 1987).

One way parents and schools may work collaboratively is in the area of monitoring. In elementary school, parents are much more likely to be engaged with the school system for various reasons: There is one consistent teacher, the school holds family-centered events, and the parent is responsible for getting his or her child to and from school-related extracurricular activities. In adolescence, however, parental involvement in schools decreases. There is no single teacher or contact person for parents, and children become less dependent on their parents for transportation and peer activities. Parental monitoring and positive support are crucial during the middle-school and high school years as youth's expanding peer interactions include issues of identity development and self-esteem. The transition to middle school can be particularly problematic for youth in early adolescence who also are struggling with autonomy from parents in addition to pubertal changes (Eccles, Lord, & Buchanan, 1996).

During adolescence, the peer group becomes more diffuse and parents are less able to track friendships and peer communication (Higgins & Parsons, 1983). Schools become larger, with more distance between teachers and students and between parents and the school. Teacher–student relationships are less positive and teachers feel less effective during this period (Eccles, Midgley, Feldlaufer, Ramon, & MacIver, 1989; Eccles et al., 1996). In the midst of a larger school and with decreases in home-to-school communication, parents and teachers lose track of how youth are functioning in the school environment (C. L. Miller et al., 1990). Rarely do parents have information about a child's homework or behavioral performance during the day. In fact, many middle and high schools do not even inform parents of minor office referrals and behavioral problems that occur during the school day. Closer communication between home and school regarding academics and classroom behavior has been shown to be beneficial for child outcomes (Blechman, Taylor, & Schrader, 1981).

Effective school-based interventions include tracking student behavior and providing the information to both parents and teachers. A functional assessment can be conducted in the school to examine behavior and its antecedents and consequences. Feedback based on this data can be given to teachers and parents, and a specific intervention plan can be developed. School-level organization of behavioral management, such as positive behavioral support (Sugai, Sprague, Horner, & Walker, 2000), can be used to decrease overall school problems. Home-to-school planning can support students in changing their behavior and can engage parents in the process of change. All of these interventions are short term and brief.

One barrier to parent–school involvement is cultural differences between the family and school environment. Schools have a clear structure that is unfamiliar to some families. Many families, regardless of their ethnicity, have difficulty entering schools and talking with staff. Issues such as language barriers and lack of a positive past school experience exacerbate these problems. Parents who have a history of negative school experiences are likely to be wary of interacting with school staff and talking with teachers.

Schools can be welcoming to families by providing a climate of support, multicultural staff to answer questions, and support for families with language barriers.

In our research, we have adapted our Adolescent Transitions Program to include a model for engaging parents in the school context. We have designed a Family Resource Center (FRC) model to provide a context within the public school environment that institutionalizes the efforts to engage and empower parents within an arena where much of development occurs or is undermined (Dishion & Kavanagh, 2003).

Derived from an ecological model of child development, the FRC model is based on a brief intervention approach to working with children and families and is embedded in the schools. The FRC is staffed with a half-time parent consultant who works collaboratively within the school to connect the school and family system. The parent consultant attends behavior support meetings, works with the assistant principal on behavior problems, and works with teachers to solve problem behavior in the classroom. When this link between the school context and home environment is made, we find that problem behavior decreases.

We have successfully implemented the FRC model in seven middle schools across two different communities, including an urban area in a large metropolitan city (Dishion & Kavanagh, 2003; Dishion, Nelson, & Kavanagh, 2003; Stormshak, Dishion, Light, & Yasui, 2005). Of relevance to this discussion are our findings related to brief interventions with youth. We tracked each contact our parent consultants had with youth in both content and time, during a 3-year study of middle-school youth. We found that many parents used a variety of modes to communicate with our parent consultant, including phone, e-mail, and in-person visits. The average family had between five and seven contacts with the parent consultant during 3 years of middle school. These contacts varied in type and length. As it turned out, these contacts with the FRC were associated with decreased involvement with deviant peers during the course of the 3 years of the study (Figure 8.4). It is interesting to note that e-mail and phone contacts accounted for 37% of all contacts with parents. These contacts were related to decreases in the growth of problem behavior during the course of 3 years, particularly for youth at risk (Stormshak et al., 2005). We also found a decline in deviant peer relationships over these 3 years for youth whose parents used the FRC service (see Figure 8.4).

By their nature, schools are a context for brief interventions, partly because of student and staff mobility. Also, schools provide a framework for the management of crisis behaviors rather than low-level problem behaviors that do not require immediate intervention. Our results support a brief intervention delivery model embedded within schools to reduce problem behavior. Most schools currently do not engage in any systematic interven-

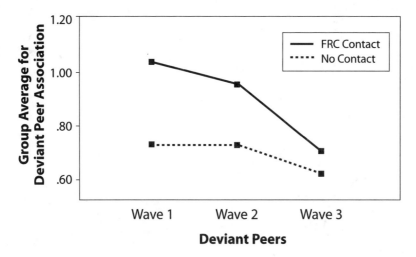

Figure 8.4. Effects of brief intervention contact on deviant peers' involvement. FRC = Family Resource Center.

tions for working directly with parents because of various factors, including limited resources and the lack of trained staff to implement such interventions. However, a family-based approach to working within schools seems to hold promise for reducing problem behavior and enhancing outcomes for youth at risk. Simple modes of communication, such as e-mail and phone calls, can effectively engage parents in the school system and concurrently reduce problem behavior.

SUMMARY

In this chapter, we describe several key parenting practices that are amenable to a brief parenting approach. We also outline a model for working with parents in brief therapy and highlight examples of effective brief, group, and school-based approaches. Brief therapy approaches show promise for working with parents in both clinic-based and community-based mental health treatment settings.

9

INTERVENTIONS WITH CHILDREN AND ADOLESCENTS

Individualized interventions with children and adolescents are often a useful complement to working with parents. A family-centered strategy for working with youth keeps the focus on improving family management and avoids interventions that directly or indirectly undermine parenting. The goal of child and adolescent interventions is essentially to support self-regulation. Parents' and teachers' use of solid behavior management practices certainly improves children's self-regulation. However, the evidence is clear that working directly with children and adolescents can reduce problem behavior and decrease depression and anxiety, presumably through improved self-regulation. This chapter provides an overview of our family-centered approach, and we discuss some process ideas in the context of a cognitive–behavioral approach to behavior change.

A child therapist faces the paradox that for therapy to be effective, the majority of therapeutic activity should primarily involve the parents. However, most child psychologists are trained to work directly and individually with children and adolescents. In general, we suggest that for the majority of children and adolescents seen in most mental health services, working with caregiving adults is the primary clinical strategy that is likely to have the longest term benefit, except perhaps when children present with pure anxiety disorders and when parents are overprotective and controlling and the therapy is in part focused on the child's self-regulatory skills, independent of the parents' influence (Kendall, Aschenbrand, & Hudson, 2003).

This child-focused strategy should not be overgeneralized for two reasons. First, the majority of the treatment research on children and adolescents involves pure samples of youth with anxiety or depression. The majority of youth who become involved in mental health services also show problematic behavior (Weisz & Weiss, 1991) and, therefore, these clinical strategies may be less effective in real-world clinical settings. The second reason for caution is that very few studies seriously evaluate the hypothesis that family dynamics associated with depression and anxiety or related disorders can be directly changed with corresponding benefits to the child or adolescent (for a notable exception, see Robin, 2003). From a developmental psychopathology framework, a program of research is needed that links pathogenic family dynamics with the onset, course, and severity of child emotional difficulties, followed by a series of intervention studies to test the hypothesis that changing those family dynamics prevents or reduces emotional distress in children and adolescents.

The paradox is that the majority of traditional mental health services for children and adolescents are actually individually focused on children, and the parents are left to sit in the waiting room. The evidence suggests that this approach to treatment is summarily ineffective. Weiss and colleagues have examined the efficacy of child-only treatments in a series of careful, systematic studies (Weiss, Catron, & Harris, 2000; Weiss, Catron, Harris, & Phung, 1999; Weisz & Weiss, 1989). In these studies, the authors randomly assigned children at risk to receive either traditional child psychotherapy or a no-treatment control condition (M age = 10 years old). They collected a variety of pre- and postmeasures on social–emotional adjustment from parents, teachers, and youth. They defined traditional psychotherapy as usual and customary treatment provided to individual children in the community. Both directly after the treatment and at a 2-year follow-up, no significant findings suggested that the treatment group was improved in any domain over the control condition. It is interesting that the authors were able to examine the sleeper effect theory at their 2-year follow-up. This theory is common among child therapists and suggests that the effects of treatment cannot be readily seen until long after the treatment has ended. In other words, perhaps the treatment in this study was not effective directly after administration but empowered parents or children to make changes after several months of processing the treatment internally. However, there was no evidence of a sleeper effect or long-term improvements in outcomes (Weiss et al., 2000).

This research on child-centered therapy is important for several reasons. First, it is clear that usual and customary practices for working directly with children are not effective at changing behavior across contexts or even internally. Second, this research debunks the popular hope of sleeper effects, which motivates many well-meaning therapists to work exclusively with children and adolescents. Last, the research finds several potentially harmful effects of child-only psychotherapy, including parents at Year 1 reporting high levels of satisfaction with the treatment, then at Year 2, parent satisfaction declining more than in control families. This finding is interesting and highlights the importance of attending to family dynamics in child treatment. Parents were initially positive about the prospect of getting treatment for their child with problems. However, when the services failed to produce changes in their child, they became dissatisfied. This pattern commonly occurs for families in community-based mental health services. Many parents move from one service to the next looking for an effective treatment, and their satisfaction with services declines each time they engage in child therapy that does not improve outcomes for their children. This problem has led to high dropout rates (as high as 40%–60%) among children and families seeking services for aggressive and antisocial behavior (Kazdin & Wassell, 1998).

A FOCUS ON CHILD SELF-REGULATION

We have argued that a common feature of effective interventions for children and adolescents is the systematic focus on self-regulation (Dishion & Kavanagh, 2003; Dishion & Patterson, 2006). Developmental, neuroscience, and clinical researchers are converging on the concept of self-regulation as central to social and emotional adaptation and maturation (Baumeister & Vohs, 2004; Eisenberg, Fabes, Guthrie, & Reiser, 2000).

There are several correlated facets of child and adolescent self-regulation (see Figure 9.1). We think the concept of entrainment is useful for understanding the automatic, unconscious quality of child and adolescent self-regulation. Entrainment simply means that self-regulation is embedded within daily routines that affect sleeping, diet, safety, trust, and healthy social interactions with families and peers. Children who live highly stressful, traumatic lives also tend to suffer from disrupted sleep, encopresis, enuresis, poor health, and chronic and heightened stress hormones (P. A. Fisher, Burraston, & Pears, 2004). The automatic entrained quality of self-regulation suggests that under some conditions, it is necessary to provide intense adult supervision and monitoring and to structure daily routines to promote the recovery or development of self-regulation among children stuck in highly disorganized and disrupted social environments.

As shown in Figure 9.1, the four salient and overlapping dimensions of child and adolescent self-regulation are hierarchically linked (i.e., hierarchical integration). First are the daily routines and practices that promote

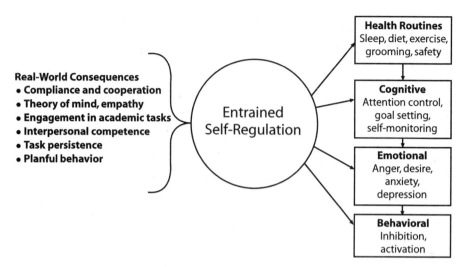

Real-World Consequences
- **Compliance and cooperation**
- **Theory of mind, empathy**
- **Engagement in academic tasks**
- **Interpersonal competence**
- **Task persistence**
- **Planful behavior**

Entrained
Self-Regulation

Health Routines
Sleep, diet, exercise,
grooming, safety

Cognitive
Attention control,
goal setting,
self-monitoring

Emotional
Anger, desire,
anxiety,
depression

Behavioral
Inhibition,
activation

Figure 9.1. A conceptual model for the intervention focus on child and adolescent self-regulation.

safety and the physical health of the child including, but not limited to, consistent practices of obtaining adequate sleep, diet, exercise, and grooming. These practices provide a context for the development of the cognitive skills necessary to regulate emotions and behavior. Recent work in neuroscience identifies effortful attention control as a fundamental dimension of children's early adaptation patterns, highly relevant to adjustment in childhood and adolescence (Kochanska, 1993; Posner, Rothbart, & Rueda, 2003; Rothbart & Bates, 1998). It is assumed that regulation of attention (i.e., dealing with sensory conflict and distractions, alerting, orienting, perseverance) is fundamental to higher order cognitive skills such as goal setting, planning, self-monitoring, and eventually developing insight for change.

Cognitive control is clearly central to the regulation of children's emotions (Lewis & Stieben, 2004). Emotional distress (anxiety, depression, anger) is understandably the primary concern for most clinicians. It is also critical to provide youth with skills of regulating desire, such as the desire to use substances (Mezzich, Tarter, Giancola, & Kirisci, 2001; Wills & Dishion, 2004), or generally to reduce impulses to engage in activities that are positively reinforced by peers (Dishion, Nelson, Winter, & Bullock, 2004; Snyder et al., 2005). It is clear that attention control is disrupted by extreme emotions. The effects are bidirectional. One key idea in the literature about self-regulation is that as children advance into adolescence, they develop skills in secondary coping strategies (Compas, Hinden, & Gerhardt, 1995; Langrock, Compas, Keller, Merchant, & Copeland, 2002).

Attention control and emotion regulation ultimately translate to be-havior change in children and adolescents. It may be necessary to induce two basic types of behavior change in children and adolescents seen in mental health clinics. The most common is behavioral inhibition, for chil-dren diagnosed with attention-deficit/hyperactivity disorder or conduct prob-lems (Barkley, Edwards, Laneri, Fletcher, & Metevia, 2001; Kazdin, 2003). However, behavioral activation, typically for interventions that target adult depression (Lewinsohn, Munoz, Youngren, & Zeiss, 1986), is also relevant to child and adolescent anxiety and depression (Clarke, DeBar, & Lewin-sohn, 2003; Kendall, Aschenbrand, & Hudson, 2003). In fact, relational frame theory (Hayes, Barnes-Holmes, & Roche, 2001) underlies the Accep-tance and Commitment Therapy, which essentially develops the capacity to accept negative feelings and at the same time engage in valued behaviors that require effort and commitment.

The voluntary control of behavior underlies the development of compe-tence, psychopathology, and physical health throughout the life span (see Figure 9.1). Bandura (1997) referred to this ability as *agency*, others call it *emotion regulation* (Izard & Harris, 1995) or *executive functioning* (Barkley, 2001). Although researchers vary in emphasis and labels, it is safe to assume that most are interested in the ability to engage (or disengage) attention and behavior according to a consciously determined goal.

Despite the appeal of the self-regulation construct for child and adoles-cent interventions, it cannot be focused on exclusively. For example, chil-dren who live in unsafe environments or whose parents cannot be trusted because of repeated betrayals (Freyd, 1996) are likely to show severe impair-ments in attention regulation strategies other than dissociation (DePrince & Freyd, 1999). The first step is to create a safe, sane environment (see chap. 13, this volume). Also, children's self-regulation is not created in a vacuum. The concept of entrainment indeed suggests that it is often embed-ded in daily routines and interactions with caregivers. In many family situa-tions, it is of dubious value to meet individually with a child when the home environment is chaotic, disorganized, and stressful. In fact, we hypoth-esize that a child-centered therapeutic approach will be most beneficial to children and adolescents who are in the healthiest environments with a less serious pattern of problem behavior.

Although child-only treatments are limited in efficacy, at times working directly with children in the context of families can be useful and may lead to changes in the overall developmental system of youth. Most empirically supported interventions for problem behavior combine a child focus on self-regulation with support for family management skills (Barkley et al., 2001; Kazdin, 2003; Lochman, Barry, & Pardini, 2003). These interventions in-clude considerations of age and gender of the client as well as unique presenting problems or contextual situations that may warrant a child-focused intervention.

Age and Gender of Child Seeking Services

Older children tend to benefit more from individual services than do younger children, and girls tend to benefit more than do boys (Durlak, Fuhrman, & Lampman, 1991; Weisz, Weiss, Han, Granger, & Morton, 1995). This situation may result from the presenting of problems of girls and boys at different ages. Males tend to present with antisocial or conduct problem behavior and females are more likely to show symptoms of depression and anxiety, although rates of comorbidity among both males and females are very high, ranging from 50% to 70% across different populations (Caron & Rutter, 1991; Kazdin, 2000). Rates of depression increase over time, with the highest rate occurring in adolescent girls (Hammen & Rudolf, 1996). In summary, adolescent girls with a primary problem of depression are most likely to benefit from individual services.

Several empirically based treatments for depression and anxiety rely on the ability of youth to have some insight into their problems and process cognitive–behavioral techniques, then to reflect on achievements over the course of the week by engaging in the therapeutic process and practicing new coping skills. These types of treatments are more effective with older youth who have the developmental capabilities to process this information and internalize changes (Holmbeck, Greenley, & Franks, 2003).

Adolescents can learn techniques in the context of therapy, such as cognitive–behavioral techniques for coping with depression, anxiety, or impulsivity problems. Therapists who have specifically focused on a protocol and administered the treatment directly to youth who are old enough to learn the protocol have been successful at teaching new coping strategies and reducing depressive symptoms (Mufson, Weissman, Moreau, & Garfinkel, 1999; Weisz, Southam-Gerow, Gordis, & Connor-Smith, 2003). However, with these programs, long-term changes in adjustment and behavior are still very limited. Primary gains include short-term reductions in problem behavior and the ability to use new skills, but not necessarily in relevant contexts. As a result, generalization of skills across contexts (from therapy to home or to school) may be limited.

Younger children (under age 10) benefit from direct instruction in skills combined with a play or game-based approach to learning. Younger children also benefit from a coordinated family-focused and child-focused approach in which the therapist coordinates the services with the child and family (e.g., assigning anger management skill exercises for both parents and children to do at home and having the family work together on those goals). Some very young children (ages 0–6) may benefit from having a supportive relationship with another adult (e.g., the therapist), but for the most part, younger children do not show gains in child-only therapy and benefit more from a parent-only model that focuses on enhancing the skills of children within a community of peers (e.g., a supportive preschool or day-care setting).

Combining Child Therapy With Family Therapy

One model that holds promise for individual practitioners stems directly from effective prevention and intervention research. In successful community intervention programs, a developmental–ecological model based on a long history of developmental research informs the intervention protocol. Children are viewed in the context of multiple systems that affect developmental outcomes, including home, school, teachers, peers, and community. Successful prevention efforts target all of these domains in a systematic, informed intervention and outcomes are measured accordingly (Conduct Problems Prevention Research Group, 1992; Dishion, Kavanagh, Schneiger, Nelson, & Kaufman, 2002; Stormshak & Dishion, 2002).

The most effective prevention and intervention programs focus interventions on parents, schools, and youth. Parents attend parenting groups or family therapy, school-based consultation with teachers is provided to facilitate home-to-school communication, and youth are given direct skills in coping, social skills, or anger management. Various research programs with both short-term and long-term outcomes are associated with this model (Conduct Problems Prevention Research Group, 1999; Dishion, Burraston, & Li, 2002; Webster-Stratton, Reid, & Hammond, 2004).

In practice, however, the model is more difficult to implement because it often requires two therapists—one to work with parents or the family and one to work with the child. Overall, this approach is preferred for delivering child interventions directly to youth. A coordinated treatment plan is developed based on an assessment of parent, child, and school problems. Goals are developed with parents and the youth, and then specific plans for intervention are implemented to target goals. Parents are informed of youth progress at each session as they work on their own goals for treatment. Regular assessment informs the clinical process, helps refine treatment goals, and leads directly to changes in targeted outcomes. One result of a coordinated treatment approach may be disengagement of the adolescent from the therapeutic process as the parent(s) gain more control over the family context. Consider the following case study:

> Marcia and her 11-year-old daughter Katy requested services to assist with Katy's negative attitude, which included talking back to her mother, refusing to comply with simple requests, and, at times, resorting to violence by throwing things at her mother and trying to grab and

hit her. Marcia was a single parent with a history of substance use, domestic violence, and depression. She was enrolled in a support group for domestic violence survivors and was receiving services for her adult depression as part of this treatment. As a result of their past, Marcia and Katy had a very close and, at times, inappropriate relationship that included Marcia using Katy as a main source of social support.

The focus in therapy was on assisting Marcia with family management skills, including consistency, monitoring, and positive engagement with Katy. Marcia also developed a new social support network and decreased her need to use Katy for emotional support. Katy worked with a therapist on anger management, peer skills, and her own depression. When Marcia began to develop the skills she needed to manage her daughter, Katy withdrew from therapy and stated, "There is no point in coming here because things are just getting worse for me." After working for an additional month with Marcia, she reported that her relationship with Katy had improved, and she had noticed a decrease in Katy's negative behaviors.

Presenting Issues and Problems

Certain childhood problems indeed are best addressed in the context of individual child psychotherapy. We have already noted that there are a variety of individual-based treatments for adolescent depression and that these interventions have been shown to be effective with this population. A range of other issues, including anxiety; death, grief, or loss; career counseling (with late adolescents); and trauma, may also warrant an individual approach.

One of the most controversial of these problems is sexual and physical abuse. Much has been written about working with abused children, yet most of it is nonempirical and unsupported in the clinical literature. Much of the writing in this area has focused on play therapy as a mode for helping children gain insight into the abuse, form a trusting relationship with another adult, and work through the trauma in the context of play. Although play therapy may be an excellent venue for developing children's self-regulation and coping with adverse events, the lack of a coherent, empirically derived framework for the process and focus of play therapy shows that more rigorous research is needed to raise the standards of this strategy to an empirically supported intervention. The goal is to develop an empirically derived curriculum and target and to show that engagement in play therapy improves some aspect of children's self-regulation, which results in improved emotional well-being and social adaptation.

The most common experience of trauma or abuse occurs in the context of a wide range of risk factors and contextual stressors, including poverty, high-crime neighborhoods, family stressors, domestic violence, substance use, and parenting problems. Research suggests that approximately 50% of children referred to community mental health clinics have experienced some traumatic event such as physical or sexual abuse (Lau & Weisz, 2003). As a result, for the therapist to focus exclusively on the traumatic event would be a mistake. Such therapies do not attend to the context of the trauma and, therefore, do not prepare the caregivers to prevent future events from occurring. More recent research in this area has begun to highlight the importance of including caregivers, such as parents or foster parents, in the treatment and systematically approaching the child's problems with a cognitive–behavioral focus that includes work on trauma only if indicated (Chamberlain & Smith, 2003). Because children vary widely in their interpretation and internalization of traumatic events, this approach to trauma is more consistent with developmental theory and research. For some children, the focus on treatment should be entirely on current functioning and behavior at home and at school with no emphasis on past trauma. For these families, a traumatic event may be one experience in a plethora of stressful, traumatic events and lifestyle occurrences that impact everyday functioning. For other children, discussion of, and work around, past traumatic events is indicated, particularly if these events are impeding the ability of the child to function at home and at school. This effect may be common in youth who have experienced less contextual stress and only one abuse or traumatic incident.

Cohen and Mannarino (1996, 1998) have developed an empirically supported treatment protocol for working with children who have experienced sexual and physical abuse. This program is called Child and Parent Trauma-Focused Cognitive Behavior Therapy, and it focuses on enhancing adaptive functioning through a cognitive approach to trauma, including stress inoculation therapy, gradual exposure, and cognitive processing (Cohen, Mannarino, Berliner, & Deblinger, 2000). The content of the protocol centers on improving individual child skills, with parent involvement, and research has shown that the program is most effective when delivered to both parents and children (Deblinger & Heflin, 1996). In two separate studies (Cohen & Mannarino, 1997, 2000), parental stress and response to the trauma significantly predicted treatment response. The parent therapy includes all of the previous components, in addition to parenting skills training. Joint family sessions are conducted, in which parents and children review and practice skills together. This treatment seems to be one of the most promising approaches for working with individual child trauma. An illustrative case history follows:

> Shannon was a 15-year-old girl with a history of sexual abuse, physical abuse, and neglect. Her mother had lost custody of her at age 3 because of drug addiction, and Shannon was currently living with her biological grandparents who had full custody. She was sexually abused by an uncle at age 12, physically abused by her biological mother, and neglected by

all caregivers in the system. Her grandparents had a history of alcoholism and domestic violence when she was younger, but her grandfather was a long-haul trucker and so was rarely at home, which led to a decrease in these problems. The family lived in poverty in a rural community with few resources. The presenting problem was anger management and impulsivity. Shannon had been kicked out of three schools and was currently enrolled in an alternative school for children with aggressive behavior. She was constantly getting into fights with her grandmother that usually ended in violence toward her grandmother (e.g., punching a wall next to her). Treatment included working directly with Shannon, directly with her grandmother and grandfather (when available), and family sessions. Treatment approaches with Shannon included social skills training, anger management skills, and future goal planning. Treatment with her grandparents included family management skills and coordinated anger management training with Shannon. Family sessions focused on a strength-based approach to these problems. There was no treatment for or focus on past trauma. After 20 sessions, Shannon and her grandparents showed improvements across all targeted domains, including aggressive outbursts at home and school attendance.

Parents Unable or Unwilling to Engage in Treatment

For some children, circumstances may prevent the therapist from working with the system of caregivers that surround the child. These circumstances, however, are not simply related to parents' lack of motivation or unwillingness to engage in parenting services. It is common for parents to come in for services believing it is the child who has the problem, and thus it is the child who needs the service. In fact, children and parents who self-refer to clinics rarely agree on the key issues, with 63% of families failing to agree on even one single problem (Yeh & Weisz, 2001). As a result, the therapist must do some work with the family and reframe the child's problem in the context of a larger system. Parents usually respond to a psychoeducation model on the development of child problems in the context of larger systems (e.g., family). After this initial reframing, the parents will typically move forward in a family model, where much of the work in therapy involves parenting and family management coordinated with child interventions.

However, sometimes parents refuse to engage in services or simply cannot for a variety of reasons. In many cases, it is best to discontinue services with families at this time, rather than to work individually with children and send a message to the parents that the problem lies within the child. Continuation of services may lead to the maintenance of unhealthy family patterns, such as triangulation and blaming the child for the family's problems.

With that said, parent refusal or disengagement from the process places therapists in a difficult situation. Does a therapist deny services to the child because the family will not commit? For children under the age of 13, the therapist should discontinue services. There is no point in working with a child this age when no work is occurring on the family system. However, older children may request services independently of their parents, which raises issues of consent, ethics, and rights of patients (see chap. 14, this volume). In many states, children can consent to individual services at age 14. In this case, therapists should still try to engage the family in therapy and then decide how to proceed on the basis of the clinical presentation of the youth.

Runaway youth are a good example of clients who pose a difficult presenting problem. Adolescents who have run away from home have begun to disengage from their families and are likely to run away again without a successful family intervention. Runaway adolescents have a range of risk factors, including sexual abuse, HIV infection, substance use, and risk-taking behavior (Tyler, Hoyt, Whitbeck, & Cauce, 2001). Runaway adolescents may also seek treatment on their own for assistance with these problems. Effective approaches to treatment involve engaging families in problem solving and family management to prevent future runaway episodes from occurring (Coco & Courtney, 2003; Riley, Greif, Caplan, & MacAulay, 2004). The therapist may work individually with the child to discuss issues of safety, temporary housing, and peer dynamics that are affecting the youth negatively. Individual work with youth in this situation may prevent future runaway episodes and lead to safety. Here's a case history to illustrate.

> Gina, a 13-year-old girl, was referred to services by the school counselor at her middle school. She had run away from home and was currently living with a friend and her friend's mother. At the initial assessment, the therapist informed Gina that to receive services at the clinic, her biological mother would need to be involved to consent to, as well as to plan for her return home. Gina reported a history of alcohol and drug use by her biological mother as well as violence during these episodes. Gina's biological mother signed consents for Gina as well as for the surrogate parent and her daughter to be involved in treatment. Gina agreed to have her mother participate but refused to sit in the room with her mother or have any physical contact.
>
> Gina's mother attended sessions to work on a plan for Gina's return and on family management skills related to runaway behavior. Gina worked with her therapist on safety issues, psychoeducation around safe sex and HIV infection, and development of a future plan. The therapist worked directly with the surrogate parent and the biological mother on effective communication between the adult caregivers in the system, who were very angry with each other and, as a result, were not facilitating

reunification for Gina and her mother. The goal was to keep Gina safe and to plan for reunification with her biological mother through a series of well controlled, planned visits over 3 months.

Marital problems are another type of presenting problem that affects the ability of therapists to work directly with youth. Marital problems are strongly associated with child behavior problems (Ingoldsby, Shaw, Owens, & Winslow, 1999) and are commonly seen in mental health clinics with a focus on child therapy, yet these problems are rarely attended to directly. Instead, parents tend to deny problems in the marital relationship and target the child as the source of the family problems; the child responds by developing a set of problem behaviors as a means of detouring the marital conflict. A comprehensive family assessment will identify marital difficulties, which should be directly addressed with feedback and intervention goals for the family. Some parents, however, are not successful in dealing with their marital problems, which results in either divorce or continued conflict in the marital system. Older youth in this situation can benefit from insight into the family dynamic and assistance in dealing with conflictual interactions in the home. Individual sessions with youth, marital sessions, and family sessions can help establish new patterns of interaction among family members and teach them new skills.

GENERAL GUIDELINES

There is a range of presenting problems and developmental issues in childhood. We now discuss a general approach to working with children and adolescents that is relevant to most child and adolescent problem behavior (see Figure 9.2). Direct interventions with children and adolescents

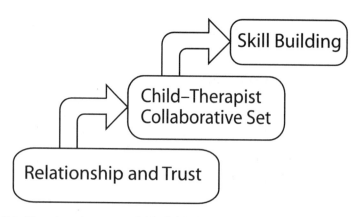

Figure 9.2. The steps to successful individual work with children and adolescents.

require a variety of skills, including knowledge of developmental research and theory as well as the ability to work with a wide range of different ages and presentations. Children are most commonly referred for treatment by their parents and, hence, they are likely to be unwilling participants in assessment and treatment. In addition, by the time a child comes into a clinic for services, he or she is used to being blamed for the problem and may therefore be defensive or withdrawn. Goals for working directly with children and adolescents include (a) building rapport and a trusting relationship with an adult, (b) developing a collaborative set with the child and adolescent regarding the focus of treatment, and (c) teaching specific skills that support improvement in the child's self-regulation deficits. It is important to note that coordination with parents and teachers is essential to successful skill development in children and adolescents, so that incentives in the natural environment will support possible changes resulting from the clinical work. With adolescents who are motivated, these three steps can be achieved readily within a few sessions. However, with young children or adolescents with severe trust and self-regulatory deficits, the goals should be more modest, with a focus on building rapport and trust and a limited concentration on skill development and training. The majority of the clinical work will be on organizing and supporting the adult executive system. We now discuss the specific skills that facilitate individual work with children and adolescents.

Building Rapport

The first step in working with children is a clinical interview. Despite very little systematic research on clinical interview techniques with children and adolescents, this is probably the most common method of obtaining information from this population and conducting a general assessment of development. On one hand, some domains of child development seem to proceed very systematically, with little variation in the population and a predictable outcome should variation occur (e.g., motor development, speech development, achievement). On the other hand, it is interesting that the social–emotional development of children can vary dramatically, even within the same age group. The way in which children think about themselves and their problems changes significantly from preschool to adolescence, and it is difficult for clinicians to assess exactly where the child's development falls within this domain (Bierman, 1990). In light of this variation, an unstructured interview session can help the therapist understand the child's social–emotional development as well as identify areas for future assessment and strengths to target during intervention. In addition, children with behavior problems often distort these problems or deny them, and this denial is related to increased risk, particularly for aggressive children

(Hughes, Cavell, & Grossman, 1997). Aggressive youth tend to distort the behavior of others by misinterpreting the intentions of peers and misattributing hostile intent to the actions of others when none exists (Dodge & Frame, 1982; Lochman & Dodge, 1998). A careful assessment of a child's perception of the problem, matched with parental report, can give therapists important information about the child's risk and likelihood of using individual services in a productive manner.

The beginning of any assessment with a child should include a discussion of confidentiality. Although many clinicians set up a confidential relationship between themselves and the child, the law in most states allows parents to have access to all information gained by a therapist in the context of child therapy. As a result, children should be informed that any information they give might be shared with parents but that the therapist will discuss this with the child should the need for information sharing arise. Most children accept this and proceed with the process.

Initial assessment sessions should also include a discussion of why services are being provided to the child. This discussion may be the most important part of the assessment, as it gives the therapist a great deal of information about the family system. Although some children will answer appropriately (e.g., "My mom says I have a problem" or "I get angry sometimes"), many children will have no idea why they are seeking mental health services, and some may have inappropriate assumptions about therapy (e.g., "My mom told me we were going to the dentist"). It is important to assess and deal with these misconceptions directly at the beginning of the process, with a statement such as "I am a person who helps families get along better, and I'm going to get some information from you and your parents today to help me understand how to help you and your family."

Most child clinicians have a variety of assessment tools they use as a standard approach to information gathering from children and families. For older children, norm-referenced behavior ratings scales should be part of the assessment battery (such as the Youth Self-Report Form; Achenbach & Edelbrock, 1981). These rating scales can be included in feedback to the family and compared with parent and teacher reports. Standardized measures of depression, trauma, and social skills should also be included.

During an interview with a younger child (under age 10), the primary goal is to assess the child's functioning across several different developmental domains (motor, language, social, physical, intellectual). Toys and games can be used to foster initial rapport building. Close-ended, nonthreatening questions help the clinician get acquainted with the child and gather basic information. Drawing pictures can be used to assess family functioning (family picture), peer functioning (school picture), and self-identity (self-portrait). In each case, the therapist gains information by talking with the child and asking questions about the drawing. Interpretations of the drawings are done by the children, not the therapist. Emotional content can be assessed with drawings of different feelings and a discussion of when the child feels that way. Open-ended questions later in the interview process lead to more information gathering and disclosure, allowing the therapist to gain insight into the child's interpretation of his or her world and perceptions of the problem.

Interviews with adolescents (ages 11 and up) should essentially proceed in the same way with developmentally appropriate toys and games. Children of any age (through age 18) perform better at unstructured clinical interviews when there are toys in the room. The game Jenga is a very good therapeutic activity for adolescents. With little structure and complexity, this game facilitates verbal communication and conversation while decreasing the seriousness of the content.

There are two common mistakes therapists can make in working with adolescents. The first is to assume the role of peer to the adolescent. Doing so can be an effective short-term strategy for engagement but will eventually undermine the therapeutic relationship. The therapist working with an adolescent must solidly assume the adult perspective but also be sensitive to the unique awkwardness and structural complexity of the adolescent life. The adult therapist does not explicitly or implicitly endorse antisocial attitudes, substance use, or other problem behavior by showing laughter, attention to, interest in, or other reactions to those behaviors. Thus, the job of joining with an adolescent can require more clinical skill than does joining with an adult. Confrontation or advice may be perceived by the adolescent client as unsympathetic and, thereby, disengage the youth from therapy. In the long run, it is better to connect as an adult with an adolescent client than to connect by becoming a peer.

One solution to this dilemma of joining with an adolescent is to become an advocate for the adolescent, especially when he or she and his or her family are participating in family therapy. By understanding the adolescent's perspective, the clinician represents the adolescent in the system or therapy. Therefore, the clinician has something to offer and can use that alliance to support and empower the adolescent's maturation and skill development in representing him- or herself. Chamberlain (1994) described the role of the youth therapist as the advocate in a comprehensive approach to treatment foster care. Treatment foster care involves temporary out-of-home treatment in a family context with trained and supportive foster parents.

The second mistake that can be made in working with adolescents involves a pitfall of the advocacy model. Often therapists assume the adolescent's perspective and begin blaming the parent. Adolescents are quick to sense collusion of the therapist against the parent. Indeed, with physically and sexually abusive families, it may be necessary to take a unilateral perspective. However, often the antagonistic perspective of the youth's therapist regarding the parents further weakens the potential for the parents to give care and guidance to their youngster. Therapists can best serve their adolescent clients by empathizing with their perspective and tactfully representing the adult point of view. Role-plays can be an engaging way for the therapist to assume the parents' perspective and allow the adolescent the emotional freedom to respond to parental behaviors in a way that promotes his or her growth and development.

Establishing a Collaborative Set

The second step in the change process is the establishment of a collaborative set. This step involves understanding where the child or adolescent client is on the stages of change continuum (Prochaska & DiClemente, 1982). Conclusions can be summarized from and reflected by a variety of verbal and nonverbal behaviors. When the relationship is established, it is more likely that clinician efforts to articulate the child's interests and concerns will result in a meaningful therapeutic interaction.

Similar to our work with parents, we use the assessment results to guide the formulation of therapeutic goals with children and adolescents. Following the feedback session of the Family Check-Up, the child and adolescent should have their own feedback session. Of course, for young children, presentation of norms and scores is not helpful or therapeutic. At times, and with consultation with parents, a videotaped feedback may be useful, as long as the caregivers are aware and approve and the feedback is coordinated with the work of the parents' therapist.

Older adolescents who are more cognitively mature can benefit from direct feedback from the assessment session, based on both the scores and videotaped feedback. Again, feedback to adolescents should fit within the general case conceptualization shared by the therapists and should be consistent with the message given to parents.

Developing a collaborative set with young children can be as simple as stating the obvious. The following script with a 7-year-old girl illustrates this point:

Therapist: Tasha, you know that your parents and I met yesterday and talked about how we can work together to help your family. Do you have any ideas about what we may have talked about?

Tasha: (shakes her head no)

Therapist: Well, lots of things. But the main thing was ideas about how you and your mom could get along better, so she and you don't get so mad when she asks you to do things.

Tasha:	She yells!
Therapist:	Yes, yelling is one of the things that we want to stop. But you know what, you are going to need to help too. So I was thinking that you and I could work together to help you learn some things to do that will help you and your mom get along better. Are you willing to meet with me for a while and we'll see how it goes?
Tasha:	(shakes her head yes)

The key skill in developing a collaborative set with a child or adolescent is pitching the goals of the intervention to fit with the child's motivation. The concepts of stress and support are relevant to all people, including children and adolescents. Clinicians can either reduce stress (conflict, fighting, strong emotions, tension) or provide support (help, be an advocate with school or parents, listen and understand the client's point of view).

When adolescents have been traumatized, placed in several foster homes or institutional settings, or exposed to multiple therapists, they may be suspicious or belligerent when a therapist suggests that he or she is going to help or advocate. However, even in these more challenging clinical situations, a therapist can often find a venue of change that is of interest and leads to a collaborative set for change. Consider this scenario:

Big John was a 16-year-old mixed-ethnicity youth who had been abused by his parents and the system. He was 6′1″ and weighed about 240 pounds. He had an anger problem. After being released from community detention, he went into treatment foster care. Because of his extensive history of both physical and sexual abuse, he had difficulty establishing a trusting relationship with his therapist. He would often escalate his problem behavior immediately following counseling sessions. From the therapist's point of view, these sessions were relatively benign. After a few disruptive outbursts with relatively benign reactions from the therapist, he began to engage. One day, when discussing some difficulties he was having with his foster parents, he blurted out, "I just want a f___ing job!" This was the third time he had mentioned work, and so the therapist pursued this line of inquiry. Big John was tired of being a child; he was ready to be treated like the man he physically appeared to be. In light of Big John's intellectual functioning and academic history, he was unlikely to be acknowledged as a young man in the school setting.

It became clear that counseling would be most successful if it were framed as job training. The therapist and Big John listed some basic skills (grooming, accepting feedback peacefully, talking, asking questions, staying calm) that he would need before he could acquire and maintain a job. The foster parents then provided weekly ratings of these skills, and in 6 months, Big John was ready for his first apprenticeship janitor position.

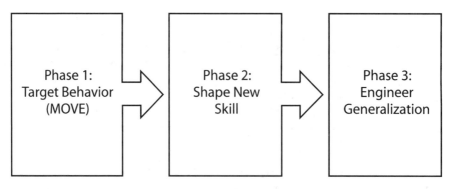

Figure 9.3. A stepwise approach to interventions with children and adolescents.

Teaching Specific Skills

Interventions that focus on developing specific skills in children and adolescents are more likely to effect meaningful clinical change (Lipsey, in press; Lipsey & Wilson, 1993; Weisz et al., 1995). There are many well-formulated empirically supported protocols for teaching children specific skills such as anger management, coping with depression, and impulsivity (Barkley et al., 2001; Brent et al., 1997; Clarke et al., 2003; Kazdin, 2003; Kendall & Braswell, 1985; Kendall et al., 2003; Sukhodolsky, Gulub, Stone, & Orban, 2005; Weisz et al., 2003). These programs offer a manual-based treatment approach to many child problems. Adaptation of the protocol to meet the needs of specific children is usually warranted, and this structure can be applied to both the parents and the child in treatment. Many children respond well to this structure and show improvements in the specific targeted skills during postassessment (Kendall, 1991). Other children, however, do not respond well to this approach and need a more individualized treatment focused specifically on the contextual factors or internal stress causing the problem. Most cognitive–behavioral interventions focus on the development of self-regulation skills and approach the task by following three phases of intervention (see Figure 9.3).

The first phase is to collaboratively set a behavior-change goal (i.e., target behavior). Stated negatively, this goal could be seen as problem identification. Selecting a behavior-change goal when working with children and adolescents is complicated. We suggest the MOVE principle for selecting target behaviors and skills: Select a behavior that is *measurable*, that has been *observed* in the child's repertoire, that is *valued* by the child, and that is *encouraged* by the social environment.

For example, in the case of Big John, we targeted a behavior we called *accepting feedback*. Although this skill was weak for John, he was capable of accepting feedback from his foster parents at times, which his foster parents had observed on previous occasions. The therapist linked getting a job and being a worker with being able to accept feedback. Because John badly wanted to work, he valued learning the skill. Finally, John's ability to accept feedback was very likely to be encouraged by the foster parents. His explosive temper made family life difficult, and having John be more open to feedback would make a dramatic difference in the task of supporting John's successful placement, healing, and growth into adulthood. To ensure that the foster parents were noticing and encouraging the *accepting feedback* behavior, the therapist met with the foster parents to support a program of immediate coaching and positive reactions and reinforcement for John's progress. The therapist clearly could not be the one who provided reinforcement at a level to make a difference in the performance of the skill in the real world.

The second phase in developing skills in children and adolescents is to provide structured opportunities for enacting the skill, whether it be inhibiting a behavior (such as accepting feedback) or activating a behavior (initiating a request or social interaction). Role-play enactments are essential for skill development with children and adolescents. Role-plays with children and adolescents should be conducted with positive affect. Humor and a playful atmosphere encourage youth engagement in the role-play. The wrong way–right way approach is optimal. First, the wrong way of responding to a situation is enacted:

> I'm going to give you some feedback. What I want you to do is get mad at me.

Children, adolescents, and adults are always ready to role-play the wrong way but are more intimidated by the right way. The next step is to encourage role-play of the skill.

For young children, this exercise can be turned into a game. We have created board games for specific clients. Many young children have played Chutes and Ladders, a game in which players turn a spinner and then move around the board, so we developed our own version. Some squares of the board might describe tricky situations, and the child or therapist must pick up a card that has a role-play. For example, in a "Walk through the neighborhood" section, a role-play of peer provocation could be designed for a child with a history of aggression.

Finally, as suggested earlier, the skill that is learned must be supported by the social environment. A close collaboration between the therapists for the child and parent and communication with parents and teachers are needed. Time should be taken to ensure that parents and teachers have specific plans to immediately reinforce any display of a skill that is the focus of treatment. It is only through repeated positive reinforcement in the natural environment that new skills get incorporated in the repertoire of the child or adolescent client.

Common Pitfalls

In work with youth, a variety of difficulties and pitfalls are worthy of discussion and attention. First, therapists tend to feel self-inflated about their work with youth, developing overly involved relationships with their clients and placing inappropriate levels of importance on the relationship and skills learned in the context of therapy. It is important to keep in mind that children are changing and growing rapidly every day, and many different interactions with family members, schools, and community members affect their development. It is the goal of child therapists to teach skills that will facilitate these outside interactions for the child. The therapeutic relationship is not usually a long-lasting, important one for most children.

A second pitfall involves the question–answer trap. As discussed, many children are resistant to therapy or just wary of talking with a stranger about their problems. It is common for children and adolescents to present as silent, refusing to talk or engage in the therapeutic relationship. A process of question–answer does not facilitate change and may lead to more resistance by the child. Games and discussions that are child directed are better for building rapport and changes over time. In working with adolescents, it is sometimes best to sit in silence rather than to ask a series of unanswered questions. For many children, direct interventions are simply not effective or useful and, as a result, many hours may be spent with children in seemingly unproductive interactions. There is a tendency among practitioners to assume that the development of rapport or a working relationship may take months with some children. In some regards, this is true, but it is not necessarily the best use of a clinician's time and energy, which, under these circumstances, may be better spent working directly with parents or teachers.

The last pitfall is to attempt to process past events with children before the child initiates conversation around the events. Most children who enter therapy have had a variety of past traumatic events and current stressors that either have created the current problem or are exacerbating the situation. In developmental terms, children are more focused on the here and now rather than the past, and sometimes overfocusing on past events can lead to additional trauma for children. Unlike adults, children are more focused on their current problems than past issues that may have caused the problems. It is common for youth to develop a variety of healthy defenses around their past issues, and many of these defense mechanisms should be seen as strengths rather than weaknesses and built on in therapy. Many children will never initiate conversations about past events such as abuse, trauma, or stressors that seem significant to therapists. Instead, a strength-based approach to working with children is indicated, which includes focusing on current strengths and problems, developing solutions that include interventions across contexts, and implementing the solutions with both parents and youth.

SUMMARY

This chapter provides a conceptual and contextual context for individual work with children and adolescents. All interventions that target children and adolescents have the implicit or explicit goal of promoting self-regulation. Developmental research confirms the importance of self-regulation in normative social and emotional adjustment. We argued that children's self-regulation is embedded within a complex ecology, and for this reason, it is critical to maintain a family-centered model when working with children and adolescents. We reviewed a general set of principles for effective clinical work with children that provides a common framework for the use of empirically supported interventions that target child and adolescent cognitive, emotional, and behavioral self-regulation.

10

FAMILY MANAGEMENT THERAPY

We propose that family management therapy is one of the most effective methods for treating a variety of child mental health problems, ranging from depression to conduct problems. In this chapter, we review some of the evidence supporting family management as a target of intervention and discuss a theoretical framework for conducting family management therapy. We then highlight some effective techniques for working with families.

Note that we refer to our work in this area as family management therapy, not family therapy. *Family therapy* is a term associated with family systems theory and corresponding literature, including early literature on family therapy techniques, by authors such as Minuchin, Haley, and Bowen, to name a few. For the most part, family systems theory is focused on working with the whole family and using family-based techniques that address family dynamics directly to effect change. There is considerable overlap between family management therapy and family systems therapy as approaches to treatment. We use a variety of techniques, some drawn from this family systems literature, to help families change and to work with parents and children together. However, our approach to working with families is derived primarily from the developmental literature, not the psychotherapy literature, and is oriented around family management skills as the main target of intervention. As such, our model is skill based and grounded in developmental theory. Sensitivity to child and family ecology mandates a focus on parents and caregivers as central to strategies that promote child and adolescent mental health. This emphasis is also consonant with systems therapies that strive to support, build, and differentiate parents as the executive system in managing and maintaining changes in the family's and in the child's behavior.

Our approach to intervening with families is guided by longitudinal and intervention research indicating that skillful family management enhances the social development and emotional well-being of children. Thus, we prioritize this emphasis in all therapeutic interactions and motivate the use of positive parenting practices that benefit children. The family ecology is addressed as a secondary issue related to family management skills. For example, we address marital problems through feedback and the promotion of mature cooperation in parenting to benefit children. Issues of depression and other forms of emotional distress are considered with respect to their effect on family functioning and parenting. Keeping this focus often requires the therapist to weave behavior change through a complex set of emotional dynamics that are potentially distracting and, at times, counterproductive for the family and child. Having a clear structure to guide intervention sessions is the best way to optimize progress.

RATIONALE FOR FAMILY MANAGEMENT

When child mental health problems are conceptualized from an ecological model, there are many different potential targets, including the child, the school, the home environment, and adult mental health problems, to name a few. Family management problems are central to all of these issues and have been shown in research to serve as a strong mediator between early childhood problems and later problem behavior (Patterson & Dishion, 1985). Family management also shows significant predictability to several other risk factors, including deviant peer formation, poor achievement, and depression (Dishion, Patterson, Stoolmiller, & Skinner, 1991; Stormshak, Bierman, McMahon, Lengua, & Conduct Problems Prevention Research Group, 2000). Developmental research clearly suggests that solid family management skills are the strongest predictor of mental health and positive outcomes for youth of all ages (see Figure 10.1).

In light of the influence that family environment, culture, and parenting have on children, it seems obvious that family management should be critical in both predicting and maintaining child mental health problems. Starting in early childhood, parents serve as regulators of child behavior in a coregulation model of development and growth. Early family management that is consistent, warm, and nonpunitive provides a predictable environment in which children can develop self-regulation and emotional compe-

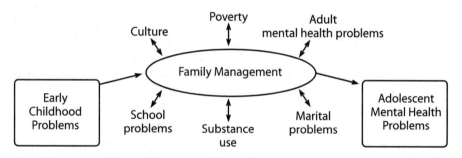

Figure 10.1. The central role of family management.

tence. Responsive parenting in infancy sets the stage for the development of appropriate communication with toddlers and young preschoolers in the form of *joint planning*, which serves as a bridge between the parent's regulation of the child and the child's development of internal regulation and control (Greenberg, Speltz, & DeKlyen, 1993). These early self-regulation capabilities, which are essentially in place by age 4 or 5, predict the development of later competence across multiple domains of functioning, including social, academic, and behavioral. In adolescence, parents build on these initial skills with effective problem solving, monitoring, and facilitation of independence. Thus, it is clear that family management therapy has relevance in both early and late childhood and serves as the target of intervention for most child mental health problems.

FAMILY MANAGEMENT THERAPY

Two primary aspects of family management could be summarized at the most basic level as skills for managing positive and negative behavior. Most families that are referred to a clinic with concerns about their children benefit from learning skills that enhance their overall level of positive interactions with their children. Second, most families also benefit from training to be more mindful of parent–child interaction contingencies and to manage contingencies that promote the child's well-being and social adaptation.

We have already discussed the Family Check-Up model, including some of the components of that model that are relevant to family management. One important element is to tailor interventions with children and families to fit their strengths and weaknesses on a systematic, comprehensive assessment. Thus, the Family Check-Up serves as the initial basis for collaboratively determining the scope, focus, and intensity of subsequent intervention activity. In contrast to many approaches to psychotherapy that are largely based on a medical model for mental health services, our model includes periodic, brief interventions with a particular emphasis on developmental and social transitions. Thus, six or eight sessions can lead to relatively large effect sizes if delivered strategically over 2 to 3 years. A second unique feature of the Family Check-Up is that we actively address the affective nature of individual well-being and relationship dynamics by integrating exposure, desensitization, and other cognitive–behavioral techniques. During the past 10 years it has become clear that most families seeking help suffer from depression, trauma, and dysregulated, coercive interactions. Thus, therapy that addresses the affective adjustment of family members is essential to promoting emotional well-being. We assume that emotional well-being and social adaptation are linked by common processes and mutual feedback loops.

Finally, the Family Check-Up model is an ecologically sensitive approach to family management in that we actively create links to social and community dynamics that will provide long-term support for social adaptation and emotional well-being. For example, for school-age children, it is important to interface interventions and assessments of children and families with those in school environments. In early childhood, we actively link family intervention services to social services that support the health and education of young children, including preschool programs such as Head Start.

Treatment with families begins after the assessment process is complete, goals have been established, and an initial working relationship has been formed with the family. We support a time-limited treatment plan that focuses on specific goals identified by both the therapist and the family. Following is an example of a beginning treatment session with a family:

1. *Establish an agenda.* At the beginning of the session, the therapist should establish the goal of the session, beginning by asking the parents what they would like to focus on during the session. If crises or other difficulties require attention, negotiate and adjust the agenda appropriately.
2. *Affirm a collaborative set.* Briefly remind parents of the agreement about the focus of the intervention, evaluate if adjustments are needed, and reiterate the understanding about the number of sessions or the focus of the sessions.
3. *Provide a brief rationale.* When introducing a new skill, provide a brief, effective rationale that is tailored to the culture, ecology, and skill level of the parent.
4. *Prepare activities and role-plays.* Come prepared with the appropriate forms, stickers, charts, and role-play scenarios to generate interest and motivation in practicing the skills.

5. *Provide behavior activation.* Suggest a behavior or assignment between sessions that will promote the successful use of the parenting behavior. The assignment should be sensitive to the abilities, motivation, culture, and ecology of the parent and child. Consider the following example:

Anna was a 10-year-old Latino girl living with her biological mother, stepfather, and new baby sister. The family had recently emigrated from Mexico, and Anna was attending school in a small city. She was having trouble adjusting to the demands of the English language, peer dynamics, and new school environment. She also expressed that she was lonely, missing her friends back home and the social connections with extended family that she had once enjoyed. Her stepfather was somewhat removed from the parenting role and pre-ferred interacting with the new baby. Her mother was overwhelmed with the stress of the new baby and expected Anna to help out with the baby as soon as she returned from school. As a result of this stress, Anna was noncompliant at home and engaged in angry out-bursts with her stepfather. The parents were also having some marital problems. During the first session of family therapy the goals set were to help them work as a parenting team with Anna and the baby as well as to educate them about some of the experiences Anna was having at school. They were motivated to change her negative behavior. They realized that the casual interactions with extended family that they were used to in Mexico were not a part of their new culture and that to increase Anna's peer experiences, she needed to do extracurricular activities away from home in the afternoons. The therapists worked with the family and what this would mean to them in the context of their own cultural values, which supported Anna as a caretaker of her new sister. They worked to get Anna into new activities and found that her noncompliance at home decreased.

THERAPIST SKILLS IN FAMILY MANAGEMENT THERAPY

Despite their best intentions, many parents simply do not have the background or skills to engage in the behaviors that would promote the social adaptation and emotional well-being of their children. When this is the case, it is imperative that the therapist actively identify this skill deficit, motivate the parents to learn, and effectively teach the parenting skill. A strength-based approach to working with families in this situation facilitates change and provides motivation, while decreasing discouragement. Such efforts are naturally collaborative but, at the same time, should be led by the therapist. Videotapes, books, and brochures may be useful in teaching new parenting skills. The following therapist skills facilitate the teaching process:

1. *Provide engaging rationales.* When teaching a new skill, the therapist should have a brief but motivating rationale for the client to acquire and, more important, to perform the skill. It may be helpful to use a chalkboard or other type of visual media or a story that motivates and engages the parent in the learning process.

2. *Break content into teachable units.* Therapists are often educated, verbal individuals. Therapists also may have a great deal of knowledge about the skills they are teaching (e.g., behavioral theory). It is important to recognize that these fundamental skills for behavior change may not be a part of the family's repertoire. Effective teaching is a give-and-take process. It is helpful to break complex skills down into manageable units for the client, tailoring them to the client's skill level and behavior-change resources at the time.

3. *Shape success.* The therapist should set up teaching so that successive gains can accumulate into larger successes for the parent and child. Again, this shaping process is tailored to the skill level, resources, culture, and ecology of the family. Small successes are motivating for clients, encouraging them to engage in the change process and build self-efficacy.

4. *Role-play.* Structured interactions within sessions that provide an opportunity for discrimination learning (i.e., wrong way and right way), practice, and skill acquisition are useful. Skillful role-plays will help the therapist accurately identify the client's current level of performance and scaffold progress toward improved performance.

5. *Proactively structure.* A therapist should be able to anticipate, precorrect, forewarn, and predict likely problems that a parent may encounter when using a new skill or in changing a behavior.

6. *Respond to feedback effectively.* Therapists should actively read implicit and explicit messages from the client about the teaching efforts and adjust accordingly to improve engagement in the learning and teaching process.

7. *Punctuate sessions.* Use verbal and nonverbal cues to demarcate the pragmatics of a teaching interaction, for example, by moving closer to the client appropriately to indicate a need for more direct communication and by signaling transitions in the interpersonal dynamics of the sessions.

8. *Balance positive feedback with correction.* Every session should have a large positive to corrective feedback ratio. A rule of thumb for client interactions is that for every episode of correc-

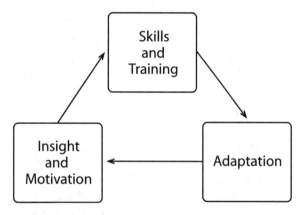

Figure 10.2. The family change cycle.

tive feedback, there should be four supportive or positive feedback interactions.

Change occurs as a cycle. It is unrealistic to think that behavior change
will occur automatically without some continued support to the client. The
habitual nature of the behavior and the emotional and ecological climate
all affect the pace and dynamics of behavior change. We see change as
unfolding in an iterative cycle that moves from insight and motivation, to
skills and training, to adaptation and change of one's life. For example,
supporting a parent's use of positive reinforcement is likely to begin with
some sense that the child and family could benefit from contingent positive
responses to the child's positive behavior. Then skills in reinforcement,
such as learning to use a sticker or point chart, are developed. Last, the
principle of reinforcement is incorporated and adapted to other aspects of
child rearing and, perhaps, to other children or other behaviors. This cycle
is shown in Figure 10.2.

The Family Check-Up sets the stage for insight and motivation. One
conclusion that may result from the feedback session with a parent is that
more support is needed to enact the change. At this stage, the therapist
becomes more actively involved in the behavior-change cycle. By and large,
therapist involvement is the most intense during the skill development stage
of an intervention. That is, the therapist takes on a leadership role in
structuring interactions that promote skill acquisition and development
within the family ecology. Once a family has developed the skill and it is
maintained, the therapist becomes less active and often follows the lead of
the parent in problem-solving difficulties and barriers. The support for change
process can be seen as circular in most families (see Figure 10.3)—that is,
all families cycle through issues, as children and parents change through

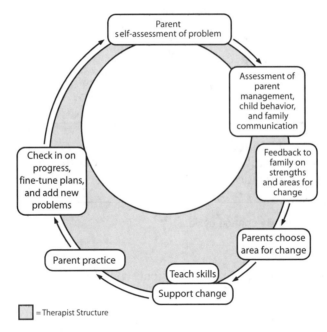

Figure 10.3. Therapist structure in the behavior-change cycle.

time. At first, the therapist may be highly involved in the change process, structuring sessions and guiding change. Although the tone is collaborative, the therapist uses highly developed interpersonal skills to structure, reframe, and support parents' efforts to make changes (Patterson, 1985). Over time, however, the therapist gradually structures less, and the parent provides more input into the content and process of each meeting. Therapist involvement may also wane in terms of the frequency of sessions (see Figure 10.3). At first, sessions may be held several times a week (Henggeler, Schoenwald, Borduin, Rowland, & Cunningham, 1998) and later, once per month or less. Within a health maintenance framework, some families may require continued support to minimize mental health problems from early childhood through adolescence.

The therapist's skill and persistence in structuring interactions and sessions are likely to reduce the client's resistance and promote the client's acceptance and commitment to a change plan. Note that it is the interaction between the parent and therapist that results in a collaborative set that leads to family change. In this way, the collaborative set is not necessarily the client's agenda or the therapist's agenda, but is a melding of both agendas by virtue of a series of interactions that involve sensitivity and structure on the part of the therapist (see Figure 10.4).

In general, the therapist and the parent should have a shared perspective about the intervention plan, which should be explicitly expressed at

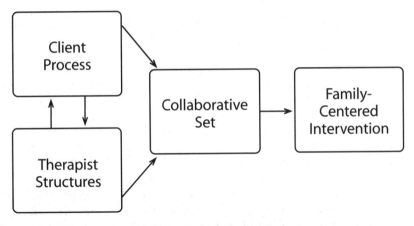

Figure 10.4. The process of change to minimize resistance.

every meeting. The outcome of the Family Check-Up leads to a shared sense of purpose that is briefly articulated at the beginning of each session. Here's an example of how that might be stated:

> Good to see you today. Let me share with you my sense of where we are. Today, we were going to focus on the bedtime routine with Rafael. We agreed that you'd like to deal with this issue in a better way. First, we were going to talk about how your evening goes and good ways to set up the routine to make it easier for Rafael to deal with bedtime. Then we were going to talk about ways for you to encourage him in compliance. Does that sound right? Is that your understanding?

HOME-BASED THERAPY

Conducting sessions within a family's home has both advantages and disadvantages. One advantage is convenience for the family. In addition, the ecology of daily family life can be more readily observed, and intervention activities such as role-plays can be actively demonstrated. The disadvantage is that chaos from telephones, visitors, television, extended family, and the like can undermine systematic work with a family. Therapists are in the leadership role in the change process, and therefore should identify barriers to a successful intervention and problem-solve for solutions. For example, bringing child care to the home or meeting with the family in a place where child care is available is often necessary for parents with one or more young children. Issues that undermine family change should be identified and addressed collaboratively with parents. We recommend that therapists always conduct at least one home visit to assess the family in their own natural environment. Home visits also can be used to assess the family's own context, including strengths and weaknesses in their ecology. Consider the following example:

> Mike and Sara came into the clinic for help with managing their four children ages 9 to 14. They were worried about arguing, angry outbursts, and noncompliance from all the children in the home. They described their limit-setting and parenting strategies and clearly seemed to need some support in refining their skills. A home visit revealed that the family was living in a small two-bedroom apartment. Although the apartment was orderly, it was very difficult for the adolescent youth in the household to maintain a sense of independence and privacy in this context, which was leading to problems in the family's interactions. With this new information, the therapist was able to integrate the contextual stress of living in a small apartment into the plan for the family. For example, activities were scheduled on alternate nights for the children to reduce the number of family members in the home at any given time. Typical interventions for youth this age, which suggest that people go to different areas of the apartment to cool off, were not suggested because they were not feasible.

A Word About Culture

To say that culture is important to consider in family management therapy is quite an understatement. Culture and family management are inextricably connected; family management skills stem directly from culture and values, and in turn cultural context affects the ability of families to use skills. In this sense, we see family management therapy as one of the most culturally sensitive treatments for children and families. Parents work with the therapist in a collaborative model that emphasizes culture and values. Parenting skills are taught in this context, and families give feedback to therapists when the content is not relevant to their own culture or values. Setbacks as well as achievements are framed in a cultural context. Consider the following example:

> Patrice was a 16-year-old African American female living with her biological mother, Angela. Patrice and Angela were having problems getting along as well as they typically had in the past. For example, Patrice stayed out all night with friends and told her mother only part of the story. A neighbor reported that she had seen Patrice at 4 a.m. at a local convenience store. A videotaped observation revealed that Patrice and Angela were extremely close, acting more like siblings or friends than mother and daughter. Angela had trouble setting limits with Patrice, and Patrice listened to her mother only when she felt it was relevant to her. Both Angela and Patrice had a strong African American ethnic identity, which was a strength for the family. Rather than build the relationship into a hierarchy, with Angela as a parent,

the therapist highlighted strengths of this relationship in the context of their culture. Communication strategies that built on their strong relationships were used in therapy.

Culture affects the closeness of family relationships and the actual parenting skills that are used in these relationships to raise children. For example, research has continually shown that spanking is related to aggression in European American youth but not African American youth (Deater-Deckard, Dodge, Bates, & Pettit, 1996). Limit setting is a difficult concept for Latino families, who more typically use positive parenting, such as warm and caring relationships with their children, to manage behavior. Children in traditional Asian families are expected to behave appropriately, and parents may use strategies such as guilt induction and shame to manage behavior. Although these illustrations are grossly generalized, they do exemplify the variation in specific parenting strategies across cultures. It is critical that therapists are aware of these differences and sensitive to cultural context as it relates to parenting.

Challenges to Working With Families

Clients, paradoxically, often later resist changes that they may have endorsed at the outset of an intervention plan. For example, when a client makes a behavior change, the therapist will quite commonly experience resistance to change in forms such as avoidance of sessions, negativity about the child or behavior-change plan, helplessness, hopelessness, or behavioral signs of distrust and premature quitting. These experiences are central to the change process and are often opportunities to address the dynamics of a family ecology that underlies the persistence of maladaptive forms of behavior and parenting.

It is critical that the therapist sensitively adjusts the intervention to fit the needs of each family, to manage transitions and parent resistance effectively, and to give appropriate dimension to skills before introducing new concepts or switching topics. Rarely do individuals change without an emotional reaction such as avoidance or some form of negativity. The therapist's reaction to these client behaviors can exacerbate or improve the change process. A variety of process tools are helpful for preventing or managing client resistance, some of which are listed here:

1. *Listen and show understanding.* Articulate an understanding of the parents' concerns, worries, and experience.
2. *Have genuine empathy and caring.* Showing understanding is helpful, but the sense that the therapist cares within the context of the professional relationship is the foundation of the therapeutic relationship.

3. *Normalize*. The therapist can share information with parents that they may not know about, whether it has to do with children's behavior, normative development, or other parents' reactions to a particular developmental stage or situation. This information may be quite helpful for guiding parents and supporting their perseverance in the change process.

4. *Use story and metaphor*. An occasional story or metaphor may provide parents with perspective about the change process if it is inspiring and fitting to their situation.

5. *Use humor*. Therapists who present themselves too seriously can distance families. However, many families have serious problems that warrant an intense, emotional demeanor. Often tension can be released, perspective gained, acceptance induced, and appropriate humility encouraged on all sides by well placed, appropriate humor.

6. *Take responsibility*. As a leader in the change process, part of the territory is accepting responsibility when change efforts go astray.

7. *Reflect and paraphrase*. During the listening process, it is often important for clients to hear how the therapist is reading the message behind their behavior, especially when feeling assured about the therapist's attentiveness is germane to the change process.

8. *Use motivational questions*. Questions that encourage clients to explore their own motivational state help enable both the client and therapist to coregulate the content and focus of the intervention session.

9. *Structure the session*. Supportive interruptions and active structuring can be especially helpful in working through session dynamics that may serve as a barrier to change, such as a parent dominating a session with his or her thoughts, feelings, or stories.

10. *Provide explicit guidance*. The therapist should ensure that the client understands the rationale and process underlying the session content or focus, as well as the therapist's behavior during the session.

11. *Contextualize*. It is important in this model that therapists actively seek opportunities to ensure that interventions are linked to the ecology of the child and family. For example, they should actively encourage problem solving and pair the intervention with relevant resources in the extended family, preschool setting, and social service agencies.

TABLE 10.1
Therapy Process Dynamics in Family Change

Client process	Behavior/ sign	Therapist reaction	Therapy solutions	Related mental health issues
Boundary problem	Blaming Zapping "Nothing works"	Defensive Critical Confrontational	Validate video feedback Reframe Problem solve	Parental depression
Detouring	Blames child for family problems	Sides with child Lacks empathy	Validate and normalize Build parents as a team	Marital discord Stepparenting
Avoid problems Neglectful	Unmotivated Passive Disengaged "I can't"	"Parenting the parent"	Small steps Incentives Positive change strategies	Substance use Depression
Cultural disconnect	Lack of trust Cancels Quits	Avoid contact Tries too hard	Show respect Query Bicultural training	Delinquency/ Maltreatment (mandated to service)

COMMON FAMILY DYNAMICS

Families resist therapy for various reasons. Four common dynamics and related problems occur in family therapy (see Table 10.1). These processes occur within the context of therapy and can lead to failure on the part of parents to connect with the therapist, engage fully in the change process, or continue with therapy. These problems can also lead to a variety of therapist pitfalls, which may exacerbate the problem. It is the therapist's task to effectively respond to patterns of client resistance in the interest of the family's well-being. Table 10.1 briefly summarizes some common forms of client resistance and some positive steps to effectively work through resistance toward lasting, adaptive change.

Enmeshment and Boundary Problems

This first family dynamic can be illustrated with the following case:

Joan and her 12-year-old son, Scott, were referred to the clinic for Scott's depression and lack of achievement at school. Joan was a single parent who worked full-time at a stable job. Scott's main problems were lack of energy, lack of positive affect, and low motivation. Scott came home every day and waited for Joan to return from work. The two of them then rented a movie and had dinner together. Joan never went out without Scott in the evenings and had few friends, relying on Scott as her primary social support. Scott played on the computer most of the afternoon and had few friends. He rarely completed his homework. Joan liked Scott to be at home and safe while she was at work. She didn't like Scott going over to other children's homes, even if their parents were home. She was angry with Scott for not doing well in school and blamed him for the problem. She did not structure homework time for Scott and expected him to be able to manage this on his own given his high level of maturity.

This dynamic is common in families in which parents rely on their children to maintain roles in the family system, such as providing social support or marital therapy, that are not consistent with their developmental age. Anger and negative emotion characterize the relationships and also represent a high level of investment on the part of parents. Pitfalls for therapists include siding with the child against the parent, which can reduce the parent's engagement with the process and lead to defensiveness. It is important for therapists to remain objective as they try to work within this system.

Effective strategies involve empathy with the parents and positive support for change in the family system. Without support, the parents may feel frustrated and continue to feel negatively toward the child. A statement such as the following may help Joan move from a negative, angry state to a more positive change state.

> It seems as if you are working hard to help Scott with this problem. You clearly care a great deal about Scott and his development. It's really hard to be a parent sometimes—you feel so invested in your child and also so helpless to make changes.

Parental Depression

Adult depression is a common problem seen in enmeshed, angry family presentations. Some of the main diagnostic features of depression can have a negative effect on parenting children. Depressed parents exhibit anger, moodiness, and a lack of social support and often fail to experience pleasure in activities. In the context of a parent–child relationship, depression may exacerbate problems with enmeshment, which in turn can lead to lack of motivation for change on the part of the parent and the child.

Therapists can often deal with depression in the context of family management therapy by supporting the parents and working directly with the family on making structured changes in the parenting system. This treatment is quite similar to typical therapies for depression, with a structured behavioral response to depression and rewards for changing behavior.

Detouring Family Problems Onto the Child

Targeting the child as the problem when another one exists is a common family dynamic that is associated with child mental health referrals. Detouring families are likely to begin the treatment process with a focus on one target child and that child's problems. They may even focus on one child's problems rather than those of another child, when the children look quite similar based on an objective assessment. The parents may be angry with that child for his or her problem behavior and often feel that if that child would behave appropriately, all the problems in the family would be solved. They are unable to see the contextual impact of the family situation on the child. They may present as angry, yet detached, because their anger seems misdirected. Here is an illustrative case example:

> Cindy and Jack (stepfather) presented to the clinic with problems managing their 8-year-old son, Devon. They described Devon as oppositional, angry, and difficult to manage. Devon's teacher reported no school problems and described Devon as a social, pleasant child. Cindy and Jack were both recovering alcoholics and this was a second marriage for each. Jack had another son, age 10, who did not live with the family but visited occasionally and did not get along well with Devon. Cindy and Jack both reported high levels of marital problems, including lack of communication and value differences. Jack was using marijuana on a regular basis in the evenings, and Cindy wanted to remain abstinent from all substances. They regularly argued over this and many other problems in Devon's presence.

For families like this one, a thorough ecological assessment can help them begin to see the context of the child's problems. Support for parents, norm-referenced assessments, and a strength-based approach can also help. When this process begins for families, they may feel as if their problems have worsened because the therapist will help the families change their focus to new problems and conflicts. It is common for detouring families to feel worse rather than better after several successful sessions, as they begin to focus on more complex problems within the family. One pitfall for the therapist could be siding with the child against the parents, which may lead to parent defensiveness and a need for parents to show the therapist how bad the child really is. This dynamic is related to a lack of ability to bring out the real problem and focus on it in the context of the assessment and therapy. It is also a mistake for the therapist to be reactive and give in to parents' anger toward the child.

It is helpful when working with a detouring presentation to use a psychoeducational model at the outset to educate the family about an ecological model of development. For some parents, this reframing of the child's problems in context can be very helpful and reduce defensiveness.

The next step is to build support for the parents by using empathy and siding with the parents. Doing this helps build up the parents as the experts on their child, and sets up the parenting dyad as the context for change. Continued support for the parents as the agents of change then begins to shift the focus of the problem off of the child and onto the parenting system. This sample conversation shows how to reduce defensiveness in a detouring family:

> Mom: Devon is just such a hard child. If you could see him at home, you'd see that he is really impossible to manage.

> Stepdad: Yes, he is very hard for me to be around.

> Therapist: He sounds really hard, and it seems that he has been that way for a long time. It also sounds as if when he starts his behavior problems, it is really upsetting to both of you. It will be hard for him to change his behavior, and he is going to need a lot of support to do so.

> Mom: Yes, I don't know what to do.

> Therapist: Devon is lucky to have parents like you who are so invested in him and understand him so well. You really know a lot about Devon and his behavior problems. You are going to be the experts at helping him change.

> Stepdad: What do you mean?

> Therapist: Together, we can focus on some things you can do, as parents, to help Devon make some changes in his behavior. The changes we make will start with you because you are the leaders of this household. We will probably try a few things before we find something that really works for you and Devon.

> Mom: But what about Devon? What is his part going to be?

> Therapist: Well, Devon will be a really important piece of our work because as you begin trying new approaches to dealing with his problem behavior, he will react to these approaches either positively or negatively. His reactions will help inform us and help us adapt our treatment. He can also be involved in planning interventions, such as rewards or incentives for positive behavior.

> Stepdad: This sounds like a lot of work.

> Therapist: Yes, it's really hard to parent a child who is having problems.

The most common detouring presentation involves a marital or step-parenting conflict, such as in the example presented, that is misdirected onto the child. We have found that many two-parent families have a history of marital conflict and distress that has not been treated or discussed, which has led to parenting problems and a focus on one child as the target. It is important not to mislead parents into thinking that the family management intervention will solve their marital problems. However, effective communication, problem solving, and parenting skills that focus on team building in the marital dyad can support the parents in beginning to work on these issues. For some families, the assessment process and direct discussions surrounding the marital discord are also helpful.

Stepparenting issues are predictable and can often be addressed with a psychoeducational model. It is often the case that stepparents have not thoroughly considered their role as new parents to a child. It is common for them to step in and parent inappropriately, distancing the child and creating conflict in the marital system. When stepparents learn about their role and consider other options, such as decreasing their parenting involvement and increasing their role as mentor or support for the family, many of these problems are solved.

Disconnected Parents

Avoidance of problems occurs when parents disconnect from their children for various reasons. The following case highlights this scenario:

> Linda was a single parent of two young girls ages 7 and 10. She had a variety of medical problems, including chronic back pain and an intestinal illness. As a result, she took a variety of pain medications on a regular basis. She was referred by the school because her 10-year-old daughter was acting out aggressively toward peers and failing several subjects. The school reported that Linda was "uninvolved" and was not responsive to their efforts to work with the family. Linda was engaged in therapy, coming in every week, but she did not follow through on homework assignments. She avoided interacting with her children in the afternoon by taking pain medication and sleeping, which resulted in her 10-year-old being at the park unsupervised one day until after dark, then being brought home by the police.

In this example, small steps and a focus on restructuring the environment were helpful to Linda. She worked on finding low-cost activities for each of the girls after school, including sports and clubs. She also worked on engaging positively with each child at least one time per day. After accomplishing these goals, she was then able to work on managing negative behavior. This presentation involves a parent who has problems with both depression and substance use, both of which can lead to detachment and apathy on the part of parents. Parents in this situation present as helpless and fragile, and therapists often react to that carefully, with limited confrontation and lowered expectations for achievement. Although small goals are important, sometimes confrontation of parents is needed to reinitialize the parenting system.

Substance use is one problem that leads to disengagement at this level because the parent spends most of his or her time either taking drugs or thinking about drugs. The parent's primary goals are not related to parenting and the children. Parents with a primary substance abuse problem should be referred for substance abuse treatment first. It is very difficult for parents who are addicts to focus on parenting their children. Many parents need assistance with motivation for treatment, which is why a thorough assessment and motivational feedback session can be so helpful with this population. Therapists in this situation must avoid the pitfall of ignoring the substance use completely without attending to its effect on parenting.

Cultural Disconnect

In this example, a major problem stems from the therapist's lack of knowledge and skills within a particular cultural group and his or her inability to apply interventions appropriately to the family as a result of this knowledge gap:

> Juanita and Jose, a Latino couple, were referred to the clinic by the school because the school was having trouble managing the behavior of their 8-year-old boy. They also had two other children, ages 4 and 9. They lived in a small apartment with Juanita's biological mother, who did most of the parenting while Juanita and Jose were at work. After weeks of work with Juanita and Jose on parenting skills, they stopped coming in for therapy. Reengagement occurred when the therapist called a meeting with Juanita, Jose, and the grandmother and began working with all three adults in the system as a parenting team.

It was ineffective to work only with Juanita and Jose because the primary caretaker was the grandmother. In all work with families it is important to work from a collaborative set that includes the parents and any other primary caregivers in the decision making for interventions. It is also critical for all therapists who work with families to have training in multicultural counseling and issues of diversity (M. C. Roberts et al., 1998).

Research has shown that two related factors—racial identity and acculturation—play a critical role in the success of ethnically diverse youth and families. Both racial identity and acculturation may mitigate risks associated with poverty, ethnic diversity, and the transition to high school (Chavous et al., 2003). Acculturation can operate as both a protective factor and a risk factor for ethnically diverse youth. Certainly, ethnically diverse youth from immigrant families that are more acculturated may find that schoolwork and peer-group adaptation are facilitated by strong English language skills and values that are consistent with mainstream American culture. Higher levels of acculturation have been found to predict lower levels of school dropout for Latino youth (Martinez & Forgatch, 2001).

However, recent acculturation research has been criticized for being overly simplistic in viewing acculturation to the mainstream American culture as purely positive. For example, both Latino and Asian families value family support, assistance, duty, and family obligation (Fuligni, 1998). Acculturation may detach youth from these family values and may in turn lead to an increase in problem behavior as youth develop values consistent with mainstream American culture and subsequent conflict with their family of origin (Coatsworth, Szapocznik, Kurtines, & Santisteban, 1997; Szapocznik et al., 1997). Recent research by Fuligni (1997) suggested that Asian and Latino youth from later generations spend less time studying and engaging with schoolwork than do students from immigrant families. In this way, acculturation may be detrimental to some youth, particularly as acculturation increases family conflict and exposure to deviant peers.

Both ethnic identity and acculturation are critical aspects of an ecological model of child adjustment. The cultural world of the child interfaces with the school and peer contexts to either promote or interfere with positive adolescent outcomes (Garrod, Ward, Robinson, & Kilkenny, 1999). Clear evidence exists to support the link between ethnic socialization at the family level and positive outcomes for youth. These positive outcomes range from enhanced cognitive and behavioral competencies in early childhood for African American youth who experience positive ethnic socialization in the home (Caughy, O'Campo, Randolph, & Nickerson, 2002) to enhanced monitoring by parents and positive communication with teens in adolescence (Frabutt, Walker, & MacKinnon-Lewis, 2002).

We suspect that the complex relations between ethnic minority status, acculturation, and mental health problems are best understood and addressed through an assessment of the specific effects on family management in early and late childhood (Catalano et al., 1992; Dishion, Owen, & Bullock, 2004; Gillmore et al., 1990; Szapocznik et al., 1997). When family interventions are tailored to address issues of acculturation and racial identity, they are successful at reducing problem behavior and enhancing positive development for young children and adolescents (Pantin et al., 2003; Santisteban et al., 2003; Szapocznik, Santisteban, Kurtines, Perez-Vidal, & Hervis, 1984).

SUMMARY

This chapter highlights our model of family management therapy, including some therapist skills and techniques for engaging a range of family presentations. Our model is contextually based and driven by developmental science that suggests family management skills are central to the system of the child and adolescent.

11

PARENT INTERVENTION GROUPS

Group-based parenting training is one of the most cost-effective and empirically validated approaches to working with parents. In this chapter, we highlight the research that supports a group approach to parent training and discuss in detail the techniques for working with parents in a group context.

DEVELOPMENTAL RESEARCH SUPPORTING PARENTING INTERVENTIONS

Considerable evidence supports the general theory that poor family management (e.g., inconsistency, lack of warmth, and punitive parenting) is associated with childhood antisocial behavior, which in turn is related to academic failure, peer rejection, and a variety of social–emotional problems (e.g., Patterson & Stouthamer-Loeber, 1984; Pettit, Bates, & Dodge, 1993; Stormshak, Bierman, McMahon, Lengua, & Conduct Problems Prevention Research Group, 2000). Furthermore, patterns of interaction learned in the context of parent–child exchanges are generalized to school settings and peer groups, which leads to the later development of problems such as drug use, delinquency, and school dropout (Loeber & Dishion, 1983; Loeber et al., 1993). As children develop into adolescents, lack of monitoring, ineffective limit setting, and parental disengagement exacerbate existing behavior problems (Dishion & McMahon, 1998). Family management problems (e.g., low levels of monitoring) then set the stage for intense involvement with a deviant peer group (Dishion, Nelson, Winter, & Bullock, 2004; Dishion, Patterson, Stoolmiller, & Skinner, 1991), which in turn is highly predictive of early-onset substance use and problem behavior (Dishion, Capaldi, Spracklen, & Li, 1995). During the transition to adolescence, further parental disengagement exacerbates peer problems and leads to growing problem behavior in youth (Dishion, Kavanagh, Schneiger, Nelson, & Kaufman, 2002). In summary, ample evidence supports parenting skills as a primary target of prevention and intervention for families. Through the parenting system, changes in family management affect proximal targets such as parenting and child behavior, as well as distal targets such as peer group affiliation and maternal depression (DeGarmo, Patterson, & Forgatch, 2004).

Parenting Intervention Research: Early Childhood

A long history of research supports working with parents in a group format. This research is based primarily on the developmental literature referenced earlier. For the most part, this research is based on a behavioral model that focuses on teaching skills to parents and using parent–peer support to effect change. Parent training approaches are effective as stand-alone clinic-based programs (Webster-Stratton, 1994), school-based programs (Fast Track; Conduct Problems Prevention Research Group, 1999), or interventions embedded in a larger multifocused program of research (Kaminski, Stormshak, Good, & Goodman, 2002).

Many programs in early, middle, and late childhood have been effective at producing both short- and long-term gains in parenting skills and child behavior. In early childhood, one of the most known and researched programs is the Incredible Years Parent Intervention (Webster-Stratton, 1980, 1992). This program uses a videotaped approach to work directly with parents in a group format. The program takes about 26 hours and is completed in 13 or 14 weekly 2-hour sessions. Two therapists typically facilitate groups of 8 to 12 parents who watch the videotaped examples and discuss the applicability of these examples to their own parenting and children. The ADVANCE parent training program delivered in conjunction with the BASIC parent training program includes content of personal self-control, communication skills, problem-solving skills, and social support (Webster-Stratton, 1990). This program has demonstrated effectiveness in improving parenting skills and attitudes, reducing parental violence and punitive parenting, and decreasing child behavior problems both directly after implementation and at follow-up (Webster-Stratton, 1994). It is interesting to note that in one research study, parents who simply watched the video program

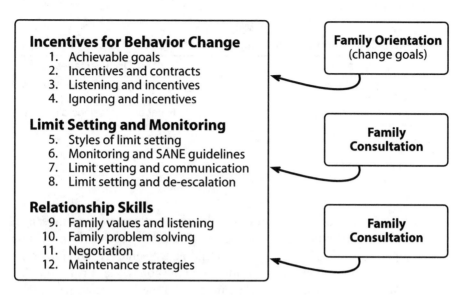

Figure 11.1. Outline for the family management curriculum.

(without group facilitation) also showed changes in behavior, suggesting that in terms of predicting changes, the content of this program may be equally as important as the process of delivery (Webster-Stratton, Kolpacoff, & Hollingsworth, 1988).

Late Childhood and Adolescence

The Adolescent Transitions Program (ATP; Dishion, Andrews, Kavanagh, & Soberman, 1996; Dishion & Kavanagh, 2002) has been used successfully to work with parents of adolescents in a group format and has been the primary approach for working with families in groups that our research and clinical teams have used. Following from the work of Webster-Stratton (1992), ATP uses a video-based approach to working with parents in groups of 8 to 10 and emphasizing family management skills (see Figure 11.1). ATP has been shown to be effective at reducing problem behavior and enhancing parenting skills both immediately after the intervention and at follow-up (Dishion, Andrews, et al., 1996).

RATIONALE FOR WORKING WITH PARENTS IN GROUPS

There are a variety of reasons to work directly with parents in a group format. First, many parents prefer the group format, which has a psychoeducational approach to learning skills. The group format decreases

TABLE 11.1
The Advantages and Disadvantages of Working With Parents in Groups

Advantages	Disadvantages
Provides social support	Group dynamics hard to control
Is cost-effective	No individual approach
Disseminates normative behavior and milestones	Number of sessions difficult to determine
Exerts informal pressure to engage and change	High dropout rate
Is community based	

the focus on any one parent and provides group support for members. In early childhood situations, groups can be particularly useful for providing social support, connecting parents with children the same age, and providing information about developmental norms and milestones. Many parents enjoy the social interactions with group members and feel supported when they learn of other families who are having similar problems with their children. Groups are also an ideal mechanism for reaching large numbers of parents in community-level interventions that are not specifically focused on children at risk. Parents with children who are developing normally may take advantage of the group format to learn new skills or to get social support from group members.

The group format also has several disadvantages, including the lack of individual planning for parents and a high dropout rate (see Table 11.1). Groups have a dynamic that is sometimes difficult for therapists to manage, which can also be a weakness. In addition, despite the cost-effective nature of groups, they are expensive to run when attendance is low, which is a common problem. For successful recruitment of parents into groups, child care and food must be provided, which increases the cost substantially.

Content, Structure, and Participants

The content, structure, and participants of parenting groups can vary widely. This flexible delivery enhances the feasibility of parenting groups. Parenting groups can include a wide range of relevant content, from divorce or stepparenting issues to sexual and physical abuse. Groups can be organized at the community level to address these specific issues and target families for whom these issues have relevance. The content of parenting groups can be adapted to meet the needs of any specific group.

Parenting groups can be structured in various ways. They can be small groups with content delivered over many weeks. These small groups are usually facilitated by therapists and may include some components of a group therapy approach, such as feedback given to parents by other parents and confrontation of disruptive or inappropriate group members. For some parents, this type of group format can be extremely beneficial and can serve as a context for learning both parenting skills content and adult interpersonal skills.

Parenting interventions can also be delivered to large groups of families, in community-based clinics or in schools. We have developed a series of topic nights for schools and Head Start centers based on effective family management skills. The series includes topics such as "Monitoring Your Adolescent," "Playing With Your Child," and "Dealing With Negative Peer Influences." We have delivered these topics to large groups of parents (25 or more) with success, and have found that this psychoeducational format is one of the most popular structures for the delivery of parenting content in community settings.

The participants in parenting groups can be drawn from normative or high-risk populations. School-based groups tend to attract a bimodal distribution of parents that includes families at high risk looking for support and families at low risk trying to supplement already existing skills. Groups can also be conducted in clinics with a clinic-based, self-referred sample of parents. These groups tend to have members who have a high level of motivation to attend and achieve in the group. Groups can also be based in community facilities, such as jails or low-income housing, to bring in certain populations for treatment. Groups that target only families and youth at high risk tend to have the lowest levels of attendance and participation.

Session Content

The next several sections will focus on the typical content of parenting skills groups aimed at decreasing or preventing disruptive behavior problems. The content of multiple curricula is summarized in Exhibit 11.1, which includes a description of typical content for both early childhood and late childhood (adolescence) groups.

EXHIBIT 11.1
Content for Early Childhood and Late Childhood Adolescent Groups

Early childhood	Late childhood/adolescence
Play skills	Monitoring
Reading to child and facilitation of learning	Using incentives
	Problem solving
Time-out	Listening skills and communication
Limit setting	Handling problem behavior
Ignoring	Supporting autonomy and independence
Consistency	Using contingencies
Managing problem behavior	Enhancing positive family relationships
Working with schools	

In early childhood (ages 0–6), groups typically start with a focus on the development of a positive relationship with the child. The content usually includes information about playing with one's child and skills for doing so, spending positive time with one's child, and early literacy. This focus was determined on the basis of both attachment research and behavioral research, which suggest that in early childhood, the relationship between parents and children can be undermined by unhealthy negative interactions and lack of attachment to the caregiver (Greenberg & Speltz, 1988). This content forms the foundation for the discussion of more complex skills. Groups then move on to discuss specific skills for managing behavior, starting with basic skills such as praise and ignoring, then moving to more difficult skills such as limit setting, time-out, and management of extreme problem behavior.

Groups for older children focus more on monitoring, management of peer groups, communication, and problem solving with adolescents. Parents who attend these groups may be dealing with serious problem behavior at home and, therefore, it is reasonable to begin these groups by narrowing the goals and discussing incentives that may be applicable to adolescents. Relationship skill building is built into the curriculum with sessions on content, including listening, communication, and problem solving. Parents of adolescents may have been attempting to manage the problem behavior of their child for many years and thus may present to parenting groups with a higher level of frustration and hopelessness than do parents of younger children.

Goals Associated With Parenting Groups

Four main goals are associated with parenting groups (see Exhibit 11.2). The first is to teach parents behavioral management skills and theory. Although these skills come naturally to some parents, for others the theory behind behavioral management is confusing and difficult to understand because it is not compatible with their own upbringing or culture. The second goal is psychoeducational. Most parents do not have access to developmental norms or milestones, particularly for social and emotional issues. Because these issues vary widely by age and by child, information sharing about

EXHIBIT 11.2
Main Goals Associated With Parenting Groups

- Teach behavioral management skills.
- Educate regarding normative development.
- Train parents to help their children in the future.
- Increase the quality of the parent–child relationship.

development is one main goal of parenting groups. The third goal involves training parents to help their own children. A parenting group is a unique form of therapy in that often the therapists have no contact with the so-called target problem (i.e., the child). The goal of parenting groups is to teach parents how to advocate and use skills that are appropriate for their own child. Last, parenting groups strive to increase the quality of the parent–child relationship by enhancing skills and promoting an increase in quality family time and positive activities shared by parents and children.

CULTURAL ISSUES IN THE CONTEXT OF PARENTING GROUPS

Parenting and culture are inextricably linked: The primary mode for the transmission of cultural values from one generation to the next is parenting. One of the greatest challenges to delivering effective interventions to parents is developing interventions that are sensitive to the diversity of families. Family interaction, by necessity, is embedded within a cultural context. As such, not all parenting strategies and family interventions will be effective with all groups of people. For example, race differences emerge in the literature linking parenting practices to child behavior problems (e.g., Deater-Deckard, Dodge, Bates, & Pettit, 1996; Florsheim, Tolan, & Gorman-Smith, 1996). In particular, physical punishments used by parents predict behavior problems for European American youth, but not for African American youth (Whaley, 2000). The result is that parenting skills interventions cannot be delivered in a vacuum; the culture and context of the parents in the groups must be considered.

Several programs for families have attempted to address this problem by providing ecologically valid and culturally sensitive interventions to diverse families. For example, the Effective Black Parenting Program (Alvy & Marigna, 1985; Myers, Taylor, Alvy, & Arrington, 1992) integrates a cognitive–behavioral parent training program with information of relevance to inner-city African American families, including discussions of "traditional black discipline" (physical punishment) versus "modern black discipline" (internalizing standards of behavior). The program also adds components such as helping one's child deal with racism at school and positive communication about ethnicity. This program has been effective at changing parenting behavior and child behavior after 1 year.

Resnicow, Soler, Braithwaite, Ahluwalia, and Butler (2000) outlined guidelines for prevention and intervention with culturally diverse families. They discussed two different types of intervention strategies related to cultural sensitivity. Surface-level strategies include matching therapists with race, using brochures, and being sensitive to the contexts in which the interventions are delivered. Deep structure strategies include attention to the developmental research, cultural heritage, and social environments that influence targeted behavior. In diverse parenting groups, discussions of culture as they relate to each skill are warranted and can help members of the group think about their own values and parenting styles that are a result of their culture. Parenting groups that target a specific culture (e.g., groups administered in Spanish) tend to be very successful in terms of attendance and participation. These groups also allow for adaptation of the curriculum to meet the specific needs of the cultural groups and have been effective in changing both parenting and child behavior (Reid, Webster-Stratton, & Beauchaine, 2001).

PROMOTING CHANGE IN GROUPS

Group work with parents requires leadership, clinical skill, and a clear focus to be productive. We use various strategies to optimize the potential for parenting groups to be helpful in the change process.

Collaborative Framework for Change

Many parents who attend parenting skills groups are there to learn new skills and to acquire basic information about child development. It thus is easy for the leaders of the group to take an expert approach to the delivery of the material. In some regards, the therapists are experts in the content; they know the curriculum and they have expertise in the skills they are teaching to parents. Many times parents will ask concrete questions about child development that elicit a direct response rather than a collaborative process (e.g., "Is a 30-minute time-out for my 2-year-old too long?"). For the most part, however, parenting itself is individualized and specific to the family and the child. It is likely that many of the skills require adaptation for each family, and thus a more individualized approach that is respectful of the parents' expertise (e.g., they know their own child best), culture, and the context of parenting is warranted.

Homework

What are the factors that lead to the increase in parenting skills delivered in a group format? One factor may be homework and outside learning. Most parenting group curricula provide homework activities to parents, and participants are encouraged to use these activities with their children and report back to the group about their effectiveness. Then the group helps the parents modify the activity for their youth. Group leaders should use caution when suggesting home practice exercises to the group.

Many parents are distanced by the idea of homework because of their own negative experiences with school or their home situations (e.g., chaotic home environment, lack of a supportive partner), which may prevent consistent follow-through. Group leaders should be sensitive to these contextual factors that may prevent consistent home practice, so that they do not alienate these members from the group.

Group Support for Behavior

Peer dynamics can be a powerful way to engage people in change, even in adulthood. Groups that are facilitated to maximize parent support for group members can support parents in making changes in their parenting. A parent-support system in which parents exchange numbers with each other and call one another for support during the week can be effective. Groups can also be supportive of positive parenting and direct in their disapproval of negative parenting strategies, which may be helpful to some parents.

Telephone Calls and Check-In

Weekly check-in by the therapists can be effective in promoting the home practice skills and maintaining engagement in the group. These check-ins should focus on the homework and content of the group session. They should be 5 minutes in length, and the therapist should be careful not to engage in extended phone therapy during these calls. Check-in calls also increase attendance and participation in the group.

Home Visits and Individual Meetings

Home visits that occur before the group begins meeting can increase attendance and decrease dropout rates in parenting groups (Dishion & Kavanagh, 2003; Szapocznik et al., 1988). There are several goals of home visits. First, the therapists have a chance to meet with the parents and discuss any individual concerns, such as substance use problems or depression, that might affect their ability to participate fully in the parenting groups. Parents also have the opportunity to meet the therapists and connect on a personal level before entering the more stressful group situation. Many parents have anxiety about attending groups, and a home visit helps to decrease this anxiety. Last, the therapists have a chance to visit the home and get a sense of other risk factors and contextual factors that may affect the parent's ability to integrate the information. The therapists can tailor a group curriculum to meet the needs of parents more effectively when they have a good sense of the members in the group.

Leadership Style

Each therapist has his or her own style of leading and managing a group. A relaxed style that encourages humor and self-reflection is the most effective for parenting groups. Many of the videotaped observations discussed previously are amusing; they show parents struggling with behaviors that are common for all caregivers, and they show children engaging in misbehavior that all parents will recognize. It is important for the group leader to laugh with parents at the videos and to lighten the discussion with humor and a relaxed demeanor. Parenting groups should be fun and engaging, not stressful and boring.

MANAGING GROUP PROCESS

Several challenges to the success of groups require specific skills and attention by the group leader. Suggestions for the major issues follow.

Attendance

Poor attendance and high dropout rates are two of the weaknesses of the parenting group model. We use several strategies to increase attendance and lower dropout rates for parents. Creating a supportive and fun environment for learning is critical for maintaining attendance. Food and child care also solve some problems that may cause parents to miss meetings. Home visits and telephone check-ins maintain engagement with the group and therapists, leading to higher attendance. Last, parental involvement in organizing the agenda and picking relevant topics for discussion can increase participation and attendance. Allowing parents to pick the topics for several sessions at the end can be useful. Incentives for parents have also been used to increase attendance (e.g., punch cards with rewards earned). These are particularly effective in community-based groups in which attendance can be low.

Personal Disclosure by the Leader

Oftentimes, the group leader has children of his or her own and may be tempted to use these children as examples in presenting the material. These examples should be used with caution in most groups, especially when the group leaders are from a different culture or demographic background than the parents. Some similarities across parents can be highlighted in groups (e.g., everyone cares about his or her child's future). However, to use one's own children as examples may be offensive to parents unless the group leader has faced similar contextual circumstances and struggles in his or her own life.

High-Risk Parenting

In parenting groups that target at-risk and high-risk youth, often some parents have engaged in high-risk parenting such as abusive episodes, neglect, or overly punitive approaches to behavioral management. Parents who share this information with the group can be quickly isolated by the group and may drop out, yet they are probably the most likely to benefit from the group process and the curriculum. Group members may be scared to confront another parent and become isolated themselves when they hear about parenting that is so different from their own. It is important to approach disclosures such as these with caution and sensitivity. Overly processing the disclosure in the group may exacerbate the situation by focusing too much on one parent and alienating others. Instead, it is better to focus on the emotions that lead to this type of parenting, such as extreme frustration with the child's behavior and anger. Most parents can relate to these feelings, which can diffuse the situation enough so that the leader can move on with the curriculum.

Confidentiality and Small Communities

Confidentiality is an important component of any group and should be discussed at the beginning of the group session. In larger cities, parents in the group may not know each other, and hence the group is safer and personal disclosure is less threatening. In small communities such as rural communities or housing projects, the families may know each other very well and may actually have a long history of interaction. In rural communities, parents may have attended school together themselves and had personal relationships with each other that may have been positive or conflictual. One approach to this context is to discuss these issues up front and assess the relatedness of the group. Open discussions about confidentiality and the relationships that parents have with each other outside of the group are important for facilitating the group process.

Group Conflict

Conflict can arise in any group process. Parenting is a sensitive issue for most people and, as a result, parents are sensitive to criticism of their skills and to the group members' lack of ability to empathize with their situation. Parenting groups conducted in small communities such as rural areas or schools may include parents who know each other and have existing conflicts between their children. The first strategy when dealing with parent conflict is to ignore the conflict unless it is impeding the group. If the therapist alerts the group to the conflict and focuses on it in the group context, the conflict can worsen. Talking with the parents who are in conflict, together and outside of the group, can also be effective. In this discussion, the therapist can ask the parents to problem-solve solutions for dealing with the conflict and staying in the group. This approach is usually effective, and parents will either deal directly with the conflict or decrease the conflict in the future.

Overly Talkative Parent

Groups commonly include both talkative and shy members. Talkative members can serve a useful purpose by engaging other parents and providing relevant examples. Sometimes, a talkative parent will disrupt the group by offering inappropriate examples of parenting to the group or by dominating the group in a way that prevents the leader from progressing with the curriculum. The group leader can use several strategies for dealing with a talkative parent. First, the leader should establish up front with the group that there are times when he or she will need to interrupt members and keep the group on track. This gives him or her the authority to do so in the future, should it become necessary. Second, the leader can make an agenda and timeline for the group, having the talker keep time and keep the group on track. Last, the leader can meet individually to discuss the problem and show sensitivity to the issues that are leading to the problem. Some parents are so distressed when they begin a parenting group that they might not even notice that they are engaging in this behavior, and they simply need some feedback from the group leader.

COMMON PRESENTING PROBLEMS AND THEMES AMONG PARENTS

Here we discuss several common themes and issues that we have encountered in running parenting groups and provide some descriptions of how to handle such problems in a group format.

Resistance to Praise

When their youth are in early childhood and adolescence, parents commonly resist the idea of praise and incentives for them. There are various reasons for this. First, many parents come to groups disengaged from their child, frustrated and tired of dealing with problem behavior. Many parents have the mindset that they should not have to reward their children for doing things that they already should be doing (such as cleaning their room). Some parents are also resistant to the idea of bribing their children to do things in the home. A discussion of the difference between bribing and rewarding is critical in the beginning of all parenting groups. Parents may also benefit from examples related to their own lives (Is a paycheck at work a reward? Would you go to work if you did not get one?). This key issue must be addressed with parents because a positive relationship with their child forms the foundation for the implementation of all the basic skills. Consider the following example:

> Jack and Diane were concerned about their son, Jason, who was 7 years old and engaged in a range of noncompliant behaviors at home and at school. One problem behavior involved not picking up toys after using them. Jason refused to clean up toys and became violent when they requested that he do so. Jack and Diane felt that rewarding Jason for picking up the toys was a bribe and that he should be able to do this on his own. When Jack and Diane learned the difference between bribes and rewards (a bribe would be administered before the cleanup had occurred), they were willing to try a reward system to change this behavior.

Lack of Understanding of Developmental Norms

In both early childhood and adolescence, many parents are not aware of developmental norms for their youth, especially in the realm of expected behavior such as attention, impulsivity, and aggression. It is common for young children to engage in some aggressive behavior, have tantrums, and lack attention skills. It is common for adolescents to lack focus, act impulsively, and engage in angry outbursts at home. We have found that one of the most common errors that parents make in understanding norms is related to the use of time-out and withdrawal of privileges. Parents of young children make errors in the length of a time-out and in the number of time-outs per day that should be administered. Parents of adolescents remove privileges for too long and then lack the ability to follow through on the consequences. This content is important to address in parenting groups for children of all ages. Other parents in the group can give feedback to parents on developmental norms. The American Academy of Pediatrics publishes several helpful books on developmental norms, including *Caring for Your Baby and Young Child*, which parents can use as a reference. Another illustrative example follows:

> Stacey is an 11-year-old girl who was failing at school because of various problem behaviors. In response to her school achievement problems, her mother expected her to sit at the table and do her homework for

3 hours straight at night, with no interruptions, until she had completed the task. This expectation created additional problems for her mother because Stacey was unable to follow through on this plan. After thinking through developmental norms and expectations, her mother was able to adapt the plan and follow through.

Inappropriate Behavior Plans

Most parents who have a child with behavior problems have developed some sort of behavior plan to manage the problem. Most of these plans, however, are not developmentally appropriate and, in fact, they exacerbate problem behavior. As a result, when the idea of behavior planning is first introduced in parenting groups, there tends to be some resistance to this idea. Most parents report that they have tried behavior planning with little success. However, their lack of success results from behavior plans that lack rewards, are too punitive, or require children to wait too long for the reward. In addition, the targeted behaviors are usually too vague (e.g., "be polite") and hence it is difficult for the child to understand the plan. Discussion of developmental norms and appropriate plans can remedy this problem, and a focus on incentives rather than removal of privileges is also warranted. Consider the following:

> Henry was an 8-year-old boy who had trouble getting along with his 2-year-old sister, Alison. Henry's parents developed a plan for Henry that involved good behavior with his sister on a daily basis. At the end of the week, if Henry had been nice to his sister all week, he would earn a reward. Henry was unable to earn even one reward with this plan, which frustrated his parents and led to hopelessness.

Commonly implemented by parents, such a plan yields a variety of problems. The plan is too vague, does not include specific behavior, and requires the child to wait too long for the reward. Parents in a group can give feedback to other parents and share behavioral plans that were effective for their youth. For instance, Henry's parents were encouraged to use a behavior plan to target Henry's problems with his sister. They specified three key behaviors they wanted Henry to work on: hitting, screaming, and sharing. Hitting and screaming were relabeled as positive behaviors (asking nicely and using a calm voice). Henry received praise from his parents when they noticed these behaviors. Each day, Henry earned a reward if his parents noticed him doing these behaviors at least three times. The rewards were small, such as an extra cookie after dinner or 15 minutes of TV at night. Henry's behavior with his sister improved within 1 week of implementing this plan.

Disengagement From Child

Many parents who have a child with problem behavior have already disengaged from the process of parenting. In groups this attitude comes across as hopelessness, with statements such as "None of this will work on my child" or "My child is really hard, and I've already tried all of these things and they haven't worked." With these parents, it is even more important to begin with the relationship components of the curriculum, including building a positive foundation for change with the child. A strength-based approach is essential with disengaged parents because it helps the parents focus on the child's strengths and build from those strengths. Usually, parents can identify one aspect or strength that they enjoy in their child. Activities and routines should be adapted to include positive time between the parent and child that highlights this strength. For some parents, this is a slow process that includes implementing a flexible approach to parenting, changing their expectations, and starting over with their child to build a working relationship. The group can facilitate this insight and process for some parents. Consider the following:

> David attended the parenting group for help with his 14-year-old son, Daniel. David could not identify anything he liked about Daniel or any strengths, except that Daniel liked computers, which was a source of much of their conflict. A plan was developed to allow Daniel complete access to the computer while David worked on the relational components of parenting. With the conflict surrounding the computer gone, David began to experience Daniel in a more positive way at home and was able to see some additional strengths and build in positive activities with his son.

Lack of Routines and Structure in the Home

Most children and adolescents perform best with predictable routines and consequences for behavior. Many adults, however, do not like this lifestyle and lack routines in their household. For some families, such as those living in poverty or without consistent employment, routines are particularly challenging to develop. This common problem is related to a variety of other child behavior problems in many households. Predictable routines, especially in early childhood, are the main solution to various problem behaviors, such as bedtime problems, eating problems, and tantrums. Adolescents also perform best within a schedule of routines, including curfews, predictable mealtimes, and homework time. Routines in adolescence set the stage for parental monitoring as well as delineate expectations for behavior. Many parents do not understand the importance of routines and have not thought through how their own preferences for lack of routines have negatively affected their child's functioning. In a group context, parents can share information about routines that work and those that do not. Parents can support each other in the development of routines in their lives. Here is another case example:

Ashley was a working single parent with two children, ages 4 and 7. She returned from work late in the evening on most days, then proceeded to feed, bathe, and care for her children before bedtime. She was frustrated that her children did not easily go to bed on most nights. However, her bedtime routine was not predictable and was based on her particular mood when she returned from work. She reported that on days when she was tired, she liked to put the kids to bed early, but on days when she was in a good mood, she liked to put them to bed late, and sometimes they went out to rent a movie or went to the store after dinner. The lack of consistency in this routine led to bedtime problems every night, which were tiring for Ashley and ended the day with her children negatively. A new, clear routine helped change this bedtime pattern.

History of Difficult Parenting

This case history serves as an illustrative example:

Robert was a single father with two boys, ages 7 and 9. His primary problem was that the boys fought all the time, engaging in extreme violence and aggression. Robert's parenting solutions also involved violence (e.g., spanking with a paddle, locking them in their rooms for an hour). In the group context, Robert shared that his own parenting had been violent and abusive. Robert was motivated not to use the same techniques with his children. Discussion of parenting histories helped Robert and the group understand his parenting behavior.

Many parents who engage in punitive parenting have been victims of the same parenting strategies when they were younger. Participation in the group usually will help parents reflect on these strategies as they relate to their own childhood, and sharing these thoughts can be positive for both the group and the parent. Most parents can identify some aspects of the way they were parented that could be improved on. This discussion can include defining the ideal parent, and examining how barriers in each parent's life make it difficult to achieve this goal.

SUMMARY

This chapter describes some of the research that supports the use of parenting groups as a means of intervention with various populations, including youth who are normative, at-risk, and at high-risk. It outlines strategies for group facilitation, common problems, and common parent presentations. As with any approach to the treatment of child problems, parenting groups should highlight both child and parent strengths as a model for changing current behavior.

12

CHILD AND ADOLESCENT
INTERVENTION GROUPS

Conducting interventions with groups of youth who share the same clinical issue is the cornerstone of child psychology and social work. Indeed, almost every institutional context has such intervention groups, and the vast majority of children and adolescents receive group interventions (Dodge, Dishion, & Lansford, in press). Elementary schools construct special classrooms such as resource rooms, or track children into classrooms that have a high density of children with behavioral or achievement difficulties. Middle schools continue these practices but add to them by forming specific intervention groups to handle anger management, drug prevention, issues of divorce, social skills training, and depression. In middle school and high school, these practices are continued, along with the addition of alternative schools designed for the youth who are at risk, disaffected, or disengaged.

GROUP INTERVENTIONS AS HELPFUL

Most treatment programs that target adolescents conduct their work in groups of youth with similar behavior and emotional issues, including drug treatment, aggressiveness, delinquency, bulimia or anorexia nervosa, anxiety, depression, sexual abuse, and sexual acting out. There are compelling reasons for grouping youth as such. It is less expensive in therapist time, and it is easier to bill insurance for a specific treatment protocol that has a set agenda, sequence, and determination of completion. There is a therapeutic rationale as well. Group work facilitates sharing of thoughts, feelings, and experiences that may underlie the behavior or emotional difficulty. Hearing that others have shared the same painful experiences can be normalizing and validating. Groups can provide a context for role-playing and skill development. Members of groups can support or confront one another to promote therapeutic progress. Indeed, group work as psychotherapy is a common, often unquestioned practice of mental health professionals serving children.

There is evidence that group interventions are helpful. For example, the work by Lochman and colleagues suggests that a cognitive–behavioral intervention targeting the aggressive behavior of boys reduces problem behavior (Lochman, 1985, 1992; Lochman, Barry, & Pardini, 2003). The Fast Track preventive intervention includes a social skills training intervention for a group of elementary students at very high risk that suggests benefits (Bierman et al., 1999). Targeting social skills in elementary school results in improvement in these skills (Walker et al., 1983). The clearest evidence of effectiveness for group treatment, however, comes in the area of cognitive–behavioral treatment for depression, which has emerged as a best practice treatment (Clarke, DeBar, & Lewinsohn, 2003; Lewinsohn & Clarke, 1990; Weisz, Southam-Gerow, Gordis, & Connor-Smith, 2003). Group interventions can also be successful in preventing and treating childhood anxiety disorders (Dadds, Spence, Holland, Barrett, & Lacrens, 1997; Kendall, Aschenbrand, & Hudson, 2003).

GROUP INTERVENTIONS AS HARMFUL

Despite the compelling economical and therapeutic rationale and the evidence of effectiveness, there is considerable reason for concern about the potential of doing harm in group interventions. For instance, a special issue of the *Journal of Abnormal Child Psychology* described several intervention studies that revealed iatrogenic effects associated with youth at high risk in groups (Dishion & Dodge, 2005). The major shortcoming of child clinical science as of this writing is a naïve realism approach to the study of intervention outcome. Researchers select variables that are directly related to the target of the intervention and, when positive effects are observed, conclude that the intervention is helpful. This approach is naïve because of the lack of appreciation for the complexity of human behavior—often individuals reduce one behavior and learn a new, maladaptive behavior. It was for this reason that Kelly (1988), in developing the concept of an ecological paradigm for mental health services, introduced the radical notion that mental health interventions could have both negative and positive side effects and that studying these should be central to evaluation of intervention services.

In a review of the literature on peer contagion effects in mental health interventions, Dodge and Sherrill (in press) revealed that prevention studies with youth at high risk for delinquency and prevention programs for females at risk for bulimia have found iatrogenic effects. In a comprehensive review of all education, mental health, and juvenile justice programs, the evidence was clear that some peer group interventions do produce positive effects, whereas others produce negative effects. It can be concluded that interventions that aggregate peers tend to reduce the effect size in the best of all conditions and, in the worst, produce negative effects (Dodge & Sherrill, in press).

Minimizing Harm

Under what conditions does working in groups of youth produce harm and under which does it seem helpful? Figure 12.1 summarizes the literature

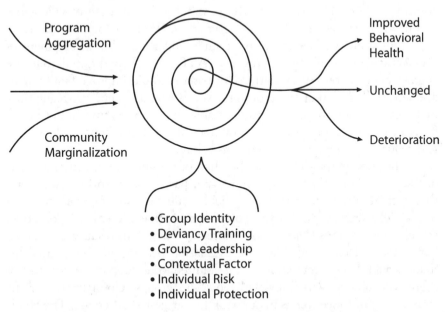

Figure 12.1. The maelstrom model for outcomes in group interventions.

on factors that undermine outcomes in group work with children and adolescents. In general, the situation can be thought of as a maelstrom, because outcomes for children are somewhat unpredictable in group settings. As shown in Figure 12.1, some youth can improve, others remain unchanged, and still others deteriorate. Because the child clinical literature reports primarily central tendencies, it is difficult to study the outcomes associated with group work. Fortunately, enough research indicates the possible candidates that undermine outcomes. As shown in Figure 12.1, factors that can impact the effectiveness of a group intervention may include group identity, group leadership styles, contextual factors, the youth's risk before entering treatment, and individual resiliency factors such as the youth's self-regulation (Dishion & Patterson, 2006).

Adolescent Transitions Program Study

Our own research on the effectiveness of group interventions with young adolescents at high risk suggested that the process of deviancy training was a probable cause of iatrogenic effects in group work with children and adolescents. We randomly assigned 120 youth to one of four groups: (a) a parent-only cognitive–behavioral group treatment, (b) a youth-only cognitive–behavioral group treatment, (c) a parent and youth group, with coordinated cognitive–behavioral treatment, or (d) a self-directed control group, which was provided with all of the informational content of the interventions in the form of newsletters and videotapes. We added a quasi-experimental control group of 39 to evaluate the possibility that the use of videotapes and newsletters was an effective intervention. We later found it was not.

This study was our initial pilot study underlying the development of the Adolescent Transitions Program (ATP). We hypothesized that the cognitive–behavioral interventions for parents would improve family management skills and that the groups for youth would benefit self-regulation. Self-regulation of youth and family management in parents would be reflected in a reduction in coercive interactions in the parent–child system and reductions in adolescent problem behavior.

The good news was that we had half of it right. In our initial analysis of the short-term effects of the youth and parent interventions, we found that each resulted in statistically reliable reductions in observed coercive interactions, in contrast to the control group that increased in observed coercive interactions (Dishion & Andrews, 1995). This result was what we hoped for and expected. Had the evaluation desisted at this point, this study would have been another randomized trial supporting the use of cognitive–behavioral therapy with youth in groups. Unfortunately, right away we began to see trends in our data that suggested otherwise. The youth reported more smoking, and teachers reported more delinquent behavior among the youth randomly assigned to the group interventions, in contrast to the parent-only and control groups (Dishion & Andrews, 1995).

Our concern about the potential iatrogenic effect of the group intervention was confirmed when we followed the data for 3 years following the randomized intervention. Poulin, Dishion, and Burraston (2001) used latent growth curve modeling to examine the specificity of iatrogenic effects on youths' growth in problem behavior (Muthén & Curran, 1997). The Muthén and Curran strategy involves two steps. The first step is estimating the normative growth (in this case, growth in the control group). Then, iatrogenic growth specific to the intervention group is estimated. There was significant iatrogenic growth in self-reported tobacco use over the course of 3 years, following random assignment to the group intervention. Statistically reliable increases were also indicated in teacher ratings of delinquent behavior over 3 years (Poulin et al., 2001).

These trends were certainly alarming to the investigative team. At the time, it was important to be especially cautious because these data were limited to one study—a pilot study at that. However, about the same time we were grappling with our iatrogenic findings, Joan McCord came to the University of Oregon to give the Leona Tyler Lecture. In her lecture, she focused on the negative effects discovered in the Cambridge-Sommerville Youth Study. During her visit, we discussed the fact that many of the boys in the treatment group were sent to summer camps—several times, in fact. The Cambridge-Sommerville Youth Study was unique in the level of statistical control incorporated in the design of the study. Pairs of youth were created by matching on a variety of characteristics including age, religion, physical stature, and history of antisocial behavior. Thus, when going back to the data, one could select out youth who received certain aspects of the program and compare their outcomes with their matched controls, as opposed to the control group in general.

This approach to design and analysis reduces the likelihood of confounding characteristics of the boys with the intervention they received. For example, it is possible that the most severe and problematic boys were sent to summer camp and that any untoward effect of summer camps on later outcomes would be confounded with the boys' tendency to be troublesome. Using the matched control design, McCord did indeed find that boys who went to at least two summer camps were 10 times more likely to experience negative life outcomes, including severe mental health problems, substance abuse, and criminal outcomes. We put our data together to provide a report to the *American Psychologist* that would alert the professional community to the possibility that group interventions with youth could potentially do harm (Dishion, McCord, & Poulin, 1999).

Iatrogenic Conditions

Following those studies, Ken Dodge formulated the Duke Executive Session on Deviant Peer Contagion. The executive sessions lasted for 3 years, resulting in a comprehensive report of the evidence (Dodge, Dishion, & Lansford, in press) as well as a series of related scientific reports published in a special issue of the *Journal of Abnormal Child Psychology* (Dishion & Dodge, 2005). This chapter benefits from the work of this group of scholars.

The evidence that group interventions potentially undermine benefits of interventions goes beyond those two studies. Lipsey (in press) conducted a comprehensive review of the literature on treatment effects for juvenile delinquency and found that effect sizes were reduced when interventions aggregated youth into groups. A recent special issue of the *Journal of Abnormal Child Psychology* presented further evidence for potential harm as a function of aggregation (Mager, Milich, Harris, & Howard, 2005).

Three sets of findings from this special issue are relevant to understanding and reducing negative effects of group treatment. First, aggregating youth into classrooms can undermine both achievement and behavioral outcomes for years afterward. Moreover, supporting first-grade public school teachers with easy-to-use behavior management practices can reduce the risk of peer aggregation into classrooms (Kellam, Ling, Merisca, Brown, & Ialongo, 1998; Schaeffer, Petras, Ialongo, Poduska, & Kellam, 2003; Warren, Schoppelrey, Moberg, & McDonald, 2005). The second relevant finding is from the Fast Track social skills intervention. Twenty-five percent of the group social skills interventions involving first and second graders at high risk became disrupted by out-of-control behavior that reduced the benefits of those sessions for all youth involved. Studies of group intervention with 10-year-old youth revealed that some youth had negative outcomes, and not necessarily in groups with youth who were homogenously high on antisocial behavior (Mager et al., 2005). In fact, heterogeneous groups tended to be more problematic than were homogenously high antisocial groups. Finally, in an effectiveness trial of the Reconnecting Youth program, there was wide variability in outcomes depending on the high school and teacher leading the classes. This selected intervention involves training teachers in a special high school classroom to specifically increase the engagement of youth who are on the verge of either dropping out of school or increasing substance use. It appeared that at least half of the classroom population actually increased their substance use and delinquent behavior compared with randomly assigned control participants.

The evidence is clear that group interventions can sometimes benefit clients and sometimes do harm. Therefore, it becomes critical for clinicians to know about the conditions that are most likely to lead to negative effects for children and adolescents. In light of the limited amount of intervention data on the specific conditions leading to negative effects, we need to consider developmental research on the social mechanisms underlying deviant peer contagion.

Developmental research is most useful for identifying mechanisms that would account for negative effects in group treatment. We return to the process referred to as deviancy training, which has been identified within adolescent friendships (discussed in chap. 3, this volume). Recall that deviancy training involves positive reactions to discussions of deviancy within peer interactions (Dishion, Spracklen, Andrews, & Patterson, 1996). Youth in friendships that selectively attend to and laugh in response to deviant talk and behavior, and ignore prosocial behavior, are those most prone to escalation in substance use, delinquent behavior, and even violence during the course of adolescence (Dishion, Capaldi, Spracklen, & Li, 1995; Dishion, Eddy, Haas, Li, & Spracklen, 1997; Dishion, Spracklen, et al., 1996). In fact, this process mediated the link between being in a deviant peer group as a young adolescent and engagement in serious problem behavior in young adulthood (Patterson, Dishion, & Yoerger, 2000). The problem is not the people who form the relationships; it's the repeated dynamics of those relationships.

It turns out that when adolescent friendships are studied, the faces change but the process remains the same (Dishion & Owen, 2002). There was a moderate level of stability ($r = .52$) over 5 years in the level of deviancy training assessed in videotaped friendship interactions even though only 10% of the participants were the same (Dishion & Owen, 2002). This level of stability in deviancy training suggests that individuals actively re-create friendship environments using deviance as an organizing dynamic (Kandel, 1996).

Until recently, it was generally assumed that deviant peer contagion was largely restricted to adolescents. Findings by Kellam and others on classroom assignment (Kellam et al., 1998) were assumed to be anomalous. Snyder et al. (2005) studied the friendship interactions of first-grade children with randomly selected classmates during a free-play episode in the classroom. They videotaped the free-play session and later coded the dynamic between each child and his or her classmate. They found that a pattern of mocking or acting out deviant themes, followed by laughter, was indeed reliably observable. It was especially alarming that these brief observations of deviancy training were negative effects and were the result of the interactions among group members and growth in covert forms of antisocial behavior both at home and at school over the ensuing year. As was similarly found in the data about adolescents, it appears that some antisocial children seek out reinforcement from peers for the deviant antics and, if they are successful in their hunt, escalate some forms of problem behavior.

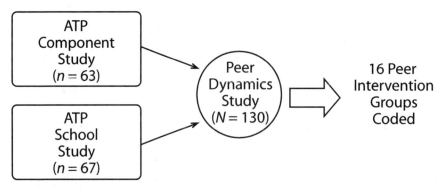

Figure 12.2. What group processes predicted iatrogenic growth?

How do these findings apply to group interventions with children and adolescents? One hypothesis suggests that therapists can inadvertently create artificial environments that reinforce the very behavior the intervention is designed to reduce. We examined this hypothesis by reanalyzing the group intervention data from our early ATP study that originally yielded iatrogenic results. Sixteen young adolescent peer intervention groups, each containing 12 sessions, were videotaped (see Figure 12.2).

We were especially interested in the informal interactions among the youth in the groups, especially when the group leaders were not structuring the session. Thus, we began coding the interactions that occurred before the group began; immediately before, during, and after the break (the 2-hour sessions included a brief 10-minute break in the middle); and toward the end of the group session. We used global ratings to describe the interactions of each child during each time sampled. We rated each youth on deviancy training with other peer group members, using items such as these: "This person got explicit group attention or status for counter-norm talk or problem behavior" or "This person engaged in counter-norm talk, problem behavior, or dressed or acted deviant." We also rated each participant on a variety of other group experiences that may have contributed to a positive or negative effect of the group on each youth's behavior (e.g., therapist-reinforced positive behavior, a positive connection with the older peer counselor, rejection by peers).

Using the statistical framework adopted for initially detecting the iatrogenic effects on smoking and delinquent behavior (Poulin et al., 2001), we entered the coded data from the videotaped peer group interactions. As shown in Figures 12.3 and 12.4, there were individual differences in youth's experiences in the groups and their escalations in problem behavior. For growth in delinquent behavior at school (as rated by teachers), the findings were quite clear. Deviancy training within the group predicted growth in delinquent behavior at school ($\beta = .34$, $p < .05$), whereas a positive relation-

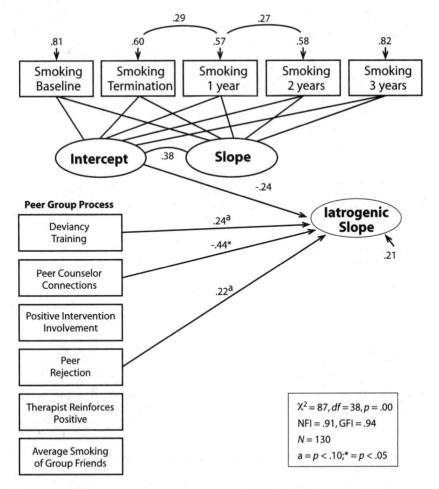

Figure 12.3. Group dynamics predictive of iatrogenic effects on smoking.

ship with the older peer counselor predicted lack of growth (β = −.37, p < .05). These findings are summarized in Figure 12.4. In addition, the youth who were less delinquent at school at the onset of the intervention escalated their behavior the most (β = −.94, p < .05).

The findings for predicting individual differences were alarmingly similar, despite the fact that one dependent variable was teacher report and the other self-report. As can be seen in Figure 12.3, deviancy training predicted growth in smoking in the 3 years following the intervention (β = .24, p < .10), as was rejection by other group members (β = .22, p < .10). In this analysis, the peer dynamics were marginally significant. However, positive connections with the peer counselor again revealed reduced growth in smoking in the 3 years following the intervention (β = −.44, p < .05). The protective effect of older peer counselors on iatrogenic growth was an

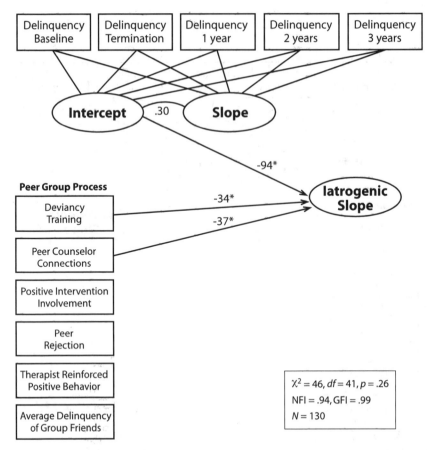

Figure 12.4. Group dynamics predictive of iatrogenic effects on delinquent behavior at school.

unexpected finding, albeit filled with practical implications for establishing guidelines for reducing the potential negative effects of peer contagion in group interventions.

Before we proceed to conjecture about how to reduce iatrogenic effects, some points about our science are in order. The ATP was really only a pilot study. The sample was rather small, and these findings may not replicate or extend to other group intervention research. We clearly need more research on group dynamics associated with both negative and positive change as a function of group interventions.

What we find compelling about the ATP findings, however, is the robustness of the trends despite the small sample and the fact that these analyses lack statistical power. It is noteworthy that the group effects were minimal and that the major trends were individual differences, which means that some youth were more likely to respond to the group intervention with iatrogenic growth. Thus, one cannot simply conclude that a poorly skilled therapist who was unable to manage young adolescents in groups was the reason for all of the negative effects. The number of youth whose behavior worsened was spread across groups. This result suggests that the processes that account for such effects are subtle and require considerable attention and skill on the part of the therapist to reduce and prevent them. Given the preponderance of group intervention activities in child and adolescent clinical and counseling psychology, we propose guidelines that we hypothesize will reduce the potential for iatrogenic effects.

SOME GUIDELINES

The general trend of current writing is that group interventions with children and adolescents are to be avoided when the focus is problem behavior—and the evidence is overwhelming that such behavior is functionally embedded within the peer environment. As we discuss in this volume, the evidence favors family-centered interventions for child and adolescent problem behavior and, therefore, this is the intervention of choice. However, as detailed in chapter 9 (this volume), direct interventions with children and adolescents are a useful adjunct to those that focus on the family and parenting practices. Work by Kazdin, Siegel, and Bass (1992) provides an example of an empirically supported approach to working with children and adolescents to develop self-regulation skills that inhibit conduct problems. This intervention does not involve groups.

Group interventions with children and adolescents are probably most justified when they address depression and anxiety among children and adolescents without comorbid problem behavior. From both a developmental and a clinical perspective, this approach makes sense. Depressed youth are likely those with a history of marginal peer relationships, and in this context, group work accomplishes two therapeutic goals: contact with peers and cognitive–behavioral skills underlying mood regulation. A similar case could be made for anxious children.

As the science of child clinical psychology progresses, we hope that researchers will be able to determine (a) under what conditions group interventions are advisable and (b) under what conditions they are highly discouraged. For example, systematic research by Waldron and Flicker (2002) found that cognitive–behavioral interventions with adolescents to reduce marijuana and other substance use showed positive effects for the group intervention. Thus, in summary, group interventions are most likely to be one part of an overall service armamentarium for children and adolescents.

One important consideration is to think contextually. Child and adolescent intervention groups are used in a variety of service settings, including

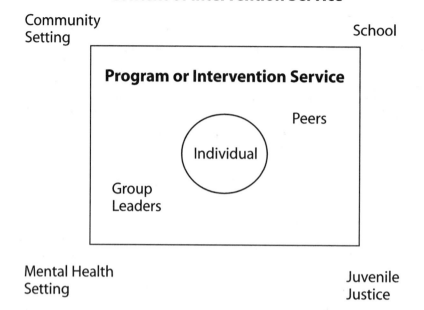

Context of Intervention Service

Community
Setting

School

Program or Intervention Service

Peers

Individual

Group
Leaders

Mental Health
Setting

Juvenile
Justice

Figure 12.5. An ecological framework for understanding and preventing deviant peer contagion.

juvenile justice centers, mental health agencies, public schools, and other community service settings. The location and service setting, in itself, may contribute or detract from its effectiveness (Dishion, McCord, & Poulin, 1999). For example, it is not uncommon to observe groups of adolescents standing outside a community mental health clinic, alternative school, or other community agency sharing a smoke or talking. They may share transportation to and from the group, which puts these youth in contact with each other in unsupervised contexts (e.g., public bus stations). From an ecological perspective, the context of a service may be as important as the service itself, with respect to facilitating or detracting from informal interactions and the formation of friendships. Thus, as shown in Figure 12.5, it is important to consider the informal and formal ecology of the group and to minimize the potential for informal interactions that would potentially undermine the goals of the intervention.

The developmental level of the individual is likely to be an important factor in his or her response to a group intervention. For example, Alcoholics Anonymous and Narcotics Anonymous are group intervention programs that provide a service supportive of abstinence that is helpful to many (W. R. Miller, 1993). Researchers have speculated that group interventions are most likely to be iatrogenic regarding problem behaviors that are functional within a given developmental period. For example, in the transition into elementary school, children at high risk assume new forms of problem behaviors, such as lying and stealing, as part of the entry process into a peer group in that school. In a similar way, studies on tobacco use (Kaplan, 1973, 1975, 1978) proposed that smoking in early adolescence enhances self-esteem. We proposed that such an effect would be most pronounced for youth with marginal peer relationships, in which smoking eased a rough social transition from middle to high school (Dishion, Capaldi, et al., 1995). One could see delinquent behavior at school serving a similar function. However, our group interventions did not have an iatrogenic effect on alcohol and marijuana use. In comparison, Duncan and colleagues (Duncan, Boisjoly, Kremer, Levy, & Eccles, 2005) found that during the transition to college, aggregating roommates with drinking histories increased heavy drinking in schools.

Thus, youth would be most vulnerable to group interventions during transition points that involve social change and when targeted behaviors are novel and potentially functional within the peer group. It is ironic that selected interventions that pull out and aggregate youth at risk may inadvertently do the most to escalate their problem behaviors.

Reducing Iatrogenic Effects

As our data suggest, these effects seem to be linked to the kinds of interactions between children and other group members. Thus, a guideline for reducing the potential for iatrogenic effects is to supervise youth closely and provide structure during sessions, as well as before, during, and after breaks. Informal interactions that reinforce deviance should be discouraged and, most important, prevented. This is easier said than done. When we were developing a code system for the analyses reported earlier, we had a very bright undergraduate student attempting to code deviancy training. He became discouraged when it became clear how subtle the dynamic could be and how challenging it would be to train other coders to see the process. For example, a 12-year-old boy who sincerely discusses quitting smoking within a group of other adolescents at risk is likely getting high dosages of reinforcement for his deviancy. Because his behavior is novel for that developmental age, he certainly experiences the rapt attention of the group members for his efforts to reduce his adultlike smoking addiction. If one were simply coding laughter in response to deviant talk, the dynamic would be rarely noted. However, group attention and interest are likely to be very reinforcing, especially for youth with a history of peer rejection and isolation. Thus, group leaders must be attentive to subtle and indirect forms of rein-forcement and curtail interactions that inadvertently give group status to individuals that are secondary to their deviant behavior.

One way to influence the implicit culture of the group is to have older peers as members of the group. In our ATP peer group interventions, we worked very hard to identify older adolescents with definable prosocial skills to model prosocial behavior. This task is not as easy as it seems. Older adolescents without a history of problem behavior are not interesting to younger adolescents at high risk. The most effective older peer counselors were those who had a history of problem behavior but had clearly changed their ways. It was especially helpful if they were socially skilled. When working with older adolescent counselors, we met before each session and practiced specific interactions that fit within the cognitive–behavioral curriculum. For example, each session had role-plays that provided practice for specific skills within the curriculum. We often used the older adolescents as strategic plants who could raise or answer questions and who could volunteer for role-play activities. It is clear that the extent to which the older peer counselors affectively engaged with their younger peers served as a protective factor, reducing iatrogenic growth.

The problem of iatrogenic effects associated with children and adolescent group interventions has several far-reaching implications for clinical and counseling psychology. The most significant is the importance of clinical training. Services for children and adolescents are often performed by community therapists with limited training (Weiss, Catron, Harris, & Phung, 1999). Perhaps one of the reasons such services are largely ineffective is a result of the lack of training (Weiss et al., 1999; Weisz, Weiss, Han, Granger, & Morton, 1995). It is our sense that effective group work with children and adolescents would require extensive training in the following four areas.

First, it is essential that clinicians understand the research on peer influence and the powerful dynamics that can emerge in unsupervised groups of children at high risk. It is important to think ecologically when offering services. A service offered in a community center may provide a context for young people to interact informally before and after the group. Group interventions in schools, however, may have more control over these informal interactions. Second, therapists must be able to identify peer interactions that are potentially supportive of deviance. As discussed, many of these interactions are likely to be subtle. Third, clinicians must have a strong set of group-leadership skills in engagement and motivation as well as redirection of problematic groups if they get off track. Finally, videotaping or audiotaping group interventions and seeking supervision for problematic group dynamics is essential for maintaining high levels of therapist performance.

Possible Extensions

The work in this chapter focuses primarily on outpatient group work with children and adolescents primarily referred for problem behaviors typically falling into the diagnostic label of disruptive behavior disorders. We simply do not yet have the data to determine to what extent iatrogenic effects apply to a variety of interventions that aggregate such as summer camps for troubled youth and groups for combatting eating disorders (e.g., bulimia and anorexia nervosa). We conjecture that there is reason to be cautious when applying a group intervention with children and adolescents as well. For example, binge eating (and purging) behaviors cluster in college dormitory houses (Crandall, 1988). It would make sense that under some conditions, bringing together adolescent girls could eventually lead to adoption of the behavior patterns one wishes to prevent. In a similar way, when suicide attempts are reported in the media an increase in adolescent suicide ensues (Gould, Jamieson, & Romer, 2003). On the basis of this observation, it would seem unwise, therefore, to bring together youth who are at high risk for suicide. Although no data indicate that iatrogenic effects necessarily follow from group interventions for these issues, there is sufficient evidence that contagion processes apply and therefore, considerable caution is in order.

SUMMARY

One of the most important implications of an ecological approach is that our research must become more sophisticated, responsible, and detailed in documenting both the benefits and the harm of interventions targeting children and adolescents. The evidence of iatrogenic effects associated with youth group interventions drives this point home and has serious implications (in both policy and practice) for several agency domains. On the basis of the available data, we suggest avoiding group intervention strategies with children and adolescents when the focus is on problem behavior, especially when the strategy is selecting out a group of children or adolescents deemed at risk. We are also cautious in recommending group intervention for any form of psychopathology that involves a behavior that may be influenced by peers, including eating disorders, sexual behavior, and possibly some forms of adolescent suicide. However, some data suggest that group interventions can be effective, especially for depression and anxiety. On the basis of our own limited research, we provide guidelines in this chapter for managing group interventions that consider both the context of the groups and the processes within the group that most likely underlie negative intervention effects.

IV

PROFESSIONAL AND ETHICAL CONSIDERATIONS

13

THE ECOLOGY OF THE CHILD
AND FAMILY THERAPIST

The move to implement empirically supported interventions for children and families often ignores the dynamics of the service delivery context regarding therapist performance and child and family change. We believe this omission is not trivial, because therapist performance is very likely maintained by a set of contingencies and supervisory support processes. It seems reasonable to assume that low pay, too many clients, poor training, lack of supervision, low morale, and an eclectic intervention model certainly would undermine the quality of therapist practice. In general, the external validity of child and adolescent clinical research, especially research on the organizational conditions related to the quality of empirically supported child and family interventions, is limited (Weisz, Doss, & Hawley, 2005). In this chapter, we discuss the features of effective interventions from the standpoint of the therapist and the context within which he or she functions, including the importance and function of a team approach to working with children and families. We also review issues related to supervision and case management in a team approach to intervention and service delivery.

It has become increasingly clear that the cornerstone of therapeutic effectiveness, even for empirically supported interventions, is the therapist. Wampold (2001) examined the role of the therapist in reducing adult depression, when the client was randomly assigned to cognitive–behavioral therapy, interpersonal therapy, and medication. Contrary to expectation, the majority of the variation in clinical outcomes was attributed to therapist effects (Wampold, 2001). This finding is often referred to as a *nonspecific factor of therapy*. It cannot be attributed to any particular school of therapy. Wampold argued that the differences often observed in community services and clinical intervention trials are a result of therapist effects and that if the community practitioners with the best client outcomes are selected out, effect sizes for community and clinical trials will be equivalent (Wampold, 2001).

This argument raises the question of what conditions produce an effective therapist. We know that changing parenting practices can be conceptualized as *working with resistance* (Stoolmiller, Duncan, Bank, & Patterson, 1993). Parents with higher levels of psychopathology are less likely to change during interventions (Kazdin & Wassell, 1998). What are the conditions that promote the high levels of performance necessary to work with the often-difficult dynamics of clinical change to produce positive outcomes for children and adolescents?

To provide an empirical account of the conditions that might lead to positive outcomes, we need research that links therapist performance to parents' change in parenting practices and to child improvement. As of this writing, only one study has accomplished all of this. Recent work by Forgatch, Patterson, and DeGarmo (2005) directly observed therapist fidelity to the Oregon Social Learning Center (OSLC) approach to parental management training. They found that direct observation of therapist fidelity to the OSLC intervention was predictive of observed improvements in parenting practices of stepfamilies at high risk. The measurement of therapist fidelity is critical in this study. Videotapes of therapist–client interactions were coded with a macro rating system that encapsulated the therapist's skills in managing parents' resistance to change. Because of the use of direct observation, this study is an important contribution to previous research, showing that adherence to multisystemic therapy predicts positive change among adolescents with multiple problems (Huey, Henggeler, Brondino, & Pickrel, 2000).

In adult models of intervention, it is common for treatments to occur within a small team, perhaps consisting of a therapist and a supervisor. In private practice situations, an individual therapist or counselor may be operating with no supervision. In this sense, adult therapy occurs in isolation from other professionals and, as a result, is vulnerable to ethical problems and malpractice.

In child and family work, this setup is less common and, in fact, may be detrimental to the health and well-being of both the family and the therapist. By nature, effective interventions with children and families demand a coordinated team approach, including group supervision. This is particularly true given the current state of mental health services for families, which are underfunded and short term, leading to chronic mental health problems and complex clinical presentations at most clinics. We argue in this chapter that child and family work requires a team approach to case management and regular supervision of therapists and professionals who work with this population.

Behavioral interventions were once thought to be a technology of change. The therapist needed only do an accurate behavioral analysis and modify the reinforcement contingencies, and change was guaranteed. This optimistic stance had many advantages compared with the psychodynamic therapy. Virtually anyone could change and benefit from mental health services, regardless of their intellectual readiness or socioeconomic status. Recall that mental health services were once designed almost exclusively for the privileged socioeconomic classes. Social work was the venue for serving the mental health needs of the poor.

The polarity between the esoteric psychodynamic view of therapy and the proletariat behavioral perspective began to shrink in the early 1980s. Patterson (1985) pointed out, for example, that effective behavioral interventions for children and families required clinical skills on the part of the therapist to achieve significant improvement in children's problem behavior. The title of this pivotal work in the behavioral psychology movement began with "Beyond technology . . . ." This work was soon followed by a series of studies about defining clinical skills that effectively navigated the waters of parents' resistance to change (e.g., Patterson & Chamberlain, 1994; Patterson & Forgatch, 1985; Stoolmiller, Duncan, et al., 1993). We reviewed much of this work in chapter 10 (this volume).

THERAPIST IN CONTEXT

Just as children and families can be viewed in light of a complex community ecology, therapists can also benefit from the same perspective. We propose that therapists require emotional, material, and social support to maintain the high levels of functioning necessary to be effective in working with children and families in distress. It is unreasonable to expect a human being to provide mental health services to large numbers of children and families without adequate support. However, literally thousands and thousands of therapists serve children and families while working under difficult circumstances without those support systems. In fact, most mental health services to children and adolescents are delivered by social service agencies because most insurance reimbursement does not cover extensive mental health treatment for children and adolescents.

The most immediate context for maintaining therapist motivation and skills is the supervisory team. Almost all agencies have staff meetings or

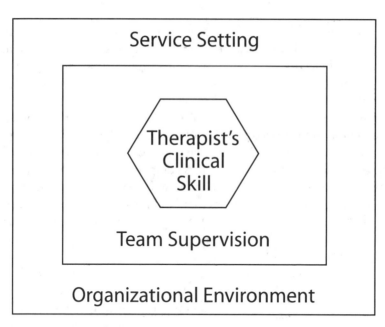

Figure 13.1. The context of therapist skills.

case conferences, usually weekly. However, how these meetings are conducted may vary from service setting to service setting. In this chapter, we discuss the function and dynamics of team supervision that are likely to lead to positive therapeutic outcomes.

The next level of influence is the organization within which an intervention service is provided. An organization that is low on resources, has poor leadership, is characterized by conflict, or is unclear in its objectives is not an optimal environment for forming an effective supervisory team. However, an organization that provides ample training, has clear objectives, is oriented toward client outcomes, and promotes accountability and support is one that is likely to provide the foundation for effective intervention teams as well as higher levels of clinical skill and child and family outcomes. The ecological perspective on therapist clinical skill is summarized in Figure 13.1.

Team Supervision

Considerable research on the characteristics of work teams applies to the function of therapeutic team supervision groups (Ilgen, Hollenbeck, Johnson, & Jundt, 2005). Team supervision serves three functions that promote effective interventions for children and families (see Figure 13.2 for overview): (a) supporting the achievement of a therapeutic perspective

Getting Perspective	Developing a Strategy	Intervention Maintenance
• Use model • Videotape • Gauge emotional reactions • Present alternative views	• Self-assess • Focus discussion • Problem solve • Model and role play • Supervise • Use date	• Develop therapeutic plan • Follow through • Support success • Review videos • Self-assess

Figure 13.2. The three functions of team supervision.

and case conceptualization, (b) problem-solving an effective intervention strategy that is likely to address both the dynamics of change and realistic change goals, and (c) maintaining an intervention strategy through the ebb and flow of the clients' change dynamics. We discuss each of these functions in some detail. In fact, therapists benefit from the supervision team in the same way clients benefit from therapeutic interventions, which will become clear throughout the discussion that follows.

Getting Perspective

One of the difficulties of clinical work in general, and child and family interventions specifically, is developing a professional perspective that is useful to the change process. When interventions are eclectic (every therapist is in charge of his or her own therapeutic approach) or exclusively one therapy (psychodynamic, behavioral, etc.), the therapist's perspective on a child and family may not always fit the family's reality. As such, change is unlikely, and therapy may even be counterproductive. We have discussed the importance of case conceptualization throughout this volume. A critical feature of case conceptualization is getting perspective on the change dynamics for any given client (see chap. 9, this volume). This aspect is especially important in interventions with culturally diverse families. Thus, the cultural representation of the client population within the therapeutic team is essential to support appropriate and sensitive interventions.

FEATURES OF A STRONG SUPERVISION TEAM

A critical feature of an effective intervention strategy is the supervision team. As with the intervention model, the function of the team is to motivate, support, and provide objective feedback.

Model-Driven Interventions

The hallmark of a team approach to intervention involves a coordinated group of service providers that are centered around one particular model or approach to working with families. In general, work groups function best when the team members have a large set of values that overlap (Ilgen et al., 2005). There are two ways to accomplish a model-driven team approach. One is to have a rigorous set of training procedures so that individuals in the team have a shared skill base. The second approach is to include in the training an overview of the empirical literature on a model underlying the intervention procedure. For example, it is helpful for a therapist team to understand that in light of the complexity of a child and family case, prioritizing interventions that target family management practices is likely to produce the best result.

The best practice for most child or family problems involves a group of therapists or providers who work closely together on different aspects of the family problem, coordinating their services and working from a team perspective with the family. Case managers or lead therapists facilitate the coordination of treatment with various aspects of the system, including parents, the individual child, and the teachers.

Using a developmental, ecological model to understand and intervene in child mental health problems necessitates a focus on the child's functioning across multiple levels (e.g., school, home, individual child, and parents). It is not feasible for one therapist to work intensely with each of these subsystems. In fact, when only one therapist is treating the family and only one area of functioning or one subsystem is targeted, the outcome is oftentimes a piecemeal approach to treatment that does not address all of the problems and potential areas for change. A team approach involves a group of service providers, each working independently on various clinical issues but coordinating the treatment with the case manager and treatment team.

In a similar manner, a team approach involves a consistent model applied to every family served in the clinic or mental health center. This approach is very different from what is suggested and even recommended by adult-based psychotherapy research. Various meta-analyses and outcome research in adult work have supported a so-called "Do-Do Bird" hypothesis—that is, all psychotherapies are equally effective in terms of their outcomes, and there are negligible differences in the effects produced by any one type of therapy over another (Wampold et al., 1997). Unfortunately, this adult-based research has been applied to child and family therapy—situations in which this hypothesis is simply not true. Some approaches to working with child and family mental health (e.g., family focused, behavioral) have been shown to be significantly more efficacious in changing child behavior than have many forms of traditional, child-focused therapy (Weisz, Weiss, Han, Granger, & Morton, 1995).

The literature contains several examples of successful team approaches, including the Oregon Multidimensional Treatment Foster Care Model (Chamberlain & Smith, 2003) and the Multisystemic Treatment approach (Henggeler, Schoenwald, Borduin, Rowland, & Cunningham, 1998). In both of these examples, the populations served are families with severe-to-chronic mental health problems in several areas of functioning. The team is organized around a model of change, the model is implemented by each member of the team, and reassessment and evaluation of the outcomes occur regularly to allow for flexibility and adaptation of the treatment approach. The treatment is manual-based, and training is provided for each of the service providers in the system. Both of these models of treatment have been successful at reducing child conduct problems in both short-term and long-term follow-up studies.

Videotaping of All Clinical Contacts

Feedback is a critical feature that maintains high levels of work performance in general (Latham & Pinder, 2005), and for therapist skills in particular (Wampold, 2001). Videotaped feedback is an especially important venue for improving therapist performance (Bernard & Goodyear, 1992; Calhoun, Moras, Pilkonis, & Rehm, 1998). All therapy sessions are videotaped, and these tapes are used in supervision to conceptualize the family, show therapy examples, and get feedback on the treatment; this includes sessions that occur in the home or school, which are taped with mobile video cameras. Videotaping may make some families and therapists uncomfortable. We feel that appropriate supervision in complex child or family cases cannot be provided without videotape available for supervisors and peers to review. Families who are concerned about taping should be assured of confidentiality and the use of tapes. Therapists concerned about videotaping may worry about being criticized for their treatment, which is a direct outcome of an unsupportive supervision team or baggage left over from academically oriented clinical training.

It is difficult, if not impossible, to get perspective on the change dynamic with a client without recording sessions. In our approach, we videotape all sessions, including those conducted in the home. Digital cameras allow for easy, unobtrusive videotaping.

It is interesting that therapists often cooperate with videotaping, yet rarely review their own videotapes. More interesting is that videotapes of sessions are often not brought to clinical meetings when cases are being discussed and team supervision elicited. This situation probably stems from clinical training that gave center stage to the client rather than the therapist.

When the therapist switches perspective and becomes concerned about providing the best service possible, then he or she wants input from supervisors and peers with respect to eliciting discussions that provide insight into the interventions most likely to be successful and well-received by a child and family. In general, seeking supervision and active self-assessment are two key features of higher levels of performance of complex tasks (Latham & Pinder, 2005). It has certainly been our experience that therapists in training advance to the highest levels when they actively review their videotapes, seek supervision parsimoniously, and have accurate self-assessments about their strengths and weaknesses in working with children and families.

Videotaping is critical for ethical practice and supervision of child or family cases in a team approach. Videotapes provide examples of interventions that are working as well as those that are less effective. Therapists can get direct feedback from supervisors and peers on the basis of the videotaped sessions. Videotapes also provide a forum for assessing a therapist's adherence to the model and treatment, as well as for examination of process issues that may be facilitating change.

Emotional Reactions

It is unrealistic to think that clinical work with children and families is not going to elicit some strong emotional reactions that may or may not interfere with the quality of service a professional provides. One important function of a trusted supervision team is to allow the therapist to feel comfortable sharing these thoughts and feelings. Giving these reactions airtime can be invaluable as a first step toward the therapist's self-regulation and development of a more constructive perspective. Effective groups often vent by using self-revealing humor. It is important that the supervision group not reinforce negative attitudes but, rather, that the therapist struggle to get perspective on his or her affective attitudes toward a client. The difference is subtle but important. If a client reminds the therapist of a negative experience in childhood, it is important that the therapist notice this and make the appropriate adjustments. Note the following example:

> *Therapist:* I need to talk about Deb a bit, as I think I have some baggage around her coming out that I need to get a handle on. I see her as being completely self-centered and neglecting her adolescent son Josh. It's as if she expects her newfound sexual orientation should be completely received with open arms by Josh.

> *Peer therapist:* I can see why you'd react that way. You know, it's not easy coming out and being a parent. Maybe this mom

would benefit from some time during which you listened and supported her stress over the past year related
to coming out; then she would be in a better place to
think about Josh's needs. Maybe this mom needs to
know that when she's undergoing stress like she is, it
is natural to be self-focused. That's why it's important
that Josh have his own therapist who is neutral to
these particular issues. Then you can focus on the
parenting dynamics and leave the processing of all the
recent changes to Josh's therapist.

In this way, the therapist moves beyond getting mad at a parent and
gains perspective from her peer. The change in perspective is an important
one. If the therapist did not address this issue, the therapist's negativity
toward Deb may eventually leak out into the interpersonal relationship and
over time undermine the change process. The more important issue is
assuring Deb that she is being supported in her efforts to refocus on her
parenting, provide support, and actually create the needed boundaries between her personal issues and the adolescent son's reactions, which may
not always meld well.

Alternative Views

As suggested, when the therapist is free to air his or her emotional
reactions to providing services to specific families, then the supervision team
can be helpful with respect to offering alternative views of the parent and
child. As we discuss in the next sections, alternative views are not competitive views of the family. For example, a dysfunctional supervision team
would compete for the floor or argue about the best way to view a child or
family situation. It is important that alternative views be offered respectfully
and that they are listened to with respect by the therapist seeking supervision.
Another example follows:

Peer supervisor: You know, one way to look at this situation is that if
we meet with the dad during this conflict, we are
inadvertently agreeing that he is the one that should
be making the decision.

Supervisor: Yes, that's what's been bothering me about this! By
playing into this couple's dynamic of letting the dad
call the shots, we are inadvertently reinforcing the
mom's helplessness. I don't think we want to do that.

The effective supervision team can brainstorm alternative views of a
family situation or build on each other's comments and perspectives. It is

not helpful, however, to argue or to assert one's perspective. If confusion remains after a team supervision meeting, then the therapist can seek supervision from the appropriate supervisor. In this case, the team was being helpful because the dynamic with a specific couple was particularly subtle and easy to miss, especially for a therapist whose emotions were being stressed to the maximum in the face of intense marital conflict.

A supervision team can also provide perspective on potential boundary problems and confusions. Effective child or family interventions do not occur in a clinic within a 50-minute time slot. They are community based and contextual, sensitive to diversity, and often require services to be delivered late in the evening or at unique locations. As a result, it is difficult for some therapists to create professional boundaries around the family that are healthy and sensitive to the needs of both the family and the professional. For example, in adult models, therapists are usually taught to address with the client the possibility of seeing the client outside of therapy (such as running into the client at the grocery store) and how they would handle the confidential relationship if that occurred. This conversation is also important to have with child or family clients; however, most children and families will readily say hello to therapists in the community. Many parents will also ask for quick parenting tips or give updates on the family's weekly functioning. We have found that this interaction is usually more uncomfortable for the therapist than for the client. Supervision can allow for processing these events and the emotions that surround them as well as discussing boundary issues in the context of treatment.

A trusted, supportive supervision team is in the best position to navigate the nuances of effectively managing the clinical change process. For example, some research suggests that therapist self-disclosure improves the therapeutic alliance and outcomes in adult therapy (Barrett & Berman, 2001). In child and family work, therapist self-disclosure is a complex issue and is often discouraged. A therapist with children in advanced placement school settings or elite sports teams could easily undermine a parent's sense of confidence. Teams can help the beginning therapist get perspective on the type and level of information to share with a client about his or her own family circumstances.

Peer Support

The very nature of this work is at times stressful and complex. More seasoned clinicians who have experience reading complex family histories and hearing about family dysfunction can support novice therapists, who may be overwhelmed simply with the content of some family histories. Peer support within a team approach is critical to the overall functioning of the family. Struggles with one aspect of the treatment can be discussed and supported across alternate systems of the treatment plan.

By nature, the team approach is grounded in a systems perspective, and hence when one component of the system changes, there will likely be changes in other aspects of the system. Some of these changes may not be positive or perceived as positive by the participants and, as such, may be stressful for the treatment provider who is working with that part of the system.

> David and Susan brought their 13-year-old daughter, Chelsea, in for treatment when they suspected she was using drugs after school with her peers. Both David and Susan work in the afternoon, and therefore they had trouble monitoring Chelsea, who was spending unsupervised time with her peers at their home and using marijuana. One day, Susan came home early from work and caught her daughter smoking with her peers. The treatment team included two therapists—one to work with David and Susan on monitoring and effective limit setting, and the other to work with Chelsea on peer relations and coping skills. David decided to change his work schedule and pick up Chelsea after school to avoid the unsupervised time and to spend some quality time with his daughter. Soon after this change, David and Susan reported feeling much better about parenting Chelsea, and Chelsea reported a decrease in substance use behavior. However, Chelsea became angry and hostile, lashing out at the therapist and blaming the therapist for all her peer problems at school. The therapist was concerned about the change and consulted the team. This anger was a result of losing her freedom in the afternoons, and the therapist worked with the treatment team and family to identify other areas of freedom for Chelsea that would facilitate her independence and growth in a safe environment.

Note that in the preceding example, a therapist working in isolation with an adolescent is much less able to accurately interpret the adolescent's anger and is also less able to activate the system to make changes that are developmentally appropriate and therapeutic for the adolescent and parents in the system.

A group process that allows for flexibility and support is critical in intervention teams. As discussed earlier, child and family mental health tends to be complicated and requires a group process that allows for sorting through the information and targeting important areas of change. The team should meet weekly and review the progress of each family, review data and assessment material to assess the success of the program, and plan for the next week of treatment. Each therapist or treatment provider should summarize his or her work for the week, and the supervisor should facilitate a coordinated discussion of cases. Data from the Parent Daily Report (discussed later in this chapter) can be used to evaluate the efficacy of the treatment for the week and to plan for the future.

DEVELOPING A STRATEGY

The second major function of a supervision team is to support the development of an intervention strategy or a treatment plan. This critical function depends on the following features:

Individual Supervision

Although team supervision is a critical feather of our model, individual supervision is indispensable. We discuss features of individual supervision that are especially helpful.

Self-Assessment

It is often thought that seeking supervision is a sign of incompetence. Of course, an unhealthy dependency between a therapist and supervisor, or supervisory team, is not optimal, because it implies that the therapist is untrained, overwhelmed, or uncomfortable with his or her leadership role in the change process.

There is virtually no correlation between years of experience as a therapist and clinical outcomes that benefit clients (Dawes, 1994). We think one critical ingredient of effective therapy, which may come with experience, is self-understanding and accurate self-assessment as it relates to therapeutic work with children and families. In our clinical training model, we ask doctoral trainees to conduct a self-assessment of their strengths and weaknesses as they pertain to child and family interventions. We often find that the trainees who are most realistic in their self-appraisals, regardless of training background, benefit most from clinical training and supervision.

It is interesting to note that useful supervision is actually driven by the supervisee. A supervisor or supervisory team cannot influence a therapist unless he or she is amenable to change and influence. Thus, taking the time to understand one's strengths and weaknesses in clinical work with children and families provides the foundation for effective service delivery and professional growth.

Thus, if a therapist tends to be more interpersonally quiet and is confronted with an assertive, chaotic family, he or she may need to self-appraise his or her natural tendencies and develop strategies that will be more effective in managing sessions.

Focused Discussion

Team supervision meetings can be extremely chaotic and irrational. It is important that both the therapist seeking supervision and the team collaborate to guide a discussion that functions to solve a clinical problem. The function of the therapist and the case presentation is to accentuate the relevant (Fischoff & Downs, 1997). The therapist can structure this discussion by his or her case presentation and framing the issue of concern.

> One of the issues I'd like some help with is navigating the joint custody situation when giving feedback to this family next week. I'm wondering if it would be more constructive to meet with each parent separately or to meet with the two of them together.

This manner of structuring a case presentation provides a prompt to the group that this is a problem-solving discussion with a specific problem to be solved. The group members need not discuss this issue, but it certainly would be helpful for group members to keep this problem in mind when asking questions and providing suggestions and support.

Problem Solving

Because a critical function of the supervisory team is to solve a problem, the group should support good problem-solving processes. Central to a group's ability to support problem solving are cohesion, positive affect, good communication, and the absence of conflict and negative affect (Cantor & Harlow, 1994; Forgatch, 1989). As discussed, it is also important that the group share an intervention model and training experiences from which they can draw when engaged in a problem-solving discussion.

There are three basic steps to problem solving (Forgatch & Patterson, 1989). The first step is developing a neutral problem statement, which can be accomplished in the case presentation and by the group in helping the therapist get perspective on a family. The second step is brainstorming solutions or, in this case, intervention strategies. Brainstorming is a very delicate process. Criticism or negativity in a group does not support brainstorming for creative solutions. If a therapist is worried about the comments or thoughts of peers, then he or she will be less likely to suggest new intervention ideas. Thus leadership in creating a group atmosphere that is nonthreatening and supportive is essential for teams to be effective in brainstorming. Humor is a wonderful tool for loosening up a group to be creative and nonjudgmental.

The final step in a problem-solving process is for the therapist to select an intervention strategy. Suggesting multiple intervention strategies is an important form of support by the supervisory team. However, arguing over the best strategy is not a form of support, and it undermines the therapist's professional autonomy. Group supervision should be structured so that the therapist is given many ideas and is left to sort through them to develop an intervention plan that is realistic and effective in light of the ecology of the child and family, the service setting, and the skills of the therapist. If a solution is difficult, the therapist should seek supervision, scheduling sessions to accommodate opportunities for it.

Supervision

A team approach to treatment involves a clear hierarchy for supervision and case coordination. In this approach, one person coordinates the services and manages all aspects of the treatment plan. Supervision is provided either by this case manager or by an outside supervisor who ensures adherence to the model and provides support for all treatment providers on the team. In our clinic, we provide several different modes of supervision, including a large-group case presentation, smaller group peer supervision, and individual supervision on an as-needed basis.

Each of these modes of supervision allows for different aspects of training and supervision that are critical to the team approach and form a pyramid of support (see Figure 13.3). The large-group supervision model (8–10 or more) provides a forum for case conceptualization and overall planning. Therapists use videotape and data to present cases and then solicit feedback from the large group. In this context, the other group members

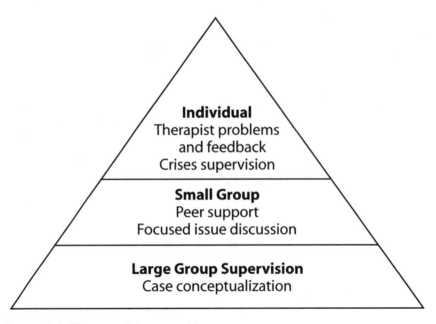

Figure 13.3. The supervision pyramid.

can help coordinate the treatment for the family. Large-group presentations are also used to discuss both successes and failures with families, which is beneficial to all the group members. Peers give feedback and support to the therapist team and learn about the family and the treatment model.

A small-group supervision model (5–6 therapists) allows for additional peer support and individual support to therapists. Cases can be discussed more in-depth, and peers can be tapped to help solve ethical dilemmas and treatment problems. Cases can be tracked weekly in small groups, and treatment progress can be assessed. Familiarity with the families helps facilitate peer discussion and feedback to therapists. Individual supervision is used to discuss personal difficulties that arise when working with families and ways to overcome the difficulties in the context of the treatment. For the most part, individual supervision is reserved for problems that cannot be adequately addressed in the group format.

Role-Plays

We often role-play with clients to provide them with the confidence and skill repertoire to make changes within their families. However, we often neglect role-playing as an important tool for supporting therapists in developing an effective intervention strategy. An indispensable tool for the therapist is to role-play an interaction with a difficult client, to attain the practice and confidence necessary for challenging client interactions (Forgatch, Bullock, & Patterson, 2004). For example, peers can help role-play a clinical scenario so that the therapist can try out a strategy before meeting with a client. If an intervention is not going to work, it is better for the family if this is determined by a supervisory team, rather than in their actual lives. Role-playing can also be an excellent medium for modeling a new skill for a therapist. It is often helpful to see and hear what an intervention would sound like with a given client before enacting it. Although rarely do interactions with clients unfold in exactly the way one anticipates, having an armamentarium of skills and strategies primes the therapist to be an active and effective participant in the change process.

Data

It is easy to work in isolation as a therapist, assuring oneself with weekly sessions that one's clients are changing and maintaining these changes in their lives. Unfortunately, without data to support these changes, this subjective experience of working with children and families is prone to distortion and is not based in reality. It is human nature to form relationships with people and to feel positive about those relationships. It is also typical for clients to exaggerate their own response to therapy to please the therapist. Regularly collecting concrete, reliable data can mitigate this problem and provide information to families about their progress. Data also allow for accountability of the treatment team.

One effective method for the systematic data collection from families is a measure called the Parent Daily Report (PDR; Chamberlain & Reid, 1987). The PDR has been used successfully in research at the OSLC as well as in clinical work as a way to track the changes in a family over the course of a week, a month, or longer. This behavior checklist can usually be quickly administered via telephone nightly. Parents respond in a yes-or-no format to a list of common behavior problems. The list can be adapted and modified to map onto the treatment goals for the family. An adolescent version of the PDR is also available. The baseline of behavior collected through the PDR, followed by weekly data during treatment, can be used to give feedback to parents on progression, reevaluate treatment goals, and assess therapist efficacy with the model.

Intervention Maintenance

The features of a supervisory team that support the therapist getting perspective and developing an intervention strategy are also critical for the maintenance of an intervention strategy. It is easy to lose one's focus when working with children and families, and the supervisory team can get a therapist back on track. An illustrative case follows:

> The "Winnebago" family was homeless and unemployed when our clinic first provided services. With four children ranging in age from 9 to 15, parenting was quite a challenge. An added stress to this challenging situation was that the stepfather was particularly motivated but unfortunately unskilled in parenting. In addition, the mother was quite depressed, and both were struggling with substance use recovery. After about 1 year of intervention activity and considerable hard work and progress by this family, the intervention seemed to lose focus. When presenting the case, the therapists and the supervisory team concluded that the intervention had lost focus because both the therapist and family had become overly attentive to the weekly crises and neglected the practice and performance of family management practices.

One additional feature of child and family work is critical to the maintenance of an intervention plan: forming a collaborative cotherapy relationship. More a process than a goal, an effective cotherapist relationship has three interconnected dimensions (see Figure 13.4):

A collaborative strategy with clear roles. When discussing and developing an intervention strategy, the cotherapy team develops a plan that involves clear roles. One obvious point of demarcation is one's role as either the child or the parent therapist. Clarifying this role is usually sufficient to avoid many potential confusions. As we have discussed throughout this volume,

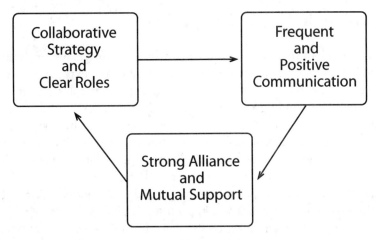

Figure 13.4. The cycle of effective cotherapy process.

however, it is important not to overidentify with either the child or parent, but rather to develop a case conceptualization and intervention strategy that accounts for each role.

Frequent and positive communication. For a cotherapy team to function well, frequent communication between the therapists and consistent communication with the family within the context of one's role are necessary. It is inappropriate, for example, for the therapist assigned to the child to communicate with and guide a parent without a previous agreement with the parent's therapist. Information to the family is channeled through the appropriate roles to avert any potential team splitting or confusion to the family.

Strong alliance and mutual support. All therapists make mistakes. What is critical to successful child and family work is the recovery from mistakes. The alliance between the therapist and cotherapist is especially useful for minimizing mistakes and developing confidence in the intervention. Therefore, it is important that in the intervention plan, the roles and alliance between the therapist and cotherapist are considered within the context of the service delivery system.

SERVICE DELIVERY SYSTEMS

All intervention activities occur within a service system such as a community mental health agency, hospital, or school. The dynamics, level of training, and organizational leadership are bound to impact the quality of intervention activities.

Paraprofessionals

The model previously described can be quite intensive, in both staff time and supervisory time. This model can also be very expensive. We have employed paraprofessionals to serve several important roles in our service delivery model, including behavior support therapists for youth, data collectors, assessment specialists, and school-based therapists who coordinate services across home and school. Paraprofessionals can be trained in a specific model and, if well supervised, can deliver a particular component of the model in the context of a treatment team. Paraprofessionals can also run parenting groups and deliver community-based educational services. However, the lack of formal education in professional issues should be addressed when working with paraprofessionals. Also, training needs to be extensive and performance monitored continually.

Training

Ongoing training and certification of therapists is a key component for the success of intervention teams (Calhoun et al., 1998). It is common for therapists to be hired to work within a particular model but then lack the training that would allow them to operate successfully from the model. A common problem is described next:

> Amy was a master's-level therapist hired to work as a parenting skills trainer and family specialist within a team of service providers. Amy was used to working from an individual model and, like most therapists, was skilled at forming relationships with families but less skilled at working directly with conflict. Amy was enlisted to work with a family in her training case who required direct feedback around parenting skills. In one conversation with the parents, they described an abusive incident that involved locking their child in a room for 1 hour. Rather than deal directly with the incident and alternatives to this behavior, Amy took an emotion-focused approach and processed the parents' feelings about the incident. Supervision and training helped Amy identify the positive aspects of her work (connecting with the parents, focusing on emotion) as well as the aspects of her work that were not consistent with the model (that the parents needed direct feedback and skills).

Training in emotion-focused processing and relationship building with clients forms the foundation of most graduate training programs in counseling and psychology. These skills are also the foundation of successful treatment, and they are critical aspects of our intervention model. However, they are not the only important aspects of treatment and, when used alone without more directive approaches, they can actually be detrimental to the family. A therapist who consistently supports parents in their abusive or inappropriate parenting skills may be building a relationship with the family but is not educating families about what may be best for their child or giving appropriate feedback to parents on their own issues. Parents may leave such a treatment feeling good about themselves, without realizing that their parenting is ineffective. We have found that therapists can find it especially difficult to give feedback regarding marital problems and substance use problems. We now provide a script of a good example of dealing directly with marital difficulties, followed by a less effective example.

Mother: It seems like every time we try to place a limit on our son, we start fighting about what that limit should be.

Therapist: Yes, I noticed in the videotaped family interaction that the two of you spent a great deal of time arguing about what to do with your son, even when he was part of the interaction.

Father: Yes, I guess we don't really think about how that might be affecting him.

Therapist: It sounds like your marital problems are interfering with your ability to parent.

Mother: Yes, we need to work on that.

Therapist: Marital problems can really lead you to parent your son in a negative way. Let's discuss how our work with your parenting can also target your marital difficulties.

This script provides an example of an approach that is less effective.

Mother: It seems like every time we try to place a limit on our son, we start fighting about what that limit should be.

Therapist: How did you feel about the videotaped family interaction?

Father: I thought it went well; it was a lot like how we are at home.

Therapist: I noticed that you were arguing in that interaction. Is that like home too?

Father: Yes, I guess we don't really think about how that might be affecting our son.

Therapist: That must be really hard for both of you.

Mother: Yes, it is really hard for me.

In the first example, the therapist addresses the marital problem directly, and the parents are given specific information related to the problem (e.g., the therapist noticed the fighting in the videotape). In the second interaction, the therapist focuses more on the process and emotion. The process leads to a discussion of how difficult the marital problem is, but the parents and therapist do not identify the marriage as an area of change and the problem is never labeled as such by the therapist.

Fidelity

We are just beginning to unpack the meaning of *therapist effects* in intervention research. The next 10 years undoubtedly will reveal many measurable components of interventionist behavior that promote change in family interactions that relate to real-world benefits to child and adolescent social adaptation and well-being. The pioneering work of Forgatch et al. (2005) is leading the way in terms of what can be expected to be fruitful areas of scientific inquiry. These findings suggest the promise of training to certification and ongoing fidelity checks to promote effective mental health service delivery to children and families. Just as in teaching, the culture of a service delivery organization will support ongoing training, videotaped feedback, fidelity criteria, and emotional and material support for child and family therapists.

SIX PILLARS OF EFFECTIVE INTERVENTIONS

Figure 13.5 summarizes the information in this chapter. The evidence to date suggests that service delivery systems that are organized and promote the following six features of child and family interventions will be effective in their goal of improving mental health. This ACCESS model is briefly delineated and summarized next:

1. *Accountability*. Therapist and agencies use assessments and data to evaluate their effectiveness in reducing mental health problems in children and families.

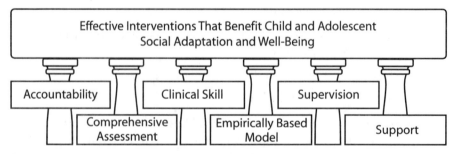

Figure 13.5. The six pillars of effective interventions: accountability, comprehensive assessment, clinical skill, empirically based model, supervision, and support (ACCESS).

2. *Comprehensive assessment.* Case conceptualizations and intervention strategies are based on comprehensive assessments of the child and family and the ecology within which they reside.
3. *Clinical skill.* The evidence is clear that clinical skill, more so than the academic degree of the therapist, is central to promoting change in children and families.
4. *Empirically based model.* Interventions that are based on a clearly specified model are more likely to be effective in both preventing and treating mental health problems.
5. *Supervision.* Child and family interventions require supervision to appropriately address the conceptual and emotional complexity of change. Team supervision in particular is an invaluable feature of a service delivery system that is focused on child and family interventions.
6. *Support.* Peer and supervisory support is critical at all phases of this work and should be provided at both the material level (workload, pay) as well as at the social–emotional level.

SUMMARY

Intervention teams are critical for successful child and family mental health service delivery. We have described a model for building and working within intervention teams in child and family therapy, including supervision and training of therapists and designing service systems that meet the objective of preventing and treating child and family mental health problems.

14

ETHICAL AND PROFESSIONAL STANDARDS IN CHILD AND FAMILY INTERVENTIONS

Mental health interventions with children and families present a set of unique ethical challenges and dilemmas compared with individual adult clinical work. The ecological approach described in this volume provides a solid foundation for decision making and for establishing a shared understanding with caregivers and children that minimizes the potential for ethical violations and dilemmas. In this chapter, we discuss (a) the ethical issues inherent in working with children and adolescents, (b) a framework for decision making when the clinician is confronted with issues of harm, and (c) the role of training in buttressing the clinician's knowledge base to optimize his or her potential to tailor and adapt interventions in response to the child and family developmental, geographic, historical, and cultural context.

First, as discussed earlier in this book, children and adolescents present with a wide range of developmental competencies, cognitive understanding, and emotional and social maturity. For example, a 15-year-old girl presenting with depression may show high levels of emotional maturity and competence, whereas a 17-year-old boy with conduct disorder and who engages in substance abuse may have limitations in maturity and insight needed for motivation to change. The majority of research suggests no linear prediction of age to competency in children and adolescents (V. A. Miller, Drotar, & Kodish, 2004).

Second, reimbursement for mental health services typically involves diagnosis. It is common practice for clinicians to base the majority of their diagnostic information on informal, unstructured interviews. In child and family work, basing decisions regarding the selection and adaptation of an intervention exclusively on unstructured interviews has serious limitations. Instead, a comprehensive set of norm-referenced assessment techniques, across multiple domains and reporters (e.g., family, school, parents, teachers), is warranted and supported by research and intervention science. In fact, some childhood diagnoses such as attention-deficit/hyperactivity disorder require that the behavior be present in multiple contexts, which would involve an objective assessment of the behavior in at least two of these contexts. And yet, there are no ethical guidelines on the best practice for assessment and diagnosis of children and families.

A particular challenge to psychologists who specialize in child and family work is the lack of ethical standards appropriate to the clinical context. Instead, adult guidelines are used to map onto the child client, and sometimes these guidelines are insufficient for this population. Moreover, current American Psychological Association (APA) ethical standards are aligned more with what therapists should not do, and less with the process with which ethical issues can be addressed in providing treatment to the child and family (Dawes, 1994).

The APA recently published a revised set of ethical guidelines for psychologists. This ethical code serves as a foundation for ethical behavior as a psychologist, but it lacks detail for child and family interventions, especially those that are ecological. An ecological intervention, as standard practice, involves multiple family members and other adults in caregiving roles. The sheer amount of information gathered through this method presents a challenge with respect to issues of disclosure, confidentiality, and professional trust.

We present this chapter as an adjunct to the APA Ethics Code (APA, 2002; see also http://www.apa.org/ethics/code2002.html), not as a replacement. In 1982 Margolin identified several unique ethical and legal issues that emerge in working with marriages and families. Since that time, there has been a dearth of activity on the ethics of child and family interventions. In the APA Ethics Code, there is virtually no mention of any ethical guidelines for working with the complex presentations of children and families. Following is an excerpt (from the APA guidelines) that addresses family therapy:

10.02 Therapy Involving Couples or Families

(a) When psychologists agree to provide services to several persons who have a relationship (such as spouses, significant others, or parents and children), they take reasonable steps to clarify at the outset (1) which of the individuals are clients/patients and (2) the relationship the psychologist will have with each person. This clarification includes the psychologist's role and the probable uses of the services provided or the information obtained.

The complexity of child and family issues has grown astronomically in the past 20 years because of the increased number of divorces and remarriages and an expanding definition of the boundaries of families. Consider this example in relation to the ethical response of a psychologist: In a divorced family, the noncustodial mother comes to the clinic seeking help for her 5-year-old child who is having behavior problems. The 5-year-old has been living with her for 5 months, and the father (per the mother's report) is emotionally abusive. Three months into therapy, the custodial father calls and wants to know what is going on in therapy. What is the psychologist's role in these transactions? Can a noncustodial parent seek parenting help when he or she is the primary caretaker of a child? What kind of information should be provided? The current ethical guidelines do not provide adequate detail or enough information to inform child and family therapists about how to proceed with these complex issues.

ETHICAL AND STRATEGIC INTERVENTION

Family work demands that the psychologist is able to negotiate complex ethical, legal, and professional issues to provide the optimal services for children and families. The clinician must also consider his or her service in juxtaposition to other services available to families and the likelihood that families would seek and engage in the necessary services after his or her intervention. We see ethical decisions in child and family services as a decision tree, as shown in Figure 14.1. The first critical question is whether

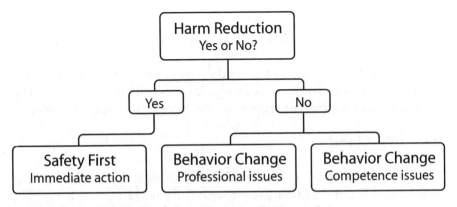

Figure 14.1. Making decisions in child and family interventions.

a family is caught in a cycle of abuse, violence, or severe neglect that requires immediate attention to reduce potential harm. If the answer to this question is yes, then the therapist is in a harm reduction mode until all family members are safe or the appropriate services and authorities have been engaged.

If the answer to this first question is a preliminary no, then therapists proceed to setting the stage for assisting the family in behavior change. Providing behavior change services involves a variety of ethics-related issues of professional behavior and competence. For several reasons, the Family Check-Up approach to child and family intervention is a solid foundation for ethical professional service delivery. First, therapists base decision making about the family's needs on a comprehensive assessment, which forms the case conceptualization. Critical to case conceptualization are decisions and communications with a family about the nature of the services (informed consent), boundaries of the service (who is the client), and the limits of professional competence when generating a service menu. In addition, to complete an assessment, one needs advance consents for consultations with teachers, ex-partners, other mental health and social service professionals, and extended family members who are involved. For decision making and professional posturing, proactively seeking information at the onset of clinical activity is generally superior to reactive engagement or responses to ethical dilemmas. The Family Check-Up also provides ample time for discussion with the family about complex ethical issues or competing perspectives during the time in which the professional relationship is being established. In addition, the structure of the Family Check-Up allows opportunities for the therapist to seek consultation and supervision on service delivery or ethical issues before commitments or agreements regarding mental health services are offered.

Following the format of Figure 14.1, we first discuss issues of harm reduction and then proceed to ethical issues related to service delivery when abuse or family violence are not the organizing concerns.

HARM REDUCTION

Harm reduction refers to the need to prioritize the intervention focus on issues such as violence, abuse, and self-harm. When the behavior and environment of a client are dangerous, the priority is to render it safe.

Who Is the Client?

This first question in child and family therapy is actually the most complicated. We operate from a family-centered model and, as such, typically view the family as the client. However, consent and billing procedures can limit the feasibility of this approach. In addition, when a family presents for therapy, multiple perspectives and a complicated picture of the problem usually emerge. For example, Hawley and Weisz (2003) found that therapists, parents, and children rarely agree on the problem to be targeted in therapy. In their study, agreement on target problems occurred less than 25% of the time. This finding suggests that thorough objective assessment must occur up front in child and family therapy, with consensus building and feedback intrinsic to the entire system of care. Consider the following scenario:

> Amy came into the clinic for support in parenting her 5-year-old son, Mike, for 3 months, but is considering using drugs again because parenting Mike is so difficult. Mike has problem behavior, including aggression and noncompliance, both at home and at school. The therapist decides that work with Amy on her depression and past sexual abuse history will facilitate a future focus in therapy on parenting.

In this scenario, it is unclear at first who the client is, but after thorough assessment and evaluation, the identified target of intervention becomes Amy, not Mike. Following this assessment, paperwork and documentation should clearly identify Amy as the client. Even though the paperwork in the file and documentation focus on Amy's personal problems, if the client is identified as Mike, then Amy's ex-husband (Mike's biological father) could have access to the records. Documentation and record keeping are critical in child and family work.

Safety First

A therapist cannot provide mental health services when there is an ongoing threat of physical or sexual abuse or severe neglect by caregivers. With experience, child and family therapists can get an initial sense that a family may be at risk for these troublesome dynamics. Often, one or more family members will actively disclose experiences that suggest abuse or neglect. In some clinical situations, abuse and neglect may be the referral problem. Many states require mandatory reporting of child abuse and neglect, which simplifies that decision for the child and family therapist. However, some states allow psychologists a certain amount of professional discretion. For example, some states (e.g., Oregon) recognize that little benefit results to a parent or child when Child Protective Services becomes involved when a family is already actively engaged in the very treatment service designed to eliminate abuse and neglect. Psychologists are allowed to use their discretion regarding reporting child abuse if the abuse incidents are acquired in the context of a privileged relationship. However, social workers, counselors, or master's-level practitioners do not have privilege and, therefore, are mandated reporters. Each state has its own laws, and we encourage therapists to check the laws that apply.

The first interactions with parents and children set the stage for addressing harm reduction. Informed consents delineate the conditions under which confidentiality is honored and how information suggesting abuse, harm, suicide, or neglect is handled. It is important that these procedures are stated clearly and that families understand the conditions under which psychologists work to promote the safety and health of all family members.

Communication

Therapists can look at harm reduction interventions in two ways. One is that therapists are outside helping-agents who are responsible for protecting children (or spouses). The operative term is *responsible*, and it justifies making unilateral decisions such as calling Child Protective Services or other legal authorities. The second perspective is that a therapist uses indications of harm as an opportunity for supporting both safety and healthy family change. Both perspectives are valid, and we suggest this sequence: (a) therapeutic interventions to reduce harm and (b) decisive, unilateral action to reduce harm. The next few paragraphs explain further.

Many parents who are abusive or neglectful behave that way because of their own inability to self-regulate their emotions and needs in the best interest of their children. It is our impression that 90% of such family episodes are shameful to the perpetrators and would be stopped if they received support and active intervention. This working assumption is helpful. Consider using the following opening statement:

> From what you've told me, there are times that things get out of control in your family, and people get hurt. I want to let you know that I'm concerned about this, as I'm sure you are. We can continue to work together under two conditions. One is that you commit to not using any form of violence in the next month when dealing with conflict. The second is that, if things get out of control again, it will be discussed openly. To heal you from these patterns, you and I are going to have to work as a team to make sure that everyone in the family is safe from harm. This may mean that we will need to bring in other resources, such as Child Protective Services, if your children are not safe. Are you able to commit to this agreement?

As discussed, the advantage of basing services on a comprehensive assessment is that issues of harm reduction are often unveiled at the beginning of forming the therapeutic relationship and, therefore, can be proactively addressed in therapy. In some cases, it may be clear that the service offered is not appropriate or secure enough to guarantee the safety of family members. Some families may require more intense support to prevent harm and violence from being perpetuated, and therapists may need to carry pagers or be on call with emergency access and the ability to respond 24 hours a day, 7 days a week. If one's service is not adequate to support a family with this level of need, then it is unethical to enter into a professional relationship with a family vulnerable to abuse or neglect.

On occasion, the Family Check-Up can be used to prevent abuse and neglect and to enhance engagement of families into the most appropriate services for their level of need. Consider the following case scenario:

> Pam is a single mother with three young children—a 6-year-old boy and two daughters, 3 and 2 years old. She is seeking services primarily to address the angry outbursts of her 6-year-old boy but acknowledges that all her children present challenges. Pam has a history of crack-cocaine use that she has worked hard to stop. She has been in recovery for more than 6 months. Pam is currently engaged in recovery treatment services, which also provide daily child care. Although these services are appropriate, Pam does not get along with the child-care providers and, recently, has become upset at their questions about her behavior.
>
> Pam's sister (who is likely using drugs) has come to live with her. Rather than use the treatment child care, Pam has asked her sister to provide child care. In the past month, Pam had gone away for a weekend and left her children in her sister's care. After an initial interview, Pam participated in a home visit with a videotaped assessment of her and her sister interacting with the children, a consultation from the drug treatment agency, and a child-care and feedback session. The focus of the feedback was to improve Pam's understanding of the recovery process, her family's current needs, and the need for more intensive ongoing support. In collaboration with Pam, it was agreed that the therapist would meet with Pam and the treatment agency to address Pam's difficulties with the treatment staff and to solidify her engagement with this comprehensive recovery and child-care service. The therapist served as an advocate for Pam within the treatment setting and alerted the treatment staff for the need to provide Pam with behavior management support, specifically for her 6-year-old.

Abusive Circumstances

Child neglect and maltreatment may be the central focus of the intervention, or emerge as an issue during work with a family. Unfortunately, sexual misconduct with and abuse of children and adolescents is not uncommon (Mullen, Martin, Anderson, Romans, & Herbison, 1996). The nature of sexual abuse is that it is covert and hidden. Thus, of all forms of abuse, this one can catch the therapist by surprise. Adults who sexually exploit children are often immature in other respects and are unwilling, at least initially, to admit and take responsibility for the severe emotional pain they inflict. In cases of sexual abuse, it is critical to mobilize the adult community who will protect a child in both the short and long run. Thus, interventions that address ongoing sexual abuse require decisive action as well as support for nonabusive (but often neglectful) caregivers. The first step in healing the trauma of sexual abuse is to identify and mobilize any member of the parenting community who can be trusted to protect a child. Consider the following case:

> Natasha and Peter had been married for 10 years and had two children—a 9-year-old boy and a 6-year-old girl. The family lived in a remote rural area, and Natasha worked sporadically as a temp. The family had been in family management therapy for 8 weeks, when Natasha disclosed to the therapists that she suspected sexual abuse by Peter. The disclosure was over the telephone on a day the family was not scheduled for an appointment. The therapist had Natasha bring the children in to the clinic to further discuss her concerns. Three very clear events that likely involved sexual abuse were described. The therapist praised Natasha for her courage in bringing this to her attention. Two courses of action were taken. First, a women's shelter was notified, and arrangements were made for the safety of Natasha and her children. Following the mobilization of a shelter service, Natasha was coached on how to call and report the incidences to the police. The therapist sat with Natasha as she called and reported the sexual abuse to police. Within 2 hours after the call was made, Peter was arrested and in police custody. Following an investigation, he was eventually tried and sentenced for child sexual abuse, and the children remained in Natasha's care.

This case provides an example of how decisive action empowers the nonabusive adult system to protect children and stop the abuse. Unfortunately, in such cases, the services and support structures in communities are often insufficient to follow up on such interventions. Shelter services are often short term, and police custody is good only until bail is set. Often the emotional characteristics of the parent (e.g., depression), which led to the neglect in the first place, lead to new, potentially abusive conditions such as cohabitating with an antisocial man. For these reasons, the interventions that address the acute conditions of abuse require diligent follow-up. However, most communities do not prioritize these kinds of child and family services, and the cycle of abuse continues. Consider the following scenario, which is more typical of community and family reactions to abuse. In this example, the therapist works with the family system to protect a child, with little support from the community.

> Maria and Marcus are Latino parents who came into the clinic because they were concerned about their 10-year-old daughter, Gina, who was having problems concentrating in school. A thorough ecological evaluation revealed that recently Marcus's two older boys from a previous marriage had moved into the household with Maria, Marcus, and their

three other children. The additional demands of two adolescents were taxing the marriage and were financially difficult for the couple. The boys were both engaging in problem behavior, including substance use and delinquency. They refused to attend school. After the second meeting with the family during the Family Check-Up, Maria pulled the therapist aside and told her that she feared the oldest boy was molesting Gina. She had observed him going into her room at night for no reason, and Gina was fearful around the boy. The therapist quickly mobilized around a safety plan for Maria and Gina, which included reporting the suspected incident to Child Protective Services (CPS) and moving Maria into Gina's room at night to sleep. Because there was no concrete evidence of abuse, CPS did not respond with urgency to the situation and no assessment was made of the family for several weeks. Limited resources for Spanish-speaking CPS workers extended the time line. There was no history of domestic violence, and Maria did not fear for her safety, so the therapist facilitated a discussion of the problem between Maria and Marcus. Marcus and Maria were supported as a parenting team to address the mental health issues of the older boy and Gina, as well as to develop safety plans at home that prevented contact between Gina and the older boy until a thorough evaluation of the situation could be conducted.

One other unique characteristic of child and family work is challenging with respect to harm reduction. As we discussed in the previous scenario, a therapist often meets separately with different family members. On such occasions, a therapist may gain information about abusive or neglectful interactions. For example, a 9-year-old boy recounts a weekend when he was left under the care of his 15-year-old sister and her boyfriend, who engaged in substance abuse. A 13-year-old girl recounts a discipline episode in which her mother bloodied her nose. An 8-year-old girl describes her parents' partying with drugs and alcohol, whereas the parents report being in recovery. Children reporting potential abuse and neglect are to be taken very seriously, with full attention given to the short- and long-term safety of all family members. Seasoned child therapists will be quick to remind children that their reports are seriously considered and that they will at times act to protect them on the basis of what they say. Thus, therapeutic trust is established and maintained. These issues require direct and clear communication. It is not unusual for a therapist to meet with a parent to discuss topics unveiled in the course of a discussion with a child. Judgment about the parent's ability to respond therapeutically to such intrusions of privacy is fundamental to how this information is used. Consider the following case and how the child and parent are addressed to investigate the bloody nose episode:

> (To the parents) We wanted to talk with you about an issue that came up when Tom was meeting with Rebecca. Rebecca reported that one

of your conflicts ended up with her getting a bloody nose. We know that must have been difficult for you, and we thought it would be good to talk this situation through. When things like this happen, it tells us that we may need to adjust the support we are giving you. Can you tell us more about this situation?

(*To Rebecca*) I'm glad you mentioned this, Rebecca. It sounds like it was pretty scary. You know, I will be talking with your mom about this, to see if there is something we can do to make sure this doesn't happen again. Do you have concerns about us talking about this? Would you like to be there?

The salient point is that in the balance of cost and benefits, information in therapy that suggests an ongoing process of potential harm to children is not kept confidential. The therapist must proactively communicate this principle to all family members to prevent violations of trust and misunderstandings about the nature of a therapeutic relationship. When families are clear about this principle at the onset, indications of potential harm can often be addressed in a way that reduces the potential risk in the future.

PROFESSIONAL AND ETHICAL STANDARDS

The basic structure of the APA guidelines is helpful for identifying the major issues of ethical conduct when working with families to promote behavior change. The basics of honesty, disclosure, confidentiality, and avoiding dual relationships are often quite clear in individual psychotherapy, but with families, the issues become much more complicated. Rarely do therapists and psychologists purposely violate ethical guidelines. Most often, unethical behavior results from lack of training, poor supervision, working in isolation, and failure to acquire appropriate consultation. The therapist's personal history can also play a role in failure to provide ethical and professional services. The personal factor can be subtle, or it can be quite severe. For example, a therapist with a history of physical abuse may inadvertently avoid engaging a father who has a threatening appearance, even though his behavior, both in the family and outside of it, is quite appropriate. Failure to engage an important caregiver can result in limited family change, or worse, lead to disruption of the family system. In a more serious vein, therapists who become intimately involved with clients are clearly playing out personal issues that are exploitative, self-centered, and harmful to the client as well as highly unethical.

In contrast to other approaches to child interventions, the ecological approach to child and family interventions in general, and the Family Check-Up in particular, provides a foundation for ethical decision making and

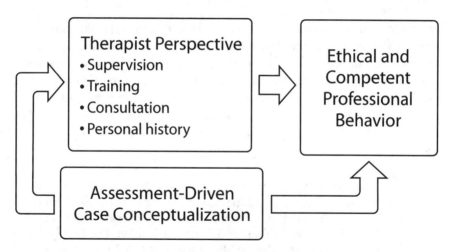

Figure 14.2. The role of assessment in ethical decision making.

professional behavior. Several features of this approach support high-quality mental health services. As shown in Figure 14.2, in work with children and families, the assessment-driven case conceptualization and ethical and competent professional behavior are linked. When case conceptualization is based on multiple inputs and psychometrically solid assessments, the personal biases of the therapist are reduced and minimized. Building in a step between assessments and feedback provides ample opportunity for supervision or consultation. Child and family therapists learn quickly that supervision and consultation are often critical for developing a case conceptualization that is helpful in providing intervention services that benefit the child and family. As discussed in chapter 13 (this volume), working in therapeutic teams provides a basis of support that allows colleagues to openly discuss concerns in cases that present a complex set of professional and ethical issues. When therapeutic teams are working well, they create a setting in which a therapist can discuss his or her personal biases and challenges about a case, and the team will mobilize to work through these issues and arrive at a more constructive therapeutic frame. Supervision groups that are competitive or acrimonious are not supportive of a therapist's mental health, nor do they provide the ambience for working through personal issues to promote quality of services or professional behavior.

In discussing treatment for marital dysfunction, Weiss and Halford (1996) articulated the need for *perceptual objectification* for healthy change in marriages. Objectification is the process of moving from one's own relationship perspective to a more objective point of view that encompasses and integrates both one's own and one's partner's point of view. For the therapist to behave professionally and ethically in child and family work, objectification is a critical step. Getting locked into a specific perspective about a family is the foundation for incompetent or unethical behavior. Therapist training is essential for simply recognizing that one's first set of reactions and perceptions may be biased, and worse, not particularly helpful for the family. Assessments, input of cotherapists, supervision, and consultation move the therapist toward objectification, which ultimately leads to improved services and professional behavior. Consider the following example:

> Dharma and her mother Rachel were being seen because Dharma was depressed, using drugs, and cutting herself. At the first session, Rachel blamed her ex-husband for Dharma's difficulties. He was angry and resentful of Rachel and dismissed Dharma as a flake. The therapist adopted Rachel's perspective on the family and failed to seek input from Dharma's father. He proceeded to conduct a Family Check-Up with just Rachel and Dharma. After seeking supervision, he expanded his perspective to potentially consider the father as a resource. He asked Rachel if it would be appropriate to contact Dharma's dad to consult on the case. She agreed. When he met with Dharma's father, a very different picture emerged. The father was hurt because their marriage was disrupted by an affair that Rachel had had with her current housemate. He worked full-time and missed his time with Dharma very much, although he resented having to deal with Rachel so frequently. The brief consultation with Dharma's father revealed an important family resource. Within two or three sessions, the therapist was able to help the family reorganize in such a way as to allow Dharma and her father to develop a relationship independent of Rachel.

From an ecological perspective, neglecting the role of key caregivers in supporting the mental health and social adaptation of children and adolescents is unethical and unprofessional. All available evidence suggests that healthy relationships with responsible caregivers promote competence and well-being in children. Providing services that focus narrowly on the child and exclude key family members may actually exacerbate the problem and, therefore, is inappropriate and unhelpful. However, current professional guidelines do not include as unethical the provision of inappropriate services resulting from lack of training by the therapist, limited use of assessments for decision making, or a personal bias of the therapist.

Ethical and professional issues emerge even regarding conditions of care and attention given to case conceptualization. We claim that the major ethical, legal, and professional issues can be addressed by attending to the following five guidelines, or the *five* Cs of professional child and family therapy: competence, custody clarification, cultural awareness, confidentiality, and collaboration versus collusion.

Competence

The foundation of competence as a psychologist is understanding the scientific principles of human behavior as they apply to development, change, and intervention effectiveness. One must understand not only the body of knowledge but also the process of scientific investigation and skepticism. Therapists must be amenable to changing practices based on the evolution of scientific knowledge.

Unfortunately, there is a tremendous amount of misinformation in clinical psychology in general, and in child clinical and counseling psychology in particular. Dawes (1994) incisively discussed some of the key myths in his classic exposition of the clinical psychology "house of cards." Often ethical behavior is thought to describe purely professional conduct, such as not sleeping with clients. However, as Dawes pointed out, professional ignorance is a major ethical violation. Not being aware of the fallibility of clinical judgment, the lack of connection between years of experience and client outcomes, and other misconceptions about the nature of clinical expertise can be seen as sources of ethical misconduct.

The clinical psychology myths are particularly problematic in child psychology for two reasons. First, solid empirical work on the entire clinical package that has been adopted from adult clinical psychology is generally lacking. For example, the field adopts the 1-hour-per-week model of change in child psychology, despite the fact that few, if any, studies document the optimal therapist–client contact strategy to promote change. When we first established our doctoral training practicum in child and family intervention at the University of Oregon, the graduate students (at the time) were appalled by two features of our approach. First, we asked doctorate-level graduate students to go to families' homes and schools and conduct ecological assessments. From the viewpoint of the cadre of doctoral students at that time, this was unacceptable. This belief is typical among clinicians who practice child and family psychology in the community: Clients are supposed to come to their office for 50 minutes, once a week. Any work that cannot be conducted during that time frame is out of their scope of practice.

The second feature of our practicum was that we conducted assessments with multiple individuals before beginning any intervention activity. Often, interviews with teachers or school assessments can take weeks to complete and coordinate. The concern was that we were delaying helping the client by doing research. Yet because the majority of children who present with mental health problems have similar school problems, these assessments are crucial. Imagine going to a medical doctor or dentist who begins drilling or operating before doing a sound assessment.

Professionals can be rather rigid and self-serving in their view of professional practice, which does not benefit the children and families they serve.

Imagine how many children with conduct problems were treated with ineffective mental health interventions (e.g., psychodynamic individual play therapy), without the parents being informed that parenting support or family management therapy is a more effective intervention (Weiss, Catron, Harris, & Phung, 1999).

Thus, it is incumbent on individuals and organizations that provide mental health interventions that serve children and families to promote principles that have a scientific basis. At the same time, we do not suggest rigidly adhering to manualized interventions or rejecting clients who do not fit neatly into diagnostic categories on which efficacious interventions are based. Attending to the scientific basis of child psychology means providing services that are informed by knowledge of child development, intervention outcome research, and developmental psychopathology. Therapists trained to work with adults cannot simply become child or adolescent clinicians without the proper training and education. Lack of training and awareness of the major issues in working with children and families could lead to harm. For example, in groups for adolescents with depression, some of whom are using drugs and involved in delinquent behavior, lack of attention to family processes and iatrogenic effects resulting from peer aggregation may mean that more harm than good results. A therapist who promotes this service could arguably be considered to be behaving unethically.

The AIM (*assessment, intervention,* and *motivation*) approach to service delivery allows agencies and therapists to evaluate their clients' outcomes on an ongoing basis. Single-subject designs are a useful tool for both the therapist and the client when the effectiveness of an intervention service is evaluated. Thus, therapist competence includes the ability to collect and evaluate change data.

Custody Clarification

Another major area of ethical and legal concern is ensuring that a mental health service addresses the issue of custody. Doing so is becoming increasingly complicated in our modern world of divorce, remarriage, and parent abdication of responsibility. Consider this case:

> Mary was 17 and was living in the house of a friend while finishing her senior year in high school. Her mother had had chronic difficulties with alcohol and marijuana abuse over the past 5 years. When her mom was using, she would occasionally "go off," and they would get into unpleasant, very negative arguments. The friend contacted the clinic to seek services for Mary. After an initial interview, Mary became the client. Mary's mother was consulted on occasion, but care was taken not to collude with the mother's agenda to have Mary move back with her, despite her recent sobriety.

At the very beginning, it is necessary to clarify who are the adults who have caregiving roles (i.e., custody) and to be clear about who the client is with respect to these adults. Often, one parent undergoing divorce will seek mental health services for a child. The role of the parent not seeking these services needs to be clarified at the beginning during the informed-consent process. On occasion, the divorce will be abusive. In these situations, it is inappropriate to consult or contact the perpetrator of abuse because of potential harm to the clients. These clinical scenarios do occur, and the intake and informed-consent protocols encourage accurate disclosure of the custody context for child and adolescent clients.

It is tempting to allow ethical and legal issues to obfuscate the goal of mental health treatment. Often the problem behavior is actually a key to the solution for a given child. Consider this case:

> Jane was a 38-year-old mother with an adolescent boy (age 13) and a 5-year-old daughter. She had recently experienced a painful divorce from a husband she perceived as overcontrolling. This divorce had had many serious consequences for Jane. She had been excommunicated from her local church, whereas her husband was included in the church community. Because the house she lived in was owned by her ex-husband's family, he came and went as he pleased and often intruded on her private life. She suspected, and the evidence seemed to confirm, that her ex-husband had tampered with her boyfriend's car's steering. Jane was concerned about her children's adjustment to this stressful postdivorce environment. She sought mental health services but demanded that her ex-husband not be involved, for fear of his intrusiveness or that she would be perceived as an incompetent mother. Services were provided to Jane, beginning with informing her of her rights as a client. The therapist began immediately identifying resources to support Jane and her children, acquiring the necessary restraining orders, changing locks on the house, and connecting Jane with new support systems.

A case such as this can easily become complicated with respect to custody and legal issues, and these issues could dominate the therapist's decision on how best to deliver services. Decisive commitment to providing services in such cases can be a tremendous benefit to both children and family. By immediately responding to an acutely stressful postdivorce scenario, the therapist can support and empower the parent during a key transition after many years of control and domination. In such a case, the need for parent training may be minimal—the service is primarily a support function.

It is not uncommon for parents to seek services with the agenda of building a case for an impending custody battle. It is extremely important to clarify for parents that custody recommendations are a professional service that is defined and endorsed by both parties involved. The ecological framework is an excellent framework for considering these complicated and emotionally laden issues; however, both parents would need to open themselves to assessment and scrutiny and be willing to accept the recommendation of the mental health professional assigned to this task. Therapists who serve only one parent in such a situation are of limited usefulness in legal situations. Agreeing to this role and testifying in court, in fact, can have an effect opposite from that intended. Clients should be apprised of the fact that seeking services in the effort to serve their self-interest in a future legal dispute is ill advised, at best, and potentially damaging for them and their child.

Cultural Awareness

Our social world is becoming increasing multicultural and diverse. Families often present with several complex value systems and cultural backgrounds that are relevant to both their concerns for their child and the relationship patterns within which their family is embedded. Here's another case history to consider:

> Jason was a 15-year-old high-school student at the time his parents sought services at the Family Resource Room within a public high school setting. His parents were concerned that Jason's grades had dropped during the previous term and that he was becoming disrespectful. In completing a home assessment, the family discussed the problem of Jason falling asleep at 8:00 p.m. before he finished doing dishes. Jason complained that getting up at 4:30 a.m. for the family prayer session, in addition to doing homework and being on the high school swim team, was too much and that in the evening he was very tired. In the family feedback session, the parents' religion was discussed in juxtaposition to what is developmentally normative for an adolescent who was undergoing pubertal changes and was physically active. Because the therapist understood and was respectful of the family's religious faith, their practices, and their church, the parents were able to accept that their expectations were unrealistic and revised their demands on Jason to allow more time for sleep and rest.

This example is provided to put forward the point that cultural diversity is not only an issue of ethnicity and race but also one of socioeconomic status and religion. Psychologists cannot be expected to know the details of every variation of diversity that is possible to serve. Cultural awareness in psychological service delivery is a process as much as a static knowledge base. However, it is imperative that child and family therapists are knowledgeable about the historical and cultural factors affecting a family's possible response to intervention services as well as their relationship, parenting strategies, and sources of family stress (Szapocznik & Kurtines, 1993). Lack of awareness and insensitivity in the provision of services could do harm and, to this extent, would be seen as unethical.

Sensitivity to cultural issues is especially relevant to activities and research related to dissemination of empirically supported interventions. Psychologists are rarely trained to appreciate historical and community issues. The history of how American Indian families have been treated provides a salient example. United States policies that directly attacked cultural transmission practices within the American Indian community involved forcing children to attend boarding schools and punishment for speaking an indigenous language (Duran & Duran, 1995). Elders and parents were forcibly removed from child-rearing and the socialization process, which were typically nonviolent and very effective. In contrast, boarding schools used harsh physical discipline to socialize American Indian children. Such practices, coupled with genocide, reservation assignment, and other forms of colonization, form the substrate of American Indian historical trauma (Duran & Duran, 1995).

In light of this historical context, imagine the reaction when American Indian communities are approached as sites for the dissemination of parenting programs of European American researchers, developed and tested on European American communities. Ignorance of the historical context as well as the strengths of indigenous practices clearly contributes to the perpetuation of colonial abuses and certainly results in harm to individuals and communities. Consider this case:

> A group of university-based researchers were testing a promising, empirically supported intervention in the context of a school exclusively serving American Indian children and families. On the day professionals within the experimental condition were to be trained on the intervention, half were randomly assigned to the university workshop versus the typical training activities for that day. The random assignment resulted in a female elder being restricted from attending the university training workshop (i.e., she was assigned to the control group). She protested and refused to leave the workshop. After some travail, the university training staff agreed to allow the elder to remain in the training workshop.

Restricting an elder in a tribal community involved in services for children and families is a perfect example of unethical behavior that results directly from lack of awareness of both the cultural dynamics and historical factors that affect children and families in the American Indian community. When we systematically interviewed various individuals across American Indian communities, it was clear that cultural insensitivity on the part of majority researchers was common and almost expected, unfortunately.

Indeed, mental health practices that target families are viewed with some concern and even distress within the American Indian community (Dionne & Dishion, 2004). However, under the proper conditions of collaboration and community input, the American Indian community has a strong interest in doing whatever is necessary to rebuild its families.

Another cultural group often affected by insensitivity to cultural issues is the African American community. Few mental health professionals are aware of the specific European American practices that were used to make slavery possible. Moreover, there is a general lack of awareness of and sensitivity to the continuation of racism and oppression in the daily lives of African American children and families. However, no matter what cultural group is involved, lack of awareness and sensitivity to historical events and current community circumstances underlies unethical practices in the provision of mental health services.

The best way to attend to cultural issues in the delivery of services is to have a multiethnic intervention team. From an ecological perspective, therapists do not have perspective when they work in isolation. Working within the context of a multicultural intervention team allows the assignment of therapists who have the most expertise for a family's ecology. In our intervention research, we found that the expertise of our diverse therapy staff contributed to the effective engagement of minority families with youth at high risk, which resulted in long-term benefits in terms of reduced substance use and other problem behaviors by age 14 (Connell, Dishion, & Kavanagh, 2005; Connell, Dishion, Yasui, & Kavanagh, in press).

Confidentiality

Child and family interventions present challenges to standard interpretations of confidentiality. In most states, children cannot consent to services, but they can assent to treatment. Care should be taken to explain in detail the limits of confidentiality to children and to their parents. In general, parents have the right to request information about their children's treatment from the therapist because their consent is required for treatment (Melton, Ehrenreich, & Lyons, 2001). Exceptions to this rule include emancipated minors (in most states), children with medical conditions such as sexually transmitted diseases and HIV infections, and those who seek procedures such as abortions. Practitioners who are rigid on either end of the spectrum—that is, disclosing all information to adults or refusing to disclose any information to adults—will probably make poor ethical decisions. They fail to take into account parents as a context for health promotion, or the individuality and autonomy of youth (C. B. Fisher, Hatashita-Wong, & Greene, 1999). Here's a relevant case example:

Seth is a 17-year-old boy who is having difficulty with his family's postdivorce adjustment. Although the divorce occurred 8 years before, the dynamics live on. His well-meaning parents are intrusive and have high standards. He is depressed and engages in seriously self-destructive behaviors, including substance abuse. Both parents are quite engaged in his life and, in fact, he feels he is constantly walking a tightrope between the two families so that the balance of power and affection does not get tipped in either direction. Because of his age and his family context, the therapist defines Seth as the client. The therapist meets occasionally with both biological parents. The therapist insists that Seth's disclosures in therapy are completely confidential, including his drug use. According to the therapist assessment, Seth would most benefit from having a therapeutic context that was private and confidential to discuss issues about his life in the postdivorce family.

In this case scenario, confidentiality is an indispensable tool for establishing therapeutic trust and establishing appropriate and safe boundaries for an adolescent male. The parents in this system, as might be expected, want more information about the youth's problem behavior. However, to provide it would lead to increased conflict between the two homes, and Seth would be caught in the middle. It is especially important for this adolescent (emotionally mature with many strengths) to have a confidential setting in which to work out his feelings about the postdivorce arrangement and to have a neutral, caring adult who can provide problem-solving support for such a complex social and emotional context. The facts of his problem behavior are deemed secondary to this therapeutic goal.

When therapists work within an ecological framework, strict confidentiality may not always be possible nor advisable. Information from multiple reporting agents is shared with discretion and with explicit permission. It is advisable to balance the needs of the child with those of the caregiving environment (Margolin, 1982). When assessments are requested, it is mandatory to inform reporting agents that their data will be shared with the family. However, even when the appropriate consents are obtained, the manner in which information is shared (e.g., from teachers) requires attention to the broader interests of the child. Specifically, it is important to build coalitions of care among adults such as the mother, father, and teachers, for example.

A family-centered approach demands that the therapist balance the needs of the family and each individual when considering issues of confidentiality. Issues of potential harm (e.g., violence, suicide, extreme forms of self-destructive behavior) are never kept confidential. The strategy for breaking confidentiality is predominantly a therapeutic one. For example, an adolescent who self-discloses would have a discussion with his or her therapist and hopefully his or her parents. Therapists might use this script:

> Given what you've said, it seems clear that you are at risk for hurting yourself. You know, this is a situation where I need to take action to make sure you are safe. I will be talking with your parent about my concerns regarding your risk for suicide. Would you like to be present?

In this way, the process of disclosure can move the parent–adolescent relationship forward, so that there is better communication between the two. On the rare occasions when it is necessary to break confidentiality, reminding the family members of the consent forms and, more important, the general therapeutic principles is essential. Consider the following example:

> The Johnson family was seeking treatment in the clinic for parenting and family management of their three adolescent children. During the course of treatment, each child was assigned an individual therapist, but the therapists worked as a team with the family. They had informed each child that therapy was confidential except under circumstances in which behavior was putting the children at risk. In these cases, the therapist would discuss the behavior with parents. Also, from the start, the therapists made it clear that they worked as a team at the clinic and had information about treatment for each member of the family. Brian, the 14-year-old boy, was running away from home and engaging in risky behavior, including sexual behavior and drug use. He disclosed to his therapist that he thought he was gay and was engaged in sexual behavior with an older man who was HIV positive. Given the age of the older male, this behavior was considered statutory rape (in Oregon). The boy was now using a condom, but he had previously neglected to do so and had had unsafe sex with this person. He asked the therapist not to tell his parents because he did not want his parents to know he is gay.

In this scenario, there are multiple issues. The child is clearly engaging in risk behavior that should be addressed with the parents because his own health and welfare are potentially at risk. However, to do so would out the child in the family and potentially destroy the therapeutic relationship.

In this case, the family therapist explored the potential for Brian's being gay with the parents without giving this information to the family. The parents shared with the therapist that they suspected Brian was gay and that they feared for his safety when he ran away. After Brian's therapist gave him this information, Brian felt comfortable sharing his sexuality with his family in a meeting facilitated by the family and child therapists. Support services for HIV prevention and testing were then put into place without disclosing the potential for HIV infection to the parents.

Collaboration Versus Collusion

A notion that is basic to all helping professionals is the need to address clients' stated needs. For example, a mother of an adolescent boy may ask for more closeness with her son, when her son would actually like to have better boundaries. The advantage of observational assessment is that these dynamics can quickly be observed in the course of the family's interactions. Taking the mother's report at face value and intervening with this goal in mind may actually do emotional harm to the adolescent. In other words, the mother's emotional intrusions become sanctioned by a therapist.

The ecological approach is by nature collaborative, but it is not collusive. For example, if a family system is seeking mental health treatment to avoid investigation by Child Protective Services for alleged sexual abuse, the therapist necessarily must be cautious and vigilant about not colluding with parents to avoid detection and sanctions for child abuse. Collusion can extend to a parent working out a marital conflict by establishing a bond with the therapist. The therapist is inadvertently colluding with the competitive parent to undermine the authority and credibility of his or her partner. Collusion is unethical; collaboration is therapeutic.

The most common form of collusion is with adolescent clients. To establish rapport and trust, the unseasoned therapist can inadvertently collude with a young client by reinforcing destructive attitudes and values about a parent, or by subtly encouraging problem behavior. If, for example, an adolescent girl is being treated for depression and the therapist inadvertently encourages problem behavior by naively believing her stories, then therapeutic gains are unlikely.

> Georgina was a 15-year-old attractive Latina whose mother had recently remarried and had a new baby. The mother was worried about Georgina's sulky moods, angry affect, and lack of sleep and referred her for treatment for adolescent depression. Georgina did report clinically significant levels of depression. However, her life was complicated by many factors, one of which was her 18-year-old boyfriend, of whom her parents disapproved. She was also involved in drug use and was known to steal. Georgina surmised that her therapist was an eager advocate and could be used to gain herself some freedom. The therapist advocated for more autonomy for Georgina, which translated to more substance use and unprotected sex with her boyfriend. Moreover, when Georgina was caught with someone's credit cards, the therapist advocated on her behalf in the

family, supporting the girl's story that she had found the credit cards and had no intention of using them. Georgina's problem behavior began to increase during the next year.

The distinction between collaboration and collusion is clear in the above example. Was the therapist's behavior unethical? It is our position that the therapist's lack of sophistication about problem behavior, family dynamics, and normal adolescent behavior potentiated harm for this adolescent and family. We hope that the harm caused by this mental health service was short lived.

A collaborative approach to working with this family would have taken quite a different form. The therapist could have empathized with the feelings of autonomy that are normative for this stage of development. To assist the young woman in addressing this issue, the therapist could have worked on family problem-solving skills. The therapist should have discussed this issue separately with the parents and then set up a discussion between Georgina and her parents. Such a discussion would have resulted in a better understanding of the rationale for the rules. In this case, the therapist likely would have worked toward a dialogue that would help Georgina understand her parents' limits as a sign of concern and protection and assisted her in accepting and living within those limits. Thus, collaboration often means providing the necessary consultation and support to the client for changing or living within a healthy family system.

TRAINING CHILD AND FAMILY PSYCHOLOGISTS

One problem in the field of child and family intervention is that many of the professionals who deliver the services have not been adequately trained. It is common for psychologists and therapists who graduate from programs in which they have primarily been trained to work with adult populations to then find themselves in community settings with a caseload of children and families. The result is unethical treatment of children and families—the result not of malfeasance but of a lack of knowledge and skills related to working with this population.

M. C. Roberts et al. (1998) developed a series of guidelines for improving the training of psychologists who provide services to children and families. The model was developed through a 1992 initiative of the National Institute of Mental Health with the formation of a task group to improve quality services for children and families. Exhibit 14.1 lists the guidelines developed by this group.

Note that content in both developmental psychology and psychopathology is recommended, as is training in assessment methods that include

EXHIBIT 14.1
Training Criteria for Psychologists Who Work With an Ecological Emphasis

- Life span developmental psychology.
- Life span developmental psychopathology.
- Child, adolescent, and family assessment methods.
- Intervention strategies.
- Research methods and systems evaluation.
- Professional, ethical, and legal issues pertaining to children, adolescents, and families.
- Issues of diversity.
- The role of multiple disciplines and service delivery systems.
- Prevention, family support, and health promotion.
- Social issues affecting children, adolescents, and families.
- Specialized, applied experiences in assessment, intervention, and consultation.

families. Intervention strategies discussed by the task force include child or adolescent individual interventions as well as parent interventions, family interventions, and school-based interventions. Issues of diversity, multicultural competence, and systems issues are also critical to understanding and intervening with this population. Training for competency in this area requires rigorous graduate training and a practicum that focuses on both content and applied work with children and families. The recent focus of most academic institutions has been to create shorter programs for students (e.g., a 1-year master's level training). Unfortunately, these programs simply do not provide adequate time to train practitioners to deliver ethical services to children and families.

SUMMARY

When services are provided within an ecological perspective, ethical and professional standards are often complex. It is often necessary to think systemically when the cost and benefits of professional behavior are considered. The current APA ethical guidelines are certainly minimal, but their application is somewhat more involved. We offer professional guidelines for child and family interventions. First, the decision is bifurcated by the safety issue: Is anyone in the family at risk for physical, sexual, or emotional harm? If the answer is yes, then the focus becomes achieving safety. If the answer is no, then the series of steps that lead to behavior change are taken. The Family Check-Up offers a framework that is also a useful strategy for making good decisions about intervention activities that minimize ethical problems for children and families. Second, in addition to the general set of procedures described in this book, we offer the five Cs as guidelines for professional behavior that minimize harm and ethical problems and maximize positive client outcomes: competence, custody clarification, cultural awareness, confidentiality, and collaboration not collusion. Finally, we stress that training in child and family intervention services must address basic developmental norms and training in norm-referenced, multi-informant assessment materials so that practitioners can fully understand the problem and context for treatment.

REFERENCES

Achenbach, T. M. (1982). *Developmental psychopathology* (2nd ed.). New York: Wiley.

Achenbach, T. M. (1992). *Manual for the Child Behavior Checklist 2/3 and 1992 profile*. Burlington: University of Vermont Department of Psychiatry.

Achenbach, T. M., & Edelbrock, C. S. (1981). *Youth Self-Report (YSR)*. Burlington: University of Vermont Press.

Achenbach, T. M., McConaughy, S. H., & Howell, C. T. (1987). Child/adolescent behavioral and emotional problems: Implications of cross-information correlations for situational specificity. *Psychological Bulletin, 101*, 213–232.

Alvy, K. T., & Marigna, M. (1985). *Cognitive-behavioral parenting skill-building program. Instructor's manual*. Studio City, CA: Center for the Improvement of Child Caring.

American Psychiatric Association. (1994). *Diagnostic and statistical manual of mental disorders* (4th ed.). Washington, DC: Author.

American Psychological Association. (2002). *Ethical principles of psychologists and code of conduct*. Retrieved May 10, 2006, from http://www.apa.org/ethics/code2002.html

Arnold, J. E., Levine, A. G., & Patterson, G. R. (1975). Changes in sibling behavior following family intervention. *Journal of Consulting and Clinical Psychology, 43*, 683–688.

Bakeman, R., & Gottman, J. M. (1986). *Observing interaction: An introduction to sequential analysis*. New York: Cambridge University Press.

Bakeman, R., & Quera, V. (1995). Log-linear approaches to lag-sequential analysis when consecutive codes may and cannot repeat. *Psychological Bulletin, 118*, 272–284.

Bandura, A. (1997). *Self-efficacy: The exercise of control*. New York: Freeman.

Barber, B. K. (1996). Parental psychological control: Revisiting a neglected construct. *Child Development, 67*, 3296–3319.

Barker, R. G. (1960). Ecology and motivation. In M. R. Jones (Ed.), *Nebraska Symposium on Motivation: Vol. 8.* (pp. 1–50). Lincoln: University of Nebraska Press.

Barker, R. G. (1968). *Ecological psychology*. Stanford, CA: Stanford University Press.

Barkley, R. A. (2001). The executive functions and self-regulation: An evolutionary neuropsychological perspective. *Neuropsychology Review, 11*, 1–29.

Barkley, R. A., Edwards, G., Laneri, M., Fletcher, K., & Metevia, L. (2001). The efficacy of problem-solving communication training alone, behavior management training alone, and the combination for parent–adolescent conflict in teenagers with ADHD and ODD. *Journal of Consulting and Clinical Psychology, 69*, 926–941.

Barmish, A. J., & Kendall, P. C. (2005). Should parents be co-clients in cognitive–behavioral therapy for anxious youth? *Journal of Clinical Child and Adolescent Psychology, 34,* 569–581.

Barrett, M. S., & Berman, J. S. (2001). Is psychotherapy more effective when therapists disclose information about themselves? *Journal of Consulting and Clinical Psychology, 69,* 597.

Baumeister, R. F., & Vohs, K. D. (Eds.). (2004). *Handbook of self-regulation: Research, theory, and applications.* New York: Guilford Press.

Bem, D. J., & Funder, D. C. (1978). Predicting more of the people more of the time: Assessing the personality of situations. *Psychological Review, 85,* 485–501.

Bernard, J. M., & Goodyear, R. K. (1992). *Fundamentals of clinical supervision.* Needham Heights, MA: Allyn & Bacon.

Bierman, K. L. (1990). Improving the peer relations of rejected children. In B. B. Lahey & A. E. Kazdin (Eds.), *Advances in clinical child psychology* (pp. 131–149). New York: Plenum Press.

Bierman, K. L., Coie, J. D., Dodge, K. A., Greenberg, M. T., Lochman, J. E., McMahon, R. J., & Pinderhughes, E. E. (1999). Initial impact of the fast track prevention trial for conduct problems: I. The high-risk sample. *Journal of Consulting and Clinical Psychology, 67,* 631–647.

Biglan, A. (1995). Choosing a paradigm to guide prevention research and practice. In C. G. Leukefeld & R. R. Clayton (Eds.), *Prevention practice in substance abuse* (pp. 149–160). New York: Haworth Press.

Biglan, A., & Taylor, T. K. (2000). Increasing the use of science to improve child-rearing. *Journal of Primary Prevention, 21,* 207–226.

Birchler, G. R., Weiss, R. L., & Vincent, J. P. (1975). Multimethod analysis of social reinforcement exchange between maritally distressed and nondistressed spouse and stranger dyads. *Journal of Personality and Social Psychology, 31,* 349–360.

Blechman, E. A., Taylor, C. J., & Schrader, S. M. (1981). Family problem solving versus home notes as early intervention with high-risk children. *Journal of Consulting and Clinical Psychology, 49,* 919–926.

Boivin, M., Poulin, F., & Vitaro, F. (1994). Depressed mood and peer rejection in childhood. *Development and Psychopathology, 6,* 483–498.

Borduin, C. M., & Henggeler, S. W. (1990). A multisystemic approach to the treatment of delinquent behavior. In R. J. McMahon & R. D. Peters (Eds.), *Behavior disorders of adolescence: Research, intervention and policy in clinical and school settings* (pp. 63–80). New York: Haworth Press.

Brendgen, M., Vitaro, F., Turgeon, L., & Poulin, F. (2002). Assessing aggressive and depressed children's social relations with classmates and friends: A matter of perspective. *Journal of Abnormal Child Psychology, 30,* 609–624.

Brent, D. A., Holder, D., Kolko, D., Birmaker, B., Baugher, M., Roth, C., et al. (1997). A clinical psychotherapy trial for adolescent depression comparing cognitive, family, and supportive therapy. *Archives of General Psychiatry, 54,* 877–885.

Brody, G. H., McBride Murry, V., Kim, S., & Brown, A. C. (2002). Longitudinal pathways to competence and psychological adjustment among African American children living in rural single-parent households. *Child Development, 73,* 1505–1516.

Bronfenbrenner, U. (1979). *The ecology of human development: Experiments by nature and by design.* Cambridge, MA: Harvard University Press.

Bronfenbrenner, U. (1986). Ecology of the family as a context for human development. *Developmental Psychology, 22,* 723–742.

Bronfenbrenner, U. (1989). Ecological systems theory. In P. Vasta (Ed.), *Annals of Child Development: Vol. 6. Six theories of child development: Revised formulations and current issues* (pp. 187–249). London: JAI Press.

Bronfenbrenner, U., & Ceci, S. J. (1994). Nature–nurture reconceptualized in developmental perspective: A bioecological model. *Psychological Review, 101,* 568–586.

Brown, J. M., & Miller, W. R. (1993). Impact of motivational interviewing on participation and outcome in residential alcoholism treatment. *Addictive Behaviors, 7,* 211–218.

Bugental, D. B., Ellerson, P. C., Rainey, B., Lin, E. K., Kokotovic, A., & O'Hara, N. (2002). A cognitive approach to child abuse prevention. *Journal of Family Psychology, 16,* 16–45.

Bullock, B. M., Bank, L., & Burraston, B. (2002). Adult sibling expressed emotion and fellow sibling deviance: A new piece of the family process puzzle. *Journal of Family Psychology, 16,* 307–317.

Bullock, B. M., & Dishion, T. J. (2002). Sibling collusion and problem behavior in early adolescence: Toward a process model for family mutuality. *Journal of Abnormal Child Psychology, 30,* 143–153.

Cairns, R. B., Perrin, J. E., & Cairns, B. D. (1985). Social structure and social cognition in early adolescence: Affiliative patterns. *Journal of Early Adolescence, 5,* 339–355.

Calhoun, K. S., Moras, K., Pilkonis, P. A., & Rehm, L. P. (1998). Empirically supported treatments: Implications for training. *Journal of Consulting and Clinical Psychology, 66,* 151–162.

Campbell, D. T., & Fiske, D. W. (1959). Conversant and discriminant validation of the multitrait and multimethod matrix. *Psychological Bulletin, 56,* 81–105.

Cantor, N., & Harlow, R. E. (1994). Personality, strategic behavior, and daily-life problem solving. *Current Directions in Psychological Science, 3,* 169–172.

Capaldi, D. M. (1992). Co-occurrence of conduct problems and depressive symptoms in early adolescent boys: II. A 2-year follow-up at Grade 8. *Development and Psychopathology, 4,* 125–144.

Capaldi, D. M., Crosby, L., & Stoolmiller, M. (1996). Predicting the timing of first sexual intercourse for at-risk adolescent males. *Child Development, 67,* 344–359.

Capaldi, D. M., Dishion, T. J., Stoolmiller, M., & Yoerger, K. (2001). Aggression toward female partners by at-risk young men: The contribution of male adolescent friendships. *Developmental Psychology, 37,* 61–73.

Capaldi, D. M., & Patterson, G. R. (1991). Relation of parental transitions to boys' adjustment problems: I. A linear hypothesis: II. Mothers at risk for transitions and unskilled parenting. *Developmental Psychology, 27,* 489–504.

Caron, C., & Rutter, M. (1991). Comorbidity in child psychopathology: Concepts, issues, and research strategies. *Journal of Child Psychology and Psychiatry, 32,* 1063–1080.

Catalano, R. F., Morrison, D. M., Wells, E. A., Gillmore, M. R., Iritani, B., & Hawkins, J. D. (1992). Ethnic differences and family factors related to early drug initiation. *Journal of Studies on Alcohol, 53,* 208–217.

Caughy, M. O., O'Campo, P. J., Randolph, S. M., & Nickerson, K. (2002). The influence of racial socialization practices on the cognitive and behavioral competence of African American preschoolers. *Child Development, 73,* 1611–1625.

Chamberlain, P. (1994). *A social interactional approach: Vol. 5. Family connections: A treatment foster care model for adolescents with delinquency.* Eugene, OR: Castalia.

Chamberlain, P., & Moore, K. J. (1998). Models of community treatment for serious offenders. In J. Crane (Ed.), *Social programs that really work* (pp. 258–276). Princeton, NJ: Russell Sage Foundation.

Chamberlain, P., & Reid, J. B. (1987). Parent observation and report of child symptoms. *Behavioral Assessment, 9,* 97–109.

Chamberlain, P., & Smith, D. K. (2003). Antisocial behavior in children and adolescents: The Oregon multidimensional treatment foster care model. In A. E. Kazdin & J. R. Weisz (Eds.), *Evidence-based psychotherapies for children and adolescents* (pp. 282–300). New York: Guilford Press.

Chavous, T. M., Bernat, D. H., Schmeelk-Cone, K., Caldwell, C. H., Kohn-Wood, L., & Zimmerman, M. A. (2003). Racial identity and academic attainment among African American adolescents. *Child Development, 74,* 1076–1090.

Chilcoate, H., Anthony, J., & Dishion, T. J. (1995). Parent monitoring and the incidence of drug sampling in multiethnic urban children. *American Journal of Epidemiology, 141,* 25–31.

Cicchetti, D. (Ed.). (1993). Developmental psychopathology: Reactions, reflections, projections. *Developmental Review, 13,* 471–502.

Cicchetti, D., & Toth, S. L. (1992). The role of developmental theory in prevention and intervention. *Development and Psychopathology, 4,* 489–493.

Clark, M. S., & Reis, H. T. (1988). Interpersonal processes in close relationships. *Annual Review of Psychology, 39,* 609–672.

Clarke, G. N., DeBar, L. L., & Lewinsohn, P. M. (2003). Cognitive–behavioral group treatment for adolescent depression. In A. E. Kazdin & J. R. Weisz (Eds.), *Evidence-based psychotherapies for children and adolescents* (pp. 120–134). New York: Guilford Press.

Coatsworth, J. D., Szapocznik, J., Kurtines, W., & Santisteban, D. A. (1997). Culturally competent psychosocial interventions with antisocial problem behavior in Hispanic youth. In D. M. Stoff, J. Breiling, & J. D. Maser (Eds.), *Handbook of antisocial behavior* (pp. 103–114). New York: Wiley.

Coco, E. L., & Courtney, L. J. (2003). A family systems approach for preventing adolescent runaway behavior. *Family Therapy, 30,* 39–50.

Cohen, J. A., & Mannarino, A. P. (1996). Factors that mediate treatment outcome of sexually abused preschool children. *Journal of the American Academy of Child and Adolescent Psychiatry, 35,* 1402–1410.

Cohen, J. A., & Mannarino, A. P. (1997). A treatment study for sexually abused preschool children: Outcome during a one-year follow-up. *Journal of the American Academy of Child and Adolescent Psychiatry, 36,* 1228–1235.

Cohen, J. A., & Mannarino, A. P. (1998). Factors that mediate treatment outcome of sexually abused preschool children: Six- and 12-month follow-up. *Journal of the American Academy of Child and Adolescent Psychiatry, 37,* 44–51.

Cohen, J. A., & Mannarino, A. P. (2000). Incest. In R. T. Ammerman & M. Hersen (Eds.), *Case studies in family violence* (2nd ed., pp. 209–229). New York: Plenum Press.

Cohen, J. A., Mannarino, A. P., Berliner, L., & Deblinger, E. (2000). Trauma-focused cognitive behavioral therapy for children and adolescents: An empirical update. *Journal of Interpersonal Violence, 15,* 1202–1223.

Collins, L. M., Murphy, S. A., & Bierman, K. L. (2004). A conceptual framework for adaptive preventive interventions. *Prevention Science, 5,* 185–196.

Compas, B. E., Hinden, B. R., & Gerhardt, C. A. (1995). Adolescent development: Pathways and processes of risk and resilience. *Annual Review of Psychology, 46,* 265–293.

Conduct Problems Prevention Research Group. (1992). A developmental and clinical model for the prevention of conduct disorders: The FAST Track program. *Development and Psychopathology, 4,* 509–527.

Conduct Problems Prevention Research Group. (1999). Initial impact of the FAST Track Prevention trial for conduct problems: I. The high-risk sample. *Journal of Consulting and Clinical Psychology, 67,* 631–647.

Conduct Problems Prevention Research Group. (2002). Evaluation of the first 3 years of the Fast Track Prevention Trial with children at high risk for adolescent conduct problems. *Journal of Abnormal Child Psychology, 30,* 19–35.

Connell, A. M., & Dishion, T. J. (2006, March). *Latent growth mixture modeling in family research: Family dynamics and depressive symptom trajectories across adolescence.* Paper presented at the Biennial Conference for the Society for Research on Adolescence, San Francisco, CA.

Connell, A. M., Dishion, T. J., & Deater-Deckard, K. (in press). Variable- and person-centered approaches to the analysis of early adolescent substance use: Linking peer, family, and intervention effects with developmental trajectories [Special issue]. *Merrill-Palmer Quarterly.*

Connell, A. M., Dishion, T. J., & Kavanagh, K. (2005). *Preventing adolescent substance use with a family-centered approach in the public school context*. Manuscript in preparation.

Connell, A. M., Dishion, T. J., Yasui, M., & Kavanagh, K. (in press). An ecological approach to family intervention to reduce adolescent problem behavior: Intervention engagement and longitudinal change. In S. Evans (Ed.), *Advances in school-based mental health: Vol 2*. Kingston, NJ: Civic Research Institute.

Connell, S., Sanders, M. R., & Markie-Dadds, C. (1997). Self-directed behavioral family intervention for parents of oppositional children in rural and remote areas. *Behavior Modification, 21*, 379–408.

Crandall, C. S. (1988). Social contagion of binge eating. *Journal of Personality and Social Psychology, 55*, 588–598.

Crick, N. R., & Dodge, K. A. (1994). A review and reformulation of social information-processing mechanisms in children's social adjustment. *Psychological Bulletin, 115*, 74–101.

Cronbach, L. J., & Glesar, G. C. (1965). *Psychological tests and personnel decisions*. Urbana: University of Illinois Press.

Cronbach, L. J., & Meehl, P. E. T. (1955). Construct validity in psychological tests. *Psychological Bulletin, 52*, 281–302.

Dadds, M. R., Spence, S. H., Holland, D. E., Barrett, P. M., & Lacrens, K. R. (1997). Prevention and early intervention for anxiety disorders: A controlled trial. *Journal of Consulting and Clinical Psychology, 65*, 627–635.

Dawes, R. M. (1994). *House of cards: Psychology and psychotherapy built on myth*. New York: Free Press.

Deater-Deckard, K., & Dodge, K. A. (1997). Spare the rod, spoil the authors: Emerging themes in research on parenting and child development. *Psychological Inquiry, 8*, 230–235.

Deater-Deckard, K., Dodge, K. A., Bates, J. E., & Pettit, G. S. (1996). Physical discipline among African-American and European-American mothers: Links to children's externalizing behaviors. *Developmental Psychology, 32*, 1065–1072.

Deblinger, E., & Heflin, A. H. (1996). *Treating sexually abused children and their nonoffending parents: A cognitive behavioral approach*. Thousand Oaks, CA: Sage.

DeGarmo, D. S., Patterson, G. R., & Forgatch, M. S. (2004). How do outcomes in a specified parent training intervention maintain or wane over time? *Prevention Science, 5*, 73–89.

DePrince, A. P., & Freyd, J. J. (1999). Dissociative tendencies, attention, and memory. *Psychological Science, 10*, 449–452.

Dionne, R., & Dishion, T. J. (2004). *Restoring the circle: An ecological perspective on parenting programs, science, and the American Indian community*. Manuscript submitted for publication.

Dishion, T. J. (1990). The family ecology of boys' peer relations in middle childhood. *Child Development, 61*, 874–892.

Dishion, T. J. (2000). Cross-setting consistency in early adolescent psychopathology: Deviant friendships and problem behavior sequelae. *Journal of Personality*, 68, 1109–1126.

Dishion, T. J., & Andrews, D. W. (1995). Preventing escalation in problem behaviors with high-risk young adolescents: Immediate and 1-year outcomes. *Journal of Consulting and Clinical Psychology*, 63, 538–548.

Dishion, T. J., Andrews, D. W., & Crosby, L. (1995). Antisocial boys and their friends in early adolescence: Relationship characteristics, quality, and interactional process. *Child Development*, 66, 139–151.

Dishion, T. J., Andrews, D. W., Kavanagh, K., & Soberman, L. H. (1996). Preventive interventions for high-risk youth: The Adolescent Transitions Program. In B. McMahon & R. D. Peters (Eds.), *Conduct disorders, substance abuse and delinquency: Prevention and early intervention approaches* (pp. 184–214). Newbury Park, CA: Sage.

Dishion, T. J., & Bullock, B. (2002). Parenting and adolescent problem behavior: An ecological analysis of the nurturance hypothesis. In J. G. Borkowski, S. Ramey, & M. Bristol-Power (Eds.), *Parenting and the child's world: Influences on intellectual, academic, and social-emotional development* (pp. 231–249). Mahwah, NJ: Erlbaum.

Dishion, T. J., Bullock, B. M., & Granic, I. (2002). Pragmatism in modeling peer influence: Dynamics, outcomes, and change processes. In D. Cicchetti & S. Hinshaw (Eds.), How prevention intervention studies in the field of developmental psychopathology can inform development theories and models [Special issue]. *Development and Psychopathology*, 14, 969–981.

Dishion, T. J., Burraston, B., & Li, F. (2002). Family management practices: Research design and measurement issues. In W. Bukowski & Z. Amsel (Eds.), *Handbook for drug abuse prevention theory, science, and practice* (pp. 587–607). New York: Plenum Press.

Dishion, T. J., Capaldi, D. M., Spracklen, K. M., & Li, F. (1995). Peer ecology of male adolescent drug use. *Development and Psychopathology*, 7, 803–824.

Dishion, T. J., & Dodge, K. A. (2005). Peer contagion in interventions for children and adolescents: Moving towards an understanding of the ecology and dynamics of change. *Journal of Abnormal Child Psychology*, 33, 395–400.

Dishion, T. J., Duncan, T. E., Eddy, J. M., Fagot, B. I., & Fetrow, R. A. (1994). The world of parents and peers: Coercive exchanges and children's social adaptation. *Social Development*, 3, 255–268.

Dishion, T. J., Eddy, J. M., Haas, E., Li, F., & Spracklen, K. (1997). Friendships and violent behavior during adolescence. *Social Development*, 6, 207–223.

Dishion, T. J., French, D. C., & Patterson, G. R. (1995). The development and ecology of antisocial behavior. In D. Cicchetti & D. J. Cohen (Eds.), *Developmental psychopathology: Vol. 2. Risk, disorder, and adaptation* (pp. 421–471). New York: Wiley.

Dishion, T. J., Gardner, K., Patterson, G. R., Reid, J. B., & Thibodeaux, S. (1983). *The Family Process Code: A multidimensional system for observing family interaction* [Unpublished coding manual]. Eugene: Oregon Social Learning Center.

Dishion, T. J., Hogansen, J., & Winter, C. E. (2000). *Macro ratings of family management and process in adolescence* [Unpublished technical manual]. Eugene: Child and Family Center, University of Oregon.

Dishion, T. J., & Kavanagh, K. (2002). The Adolescent Transitions Program: A family-centered prevention strategy for schools. In J. B. Reid, J. J. Snyder, & G. R. Patterson (Eds.), *Antisocial behavior in children and adolescents: A developmental analysis and model for intervention* (pp. 257–272). Washington, DC: American Psychological Association.

Dishion, T. J., & Kavanagh, K. (2003). *Intervening in adolescent problem behavior: A family-centered approach.* New York: Guilford Press.

Dishion, T. J., Kavanagh, K., & Christianson, S. (1995). *Parenting in the teenage years* [Video]. Eugene, OR: Intervision.

Dishion, T. J., Kavanagh, K., Schneiger, A., Nelson, S. E., & Kaufman, N. (2002). Preventing early adolescent substance use: A family-centered strategy for the public middle-school ecology. In R. L. Spoth, K. Kavanagh, & T. J. Dishion (Eds.), Universal family-centered prevention strategies: Current findings and critical issues for public health impact [Special issue]. *Prevention Science, 3,* 191–201.

Dishion, T. J., McCord, J., & Poulin, F. (1999). When interventions harm: Peer groups and problem behavior. *American Psychologist, 54,* 755–764.

Dishion, T. J., & McMahon, R. J. (1998). Parental monitoring and the prevention of child and adolescent problem behavior: A conceptual and empirical formulation. *Clinical Child and Family Psychology Review, 1,* 61–75.

Dishion, T. J., Nelson, S. E., & Bullock, B. M. (2004). Premature adolescent autonomy: Parent disengagement and deviant peer process in the amplification of problem behavior. *Journal of Adolescence, 27,* 515–530.

Dishion, T. J., Nelson, S. E., & Kavanagh, K. (2003). The Family Check-Up for high-risk adolescents: Motivating parenting monitoring and reducing problem behavior. In J. E. Lochman & R. Salekin (Eds.), Behavior oriented interventions for children with aggressive behavior and/or conduct problems [Special issue]. *Behavior Therapy, 34,* 553–571.

Dishion, T. J., Nelson, S. N., Winter, C., & Bullock, B. M. (2004). Adolescent friendship as a dynamic system: Entropy and deviance in the etiology and course of male antisocial behavior. *Journal of Abnormal Child Psychology, 32,* 651–663.

Dishion, T. J., Nelson, S. E., & Yasui, M. (2005). Predicting early adolescent gang involvement from middle school adaptation. *Journal of Clinical Child and Adolescent Psychology, 34,* 62–73.

Dishion, T. J., & Owen, L. D. (2002). A longitudinal analysis of friendships and substance use: Bidirectional influence from adolescence to adulthood. *Developmental Psychology, 38,* 480–491.

Dishion, T. J., Owen, L. D., & Bullock, B. N. (2004). Like father, like son: Toward a developmental model for the transmission of male deviance across generations. *European Journal of Developmental Psychology, 1,* 105–126.

Dishion, T. J., & Patterson, G. R. (1992). Age effects in parent training outcome. *Behavior Therapy, 23,* 719–729.

Dishion, T. J., & Patterson, G. R. (1993). Antisocial behavior: Using a multiple gating strategy. In M. I. Singer, L. T. Singer, & T. M. Anglin (Eds.), *Handbook for screening adolescents at psychosocial risk* (pp. 375–399). New York: Lexington Books.

Dishion, T. J., & Patterson, S. G. (1996). *Preventive parenting with love, encouragement, and limits: The preschool years.* Eugene, OR: Castalia.

Dishion, T. J., & Patterson, G. R. (1999). Model-building in developmental psychopathology: A pragmatic approach to understanding and intervention. *Journal of Clinical Child Psychology, 28,* 502–512.

Dishion, T. J., & Patterson, S. G. (2005). *Parenting young children with love, encouragement, and limits: The preschool years.* Champaign, IL: Research Press.

Dishion, T. J., & Patterson, G. R. (2006). The development and ecology of antisocial behavior. In D. Cicchetti & D. J. Cohen (Eds.), *Developmental psychopathology, Vol. 3: Risk, disorder, and adaptation* (2nd ed., pp. 503–541). New York: Wiley.

Dishion, T. J., Patterson, G. R., & Kavanagh, K. (1992). An experimental test of the coercion model: Linking theory, measurement, and intervention. In J. McCord & R. Tremblay (Eds.), *The interaction of theory and practice: Experimental studies of intervention* (pp. 253–282). New York: Guilford Press.

Dishion, T. J., Patterson, G. R., Stoolmiller, M., & Skinner, M. (1991). Family, school, and behavioral antecedents to early adolescent involvement with antisocial peers. *Developmental Psychology, 27,* 172–180.

Dishion, T. J., Poulin, F., & Burraston, B. (2001). Peer group dynamics associated with iatrogenic effects in group interventions with high-risk young adolescents. In C. Erdley & D. W. Nangle (Eds.), *New directions for child and adolescent development: Vol. 81. The role of friendship in psychological adjustment* (pp. 79–92). San Francisco: Jossey-Bass.

Dishion, T. J., Poulin, F., & Medici Skaggs, N. (2000). The ecology of premature adolescent autonomy: Biological and social influences. In K. A. Kerns, S. M. Contreras, & A. M. Neal-Barnett (Eds.), *Explaining associations between family and peer relationships* (pp. 27–45). Westport, CT: Praeger Publishers.

Dishion, T. J., Spracklen, K. M., Andrews, D. M., & Patterson, G. R. (1996). Deviancy training in male adolescent friendships. *Behavior Therapy, 27,* 373–390.

Dodge, K. A. (1991). The structure and function of reactive and proactive aggression. In D. J. Pepler & K. H. Rubin (Eds.), *The development and treatment of childhood aggression* (pp. 201–218). Hillsdale, NJ: Erlbaum.

Dodge, K., Dishion, T. J., & Lansford, J. (in press). *Deviant peer influences in programs for youth: Problems and solutions.* New York: Guilford.

Dodge, K. A., & Frame, C. L. (1982). Social cognitive biases and deficits in aggressive boys. *Child Development, 53,* 620–635.

Dodge, K. A., Lochman, J. E., Harnish, J. D., Bates, J. E., & Pettit, G. S. (1997). Reactive and proactive aggression in school children and psychiatrically impaired chronically assaultive youth. *Journal of Abnormal Psychology, 106,* 37–51.

Dodge, K. A., & Sherrill, M. (in press). Deviant peer-group effects in youth mental health interventions. In K. Dodge, T. Dishion, & J. Lansford (Eds.). *Deviant peer influences in programs for youth: Problems and solutions.* New York: Guilford Press.

Duncan, G. J., Boisjoly, J., Kremer, M., Levy, D. M., & Eccles, J. (2005). Peer effects in drug use and sex among college students. *Journal of Abnormal Child Psychology, 33,* 375–385.

Duran, E., & Duran, B. (1995). *Native American postcolonial psychology.* Albany: State University of New York Press.

Durlak, J. A., Fuhrman, T., & Lampman, C. (1991). Effectiveness of cognitive–behavioral therapy for maladapting children: A meta-analysis. *Psychological Bulletin, 110,* 204–214.

Dwyer, J. H. (1983). *Statistical models for the social and behavior sciences.* New York: Oxford University Press.

Eccles, J. S., Lord, S., & Buchanan, C. M. (1996). School transitions in early adolescence: What are we doing to our young people? In J. A. Graber, J. Brooks-Gunn, & A. C. Petersen (Eds.), *Transitions through adolescence: Interpersonal domains and context* (pp. 251–284). Mahwah, NJ: Erlbaum.

Eccles, J. S., Midgley, C., Feldlaufer, H., Ramon, W. A., & MacIver, D. (1989, April). *Junior high school transitions: Evidence of a developmental mismatch.* Paper presented at the biennial meeting of the Society for Research in Child Development, Kansas City, MO.

Eddy, J. M., & Chamberlain, P. (2000). Family management and deviant peer association as mediators of the impact of treatment condition on youth antisocial behavior. *Journal of Child Clinical Psychology, 5,* 857–863.

Eddy, J. M., Reid, J. B., Stoolmiller, M., & Fetrow, R. A. (2003). Outcomes during middle school for an elementary school-based preventive intervention for conduct problems: Follow-up results from a randomized trial. *Behavior Therapy, 34,* 535–552.

Eisenberg, N., Carlo, G., Murphy, B., & Van Court, P. (1995). Prosocial development in late adolescence: A longitudinal study. *Child Development, 66,* 1179–1197.

Eisenberg, N., Fabes, R. A., Guthrie, I. K., & Reiser, M. (2000). Dispositional emotionality and regulation: Their role in predicting quality of social functioning. *Journal of Personality and Social Psychology, 78,* 136–157.

Elder, G. H., Jr., Van Nguyen, T., & Caspi, A. (1985). Linking family hardship to children's lives. *Child Development, 56,* 361–375.

Elliott, D. S., Huizinga, D., & Ageton, S. S. (1985). *Explaining delinquency and drug use.* Beverly Hills, CA: Sage.

Ellis, S., Rogoff, B., & Cromer, C. (1981). Age segregation in children's interactions. *Developmental Psychology, 17,* 399–407.

Falloon, I. R. H., Boyd, J. L., McGill, C. W., Williamson, M., Razani, J., Moss, H. B., et al. (1985). Family management in the prevention of morbidity of schizophrenia. *Archives of General Psychiatry, 42,* 887–896.

Felner, R. D., & Felner, T. Y. (1989). Primary prevention programs in the educational context: A transactional-ecological framework and analysis. In L. A. Bond & B. E. Compas (Eds.), *Primary prevention and promotion in the schools: Vol 12. Primary prevention of psychopathology* (pp. 13–49). Thousand Oaks, CA: Sage.

Fischoff, B., & Downs, J. (1997). Accentuate the relevant. *Psychological Science, 8,* 154–158.

Fisher, C. B., Hatashita-Wong, M., & Greene, L. I. (Eds.). (1999). *Ethical and legal issues.* Needham, MA: Allyn & Bacon.

Fisher, P. A., Burraston, B., & Pears, K. (2004). The early intervention foster-care program: Permanent placement outcomes from a randomized trial. *Journal of Child Maltreatment, 8,* 1–111.

Fisher, P. A., & Stormshak, E. A. (2000). Interventions for parents and families: A developmental psychopathology perspective. In M. Gelder, J. Lopez-Ibor, & N. Andreason (Eds.), *The new Oxford textbook of psychiatry* (pp. 1899–1904). Oxford, England: Oxford University Press.

Fletcher, A. C., Darling, N., & Steinberg, L. (1995). Parental monitoring and peer influences on adolescent substance use. In J. McCord (Ed.), *Coercion and punishment in long-term perspectives* (pp. 259–271). New York: Cambridge University Press.

Florsheim, P., Tolan, P. H., & Gorman-Smith, D. (1996). Family processes and risk for externalizing behavior problems among African American and Hispanic boys. *Journal of Consulting and Clinical Psychology, 64,* 1222–1230.

Forgatch, M. S. (1984). *A two-stage analysis of family problem solving: Global and microsocial.* Unpublished doctoral dissertation, University of Oregon, Eugene.

Forgatch, M. S. (1989). Patterns and outcome in family problem-solving: The disrupting effect of negative emotion. *Journal of Marriage and Family, 51,* 115–124.

Forgatch, M. S. (1991). The clinical science vortex: Developing a theory for antisocial behavior. In D. J. Pepler & K. H. Rubin (Eds.), *The development and treatment of childhood aggression* (pp. 291–315). Hillsdale, NJ: Erlbaum.

Forgatch, M. S., Bullock, B. M., & Patterson, G. R. (2004). From theory to practice: Increasing effective parenting through role play. The Oregon Model of Parent Management Training (PMTO). In H. Steiner, K. Chang, J. Lock, & J. Wilson (Eds.), *Handbook of mental health interventions in children and adolescents: An integrated development approach* (pp. 782–812). San Francisco: Jossey-Bass.

Forgatch, M. S., & DeGarmo, D. S. (1999). Parenting through change: An effective prevention program for single mothers. *Journal of Consulting and Clinical Psychology, 67,* 711–724.

Forgatch, M. S., & DeGarmo, D. (2002). Extending and testing the social interaction learning model with divorce samples. In J. B. Reid & G. R. Patterson (Eds.), *Antisocial behavior in children and adolescents: A developmental analysis and model for intervention* (pp. 235–256). Washington, DC: American Psychological Association.

Forgatch, M. S., & Patterson, G. R. (1989). *Parents and adolescents living together: Part 2: Family problem-solving.* Eugene, OR: Castalia.

Forgatch, M. S., Patterson, G. R., & DeGarmo, D. S. (2005). Evaluating fidelity: Predictive validity for a measure of competent adherence to the Oregon Model of Parent Management Training. *Behavior Therapy, 36,* 3–13.

Frabutt, J. M., Walker, A. M., & MacKinnon-Lewis, C. (2002). Racial socialization messages and the quality of mother/child interactions in African American families. *Journal of Early Adolescence, 22,* 200–217.

French, S. A., Story, M., Downes, B., Resnick, M. D., & Blum, R. W. (1995). Frequent dieting among adolescents: Psychosocial and health behavior correlates. *American Journal of Public Health, 85,* 695–701.

Freyd, J. J. (1996). *Betrayal trauma.* Cambridge, MA: Harvard University Press.

Fuligni, A. J. (1997). The academic achievement of adolescents from immigrant families: The roles of family background, attitudes, and behavior. *Child Development, 68,* 351–363.

Fuligni, A. J. (1998). Authority, autonomy, and parent–adolescent conflict and cohesion: A study of adolescents from Mexican, Chinese, Filipino, and European backgrounds. *Developmental Psychology, 34,* 782–792.

Gardner, F. E. M., & Griffin, W. A. (1989). Methods for the analysis of parallel streams of continuously recorded social behaviors. *Psychological Bulletin, 105,* 446–455.

Garrod, A., Ward, J. V., Robinson, T. L., & Kilkenny, R. (1999). *Souls looking back: Life stories of growing up black.* New York: Routledge.

Ge, X., Conger, R. D., & Elder, G. H., Jr. (1996). Coming of age too early: Pubertal influences on girls' vulnerability to psychological distress. *Child Development, 67,* 3386–3400.

Gifford-Smith, M., Dodge, K. A., Dishion, T. J., & McCord, J. (2005). Peer influence in children and adolescents: Crossing the bridge from developmental to intervention science. *Journal of Abnormal Child Psychology, 33,* 255–265.

Gillmore, M. R., Catalano, R. F., Morrison, D. M., Wells, E. A., Iritani, B., & Hawkins, J. D. (1990). Racial differences in acceptability and availability of drugs and early initiation of substance use. *American Journal of Drug and Alcohol Abuse, 16,* 185–206.

Gottfredson, D. C., Gottfredson, G. D., & Hybl, L. G. (1993). Managing adolescent behavior: A multiyear, multischool study. *American Educational Research Journal, 30,* 179–215.

Gottman, J. M. (1980). Analyzing for sequential connection and assessing interobserver reliability for the sequential analysis of observational data. *Behavioral Assessment, 2,* 361–368.

Gottman, J. M. (1983). How children become friends. *Monographs of the Society for Research in Child Development, 48*(3, Serial No. 108).

Gottman, J. M. (1991). Chaos and regulated change in families: A metaphor for the study of transitions. In P. A. Cowan & M. Hetherington (Eds.), *Family transitions* (pp. 247–372). Hillsdale, NJ: Erlbaum.

Gottman, J. M., & Levenson, R. W. (1986). Assessing the role of emotion in marriage. *Behavioral Assessment, 8,* 31–48.

Gottman, J. M., & Roy, A. K. (1990). *Sequential analysis: A guide for behavioral researchers.* Cambridge, NY: Cambridge University Press.

Gould, M. S., Jamieson, P., & Romer, D. (2003). Media contagion and suicide among the young. *American Behavioral Scientist, 46,* 1269–1284.

Granic, I., & Dishion, T. J. (2003). Deviant talk in adolescent friendships: A step toward measuring a pathogenic attractor process. *Social Development, 12,* 314–334.

Granic, I., & Lamey, A. V. (2002). Combining dynamic systems and multivariate analyses to compare the mother–child interactions of externalizing subtypes. *Journal of Abnormal Child Psychology, 30,* 265–283.

Greenberg, M. T., & Speltz, M. L. (1988). Contributions of attachment theory to the understanding of conduct problems during the preschool years. In J. Belsky & T. Negworski (Eds.), *Clinical implications of attachment* (pp. 177–218). Hillsdale, NJ: Erlbaum.

Greenberg, M. T., Speltz, M. L., & DeKlyen, M. (1993). The role of attachment in the early development of disruptive behavior problems. *Development and Psychopathology, 5,* 191–213.

Greenwood, G. E., & Hickman, C. W. (1991). Research and practice in parent involvement: Implications for teacher education. *Elementary School Journal, 91,* 279–287.

Gross, D., Fogg, L., Webster-Stratton, C., Garvey, C., Julion, W., & Grady, J. (2003). Parent training of toddlers in day care in low-income urban communities. *Journal of Consulting and Clinical Psychology, 71,* 261–278.

Haley, J. (Ed.). (1971). *Changing families.* New York: Grune & Stratton.

Hammen, C., & Rudolph, K. D. (1996). Childhood depression. In E. J. Mash & R. A. Berkley (Eds.), *Child psychopathology* (pp. 153–195). New York: Guilford Press.

Harkness, S., & Super, C. M. (1990). Culture and psychopathology. In M. Lewis & S. M. Miller (Eds.), *Handbook of developmental psychopathology* (pp. 41–52). New York: Plenum.

Harris, J. R. (1998). *The nurture assumption: Why children turn out the way they do.* New York: Free Press.

Harter, S. (1990). Process underlying adolescent self-concept formation. In R. Montemayor, G. R. Adams, & T. P. Gullotta (Eds.), *From childhood to adolescence: A transitional period* (pp. 205–239). Newbury Park, CA: Sage.

Harter, S. (1992). Developmental analysis of conflict caused by opposing attributes in the adolescent self-portrait. *Developmental Psychology, 28,* 251–260.

Hawkins, J. D., Catalano, R. F., Morrison, D. M., O'Donnell, J., Abbott, R. D., & Day, L. E. (1992). Effects of the first four years on protective factors and problem behaviors. In J. McCord & R. E. Tremblay (Eds.), *The prevention of antisocial behavior in children* (pp. 139–162). New York: Guilford Press.

Hawley, K. M., & Weisz, J. R. (2003). Child, parent and therapist (dis)agreement on target problems in outpatient therapy: The therapist's dilemma and its implications. *Journal of Consulting and Clinical Psychology, 71,* 62–70.

Hayes, S. C. (1987). Language and the incompatibility of evolutionary and psychological continuity. *Behavioral Analysis, 22,* 49–55.

Hayes, S. C. (1992). Verbal relations, times, and suicide. In S. C. Hayes & L. J. Hayes (Eds.), *Understanding verbal relations* (pp. 109–118). Reno, NV: Context Press.

Hayes, S. C., Barnes-Holmes, D., & Roche, B. (Eds.). (2001). *Relational frame theory: A post-Skinnerian account of human language and cognition.* New York: Kluwer Academic.

Heller, L. R., & Fantuzzo, J. W. (1993). Reciprocal peer tutoring and parent partnership: Does parent involvement make a difference? *School Psychology Review, 22,* 517–534.

Henggeler, S. W., Schoenwald, S. K., Borduin, C. M., Rowland, M. D., & Cunningham, P. B. (1998). *Multisystemic treatment of antisocial behavior in children and adolescents.* New York: Guilford Press.

Higgins, E. T., & Parsons, J. E. (1983). Social cognition and the social life of the child: Stages as subcultures. In E. T. Higgins, D. W. Ruble, & W. W. Hartup (Eds.), *Social cognition and social behavior: Developmental issues* (pp. 15–62). New York: Cambridge University Press.

Holmbeck, G. N., Greenley, R. N., & Franks, E. A. (2003). Developmental issues and considerations in research and practice. In A. E. Kazdin & J. R. Weisz (Eds.), *Evidence-based psychotherapies for children and adolescents* (pp. 21–40). New York: Guilford Press.

Hops, H., Biglan, A., Sherman, L., Arthur, J., Friedman, L., & Osteen, V. (1987). Home observations of family interactions of depressed women. *Journal of Consulting and Clinical Psychology, 55,* 341–346.

Hops, H., Sherman, L., & Biglan, A. (1990). Maternal depression, marital discord, and children's behavior: A developmental perspective. In G. R. Patterson (Ed.), *Depression and aggression in family interaction* (pp. 18–308). Hillsdale, NJ: Erlbaum.

Huey, S. J., Jr., Henggeler, S. W., Brondino, M. J., & Pickrel, S. G. (2000). Mechanisms of change in multisystemic therapy: Reducing delinquent behavior through therapist adherence and improved family and peer functioning. *Journal of Consulting and Clinical Psychology, 68,* 451–467.

Hughes, J. N., Cavell, T. A., & Grossman, P. A. (1997). A positive view of self: Risk or protection for aggressive children? *Development and Psychopathology, 9,* 75–94.

Ialongo, N., Poduska, J., Werthamer, L., & Kellam, S. (2001). The distal impact of two first-grade preventive interventions on conduct problems and disorder in early adolescence. *Journal of Emotional and Behavioral Disorders, 9*, 146–160.

Ilgen, D. R., Hollenbeck, J. R., Johnson, M., & Jundt, D. (2005). Teams in organizations: From input-process-output models to IMOI models. *Annual Review of Psychology, 56*, 517–543.

Ingoldsby, E. M., Shaw, D. S., Owens, E. B., & Winslow, E. B. (1999). A longitudinal study of interparental conflict, emotional and behavioral reactivity, and preschoolers' adjustment problems among low-income families. *Journal of Abnormal Child Psychology, 27*, 343–356.

Izard, C. E., & Harris, P. (1995). Emotional development and developmental psychopathology. In D. Cicchetti & D. J. Cohen (Eds.), *Developmental psychopathology: Risk, disorder, and adaptation* (Vol. 2, pp. 467–503). New York: Wiley.

Jabson, J., & Dishion, T. J. (2005). *Relationship Process Code.* (Available from Child and Family Center, 195 West 12th Avenue, Eugene, OR 97401)

Jacob, T., Tennenbaum, D., Seilhamer, R. A., Bargiel, K., & Sharon, T. (1994). Reactivity effects during naturalistic observation of distressed and nondistressed families. *Journal of Family Psychology, 8*, 354–363.

Jacobsen, N. S., & Truax, P. (1991). Clinical significance: A statistical approach to defining meaningful change in psychotherapy research. *Journal of Consulting and Clinical Psychology, 59*, 12–19.

Johnson, S. M., & Bolstad, O. D. (1975). Reactivity to home observation: A comparison of audio recorded behavior with observers present or absent. *Journal of Applied Behavior Analysis, 8*, 181–185.

Kaminski, R., Stormshak, E. A., Good, R., & Goodman, M. R. (2002). Prevention of substance abuse with rural Head Start children and families: Results of Project STAR. *Journal of Addictive Behaviors, 16*, 511–526.

Kandel, D. B. (1996). The parental and peer contexts of adolescent deviance: An algebra of interpersonal influences. *Journal of Drug Issues, 26*, 289–315.

Kaplan, H. B. (1973). Self-derogation and social position: Interaction effects of sex, race, education, and age. *Social Psychiatry, 8*, 92–99.

Kaplan, H. B. (1975). Increase in self-rejection as an antecedent of deviant responses. *Journal of Youth and Adolescence, 4*, 281–292.

Kaplan, H. B. (1978). Deviant behavior and self-enhancement in adolescence. *Journal of Youth and Adolescence, 7*, 253–277.

Kavanagh, K., Burraston, B., Dishion, T. J., & Schneiger, A. (2000, March). *Identification of middle school students' risk behavior: Contextual influences of gender and ethnicity.* Poster session presented at the biennial meeting of the Society for Research on Adolescence, Chicago.

Kazdin, A. E. (1990). Conduct disorder in childhood. In M. Hersen & C. G. Last (Eds.), *Pergamon General Psychology Series: Vol. 161. Handbook of child and adult psychopathology: A longitudinal perspective* (pp. 295–305). Elmsford, NY: Pergamon Press.

Kazdin, A. E. (1993). Treatment of conduct disorder: Progress and directions in psychotherapy research. *Development and Psychopathology, 5,* 277–310.

Kazdin, A. E. (1995). Bridging child, adolescent, and adult psychotherapy: Directions for research. *Psychotherapy Research, 5,* 258–277.

Kazdin, A. E. (1996). Developing effective treatments for children and adolescents. In E. D. Hibbs & P. S. Jensen (Eds.), *Psychosocial treatments for child and adolescent disorders: Empirically based strategies for clinical practice* (pp. 9–18). Washington, DC: American Psychological Association.

Kazdin, A. E. (1999). Current (lack of) status of theory in child and adolescent psychotherapy research. *Journal of Clinical Child Psychology, 28,* 533–543.

Kazdin, A. E. (2000). Predictors of barriers to treatment and therapeutic change in outpatient therapy for antisocial children and their families. *Mental Health Services Research, 2,* 27–40.

Kazdin, A. E. (2002). Psychosocial treatments for conduct disorder in children and adolescents. In P. E. Nathan & J. M. Gorman (Eds.), *A guide to treatments that work* (2nd ed., pp. 57–85). London: Oxford University Press.

Kazdin, A. E. (2003). Problem-solving skills training and parent management training for conduct disorder. In A. E. Kazdin & J. R. Weisz (Eds.), *Evidence-based psychotherapies for children and adolescents* (pp. 241–262). New York: Guilford Press.

Kazdin, A. E., Siegel, T. C., & Bass, D. (1992). Cognitive problem-solving skills training and parent management training in the treatment of antisocial behavior in children. *Journal of Consulting and Clinical Psychology, 60,* 733–747.

Kazdin, A. E., & Wassell, G. (1998). Treatment completion and therapeutic change among children referred for outpatient therapy. *Professional Psychology: Research and Practice, 29,* 332–340.

Kazdin, A. E., & Weisz, J. R. (1998). Identifying and developing empirically supported child and adolescent treatments. *Journal of Consulting and Clinical Psychology, 66,* 19–36.

Kazdin, A. E., & Weisz, J. R. (Eds.). (2003). *Evidence-based psychotherapies for children and adolescents.* New York: Guilford Press.

Kellam, S. G. (1990). Developmental epidemiological framework for family research on depression and aggression. In G. R. Patterson (Ed.), *Depression and aggression in family interaction* (pp. 11–48). Hillsdale, NJ: Erlbaum.

Kellam, S. G., Ling, X., Merisca, R., Brown, C. H., & Ialongo, N. (1998). The effect of the level of aggression in the first grade classroom on the course and malleability of aggressive behavior into middle school. *Development and Psychopathology, 10,* 165–185.

Kellam, S. G., Rebok, G. W., Ialongo, N., & Mayer, L. S. (1994). The course and malleability of aggressive behavior from early first grade into middle school: Results of a developmental epidemiologically-based preventive trial. *Journal of Child Psychology and Psychiatry, 35,* 259–281.

Kelly, J. G. (1988). *A guide to conducting preventive research in the community: First steps.* New York: Haworth Press.

Kendall, P. C. (1991). Guiding theory for therapy with children and adolescents. In P. C. Kendall (Ed.), *Child and adolescent therapy: Cognitive–behavioral procedures* (pp. 3–22). New York: Guilford Press.

Kendall, P. C., Aschenbrand, S. G., & Hudson, J. L. (2003). Child-focus treatment of anxiety. In A. E. Kazdin & J. R. Weisz (Eds.), *Evidence-based psychotherapies for children and adolescents* (pp. 81–100). New York: Guilford Press.

Kendall, P. C., & Braswell, L. (1985). Cognitive–behavioral therapy for impulsive children. New York: Guilford Press.

Kerr, M., & Stattin, H. (2000). What parents know, how they know it, and several forms of adolescent adjustment: Further support for a reinterpretation of monitoring. *Developmental Psychology, 36,* 366–380.

King, N. J., Ollendick, T. H., & Gullone, E. (1991). Negative affectivity in children and adolescents: Relations between anxiety and depression. *Clinical Psychology Review, 11,* 441–459.

Kitzman, H., Olds, D. L., Henderson, C. R., Hanks, C., Cole, R., Tatelbaum, R., et al. (1997). Effects of prenatal and infancy home visitation by nurses on pregnancy outcomes, childhood injuries, and repeated childbearing. *Journal of the American Medical Association, 278,* 644–652.

Kochanska, G. (1993). Toward a synthesis of parental socialization and child temperament in early development of conscience. *Child Development, 64,* 325–347.

Kolb, B. G. R., & Robinson, T. E. (2003). Brain plasticity and behavior. *Current Directions in Psychological Science, 12,* 1–5.

Kumpfer, K. L., Molgaard, V., & Spoth, R. (1996). The Strengthening Families Program for the prevention of delinquency and drug abuse. In R. D. Peters & R. J. McMahon (Eds.), *Preventing childhood disorders, substance abuse, and delinquency* (pp. 241–267). Newbury Park, CA: Sage.

Langrock, A. M., Compas, B. E., Keller, G., Merchant, M., & Copeland, M. E. (2002). Coping with the stress of parental depression: Parents' reports of children's coping, emotional, and behavioral problems. *Journal of Clinical Child and Adolescent Psychology, 31,* 312–324.

Latham, G. P., & Pinder, C. C. (2005). Work motivation theory and research at the dawn of the twenty-first century. *Annual Review of Psychology, 56,* 485–516.

Lau, A. S., & Weisz, J. R. (2003). Reported maltreatment among clinic-referred children: Implications for presenting problems, treatment attrition, and long-term outcomes. *Journal of the American Academy of Child and Adolescent Psychiatry, 42,* 1327–1334.

Lewinsohn, P. M., & Clarke, G. N. (1990). Cognitive-behavioral treatment for depressed adolescents. *Behavior Therapy, 19,* 385–401.

Lewinsohn, P. M., Munoz, R. F., Youngren, M. A., & Zeiss, A. M. (1986). *Control your depression.* New York: Prentice Hall.

Lewis, M. D. (2000). The promise of dynamic systems approaches for an integrated account of human development. *Child Development, 71*, 36–43.

Lewis, M. D., & Stieben, J. (2004). Emotion regulation in the brain: Conceptual issues and directions for developmental research. *Child Development, 75*, 371–376.

Lezak, M. D. (1995). Neuropsychological assessment (3rd ed.). New York: Oxford University Press.

Liddle, H. A. (1999). Theory in a family-based therapy for adolescent drug abuse. *Journal of Clinical Child Psychology, 28*, 521–532.

Lim, M., Stormshak, E. A., & Dishion, T. J. (2005). A one-session intervention for parents of young adolescents: Videotape modeling and motivational group discussion. *Journal of Emotional and Behavioral Disorders, 13*, 194–199.

Lipsey, M. W. (in press). The effects of community-based group treatment for delinquency: A meta-analytic search for cross-study generalizations. In K. Dodge & T. J. Dishion, & J. Lansford (Eds.), *Deviant peer influences in programs for youth: Problems and solutions*. New York: Guilford Press.

Lipsey, M. W., & Wilson, D. B. (1993). The efficacy of psychological, educational and behavioral treatment: Confirmation from meta-analysis. *American Psychologist, 48*, 1181–1209.

Lochman, J. E. (1985). Effects of different treatment lengths in cognitive behavioral interventions with aggressive boys. *Child Psychiatry and Human Development, 16*, 45–66.

Lochman, J. E. (1992). Cognitive–behavioral intervention with aggressive boys: Three-year follow-up and preventive effects. *Journal of Consulting and Clinical Psychology, 60*, 426–432.

Lochman, J. E., Barry, T. D., & Pardini, D. A. (2003). Anger control training for aggressive youth. In A. E. Kazdin & J. R. Weisz (Eds.), *Evidence-based psychotherapies for children and adolescents* (pp. 263–281). New York: Guilford Press.

Lochman, J. E., Burch, P. R., Curry, J. F., & Lampron, L. B. (1984). Treatment and generalization effects of cognitive–behavioral and goal-setting interventions with aggressive boys. *Journal of Consulting and Clinical Psychology, 52*, 915–916.

Lochman, J. E., & Dodge, K. A. (1998). Distorted perceptions in dyadic interactions of aggressive and nonaggressive boys: Effects of prior expectations, context, and boys' age. *Development and Psychopathology, 10*, 495–512.

Lochman, J. E., Lampron, L. B., Burch, P. R., & Curry, J. F. (1985). Client characteristics associated with behavior change for treated and untreated aggressive boys. *Journal of Abnormal Child Psychology, 13*, 527–538.

Loeber, R., & Dishion, T. J. (1983). Early predictors of male delinquency: A review. *Psychological Bulletin, 94*, 68–99.

Loeber, R., & Dishion, T. J. (1984). Boys who fight at home and school: Family conditions influencing cross-setting consistency. *Journal of Consulting and Clinical Psychology, 52*, 759–768.

Loeber, R., Dishion, T. J., & Patterson, G. R. (1984). Multiple gating: A multistage assessment procedure for identifying youths at risk for delinquency. *Journal of Research in Crime and Delinquency, 21*, 7–32.

Loeber, R., Wung, P., Keenan, K., Giroux, B., Stouthamer-Loeber, M., van Kammen, W. B., & Baughan, B. (1993). Developmental pathways in disruptive child behavior. *Development and Psychopathology, 5*, 103–133.

Mager, W., Milich, R., Harris, M. J., Howard, A. (2005). Intervention groups for adolescents with conduct problems: Is aggregation harmful or helpful? *Journal of Abnormal Child Psychology, 33*, 349–362.

Magnusson, D., Stattin, H., & Allen, D. L. (1985). Biological maturation and social development: A longitudinal study of some adjustment processes from mid-adolescence to adulthood. *Journal of Youth and Adolescence, 14*, 267–283.

Margolin, G. T. (1982). Ethical and legal considerations in marital and family therapy. *American Psychologist, 37*, 788–801.

Margolin, G., & Wampold, B. E. (1981). Sequential analysis of conflict and accord in distressed and nondistressed marital partners. *Journal of Consulting and Clinical Psychology, 49*, 554–567.

Martinez, C. R., Jr., & Forgatch, M. S. (2001). Preventing problems with boys' noncompliance: Effects of a parent training intervention for divorcing mothers. *Journal of Consulting and Clinical Psychology, 69*, 416–428.

Mash, E. J., & Terdal, L. G. (Eds.). (1997). *Assessment of childhood disorders* (3rd ed.). New York: Guilford Press.

McMahon, R. J., Slough, N., & Conduct Problems Prevention Research Group. (1996). Family-based intervention in the FAST Track Program. In R. D. Peters & R. J. McMahon (Eds.), *Preventing childhood disorders, substance abuse, and delinquency* (pp. 90–110). Thousand Oaks, CA: Sage.

McWhirter, B. T., Gragg, K. M., Hayashino, D. S., Torres, D. M., & Kaufman, N. (2001). Collaborative and community-based research supporting counseling prevention efforts: An ecological model guiding prevention practice and research. *Division 17 Prevention Section Newsletter, 8*.

Measelle, J. R., Ablow, J. C., Cowan, P. A., & Cowan, C. P. (1998). Assessing young children's self-perceptions of their academic, social and emotional lives: An evaluation of the Berkeley Puppet Interview. *Child Development, 69*, 1556–1576.

Meehl, P. E. (1973). *Psychodiagnosis, selected papers.* New York: Norton.

Meehl, P. E. (1978). Theoretical risks and tabular asterisks: Sir Karl, Sir Ronald, and the slow progress of soft psychology. *Journal of Consulting and Clinical Psychology, 46*, 806–834.

Melton, G. B., Ehrenreich, N. S., & Lyons, P. M. (2001). Ethical and legal issues in mental health services for children. In E. C. Walker & M. C. Roberts (Eds.), *Handbook of clinical child psychology* (3rd ed., pp. 1074–1093). New York: Wiley.

Mezzich, A. C., Tarter, R. E., Giancola, P. R., & Kirisci, L. (2001). The dysregulation inventory: A new scale to assess risk for substance use disorder. *Journal of Child and Adolescent Substance Abuse, 10*, 5–43.

Miller, C. L., Eccles, J. S., Flanagan, C., Midgley, C., Feldlaufer, H., & Harold, R. D. (1990). Parents' and teachers' beliefs about adolescents: Effects of sex and experience. *Journal of Youth and Adolescence, 19*, 363–394.

Miller, V. A., Drotar, D., & Kodish, E. (2004). Children's competence for assent and consent: A review of empirical findings. *Ethics and Behavior, 14*, 255–295.

Miller, W. R. (1987). Motivation and treatment goals. *Drugs and Society, 1*, 133–151.

Miller, W. R. (1989). Increasing motivation for change. In R. K. Hester & W. R. Miller (Eds.), *Handbook of alcoholism treatment approaches: Effective alternatives* (pp. 67–80). Elmsford, NY: Pergamon Press.

Miller, W. R. (1993). What I would most like to know: What really drives change? *Addiction, 88*, 1479–1480.

Miller, W. R. (2002). *Motivational interviewing.* New York: Guilford Press.

Miller, W. R., & Rollnick, S. (1991). *Motivational interviewing: Preparing people for change.* New York: Guilford Press.

Miller, W. R., & Rollnick, S. (2002). *Motivational interviewing: Preparing people to change addictive behavior* (2nd ed.). New York: Guilford Press.

Miller, W. R., & Sovereign, R. G. (1989). The checkup: A model for early intervention in addictive behaviors. In T. Loberg, W. R. Miller, P. E. Nathan, & G. A. Marlatt (Eds.), *Addictive behaviors: Prevention and early intervention* (pp. 219–231). Amsterdam: Swets & Zeitlinger.

Minuchin, S. (1974). *Families and family therapy.* Cambridge, MA: Harvard University Press.

Minuchin, S., & Fishman, H. C. (1981). *Family therapy techniques.* Cambridge, MA: Harvard University Press.

Minuchin, S., Rosman, B. L., & Baker, L. (1978). *Psychosomatic families: Anorexia nervosa in context.* Cambridge, MA: Harvard University Press.

Monroe, S. M., & Harkness, K. L. (2005). Life stress, the "Kindling" hypothesis, and the recurrence of depression: Considerations from a life stress perspective. *Psychological Review, 112*, 417–445.

Mufson, L., Weissman, M. M., Moreau, D., & Garfinkel, R. (1999). Efficacy of interpersonal psychotherapy for depressed adolescents. *Archives of General Psychiatry, 56*, 573–579.

Mullen, P. E., Martin, J. L., Anderson, J. C., Romans, S. E., & Herbison, G. P. (1996). The long-term impact of the physical, emotional, and sexual abuse of children: A community study. *Child Abuse and Neglect, 20*, 7–21.

Muthén, B. O., & Curran, P. J. (1997). General longitudinal modeling of individual differences in experimental designs: A latent variable framework for analysis and power estimation. *Psychological Methods, 2*, 371–402.

Myers, H. F., Taylor, S., Alvy, K. T., & Arrington, A. (1992). Parental and family predictors of behavior problems in inner-city Black children. *American Journal of Community Psychology, 20,* 557–576.

NICHD Early Childcare Research Network. (2002). Child-care structure to process to outcome: Direct and indirect effects of childcare quality on young children's development. *Psychological Science, 13,* 199–206.

Nelson, S. E., & Dishion, T. J. (2004). From boys to men: Predicting adult adaptation from middle childhood sociometric status. *Development and Psychopathology 16,* 441–459.

Nunnally, J. C. (1978). *Psychometric theory* (2nd ed.). New York: McGraw-Hill.

Oden, S., Herzberger, S. D., Mangione, P. L., & Wheeler, V. A. (1984). Children's peer relationships: An examination of social processes. In J. C. Masters & K. Yarkin-Levin (Eds.), *Boundary areas in social and developmental psychology* (pp. 131–158). New York: Academic Press.

O'Donnell, J., Hawkins, J. D., Catalano, R., Abbott, R. D., & Day, L. E. (1995). Preventing school failure, drug use, and delinquency among low income children: Long-term intervention in elementary schools. *American Journal of Orthopsychiatry, 65,* 87–100.

Offord, D. R. (1989, February). *The epidemiology of childhood psychopathology.* Paper presented at the annual meeting of the Society for Research in Child and Adolescent Psychopathology, Miami, FL.

Olds, D. L., Eckenrode, J., Henderson, C. R., Kitzman, H., Powers, J., Cole, R., et al. (1997). Long-term effects of home visitation on maternal life course and child abuse and neglect. *Journal of the American Medical Association, 278,* 637–643.

Olds, D. L., Hill, P., Robinson, J., Song, N., & Little, C. (2000). Update on home visiting for pregnant women and parents of young children. *Current Problems in Pediatrics, 30,* 110–114.

O'Leary, C. C. (1999). *Prevention of child psychopathology in early childhood: The Family Check-Up.* Unpublished doctoral dissertation, University of Oregon, Eugene.

O'Leary, C. C. (2000). *A brief family intervention for high-risk preschool-aged children.* Unpublished doctoral dissertation, University of Oregon, Eugene.

Olson, S. L., Bates, J. E., & Bayles, K. (1990). Early antecedents of child impulsivity: The role of parent-child interaction, cognitive competence, and temperament. *Journal of Abnormal and Child Psychology, 18,* 317–334.

Othmer, E., & Othmer, S. C. (1994). *The clinical interview using DSM–IV: Fundamentals* (Vol. 1). Washington, DC: American Psychiatric Press.

Pantin, H., Coatsworth, J. D., Feaster, D. J., Newman, F. L., Briones, E., Prado, G., et al. (2003). Familias unidas: The efficacy of an intervention to promote parental investment in Hispanic immigrant families. *Prevention Science, 4,* 189–201.

Patterson, G. R. (1974). Interventions for boys with conduct problems: Multiple settings, treatments, and criteria. *Journal of Consulting and Clinical Psychology, 42,* 471–481.

Patterson, G. R. (1977). A three-stage functional analysis for children's coercive behaviors: A tactic for developing a performance theory. In D. Baer, B. C. Etzel, & J. M. LeBlanc (Eds.), *New developments in behavioral research: Theory, methods, and applications. In honor of Sidney W. Bijou* (pp. 59–79). Hillsdale, NJ: Erlbaum.

Patterson, G. R. (1982). *A social learning approach: III. Coercive family process.* Eugene, OR: Castalia.

Patterson, G. R. (1983). Stress: A change agent for family process. In N. Garrezy & M. Rutter (Eds.), *Stress, coping, and development in children* (pp. 235–264). New York: McGraw-Hill.

Patterson, G. R. (1984). Siblings: Fellow travelers in a coercive system. In R. J. Blanchard & D. C. Blanchard (Eds.), *Advances in the study of aggression* (Vol. 1, pp. 173–215). New York: Academic Press.

Patterson, G. R. (1985). Beyond technology: The next stage in the development of a parent training technology. In L. Abate (Ed.), *Handbook of family psychology and therapy* (Vol. 2, pp. 1344–1379). Homewood, IL: Dorsey Press.

Patterson, G. R. (1993). Orderly change in a stable world: The antisocial trait as a chimera. *Journal of Consulting and Clinical Psychology, 61,* 911–919.

Patterson, G. R., & Chamberlain, P. (1994). A functional analysis of resistance during parent training therapy. *Clinical Psychology: Science and Practice, 1,* 53–70.

Patterson, G. R., Chamberlain, P., & Reid, J. B. (1982). A comparative evaluation of parent training procedures. *Behavior Therapy, 13,* 638–650.

Patterson, G. R., & Cobb, J. A. (1971). A dyadic analysis of "aggressive" behaviors. In J. P. Hill (Ed.), *Minnesota symposia on child psychology* (Vol. 5, pp. 72–129). Minneapolis: University of Minnesota.

Patterson, G. R., & Cobb, J. A. (1973). Stimulus control for classes of noxious behaviors. In J. F. Knutson (Ed.), *The control of aggression: Implications from basic research* (pp. 144–199). Chicago: Aldine.

Patterson, G. R., & Dishion, T. J. (1985). Contributions of families and peers to delinquency. *Criminology, 23,* 63–79.

Patterson, G. R., Dishion, T. J., & Bank, L. (1984). Family interaction: A process model of deviancy training. *Aggressive Behavior, 10,* 253–267.

Patterson, G. R., Dishion, T. J., & Chamberlain, P. (1993). Outcomes and methodological issues relating to treatment of antisocial children. In T. R. Giles (Ed.), *Effective psychotherapy: A handbook of comparative research* (pp. 43–88). New York: Plenum Press.

Patterson, G. R., Dishion, T. J., & Yoerger, K. (2000). Adolescent growth in new forms of problem behavior: Macro- and micro-peer dynamics. *Prevention Science, 1,* 3–13.

Patterson, G. R., & Forgatch, M. S. (1985). Therapist behavior as a determinant for client resistance: A paradox for the behavior modifier. *Journal of Consulting and Clinical Psychology, 53,* 846–851.

Patterson, G. R., Littman, R. A., & Bricker, W. (1967). Assertive behavior in children: A step toward a theory of aggression. *Monographs of the Society for Research in Child Development, 32*(5, Serial No. 113).

Patterson, G. R., & Reid, J. B. (1984). Social interactional processes within the family: The study of moment-by-moment family transactions in which human social development is imbedded. *Journal of Applied Developmental Psychology, 5,* 237–262.

Patterson, G. R., Reid, J. B., & Dishion, T. J. (1992). *A social learning approach: Vol. 4. Antisocial boys.* Eugene, OR: Castalia.

Patterson, G. R., Reid, J. B., Jones, R. R., & Conger, R. E. (1975). *A social learning approach to family intervention: Vol. 1. Families with aggressive children.* Eugene, OR: Castalia.

Patterson, G. R., Reid, J. B., & Maerov, S. L. (1978). The observation system: Methodological issues and psychometric properties. In J. B. Reid (Ed.), *A social learning approach to family intervention: Vol. 2. Observation in home settings* (pp. 11–19). Eugene, OR: Castalia.

Patterson, G. R., & Stoolmiller, M. (1991). Replications of a dual failure model for boys' depressed mood. *Journal of Consulting and Clinical Psychology, 59,* 491–498.

Patterson, G. R., & Stouthamer-Loeber, M. (1984). The correlation of family management practices and delinquency. *Child Development, 55,* 1299–1307.

Paul, G. L., & Menditto, A. A. (1992). Effectiveness of inpatient treatment programs for mentally ill adults in public psychiatric facilities. *Applied & Preventive Psychology, 1,* 41–63.

Peterson, A. C., Silbereisen, A. K., & Sorenson, S. (1996). Adolescent development: A global perspective. In K. Hurrelmann & S. F. Hamilton (Eds.), *Social problems and social contexts in adolescence: Perspective across boundaries* (pp. 3–38). New York: De Gruyter.

Peterson, D. R. (1979). Assessing interpersonal relationships by means of interaction records. *Behavioral Assessment, 1,* 221–236.

Pettit, G. S., & Bates, J. (1989). Family interaction patterns and children's behavior problems from infancy to 4 years. *Developmental Psychology, 25,* 413–420.

Pettit, G. S., Bates, J. E., & Dodge, K. A. (1993). Family interaction patterns and children's conduct problems at home and school: A longitudinal perspective. *School Psychology Review, 22,* 403–420.

Pettit, G. S., Bates, J. E., Dodge, K. A., & Meece, D. W. (1999). The impact of after-school peer contact on early adolescent externalizing problems is moderated by parental monitoring, perceived neighborhood safety, and prior adjustment. *Child Development, 70,* 768–778.

Piehler, T. F., & Dishion, T. J. (in press). Interpersonal dynamics within adolescent friendship: Dyadic mutuality and deviant talk in the development of antisocial behavior. *Child Development.*

Posner, M. I., Dehaene, S., He, S., Cavanagh, P., Intriligator, J., Volpe, B. T., et al. (2000). Part III: Attention. In M. S. Gazzaniga (Ed.), *Cognitive neuroscience: A reader* (pp. 153–187). Malden, MA: Blackwell Publishers.

Posner, M. I., Rothbart, M. K., & Rueda, M. R. (2003). *Brain mechanisms and learning of high level skills*. Paper presented at the Brain and Education Commemorative Session on the occasion of the 400th anniversary of the founding of the Papal Academy of Sciences, Vatican City, Rome, Italy.

Poulin, F., & Boivin, M. (2000). The formation and development of friendship in childhood: The role of proactive and reactive aggression. *Developmental Psychology, 36*, 233–240.

Poulin, F., Dishion, T. J., & Burraston, B. (2001). 3-year iatrogenic effects associated with aggregating high-risk adolescents in preventive interventions. *Applied Developmental Science, 5*, 214–224.

Prochaska, J. O. (1993). An eclectic and integrative approach: Transtheoretical therapy. In A. S. Gurman & S. B. Messer (Eds.), *Essential psychotherapies: Theory and practice* (pp. 403–439). New York: Guilford Press.

Prochaska, J. O., & DiClemente, C. (1982). Transtheoretical therapy: Toward a more integrated model of change. *Psychotherapy: Theory, Research, and Practice, 19*, 276–288.

Prochaska, J. O., & DiClemente, C. (1986). Toward a comprehensive model of change. In W. Miller & N. Heather (Eds.), *Treating addictive behaviors: Processes of change* (pp. 3–27). New York: Plenum Press.

Prochaska, J. O., & Norcross, J. G. (1999). *Systems of psychotherapy*. Pacific Grove, CA: Brooks/Cole.

Prochaska, J. O., Velicer, W. F., Guadagnoli, E., & Rossi, J. S. (1991). Patterns of change: Dynamic typology applied to smoking cessation. *Multivariate Behavioral Research, 26*, 83–107.

Pynoos, R. S., Steinberg, A. N., & Wraith, R. (1995). Developmental model of childhood traumatic stress. In D. Cicchetti & D. J. Cohen (Eds.), *Developmental psychopathology: Risk, disorder, and adaptation* (pp. 72–95). New York: Wiley.

Rao, S. A. (1998). *The short-term impact of the Family Check-Up: A brief motivational intervention for at-risk families*. Unpublished doctoral dissertation, University of Oregon, Eugene.

Rappaport, M., Hopkins, H. K., Hall, K., Belleza, T., & Silverman, J. (1978) Are there schizophrenics for whom drugs may be unnecessary or contraindicated? *International Pharmacopsychiatry, 13*, 100–111.

Reid, J. B. (1978). The development of specialized observation systems. In J. B. Reid (Ed.), *A social learning approach to family intervention: Vol. 2. Observation in home settings* (pp. 43–49). Eugene, OR: Castalia.

Reid, J. B. (1982). Observer training in naturalistic research. In D. Hartmann (Ed.), *Using observers to study behavior: New directions for methodology of social and behavioral science* (Vol. 14, pp. 37–50). San Francisco: Jossey-Bass.

Reid, J. B. (1993). Prevention of conduct disorder before and after school entry: Relating interventions to development findings. *Journal of Development and Psychopathology, 5*, 243–262.

Reid, J. B., & Eddy, J. M. (1997). Can we afford to prevent violence, and can we afford not to? In E. L. Rubin (Ed.), *Minimizing harm as a goal for crime policy in California*. Paper prepared for the University of California Policy Seminar Crime Project, University of California, Berkeley.

Reid, J. B., Patterson, G. R., & Snyder, J. (Eds.). (2002). *Antisocial behavior in children and adolescents: A developmental analysis and model for intervention*. Washington, DC: American Psychological Association.

Reid, M. J., Webster-Stratton, C., & Beauchaine, T. P. (2001). Parent training in Head Start: A comparison of program response among African American, Asian American, Caucasian, and Hispanic mothers. *Prevention Science, 2,* 209–227.

Rende, R., & Plomin, R. (1992). Diathesis-stress models of psychopathology: A quantitative genetic perspective. *Applied & Preventive Psychology, 1,* 177–182.

Resnicow, K., Soler, R., Braithwaite, R. L., Ahluwalia, J. S., & Butler, J. (2000). Cultural sensitivity in substance use prevention. *Journal of Community Psychology, 28,* 271–290.

Riley, D. B., Greif, G. L., Caplan, D. L., & MacAulay, H. K. (2004). Common themes and treatment approaches in working with families of runaway youths. *American Journal of Family Therapy, 32,* 139–153.

Roberts, G. C., Block, J. H., & Block, J. (1984). Continuity and change in parents' child-rearing practices. *Child Development, 55,* 586–597.

Roberts, M. C., Carlson, C. I., Erickson, M. T., Friedman, R. M., La Greca, A. M., Lemanek, K. L., et al. (1998). A model for training psychologists to provide services for children and adolescents. *Professional Psychology: Research and Practice, 29,* 293–299.

Robin, A. L. (2003). Behavioral family systems therapy for adolescents with anorexia nervosa. In A. E. Kazdin & J. R. Weisz (Eds.), *Evidence-based psychotherapies for children and adolescents* (pp. 358–373). New York: Guilford Press.

Robins, M. S., Alexander, J. F., Newell, R. N., & Turner, C. W. (1996). The immediate effect of reframing on client attitude and family therapy. *Journal of Family Psychology, 10,* 28–34.

Rogers, C. R. (1940). The process of therapy. *Journal of Consulting Psychology, 4,* 161–164.

Rogers, C. R. (1957). The necessary and sufficient conditions of therapeutic personality change. *Journal of Consulting Psychology, 21,* 95–103.

Rogoff, B. (1994). Developing understanding of the idea of communities of learners. *Mind, Culture, and Activity, 1,* 209–229.

Rothbart, M. K., & Bates, J. E. (1998). Temperament. In W. Damon (Series Ed.) & N. Eisenberg (Vol. Ed.), *Handbook of child psychology: Vol. 3. Social, emotional and personality development* (5th ed., pp. 105–106) New York: Wiley.

Rothbart, M. K., & Posner, M. I. (2006). Temperament, attention, and developmental psychopathology. In D. Cicchetti & D. J. Cohen (Eds.), *Developmental psychopathology: Vol. 2. Developmental neuroscience* (2nd ed., pp. 465–501). New York: Wiley.

Rusby, J., Estes, A., & Dishion, T. (1990). *School observations and Family Interaction Task: Interpersonal Process Code (IPC)* [Unpublished coding system]. Oregon Social Learning Center, Eugene.

Rutter, M. (1985). Family and school influences on behavioural development. *Journal of Child Psychology and Psychiatry and Allied Disciplines, 26,* 349–368.

Rutter, M., Dunn, J., & Simonoff, G. (1997). Integrating nature and nurture: Implications of person–environment correlations and interactions for developmental psychopathology. *Development and Psychopathology, 9,* 335–364.

Rutter, M., Maughan, B., Mortimore, P., Ouston, J., & Smith, A. (1979). *Fifteen thousand hours: Secondary schools and their effects on children.* Cambridge, MA: Harvard University Press.

Sameroff, A. J. (1981). Development and the dialectic: The need for a systems approach. In W. A. Collins (Ed.), *Minnesota symposium on child psychology* (pp. 83–103). Hillsdale, NJ: Erlbaum.

Sanders, M. R. (1999). Triple P-Positive Parenting Program: Towards an empirically validated multilevel parenting and family support strategy for the prevention of behavior and emotional problems in children. *Clinical Child and Family Psychology Review, 2,* 71–90.

Sanders, M. R., & Lawton, J. M. (1993). Discussing assessment findings with families: A guided participation model of information transfer. *Child and Family Behavior Therapy, 15,* 5–33.

Santisteban, D. A., Coatsworth, J. D., Perez-Vidal, A., Kurtines, W. M., Schwartz, S. J., LaPerrierre, A., & Szapocznik, J. (2003). Efficacy of brief strategic family therapy in modifying Hispanic adolescent behavior problems and substance use. *Journal of Family Psychology, 17,* 121–133.

Scarr, S., & McCartney, K. (1983). How people make their own environments: A theory of genotype to environment effects. *Child Development, 54,* 424–435.

Schaeffer, C. M., Petras, H., Ialongo, N., Poduska, J., & Kellam, S. (2003). Modeling growth in boys' aggressive behavior across elementary school: Links to later criminal involvement, conduct disorder, and antisocial personality disorder. *Developmental Psychology, 39,* 1020–1035.

Senechal, M., & LeFevre, J. (2002). Parental involvement in the development of children's reading skill: A five year longitudinal study. *Child Development, 73,* 445–460.

Shaw, D. S., Dishion, T. J., Supplee, L., Gardner, F. E. M., & Arnds, K. (in press). A family-centered approach to the prevention of early conduct problems: Two-year effects of a randomized trial of the Family Check Up in early childhood. *Journal of Consulting and Clinical Psychology.*

Shaw, D. S., Gilliom, M., Ingoldsby, E. M., & Nagin, D. (2003). Trajectories leading to school-age conduct problems. *Developmental Psychology, 39,* 189–200.

Shaw, D. S., Winslow, E. B., Owens, E. B., Vondra, J. I., Cohn, J. F., & Bell, R. Q. (1998). The development of early externalizing problems among children from low-income families: A transformational perspective. *Journal of Abnormal Child Psychology, 26,* 95–107.

Sheeber, L., Hops, H., Andrews, J., Alpert, T., & Davis, B. (1998). Interactional processes in families with depressed and non-depressed adolescents: Reinforcement of depressive behavior. *Behavior and Research Therapy, 36,* 417–427.

Sheeber, L., Hyman, H., & Davis, B. (2001). Family processes in adolescent depression. *Clinical Child and Family Psychology Review, 4,* 19–35.

Skinner, B. F. (1945). The operational analysis of psychological terms. *Psychological Review, 52,* 270–277.

Snyder, J., Edwards, P., McGraw, K., Kilgore, K., & Holton, A. (1994). Escalation and reinforcement in mother–child conflict: Social processes associated with the development of physical aggression. *Development and Psychopathology, 6,* 305–321.

Snyder, J., Reid, J. B., & Patterson, G. R. (2003). A social learning model of child and adolescent antisocial behavior. In B. B. Lahey, T. E. Moffitt, & A. Caspi (Eds.), *Causes of conduct disorder and juvenile delinquency* (pp. 27–48). New York: Guilford Press.

Snyder, J., Schrepferman, L., Oeser, J., Patterson, G., Stoolmiller, M., Johnson, K., & Snyder, A. (2005). Deviancy training and association with deviant peers in young children: Occurrence and contribution to early-onset conduct problems. *Development and Psychopathology, 17,* 397–413.

Snyder, J., West, L., Stockemer, V., Givens, S., & Almquist-Parks, L. (1996). A social learning model of peer choice in the natural environment. *Journal of Applied Developmental Psychology, 17,* 215–237.

Spoth, R., Redmond, C., Shin, C., Lepper, H., Haggerty, K., & Wall, M. (1998). Risk moderation of parent and child outcomes in a preventative intervention: A test and replication. *American Journal of Orthopsychiatry, 68,* 565–579.

Spoth, R. L., Kavanagh, K., & Dishion, T. J. (2002). Family-centered preventive intervention science: Toward benefits to larger populations of children, youth, and families [Special issue]. *Prevention Science, 3,* 145–152.

Sroufe, L. A., & Rutter, M. (1984). The domain of developmental psychopathology. *Child Development, 55,* 17–29.

Stanger, C., Higgins, S. T., Bickel, W. K., Elk, R., Grabowski, J., Schmitz, J., et al. (1999). Behavioral and emotional problems among children of cocaine- and opiate-dependent parents. *Journal of the American Academy of Child and Adolescent Psychiatry, 38,* 421–428.

Staton, B., Cole, M., Galbraith, J., Li, X., Pendleton, S., Cottrel, L., et al. (2004). Randomized trial of a parent intervention. *Archives of Pediatrics and Adolescent Medicine, 158,* 947–955.

Stevenson, D. L., & Baker, D. P (1987). The family–school relation and the child's school performance. *Child Development, 58,* 1348–1357.

Stoolmiller, M. (2001). Synergistic interaction of child manageability problems and parent-discipline tactics in predicting future growth in externalizing behavior for boys. *Developmental Psychology, 37*, 814–825.

Stoolmiller, M., Duncan, T., Bank, L., & Patterson, G. (1993). Some problems and solutions in the study of change: Significant patterns of client resistance. *Journal of Consulting and Clinical Psychology, 61*, 920–928.

Stormshak, E. A., Bellanti, C. J., Bierman, K. L., & Conduct Problems Prevention Research Group. (1996). The quality of sibling relationships and the development of social competence and behavioral control in aggressive children. *Developmental Psychology, 32*, 79–89.

Stormshak, E. A., Bierman, K. L., Bruschi, C. J., Dodge, K. A., Coie, J. D., & Conduct Problems Prevention Research Group. (1999). The relation between behavior problems and peer preference in different classroom contexts. *Child Development, 70*, 169–182.

Stormshak, E. A., Bierman, K. L., Coie, J. D., Dodge, K. A., Greenberg, M. T., Lochman, J. E., & Mahon, R. J. (1998). The implications of different developmental patterns of disruptive behavior problems for school adjustment. *Development and Psychopathology, 10*, 451–467.

Stormshak, E. A., Bierman, K. L., McMahon, R. J., Lengua, L., & Conduct Problems Prevention Research Group. (2000). Parenting practices and child disruptive behavior problems in early elementary school. *Journal of Clinical Child Psychology, 29*, 17–29.

Stormshak, E. A., Comeau, C. A., & Shepard, S. A. (2004). The relative contribution of sibling deviance and peer deviance in the prediction of substance use across middle childhood. *Journal of Abnormal Child Psychology, 32*, 635–649.

Stormshak, E. A., & Dishion, T. J. (2002). An ecological approach to child and family clinical and counseling psychology. *Clinical Child and Family Psychology Review, 5*, 197–215.

Stormshak, E. A., Dishion, T. J., Light, J., & Yasui, M. (2005). Implementing family-centered interventions within the public middle school: Linking service delivery to change in problem behavior. *Journal of Abnormal Child Psychology, 33*, 723–733.

Stormshak, E. A., Kaminski, R., & Goodman, M. R. (2002). Enhancing the parenting skills of Head Start families during the transition to kindergarten. *Prevention Science, 3*, 223–234.

Stormshak, E. A., Speltz, M. L., DeKlyen, M., & Greenberg, M. T. (1997). Observed family interaction during clinical interviews: A comparison of families containing preschool boys with and without disruptive behavior. *Journal of Abnormal Child Psychology, 25*, 345–357.

Stouthamer-Loeber, M., Loeber, R., van Kammen, W. B., & Zhang, Q. (1995). Uninterrupted delinquent careers: The timing of parental help-seeking in juvenile court contact. *Studies on Crime and Crime Prevention, 4*, 236–251.

Sugai, G., Sprague, J. R., Horner, R. H., & Walker, H. M. (2000). Preventing school violence: The use of office discipline referrals to assess and monitor school-wide discipline interventions. *Journal of Emotional and Behavioral Disorders, 8,* 94–101.

Sukhodolsky, D. G., Gulub, A., Stone, E. C., & Orban, L. (2005). Dismantle and anger control training for children: A randomized pilot study of social problem solving versus social skills training components. *Behavior Therapy, 36,* 15–23.

Sullivan, H. S. (1953). *The interpersonal theory of psychiatry.* New York: Norton.

Szapocznik, J., & Kurtines, W. M. (1989). *Breakthroughs in family therapy with drug-abusing and problem youth.* New York: Springer Publishing Company.

Szapocznik, J., & Kurtines, W. M. (1993). Family psychology and cultural diversity: Opportunities for theory, research, and application. *American Psychologist, 48,* 400–407.

Szapocznik, J., Kurtines, W., Santisteban, D. A., Pantin, H., Scopetta, M., Mancilla, Y., et al. (1997). The evolution of structural ecosystemic theory for working with Latino families. In J. G. Garcia & M. C. Zea (Eds.), *Psychological interventions and research with Latino populations* (pp. 166–190). Needham Heights, MA: Allyn & Bacon.

Szapocznik, J., Perez-Vidal, A., Brickman, A. L., Foote, F. H., Santisteban, D., & Hervis, O. (1988). Engaging adolescent drug abusers and their families in treatment: A strategic structural systems approach. *Journal of Consulting and Clinical Psychology, 56,* 552–557.

Szapocznik, J., Santisteban, D., Kurtines, W., Perez-Vidal, A., & Hervis, O. (1984). Bicultural effectiveness training: A treatment intervention for enhancing intercultural adjustment. *Hispanic Journal of Behavioral Sciences, 6,* 317–344.

Szapocznik, J. F., & Williams, R. A. (2000). Brief strategic family therapy: Twenty-five years of interplay among theory, research and practice in adolescent behavior problems and drug abuse. *Clinical Child and Family Psychology Review, 3,* 117–134.

Tremblay, R. E. (2000). The development of aggressive behaviour during childhood: What have we learned in the past century? *International Journal of Behavioral Development, 24,* 129–141.

Trickett, E. J., & Birman, D. (1989). Taking ecology seriously: A community development approach to individually based preventive interventions in schools. In L. A. Bond & B. E. Compas (Eds.), *Primary prevention and promotion in the schools: Vol. 12. Primary prevention of psychopathology* (pp. 361–390). Newbury Park, CA: Sage.

Trimble, J. E. (1990). Ethnic specification, validation prospects, and the future of drug use research. *International Journal of the Addictions, 25*(2A), 149–170.

Tversky, A., & Kahneman, D. (1974). Judgment under uncertainty: Heuristics and biases. *Science, 185,* 1124–1131.

Tyler, K. A., Hoyt, D. R., Whitbeck, L. B., & Cauce, A. M. (2001). The effects of a high-risk environment on the sexual victimization of homeless and runaway youth. *Violence and Victims, 16,* 441–455.

Vitaro, F., Brendgen, M., & Tremblay, R. E. (2002). Reactively and proactively aggressive children: Antecedent and subsequent characteristics. *Journal of Child Psychology and Psychiatry, 43*, 495–505.

Volkmar, F. R., Becker, D. F., King, R. A., & McGlashan, T. H. (1995). Psychotic processes. In D. Cicchetti & D. J. Cohen (Eds.), *Developmental psychopathology: Vol. 2. Risk, disorder, and adaptation* (pp. 512–534). Oxford, England: Wiley.

Waldron, H. B., & Flicker, S. M. (2002). Alcohol and drug abuse. In M. Hersen (Ed.), *Clinical behavior therapy: Adults and children* (pp. 474–490). New York: Wiley.

Walker, H. M., McConnell, S., Walker, J., Clarke, J. Y., Todis, B., Cohon, G., & Rankin, R. (1983). Initial analysis of the ACCEPTS curriculum: Efficacy of instrumental and behavior management procedures for improving the social adjustment of handicapped children. *Analysis and Intervention in Developmental Disabilities, 3*, 105–127.

Walker-Barnes, C. J. (2003). Developmental epidemiology: The perfect partner for clinical practice. *Journal of Clinical Child and Adolescent Psychology, 32*, 181–186.

Wampold, B. E. (2001). *The great psychotherapy debate: Models, methods, and findings.* Mahwah, NJ: Erlbaum.

Wampold, B. E., Mondin, G. W., Moody, M., Stich, F., Benson, K., & Ahn, H. (1997). A meta-analysis of outcome studies comparing bona fide psychotherapies: Empirically, "all must have prizes." *Psychological Bulletin, 122*, 203–215.

Warren, K., Schoppelrey, S., Moberg, D. P., & McDonald, M. (2005). A model of contagion through competition in the aggressive behaviors of elementary school students. *Journal of Abnormal Child Psychology, 33*, 283–292.

Watson, D., & Clark, L. A. (1984). Negative affectivity: The disposition to experience aversive emotional states. *Psychological Bulletin, 96*, 465–490.

Watson, D., Clark, L. A., & Tellegen, A. (1988). Development and validation of brief measures of positive and negative affect: The PANAS scales. *Journal of Personality and Social Psychology, 54*, 1063–1070.

Watzlawick, P., Weakland, J., & Fisch, R. (1974). *Change.* New York: Norton.

Weber, F. D. (1998). *The dose-effect relationship in family therapy for conduct disordered youth.* Unpublished doctoral dissertation, University of Oregon, Eugene.

Webster-Stratton, C. (1990). Long-term follow-up of families with young conduct problem children: From preschool to grade school. *Journal of Clinical Child Psychology, 19*, 144–149.

Webster-Stratton, C. (1992). Individually administered videotape parent training: "Who benefits?" *Cognitive Therapy and Research, 16*, 31–52.

Webster-Stratton, C. (1994). Advancing videotape parent training: A comparison study. *Journal of Consulting and Clinical Psychology, 62*, 583–593.

Webster-Stratton, C., Kolpacoff, M., & Hollingsworth, T. (1988). Self-administered videotape therapy for families with conduct-problem children: Comparison with two cost-effective treatments and a control group. *Journal of Consulting and Clinical Psychology, 56,* 558–566.

Webster-Stratton, C., Reid, M. J., & Hammond, M. (2004). Treating children with early-onset conduct problems: Intervention outcomes for parent, child, and teacher training. *Journal of Clinical Child and Adolescent Psychology, 33,* 105–124.

Weiss, B., Catron, T., & Harris, V. (2000). A 2-year follow-up of the effectiveness of traditional child psychotherapy. *Journal of Consulting and Clinical Psychology, 68,* 1094–1101.

Weiss, B., Catron, T., Harris, V., & Phung, T. M. (1999). The effectiveness of traditional child psychotherapy. *Journal of Consulting and Clinical Psychology, 67,* 82–94.

Weiss, R. L., & Halford, W. K. (1996). Marital dysfunction. In M. Hersen & V. B. van Hasselt (Eds.), *Sourcebook of psychological treatment manuals for adults* (pp. 489–537). New York: Plenum Press.

Weisz, J. R., Doss, A. J., & Hawley, K. M. (2005). Youth psychotherapy outcome research: A review and critique of the evidence base. *Annual Review of Psychology, 56,* 337–363.

Weisz, J. R., Southam-Gerow, M. A., Gordis, E. B., & Connor-Smith, J. (2003). Primary and secondary control enhancement training for youth depression: Applying the deployment-focused model of treatment development and testing. In A. E. Kazdin & J. R. Weisz (Eds.), *Evidence-based psychotherapies for children and adolescents* (pp. 165–182). New York: Guilford Press.

Weisz, J. R., & Weiss, B. (1989). Assessing the effects of clinic-based psychotherapy with children and adolescents. *Journal of Consulting and Clinical Psychology, 57,* 741–746.

Weisz, J. R., & Weiss, B. (1991). Studying the "referability" of child clinical problems. *Journal of Consulting and Clinical Psychology, 59,* 266–273.

Weisz, J. R., Weiss, B., Han, S. S., Granger, D. A., & Morton, T. (1995). Effects of psychotherapy with children and adolescents revisited: A meta-analysis of treatment outcome studies. *Psychological Bulletin, 117,* 450–468.

Weschler, D. (1974). *Manual for the Weschler Intelligence Scale for Children—Revised.* San Antonio, TX: Psychological Corporation.

Whaley, A. L. (2000). Sociocultural differences in the developmental consequences of the use of physical discipline during childhood for African Americans. *Cultural Diversity and Ethnic Minority Psychology, 6,* 5–12.

Whiting, B. B., & Whiting, J. M. (1975). *Children of six cultures: A psychocultural analysis.* Cambridge, MA: Harvard University Press.

Wiggins, J. S. (1973). *Personality and prediction: Principles of personality assessment.* Reading, MA: Addison Wesley.

Wills, T. A., & Dishion, T. J. (2004). Temperament and adolescent substance use: A transactional analysis of emerging self-control. In P. Frick & W. Silverman

(Eds.), Temperament and childhood psychopathology [Special issue]. *Journal of Clinical Child and Adolescent Psychology 33*, 69–81.

Wing Sue, D., Bingham, R. P., Porche, L., & Vasquez, M. (1999). The diversification of psychology: A multicultural revolution. *American Psychologist, 54*, 1061–1069.

Wright, J. C., Zakriski, A. L., & Drinkwater, M. (1999). Developmental psychopathology and the reciprocal patterning of behavior and environment: Distinctive situational and behavioral signatures of internalizing, externalizing, and mixed-syndrome children. *Journal of Consulting and Clinical Psychology, 67*, 95–107.

Yeh, M., & Weisz, J. R. (2001). Why are we here at the clinic? Parent–child (dis)agreement on referral problems at outpatient treatment entry. *Journal of Consulting and Clinical Psychology, 69*, 1018–1025.

Zinbarg, R. E. (1990). Individual differences in instrumental conditioning. *Dissertation Abstracts International, 50*, 4266B.

AUTHOR INDEX

Abbott, R. D., 7
Ablow, J. C., 83
Achenbach, T. M., 5, 19, 20, 23, 56, 97, 154
Ageton, S. S., 62
Ahluwalia, J. S., 189
Alexander, J. F., 82, 110
Allen, D. L., 63
Almquist-Parks, L., 37
Alpert, T., 36
Alvy, K. T., 189
American Academy of Pediatrics, 195
American Psychiatric Association, 53
American Psychological Association (APA), 242
Anderson, J. C., 247
Andrews, D. M., 37, 43, 207
Andrews, D. W., 33, 35, 37, 45, 56, 185, 204, 205
Andrews, J., 36
Anthony, J., 28
Arnds, K., 7, 132
Arnold, J. E., 28
Arrington, A., 189
Aschenbrand, S. G., 144, 202

Bakeman, R., 45
Baker, D. P., 136
Baker, L., 24
Bandura, A., 145
Bank, L., 38, 220
Barber, B. K., 62
Bargiel, K., 42
Barker, R. G., 4, 40
Barkley, R. A., 145, 158
Barmish, A. J., 7
Barnes-Holmes, D., 145
Barrett, M. S., 228
Barrett, P. M., 53, 202
Barry, T. D., 145, 202
Bass, D., 53, 95, 211
Bates, J. E., 19, 28, 32, 42, 95, 144, 173, 183, 189

Baumeister, R. F., 143
Bayles, K., 32
Beauchaine, T. P., 190
Becker, D. F., 5
Bellanti, C. J., 38
Belleza, T., 23
Bem, D. J., 22
Berliner, L., 149
Berman, J. S., 228
Bernard, J. M., 225
Bierman, K. L., 38, 50, 102, 153, 164, 183, 202
Biglan, A., 7, 25, 35, 59
Bingham, R. P., 99
Birchler, G. R., 41
Birman, D., 25
Blechman, E. A., 26, 137
Block, J., 63
Block, J. H., 63
Blum, R. W., 32
Boisjoly, J., 213
Boivin, M., 19, 38, 53
Bolstad, O. D., 42
Borduin, C. M., 6, 15, 32, 66, 80, 170, 225
Braithwaite, R. L., 189
Braswell, L., 158
Brendgen, M., 19, 38
Brent, D. A., 158
Bricker, W., 43
Brody, G. H., 6
Brondino, M. J., 220
Bronfenbrenner, U., 4, 16, 18
Brown, A. C., 6
Brown, C. H., 54, 206
Brown, J. M., 59, 112
Buchanan, C. M., 137
Bugental, D. B., 6
Bullock, B. M., 18, 37, 38, 45, 101, 102, 132, 181, 184, 233
Burch, P. R., 53, 95
Burraston, B., 8, 38, 40, 98, 102, 143, 147, 205
Butler, J., 189

Cairns, B. D., 26
Cairns, R. B., 26
Calhoun, K. S., 225, 236
Campbell, D. T., 95, 96
Cantor, N., 231
Capaldi, D. M., 19, 20, 38, 46, 62, 184,
    207, 213
Caplan, D. L., 151
Carlo, G., 95
Caron, C., 146
Caspi, A., 40
Catalano, R. F., 6, 181
Catron, T., 142, 214, 254
Cauce, A. M., 151
Caughy, M. O., 181
Cavell, T. A., 154
Ceci, S. J., 18
Chamberlain, P., 6, 15, 20, 43, 50, 59,
    74, 95, 149, 155, 221, 225, 234
Chavous, T. M., 180
Chilcoate, H., 28
Christianson, S., 136
Cicchetti, D., 5
Clark, G. N., 53, 202
Clark, L. A., 19
Clark, M. S., 32
Clarke, G. N., 145, 158, 202
Coatsworth, J. D., 181
Cobb, J. A., 32, 39
Coco, E. L., 151
Cohen, J. A., 149
Collins, L. M., 50
Comeau, C. A., 38
Compas, B. E., 144
Conduct Problems Prevention Research
    Group, 6, 25, 38, 102, 136, 147,
    164, 183, 184
Conger, R. D., 36
Conger, R. E., 24
Connell, A. M., 8, 54, 258
Connell, S., 132
Connor-Smith, J., 146, 202
Copeland, M. E., 144
Courtney, L. J., 151
Cowan, C. P., 83
Cowan, P. A., 83
Crandall, C. S., 32, 215
Crick, N. A., 18
Cromer, C., 37
Cronbach, L. J., 91, 93
Crosby, L., 19, 33, 37, 43, 45

Cunningham, P. B., 6, 15, 32, 66, 80,
    170, 225
Curran, P. J., 205
Curry, J. F., 53, 95

Dadds, M. R., 53, 202
Darling, N., 28
Davis, B., 8, 36
Dawes, R. M., 91, 104, 230, 242, 253
Day, L. E., 7
Deater-Deckard, K., 54, 101, 173, 189
DeBar, L. L., 145, 202
Deblinger, E., 149
DeGarmo, D. S., 6, 8, 12, 48, 49, 184,
    220
DeKlyen, M., 42, 165
DePrince, A. P., 145
DiClemente, C., 58, 79, 111, 112, 156
Dionne, R., 258
Dishion, T. J., 4–9, 11, 15, 18–20, 22–26,
    28, 31, 32–35, 37–40, 43–46, 48,
    49, 50, 52–57, 60, 62–64, 84, 91,
    93, 94, 95, 98, 101, 102, 104,
    109, 113, 116, 122, 128, 130,
    132, 136, 138, 143, 144, 147,
    164, 181, 183–185, 191, 201,
    202, 204–207, 212, 213, 258
Dodge, K. A., 5, 18, 19, 26, 28, 101, 154,
    173, 183, 189, 201, 202, 203, 206
Doss, A. J., 219
Downes, B., 32
Downs, J., 231
Drinkwater, M., 4
Drotar, D., 241
Duncan, G. J., 213
Duncan, T. E., 25, 33, 220, 221
Dunn, J., 9, 18
Duran, B., 28, 64, 101, 257
Duran, E., 28, 64, 101, 257
Durlak, J. A., 146
Dwyer, J. H., 96

Eccles, J. S., 137, 213
Eddy, J. M., 6, 25, 26, 32, 33, 54, 207
Edelbrock, C. S., 154
Edwards, G., 145
Edwards, P., 35
Ehrenreich, N. S., 258
Eisenberg, N., 95, 143

Elder, G. H., Jr., 36, 40
Elliott, D. S., 62
Ellis, S., 37
Estes, A., 43

Fabes, R. A., 143
Fagot, B. I., 25, 33
Falloon, I. R. H., 7, 12
Fantuzzo, J. W., 26
Feldlaufer, H., 137
Felner, R. D., 15
Felner, T. Y., 15
Fetrow, R. A., 25, 32, 54
Fisch, R., 8
Fischoff, B., 231
Fisher, C. B., 258
Fisher, P. A., 5, 143
Fishman, H. C., 8, 51
Fiske, D. W., 95, 96
Fletcher, A. C., 28
Fletcher, K., 145
Flicker, S. M., 211
Florsheim, P., 189
Forgatch, M. S., 5, 6, 8, 12, 15, 34, 35,
        41, 48, 49, 52, 59, 62, 110, 180,
        184, 220, 221, 231, 233, 238
Frabutt, J. M., 181
Frame, C. L., 154
Franks, E. A., 146
French, D. C., 39, 93, 94
French, S. A., 32
Freyd, J. J., 145
Fuhrman, T., 146
Fuligni, A. J., 181
Funder, D. C., 22

Gardner, F. E. M., 7, 35, 132
Gardner, K., 43, 56
Garfinkel, R., 146
Garrod, A., 181
Ge, X., 36
Gerhardt, C. A., 144
Giancola, P. R., 144
Gifford-Smith, M., 26
Gilliom, M., 65
Gillmore, M. R., 181
Givens, S., 37
Glesar, G. C., 91
Good, R., 184

Goodman, M. R., 135, 184
Goodyear, R. K., 225
Gordis, E. B., 146, 202
Gorman-Smith, D., 189
Gottfredson, D. C., 25
Gottfredson, G. D., 25
Gottman, J. M., 34, 43, 45, 46
Gould, M. S., 215
Gragg, K. M., 15
Granger, D. A., 146, 214, 225
Granic, I., 4, 20, 28, 36, 37
Greenberg, M. T., 42, 165, 188
Greene, L. I., 258
Greenley, R. N., 146
Greenwood, G. E., 136
Greif, G. L., 151
Griffin, W. A., 35
Gross, D., 24
Grossman, P. A., 154
Guadagnoli, E., 58
Gullone, E., 19
Gulub, A., 158
Guthrie, I. K., 143

Haas, E., 32, 207
Haley, J., 8, 51, 61
Halford, W. K., 251
Hall, K., 23
Hammen, C., 146
Hammond, M., 147
Han, S. S., 146, 214, 225
Harkness, K. L., 9
Harkness, S., 16
Harlow, R. E., 231
Harnish, J. D., 19
Harris, J. R., 62
Harris, M. J., 206
Harris, P., 145
Harris, V., 142, 214, 254
Harter, S., 84
Hatashita-Wong, M., 258
Hawkins, J. D., 6
Hawley, K. M., 4, 219, 245
Hayashino, D. S., 15
Hayes, S. C., 43, 145
Heflin, A. H., 149
Heller, L. R., 26
Henggeler, S. W., 6, 15, 24, 32, 66, 80,
        170, 220, 225
Herbison, G. P., 247

Hervis, O., 181
Herzberger, S. D., 32
Hickman, C. W., 136
Higgins, E. T., 137
Hill, P., 80
Hinden, B. R., 144
Hogansen, J., 45, 94
Holland, D. E., 53, 202
Hollenbeck, J. R., 222
Hollingsworth, T., 185
Holmbeck, G. N., 146
Holton, A., 35
Hopkins, H. K., 23
Hops, H., 35, 36
Horner, R. H., 137
Howard, A., 206
Howell, C. T., 56
Hoyt, D. R., 151
Hudson, J. L., 144, 202
Huey, S. J., Jr., 220
Hughes, J. N., 154
Huizinga, D., 62
Hybl, L. G., 25
Hyman, H., 8

Ialongo, N., 26, 54, 206
Ilgen, D. R., 222, 224
Ingoldsby, E. M., 65, 152
Izard, C. E., 145

Jabson, J., 44
Jacob, T., 42
Jacobsen, N. S., 56
Jamieson, P., 215
Johnson, M., 222
Johnson, S. M., 42
Jones, R. R., 24
Jundt, D., 222

Kahneman, D., 106
Kaminski, R., 135, 184
Kandel, D. B., 207
Kaplan, H. B., 213
Kaufman, N., 11, 15, 128, 147, 184
Kavanagh, K., 6–9, 11, 20, 26, 28, 34,
        35, 48, 50, 52, 54, 55, 63, 64,
        102, 104, 109, 113, 116, 122,
        128, 132, 136, 138, 143, 147,
        184, 185, 191, 258

Kazdin, A. E., 3–6, 20, 50, 53, 57, 58,
        95, 125, 143, 145, 146, 158, 211,
        220
Kellam, S. G., 25, 26, 54, 94, 206, 207
Keller, G., 144
Kelly, J. G., 15, 24, 202
Kendall, P. C., 7, 145, 158, 202
Kerr, M., 128
Kilgore, K., 35
Kilkenny, R., 181
Kim, S., 6
King, N. J., 19
King, R. A., 5
Kirisci, L., 144
Kitzman, H., 24
Kochanska, G., 95, 144
Kodish, E., 241
Kolb, B. G. R., 18
Kolpacoff, M., 185
Kremer, M., 213
Kumpfer, K. L., 6
Kurtines, W. M., 6, 51, 181, 257

Lacrens, K. R., 53, 202
Lamey, A. V., 4, 20, 36
Lampman, C., 146
Lampron, L. B., 53, 95
Laneri, M., 145
Langrock, A. M., 144
Lansford, J., 201, 206
Latham, G. P., 225, 226
Lau, A. S., 149
Lawton, J. M., 52
LeFevre, J., 136
Lengua, L., 102, 164, 183
Levenson, R. W., 34
Levine, A. G., 28
Levy, D. M., 213
Lewinsohn, P. M., 53, 145, 202
Lewis, M. D., 18, 144
Lezak, M. D., 91, 92
Li, F., 19, 32, 98, 147, 184, 207
Liddle, H. A., 6
Light, J., 7, 138
Lim, M., 136
Ling, X., 54, 206
Lipsey, M. W., 158, 206
Little, C., 80
Littman, R. A., 43
Lochman, J. E., 19, 53, 95, 145, 154, 202

Loeber, R., 5, 19, 22, 23, 28, 53, 82, 94, 183
Lord, S., 137
Lyons, P. M., 258

MacAulay, H. K., 151
MacIver, D., 137
MacKinnon-Lewis, C., 181
Maerov, S. L., 48
Mager, W., 206
Magnusson, D., 63
Mangione, P. L., 32
Mannarino, A. P., 149
Margolin, G. T., 34, 258
Marigna, M., 189
Markie-Dadds, C., 132
Martin, J. L., 247
Martinez, C. R., Jr., 34, 180
Mash, E. J., 91
Maughan, B., 18
Mayer, L. S., 26
McBride Murry, V., 6
McCartney, K., 46
McConaughy, S. H., 56
McCord, J., 24, 26, 40, 53, 205, 212
McDonald, M., 22, 206
McGlashan, T. N., 5
McGraw, K., 35
McMahon, R. J., 60, 102, 136, 164, 183, 184
McWhirter, B. T., 15
Measelle, J. R., 83
Medici Skaggs, N., 28, 34, 46, 94
Meece, D. W., 28
Meehl, P. E. T., 91, 93, 105
Melton, G. B., 258
Menditto, A. A., 91, 104
Merchant, M., 144
Merisca, R., 54, 206
Metevia, L., 145
Mezzich, A. C., 144
Midgley, C., 137
Milich, R., 206
Miller, C. L., 137
Miller, V. A., 241
Miller, W. R., 9, 50–52, 59, 77, 79, 112, 113, 212
Minuchin, S., 8, 24, 51, 61
Moberg, D. P., 22, 206
Molgaard, V., 6

Monroe, S. M., 9
Moore, K. J., 15
Moras, K., 225
Moreau, D., 146
Mortimore, P., 18
Morton, T., 146, 214, 225
Mufson, L., 146
Mullen, P. E., 247
Munoz, R. F., 145
Murphy, B., 95
Murphy, S. A., 50
Muthén, B. O., 205
Myers, H. F., 189

Nagin, D., 65
Nelson, S. E., 8, 11, 18, 28, 33, 147, 138
Nelson, S. N., 37, 128, 144, 184
Newell, R. N., 82, 110
NICHD Early Child Care Research Network, 24
Nickerson, K., 181
Norcross, J. G., 9
Nunnally, J. C., 91

O'Campo, P. J., 181
Oden, S., 32
O'Donnell, J., 6
Offord, D. R., 16
Olds, D. L., 7, 24, 80
O'Leary, C. C., 44, 132
Ollendick, T. H., 19
Olson, S. L., 32
Orban, L., 158
Othmer, E., 8
Othmer, S. C., 8
Ouston, J., 18
Owen, L. D., 37, 38, 181, 207
Owens, E. B., 152

Pantin, H., 181
Pardini, D. A., 145, 202
Parsons, J. E., 137
Patterson, G. R., 5–8, 9, 11, 12, 15, 18, 20, 23–26, 28, 31, 32, 34, 35, 37–41, 43, 45–50, 52–54, 56–59, 62, 63, 65, 91, 93–95, 98, 101, 110, 143, 164, 170, 183, 184, 204, 207, 220, 221, 231, 233
Patterson, S. G., 63, 64, 84, 130

Paul, G. L., 91, 104
Pears, K., 143
Perez-Vidal, A., 181
Perrin, J. E., 26
Peterson, A.C., 10
Peterson, D. R., 42
Petras, H., 206
Pettit, G. S., 19, 42, 173, 183, 189
Pettit, J. S., 28
Phung, T. M., 142, 214, 254
Pickrel, S. G., 220
Piehler, T. F., 46
Pilkonis, P. A., 225
Pinder, C. C., 225, 226
Plomin, R., 54
Poduska, J., 54, 206
Porche, L., 99
Posner, M. I., 18, 144
Poulin, F., 8, 19, 24, 28, 34, 38, 40, 46,
    53, 94, 205, 212, 208
Prochaska, J. O., 9, 58, 79, 111, 156
Pynoos, R. S., 5

Quera, V., 45

Ramon, W. A., 137
Randolph, S. M., 181
Rao, S. A., 132
Rappaport, M., 23
Rebok, G. W., 26
Rehm, L. P., 225
Reid, J. B., 5, 8, 15, 24, 25, 26, 31, 34,
    39, 40, 43, 48, 49, 50, 54, 56, 74,
    93, 94, 234
Reid, M. J., 147, 190
Reis, H. T., 32
Reiser, M., 143
Rende, R., 54
Resnick, M. D., 32
Resnicow, K., 189
Riley, D. B., 151
Roberts, G. C., 63
Roberts, M. C., 180, 262
Robin, A. L., 7, 142
Robins, M. S., 82, 86, 110
Robinson, J., 80
Robinson, T. E., 18
Robinson, T. L., 181

Roche, B., 145
Rogers, C. R., 72, 112
Rogoff, B., 37, 44
Rollnick, S., 9, 50, 51, 59, 77, 79, 112
Romans, S. E., 247
Romer, D., 215
Rosman, B. L., 24
Rossi, J. S., 58
Rothbart, M. K., 18, 95, 144
Rowland, M. D., 6, 15, 32, 66, 80, 170,
    225
Roy, A. K., 45
Rudolf, K. D., 146
Rueda, M. R., 144
Rusby, J., 43
Rutter, M., 5, 9, 18, 25, 146

Sameroff, A. J., 9
Sanders, M. R., 6, 52, 54, 132
Santisteban, D. A., 181
Scarr, S., 46
Schaffer, C. M., 206
Schneiger, A., 11, 102, 128, 147, 184
Schoenwald, S. K., 6, 15, 32, 66, 80,
    170, 225
Schoppelrey, S., 22, 206
Schrader, S. M., 26, 132
Seilhamer, R. A., 42
Senechal, M., 136
Sharon, T., 42
Shaw, D. S., 7, 25, 35, 65, 152
Sheeber, L., 8, 36, 39
Shepard, S. A., 38
Sherman, L., 35
Sherrill, M., 203
Shoenwald, S. K., 15, 32, 66
Siegel, T. C., 53, 95, 211
Silbereisen, A. K., 10
Silverman, J., 23
Simonoff, G., 9, 18
Skinner, B. F., 45
Skinner, M., 164, 184
Slough, N., 136
Smith, A., 18
Smith, D. K., 149, 225
Snyder, J., 8, 22, 34, 35, 37, 38, 39, 50,
    144, 207
Soberman, L. H., 185
Soler, R., 189
Song, N., 80

Sorenson, S., 10
Southam-Gerow, M. A., 146, 202
Sovereign, R. G., 59, 112, 113
Speltz, M. L., 42, 165, 188
Spence, S. H., 53, 202
Spoth, R. L., 6, 7
Spracklen, K. M., 19, 32, 37, 46, 184, 207
Sprague, J. R., 137
Sroufe, L. A., 5
Stanger, C., 20
Staton, B., 7
Stattin, H., 63, 128
Steiben, J., 144
Steinberg, A. N., 5
Steinberg, L., 28
Stevenson, D. L., 136
Stockemer, V., 37
Stone, E. C., 158
Stoolmiller, M., 19, 32, 38, 46, 54, 164, 184, 220, 221
Stormshak, E. A., 5, 7, 9, 22, 38, 42, 46, 50, 52, 53, 97, 102, 135, 136, 138, 147, 164, 183, 184
Story, M., 32
Stouthamer-Loeber, M., 82, 183
Sugai, G., 137
Sukhodolsky, D. G., 158
Sullivan, H. S., 77
Super, C. M., 16
Supplee, L., 7, 132
Szapocznik, J. F., 6, 7, 51, 181, 191, 257

Tarter, R. E., 144
Taylor, C. J., 26, 132
Taylor, S., 189
Taylor, T. K., 7, 59
Tellengen, A., 19
Tennenbaum, D., 42
Terdal, L. G., 91
Thibodeaux, S., 43, 56
Tolan, P. H., 189
Torres, D. M., 15
Toth, S. L., 5
Tremblay, R. E., 19
Trickett, E. J., 25
Trimble, J. E., 100
Truax, P., 56
Turgeon, L., 38

Turner, C. W., 82, 110
Tversky, A., 106
Tyler, K. A., 151

Van Court, P., 95
van Kammen, W. B., 82
Van Nguyen, T., 40
Vasquez, M., 99
Velicer, W. F., 58
Vincent, J. P., 41
Vitaro, F., 19, 38
Vohs, K. D., 143
Volkmar, F. R., 5

Waldron, H. B., 211
Walker, A. M., 181
Walker, H. M., 137, 202
Walker-Barnes, C. J., 16
Wampold, B. E., 34, 71, 219, 220, 224, 225
Ward, J. V., 181
Warren, K., 22, 206
Wassell, G., 143, 220
Watson, D., 19
Watzlawick, P., 8
Weakland, J., 8
Weber, F. D., 55, 56
Webster-Stratton, C., 6, 24, 147, 184, 185, 190
Weiss, B., 142, 146, 214, 225, 254
Weiss, R. L., 41
Weissman, M. M., 146
Weisz, J. R., 4, 5, 57, 142, 146, 149, 150, 158, 202, 214, 219, 225, 245
Werthamer, L., 54
Weschler, D., 91
West, L., 37
Whaley, A. L., 189
Wheeler, V. A., 32
Whitbeck, L. B., 151
Whiting, B. B., 64
Whiting, J. M., 64
Wiggins, J. S., 91
Williams, R. A., 7
Wills, T. A., 144
Wilson, D. B., 158
Wing Sue, D., 99
Winslow, E. B., 152
Winter, C. E., 37, 45, 94, 144, 184

Wraith, R., 5
Wright, J. C., 4

Yasui, M., 7, 8, 54, 138, 258
Yeh, M., 150
Yoerger, K., 28, 46, 207
Youngren, M. A., 145

Zakriski, A. L., 4
Zeiss, A. M., 145
Zhang, Q., 82
Zinbarg, R. E., 39

SUBJECT INDEX

ABC model of change, 133
Abuse
    children, 77
    contexts of, 148
    and ethics, 245–247
    physical, 148
    sexual, 148, 247–249
Abusive circumstances, 247–250
Abusive relationships, 74
Acceptance and Commitment Therapy, 145
Accepting feedback (behavior), 158–159
ACCESS model, 238–239
Accountability, 66, 238
Acculturation, 179–180
Adaptive interventions, 50
ADHD (attention-deficit/hyperactivity disorder), 96
Adolescence
    developmental norms in, 195–196
    and deviancy training, 207
    emotional distress in, 20
    and group-based parent training, 185, 187, 188
    and group interventions, 213
    monitoring during, 137–138
    parent/peer relationships in, 18
    routines in, 197
    social maladaptation in, 19
Adolescents. See also Child and adolescent interventions
    advocacy for, 85, 155
    clinical interview techniques with, 153–156
    and disengagement, 147
    interview techniques with, 153–156
    motivational interviewing of, 113
    parental control of, 147–148
    toys/games used with, 155
Adolescent Transitions Program (ATP), 64–65, 97, 98, 104, 138, 185, 204–205, 208–210, 214
Adult-derived models, 3

Adults
    behavior defined by, 16
    depression in, 71, 176, 219–220
ADVANCE parent training program, 184
Advice, 112
Advocacy
    for adolescents, 85, 155
    through parenting groups, 189
African Americans, 100–103, 180, 189, 258
Age
    self-regulation affected by, 146–147
    and treatment efficacy, 57
Agency, 145
Agenda, 166
Aggression, 19
    and coercive interactions, 65
    against female partners, 46
    group therapy for treating, 202
    and role-play, 159
AIM approach. See Assessment, intervention, and motivation approach
Alcoholics Anonymous, 212
Alliance, 235
American Academy of Pediatrics, 195
American Indians, 100–101, 257–258
American Psychological Association (APA), 242
American Psychologist, 205
Anger management, 158
Antecedent inventory, 133
Antisocial behavior, 35, 146
Anxiety, 7, 202, 211
APA (American Psychological Association), 242
APA Ethics Code, 242–243
Appropriate dress, 72
Asperger's syndrome, 23
Assertive limit setting, 101
Assessment, intervention, and motivation (AIM) approach, 52, 66, 106, 107, 254
Assessment-driven approach, 8, 131–132

Assessments, 91–107
    benefits of, 52
    case conceptualization of, 104–107
    clinical, 104
    comprehensive, 239
    and confidentiality, 154
    and cultural relativity, 99–103
    deficit model of, 91–92
    of developmental milestones, 77
    and diagnosis, 242
    domains of, 93
    and ethical decision making, 251
    linking interview concerns to, 81–82
    method/trait variance, 95–96
    need for, 88
    of parenting traits, 98–100
    problem-focused, 133–134
    standardized, 92
    trait, 96–98
Assessment tools, 154–155
ATP. See Adolescent Transitions
    Program
Attendance (at parenting groups), 192
Attention-deficit/hyperactivity disorder
    (ADHD), 96
Autism, 23
Autonomy, premature, 18, 34
Avoid punishing parents (SANE guide-
    lines), 64, 130
Awareness, 39, 52, 63

BASIC parent training program, 184
Behavior
    accepting feedback as, 158–159
    antisocial, 35, 146
    of child defined by adults, 16
    measurable/observed/valued/
      encouraged, 158
Behavior activation, 167
Behavioral control, 144–145
Behavioral theory, 133
Behavior-change goal, 158
Behavior management, 4
    in family management, 60, 61
    positive approach to, 63–64
    teaching skills in, 188
    therapist skills in, 84
Behavior plans, inappropriate, 196
Behavior problems, 4. See also Problem
    behavior

Berkeley Puppet Interview, 83–84
Bias, rater, 102–104
Binge eating, 215
Biological issues, 18
Biological maturation transitions, 10
Bipolar disorder, 23
Birth trauma, 23
Blame, 73, 110, 117
Boundary problems
    and enmeshment, 175–176
    for therapist, 228
Boys, 20, 205
Brainstorming, 121, 227, 231
Brevity, 86
Bribing, 195
Brief family intervention model, 131–135
    assessment-driven foci/goals in,
      131–132
    defining collaborative set of interven-
      tion goals in, 132
    evaluating outcomes/generating alter-
      native solutions in, 134
    identifying/narrowing goals in,
      132–133
    identifying possible solutions in, 134
    motivating family to seek further ser-
      vices in, 135
    problem-focused assessment in,
      133–134
    summarizing/terminating, 134–135
Brief interventions, 50, 131–139
    definitions of, 126
    for families, 131–135
    group approaches to, 135–136
    in schools, 136–139
Bulimia, 203
Bullying, 19

Cambridge-Sommerville Youth Study,
    205
Caregivers, 5–7. See also Parents
    initial contact with, 73
    interventions designed to work with,
      24
    role of key, 252
    and self-regulation, 145
    self-regulation affected by, 145
Caregiver strategies, 4
Caring, 173

Caring for Your Baby and Young Child
(American Academy of Pediatrics), 195
Case conceptualization
in assessment, 104–107
comprehensive assessment as basis
for, 244
and ethics, 251
principles/objectives guiding, 52
principles of, 114–116
Change
ABC model of, 133
addressing, 52–54
collaborative framework for, 190
cycle of family, 169, 170
ecology of, 58–60
group work promoting, 190–192
initial contacts and process of, 72
menu of options for. See Menu of
change options
minimizing resistance to, 170, 171
motivation to. See Motivation to
change
parent–child relationship central to
process of, 34
resistance to. See Resistance to
change
stages of, 112
steps of, 59–60
technology of, 221
Change agents, 52–53
Changes in context, 10
Check-in, 191
Child abuse, 77
Child and adolescent interventions,
141–161
challenges within, 160–161
collaborative set established in,
156–157
emotional distress prevented
through, 142
and family dynamics, 142
with family therapy, 147–148
goal of, 141
group-based. See Group-based child
and adolescent interventions
guidelines for, 152–161
immediate traumatic events in,
149
marital problems affecting, 152
parental disengagement in, 150–152

parents' engagement in treatment,
150–152
past traumatic events in, 149
presenting issues/problems during,
148–150
rapport in, 153–156
reframing used in, 150
self-regulation focus of, 143–147
teaching specific skills within,
158–159
and traumatic events, 149, 160
Child and Family Center, 114–115
Child and Parent Trauma-Focused Cognitive Behavior Therapy, 149
Child Behavior Checklist, 114, 119
Child-centered therapy, 142–143
Child-focused approach, 146
Child-focused approach to learning, 146
Childhood
developmental issues in, 152–161
presenting problems in, 152–161
Child interviews, 83–87
of adolescents, 84
brief/slow start in, 86–87
and developmental issues, 83
linking concerns with assessments
in, 86
normalizing experiences in, 85
optimistic framing of situation in, 86
respecting space/privacy during, 84–85
of young children, 83–84
Child-only treatments, 142, 143, 146
Children
and benefit from direct instruction
in skills, 146
clinical interview techniques with,
153–156
and confidentiality, 153, 154
and denial, 153–154
emotional distress in, 19–20
and game-based approach to learning, 146
perspective of, on family difficulties,
76
social–emotional development of,
153–156
social maladaptation in, 19
strength-based approach used with,
160
toys/games used with, 154, 155, 159
and traumatic events, 149, 160

Child report reliability, 83
Child Well-Being Profile, 116
Chutes and Ladders (game), 159
Clarification, 118
Clear boundaries, 72
Client identification, 244–245
Clinical assessment, 104
Clinical interview techniques
    with adolescents, 153–156
    with children, 153–156
    with children/adolescents, 153–156
Clinical skill, 239
Closeness, 32–33, 72, 173
Coding of interpersonal process,
    43–45
Coercive behavior
    and client motivation, 65
    and family dynamics, 39
    observation of, 204
    and relationships, 33–36
    by siblings, 38
Coercive interactions, 8
Cognitive–behavioral therapy, 146, 149,
    204, 211
Cognitive skills, 144
Collaboration
    collusion vs., 261–262
    of family members, 75
    with teachers, 75
Collaborative problem solving, 62
Collaborative sets
    affirming, 166
    in child/adolescent interventions,
        156–157
    establishing, 59, 60
    of intervention goals, 132
    parent–therapist interchange result-
        ing in, 170
Collaborative strategy, 234–235
Collusion, 85, 261–262
Common ground activity, 46
Communication
    attention to skills of, 62
    effectiveness of, 126–127
    and emotion, 62
    frequent/positive, 235
    and harm reduction, 246–247
    parent–school, 25–26
    pragmatics of, 45
    between school and home,
        137

Community factors, 27, 60
Comorbidity
    and deviancy training, 38
    and family dynamics, 36
    heterotypic, 27
    and interventions with children, 53
    of social maladaptation/emotional
        distress, 20
Competence, 253–254
Comprehensive assessments, 239
Confidentiality
    with children, 154
    in groups, 193
    and harm reduction, 246, 250
    importance of, 154
    standards regarding, 258–261
    and videotaping, 225
Conflict
    group, 193–194
    marital. See Marital conflict
Conflict control, 36, 39
Consent, 151, 244, 246, 255, 258, 260
Consequences, 64, 130, 133
Contemplation stage, 79
Content, process and, 76
Context, 16–17
    of abuse, 148
    changes in, 10
    factors of, 81, 158
    of group therapy, 211–212
    sensitivity of, 20–23
    therapist in, 221–223
    and trait assessment, 96
Contextualization, 174
Contingent positive reaction, 129
Cooperation, parent–school, 25–26
Coordinated treatment, 147, 224
Coping, 79, 146, 158
Corrective feedback, 168, 169
Cotherapy team, 234–235
Crisis management, 80
Cultural awareness, 256–258
Cultural disconnect, 180–181
Cultural diversity, 41–42, 137–138
Cultural issues
    and ecology of development/change,
        27
    and home-based therapy, 172–173
    in parenting groups, 189–190
Cultural relativity, 99–103
Cultural sensitivity, 51, 72

Custody, joint, 74
Custody clarification, 254–256

Data collection, 233–234
Daycare, 24
Decision tree, 243
Deficit model, 91–92
Delinquency
    and ATP Study, 205, 208, 210
    and deviant talk, 46
    and group interventions, 203, 206,
        213
Democratic limit setting, 101
Denial, 153–154
Dental metaphor, 53, 65
Depression, 7, 8
    in adolescent girls, 146
    adult, 71, 176, 219–220
    in childhood, 20
    and conflict control, 36
    and family dynamics, 39
    and family management therapy,
        26–27
    group therapy for treating, 202, 211
    parental, 176
    and peer dynamics, 38
Detouring family problems onto child,
    177–179
Development
    and assessment, 93–94
    group interventions and level of,
        212–213
    life span view of, 24, 25
    and relationship processes, 94–95
    social–emotional, 149
    wide range of, 241
Developmental domains, 154
Developmental–ecological model, 147
Developmental issues
    in childhood, 152–161
    and child interviews, 83
    in initial contacts, 77
Developmental norms, 195–196
Developmental outcomes in children,
    147
Developmental psychopathology litera-
    ture, 15
Developmental variation, 3–4
Deviancy training, 8
    factors in, 37–38

and group interventions, 204,
    207–209
and verbal schemas, 45–46
Deviant peer contagion, 203–212
Deviant peer involvement, 26
Deviant talk, 37, 46, 207
Diagnosis, 242
Diagnostic classifications, 23
Diary method, 42
Difficult parenting, history of, 198
Dimensionality, 43
Direct observation, 96
Disclosure
    by group leader, 192–193
    self-, 228
Disconnect, cultural, 180–181
Disconnected parents, 179–180
Discrepancies during initial interview, 81
Discussion, focused, 231
Disengagement
    adolescent, 147
    and age of child, 151
    from child, 197
    from child/adolescent interventions,
        150–152
    parental, 150–151
Distress
    emotional. See Emotional distress
    and reactivity, 42
    separation, 19
Diversity
    in assessment models, 100
    cultural, 41–42, 137–138
    and cultural awareness, 256
Divorce, 10
"Do-Do Bird" hypothesis, 224
Domestic violence, 77
Dosage, 55–57
Drawings, 154–155
Dress, appropriate, 72
Drinker's Check-Up, 59
Dropping out of school, 206
Duke Executive Session on Deviant Peer
    Contagion, 206
Dynamics, family. See Family dynamics

Early childhood, 184, 185, 187, 188, 195
Early Head Start, 51
Eating disorders, 7, 203, 215

EcoFIT model. See Ecological family intervention model
Ecological approach, 4
Ecological family intervention (EcoFIT) model, 3–10, 49–67
  assessment-driven, 8
  and change, ecology of, 58–60
  change addressed in, 52–54
  client motivation management in, 65–66
  empirically based, 5–6
  entrained self-regulation in, 54
  family-centered, 6–7
  and health-maintenance framework, 9–10
  influences on, 49–50
  measuring outcomes in, 55–58
  motivation to change addressed by, 9
  need for, 3–4
  sensitivity in, 51–52
  social interactions addressed by, 8–9
  support structuring in, 60–65
  unique aspects of, 50–51
Ecology of development and change, 15–29, 58–60
  family-centered model of, 24–29
  as heuristic framework, 17–18
  and psychopathology, 19–23
Effective Black Parenting Program, 173
Effective consequences (SANE guidelines), 64, 130
Emotional charge, 32–33
Emotional distress, 19–23
  and child/adolescent interventions, 142
  context sensitivity of, 20–23
  and family dynamics, 36
  internalizing disorder as, 97
  and peer dynamics, 38
Emotional reactions, 226–227
Emotional well-being, 166
Emotion-focused approach, 236–238
Empathy, 72, 80–81, 112, 156, 173, 176, 178
Empirically-based model, 239
Empirical model, 5–6
Encouragement, 129
Engagement, lack of, 73–74
Enmeshment, boundary problems and, 175–176

Entrained biosocial traits, 18
Entrained self-regulation, 54, 144
Entrainment, 18, 143
Environment
  self-regulation affected by, 145
  as system, 4
Escape conditioning, 36, 43, 47
Ethics, 241–264
  and age of child, 151
  APA guidelines for, 242–243
  of harm reduction, 244–250
  and standards, 250–262
  and strategic intervention, 243–244
  and training, 262–263
Ethnic identity, 180
Evaluating outcomes, 134
Event-duration coding, 44
Executive functioning, 145
Executive system (within family), 61
Expressed emotion, 114
Externalizing disorders, 19, 36, 97

Family, initial contacts with, 73
Family-centered approach, 6–7, 24–29, 141
Family change cycle, 169, 170
Family Check-Up (FCU), 9, 10, 109–122
  annual basis for, 54
  and brief family intervention, 131–132
  case conceptualization in, 114–116
  and ethics, 244, 247
  and family management therapy, 165–166
  feedback session in, 116–122
  motivational interviewing in, 109–113
  as steps of change, 60
Family dynamics, 34–38
  and child/adolescent interventions, 142
  and cultural disconnect, 180–181
  and detouring family problems onto child, 177–179
  and disconnected parents, 179–180
  enmeshment/boundary problems in, 175–176
  and family management therapy, 175–181
  initial contacts affected by, 73–74
  and parental depression, 176

Family ecology, 51, 52
Family-focused approach to learning, 146
Family Intake Questionnaire (FIQ), 74, 77
Family intervention model, brief. See Brief family intervention model
Family management, 5–7
  and Adolescent Transitions Program, 204
  central role of, 164–165
  curriculum for, 185
  measurement of, 45
Family management therapy, 163–181
  beginning session of, 166–167
  and cultural disconnect, 180–181
  and detouring family problems onto child, 177–179
  and disconnected parents, 179–180
  and dynamics of families, 175
  enmeshment/boundary problems in, 175–176
  and Family Check-Up, 165–166
  family therapy vs., 163
  home-based, 171–174
  and parental depression, 176
  rationale for, 164–165
  therapist skills in, 167–171
Family problems, 177–179
Family Process Code, 43, 56
Family relationships, 4
  dynamics of, 34–38
  measurement of, 40–47
  types of, 32–34
Family Resource Center (FRC), 138
Family resource room, 26
Family systems theory, 8, 163
Family therapy
  APA Ethics Code regarding, 242–243
  and child/adolescent interventions, 147–148
  family management therapy vs., 163
Fast Track program, 25, 206
Fate control, 37
Fathers
  antisocial behaviors encouraged by, 38
  and initial contacts, 73–74
  role of, 78–79
FCU. See Family Check-Up
Feedback, 112
  accepting, 158–159
  direct, 156
  effective response to, 168
  ratio of positive/corrective, 168, 169
  tailoring, 115–116
  videotaping used for, 156, 225–226
Feedback session, 116–122
  feedback phase of, 117–120
  menu of change options in, 120–122
  self-assessment phase of, 116–117
  support/clarification phase of, 117
  work of, 113–114
Fidelity, 238
FIQ. See Family Intake Questionnaire
Five Cs of professional child and family therapy, 252
Focused discussion, 231
FRAMES model, 112–113
FRC (Family Resource Center), 138
Friend–child interactions, 33

Game-based approach to learning, 146
Games, 154, 155, 159
Gender differences
  in emotional distress, 20
  in risk ratings, 103
  in self-regulation, 146–147
Generalization of skills, 146
Genetic factors, 16, 23
Girls, 20, 146, 215
Goals
  assessment-driven, 131–132
  defining collaborative set of, 132
  of group-based parenting training, 188–189
  identifying/narrowing, 132–133
Group-based child and adolescent interventions, 201–215
  advantages of, 201–202
  disadvantages of, 202–211
  guidelines for, 211–215
Group-based parenting training, 183–199
  advantages/disadvantages of, 186
  and attendance, 192
  brief, 135–136
  and check-ins, 191
  and confidentiality, 193
  conflict in, 193–194
  content/structure/participants, 186–187

Group-based parenting training, *continued*
    cultural issues in context of,
        189–190
    curriculum for, 185
    and disengagement from child, 197
    goals of, 188–189
    and high-risk parenting, 193
    and history of difficult parenting,
        198
    and home visits/meetings, 191
    homework for, 190–191
    and inappropriate behavior plans,
        196
    and knowledge of developmental
        norms, 195–196
    and lack of routines/structure in
        home, 197–198
    and leadership style, 192
    managing, 192–194
    and personal disclosure by leader,
        192–193
    promoting change in, 190–192
    rationale for, 185–186
    research supporting, 183–185
    and resistance to praise, 194–195
    session content, 187–188
    talkativeness in, 194
Group conflict, 193–194
Group leaders, 192–193
Guilt induction, 173

Happiness, 62
Harm reduction, 244–250
    and abusive circumstances, 247–250
    and case conceptualization, 52, 115
    and client identification, 244–245
    and confidentiality, 250, 259–260
    in group therapy, 203–204
    safety as priority of, 245–246
Head Start, 51
Health maintenance model, 9–10
    AIM clinical model as, 53
    EcoFIT similar to, 50
Health routines, 144
Heterotypic comorbidity, 27
Hierarchical integration, 94, 143
Hierarchy
    among parenting practices, 61–62
    in parent–child relationships, 33
High-risk parenting, 193

HIV, 260–261
Home-based therapy, 171–174
    advantages/disadvantages of, 171
    and culture, 172–173
    need for, 171–172
Home context, 20–22, 28
Home sessions, 66
Home visits, 80, 191
Homework, 190–191
Hostile attitudes toward women, 46
"House of cards," 253
Humor, 174, 192, 226, 231

Identification
    of goals, 132–133
    of possible solutions, 134
    of strengths, 116
Impulsivity, 158
Inappropriate behavior plans, 196
Incentives, 192, 196
Incredible Years Parent Intervention, 184
Individual supervision, 230–234
Informed consent, 246, 255
Initial contacts, 71–89
    channeling perspectives in, 74–76
    with children, 83–87
    clinical observation from, 87–88
    concluding, 88
    logistics of, 73
    nonspecific factors in, 71–76
    with parents, 76–82
    settings/circumstances of, 72
Insurance reimbursement, 221
Interdependent relationships
    and deviancy training, 46
    and escape conditioning, 47
    in families, 32, 33
Internalizing disorders, 19, 97
Interpersonal Process Code, 43
Intervention maintenance, 234–235
Interviewing
    of children/adolescents, 153–156
    motivational. See Motivational
        interviewing
    of parents, 76–82
    and respect, 74
    strategies for, 80–82
Intimate partner selection, 46
Involvement of family members, 73–74

Jenga (game), 155
Joint custody, 74
Joint feedback session, 120
Joint planning, 165
Journal of Abnormal Child Psychology, 202, 206
Judgment(s)
    about parenting practices, 73
    parents' initial, 74

Large-group supervision model, 232, 233
Late childhood, 185, 187
Laughter, 33
Leadership, 61, 65–66
Leadership style, 192
Learning, 146
Lecture series, 135
Life span view of development, 24, 25
Limit setting, 129–131
    assertive vs. democratic, 101
    and culture, 101–102, 173
    difficulties of, 64
    and EcoFIT approach, 50
    and monitoring, 98, 99
Listener reactions, 45
Listening, 126, 173
Long-term interventions, 125–126
Lying, 19

Maelstrom model, 203–204
Mandatory reporting, 245
Manual-based treatment approach, 158
Marital conflict
    and children and adolescent interventions, 152
    detouring, onto child, 177–179
    and feedback session, 119–120
    and parenting, 63
    and perceptual objectification, 251
    script for dealing with, 237
Marital interactions, 41
McCord, Joan, 205
Mean level analysis, 99–101
Measurable/observed/valued/encouraged (MOVE) behavior principle, 158
Measurement, 40–47
    dimensionality of, 43
    issues with, 40–42

process of, 43–45
    verbal schemas in, 45–47
Medication, 23
Mental retardation, 23
Menu of change options, 112, 120–122
Metaphors, 174
Method variance, 95
Minority status, 42, 100–103
Model-driven interventions, 224–225
"Modern black discipline," 173
Monitoring, 128
    and deviant peers, 18
    and EcoFIT approach, 60, 61
    and limit setting, 98, 99
    parental, 35–36
    and peer influence, 115
    and school programs, 136–137
Mood disorders, 20
Mother(s)
    absence of, 79
    early relationships with, 94
    and initial contacts, 73–74
    interventions with young, 24
    reporting by, 21
Motivating family to seek further services, 135, 136
Motivational interviewing, 9, 109–113
    in initial interview, 79
    reframing in, 110–111
    role of assessment in, 111
    and therapist interactions, 59
    transtheoretical view in, 111–112
Motivational questions, 174
Motivation to change, 9
    managing, 65–66
    support for, 51, 52
    supporting, 116
    and therapist interactions, 58, 59
MOVE (measurable/observed/valued/encouraged) behavior principle, 158
Multimethod trait approach, 98–100
Multisystemic Treatment approach, 225

Narcotics Anonymous, 212
National Institute of Mental Health, 262
Negative reciprocity, 45
Negativity, 95
Neglect, 245–247

Never abuse children or adolescents
(SANE guidelines), 64, 130
Night terrors, 20
Nomological network, 93
Nonspecific factor of therapy, 220
Nonverbal cues, 168
Normalization, 174
of child's experiences, 85
of problems for parents, 82
Norm-referenced behavior ratings scales,
154–155
Norm Validation Code, 46–47

Objectification, 251–252
Observation
direct, 96
of initial contacts, 87–88
Open-ended questions, 155
Oppositional behavior, 35
Optimistic framing, 82, 86
Oregon Multidimensional Foster Care
Model, 225
Oregon Social Learning Center (OSLC),
40, 49, 220
Oregon Youth Study, 33
OSLC. See Oregon Social Learning
Center

Pain control, 34
Paraphrasing, 174
Paraprofessionals, 236
Parental control, 147–148
Parental monitoring. See Monitoring
Parent–child relationships
hierarchy of, 33
influence of peers on, 34
Parent consultant, 138
Parent Daily Report (PDR), 74, 229–230,
234
Parenting
high-risk, 193
history of difficult, 198
priority of, 115
punitive, 102, 198
responsive, 164–165
step-, 179
Parenting interventions, 125–135
brief, 131–135
for early childhood, 24, 25

group-based. See Group-based parenting training
targets for, 126–131
Parenting in the Teenage Years, 136
Parenting practice(s), 5, 126–131
communication effectiveness as,
126–127
importance of, 130, 131
limit setting as, 129–131
monitoring as, 128
positive reinforcement as, 129
proactive structuring as, 127–128
relationship building as, 128
Parenting skills, 60, 61
Parenting traits, 98–100
Parent interviews, 76–82
collaborative relationship established
in, 78
discrepancies during, 81
empathy/understanding in, 80
linking concerns to assessment in,
81–82
normalizing problems in, 82
optimistic framing of situation, 82
paraphrase parent concerns in, 80
and previous professional experiences, 82
priority of, 78
process/content in, 76
two therapists for, 77–78
validating parenting efforts, 80
Parent Management Training, Oregon
model, 49
Parents. See also Caregivers
antisocial behaviors encouraged by,
38
avoid punishing, 64, 130
depression in, 176
disconnected, 179–180
initial contacts, 76–82
motivation to change of, 51
reporting by, 97
Parent-support system, 191
Past events, 149, 160
Patients' rights, 151
PDR. See Parent Daily Report
Peer aggregation, 206
Peer dynamics, 36–38
Peer provocation, 159
Peer relationships
and brief intervention, 138, 139

dynamics of, 36–38
parent–child relationships affected
   by, 34, 62–63
verbal schemas of, 45–47
Peers, 8
   and group therapy, 203
   older, 214
   and parent monitoring, 18, 28
   role of, 115
   school behavior influenced by, 21, 22
   and social adaptation, 26
   and social maladaptation, 19
Peer support (for therapist), 228–230
Perceptual objectification, 251–252
Permissive close relationships, 64
Personal disclosure by group leader,
   192–193
Perspective(s), 223
   channeling, 74–76
   child's, 76
   parents', 119
Phobias, 20
Physical abuse, 148
Physical aggression, 102
Physical punishment, 173, 189
PIE recipe, 129
Play therapy, 148–150
Positive feedback, 168, 169
Positive reinforcement, 37, 47, 63–64,
   98, 99, 129, 159, 169
Pragmatics of communication, 45
Praise, resistance to, 194–195
Praise-to-correction ratio, 116
Precontemplation stage, 79
Premature autonomy, 18, 34
Preschool, 24
Presenting problems (in childhood),
   152–153
Privacy, 84
Privileges, removal of, 195
Proactive approach, 7
Proactive structure, 168
Proactive structuring, 127–128
Problem behavior, 4–6
   externalizing disorder as, 97
   group therapy contraindicated for,
      211
   science of, 15
Problem-focused assessment, 133–134
Problem normalizing, 82
Problem solving, 62, 98, 99, 231–232

Process, content and, 76
Professional and ethical standards,
   250–262
   for collaboration vs. collusion,
      261–262
   for competence, 253–354
   for confidentiality, 258–261
   for cultural awareness, 256–258
   for custody clarification, 254–256
   five Cs of, 252
Professional experiences, 82
Professional ignorance, 253
Prosocial behavior, 62–63
Prosocial talk, 37
Psychoeducational model, 177, 179, 185,
   187, 188
Psychopathology
   in children/adolescents, 19–23
   differences in, 95
   literature on developmental, 15
   threshold warranting diagnosis of, 16
Psychoses, 23
Puberty, 94
Punitive parenting, 102, 198
Puppet interview, 84

Question–answer process, 160

Racial identity, 179
Rapport, 153–156
Reactivity, 42
Real situations, hypothetical vs., 41
Reconnecting Youth program, 206
Record keeping, 245
Reflection, 174
Reframing, 110–111, 150
Reimbursement policies, 126, 221, 242
Reinforcement, positive. See Positive
   reinforcement
Relationship building, 60–64, 128
Relationship Process Code, 44
Relationship processes, 94
Relationship quality, 98, 99
Relationships, 4
   of groups in small communities, 193
   lack of correlation across, 33, 34
   quality of, 189
   systems of, 16
   types of, 32–34

Remarriage, 10
Report, FCU, 122
Requests, making effective, 126–127
Resistance to change, 52
    minimizing, 170, 171
    and motivation, 65
    and therapist, 220
    tools for preventing/managing,
        173–174
Resistance to praise, 194–195
Resistance to therapy, 160
Resources, knowledge of available, 121
Respect, 72, 74, 119
Responsibility
    of client, 112
    of therapist, 174, 246
Responsive parenting, 165
Restraining orders, 77
Rewards, 63, 129, 194–196
Rights of patient, 151
Risk, 153–154
Role-play, 156, 159, 166, 168, 214, 233
Routines, 197–198
RUM approach, 63
Runaway children, 115

Safety, 245–246
Salience, 44
SANE guidelines, 64, 129–130
Schizophrenia, 7, 23
School(s), 7
    brief family-based interventions in,
        136–139
    context of, 20–22, 28, 75
    group-based child/adolescent inter-
        ventions in, 201
    group-based parenting training in,
        187
    interventions delivered in, 25
School assessment, 75
School phobias, 20
Self-assessment, 116–118, 226, 230
Self-disclosure, 228
Self-efficacy, 112, 113
Self-reflection, 192
Self-regulation, 28, 141, 143–147, 204
    age/gender affecting, 146–147
    caregiver role in, 145
    entrained, 54, 144
    environmental effect on, 145

facets of, 143–144
    interventions to support, 141
    and negativity, 95
    and responsive parenting, 164–165
    of therapist, 226–227
Sensitivity, 51–52
Separation distress, 19
Service delivery system, 59, 235–238
Sexual abuse, 148, 247–249
Sexual activity, 22, 28
Shame, 173
Shyness, 20
Siblings, 38, 46
Skills
    cognitive, 144
    coping, 146, 158
    development of, 167–171, 239
    generalization of, 146
    social environment for reinforcing
        new, 159
    teaching specific, 158–159
Skinner, B. F., 45
Sleeper effect theory, 142
Small consequences (SANE guidelines),
        64, 130
Small-group supervision model, 232, 233
Smokers, 112
Smoking, 205, 208, 209, 213
Social development, 24
Social–emotional development, 153–156
Social-events approach, 42
Social interactions, 31–48
    awareness of, 31, 39–40
    change patterns of, 52
    and contexts, 40
    dynamics in, 34–38
    and EcoFIT model, 8–9
    measurement of, 40–47
    and psychopathology, 39
    types of relationships in, 32–34
Socialization systems, 28
Social maladaptation, 19
    context sensitivity of, 20–23
    and family dynamics, 34–36
    and peer affiliations, 36–38
    referrals for, 20
Social phobia, 20
Social skills, 202, 206
Solutions
    generating alternative, 134
    identifying possible, 134

Space, respecting client's, 84
Spanking, 173
Stability, 94
Standards, professional and ethical. See
    Professional and ethical standards
Stealing, 19
Stepparenting, 179
Stories, 174
Strength-based approach, 160, 167
Strengths, identifying, 116
Structural equation modeling, 96
Structural family therapy, 60, 61
Structure
    and group interventions, 213
    and routine, 197–198
Structured opportunities, 159
Structuring
    of case presentations, 231
    as function, 44–45
    proactive. See Proactive structuring
    of sessions, 174
Student Self-Check, 122
Substance use
    in adolescence, 19
    and comorbidity, 28
    and deviancy training, 46
    and disengaged parents, 179–180
    and EcoFIT model, 54
    and group interventions, 206, 211,
      213
    and monitoring, 26
Success, shaping, 168
Suicide attempts, 215, 246
Summarizing/terminating, 134–135
Summer camp, 205, 215
Supervision
    hierarchy of, 232–233
    individual, 230–234
    as pillar of effective interventions,
      239
Supervision pyramid, 232
Supervision team, 221–230
    alternative views of, 227–228
    context for, 221–223
    emotional reactions of, 226–227
    model-driven interventions used by,
      224–225
    peer support from, 228–230
    videotaping of all contacts by,
      225–226
Supervisors, 220

Support, 52
    for family mental health, 60
    mutual, 235
    as pillar of effective interventions,
      239
    by therapist, 169, 176
    therapist's role in, 80
Support and clarification process, 118

Talkative parents, 194
Teachable units, 168
Teachers
    behavior-management practices for,
      206
    bias of, 103
    initial contacts, 75
    relationships with, 31, 34
    reporting by, 21, 97
    school behavior influenced by, 22
Teaching interactions, 44
Team approach, 220–221
Team supervision, 222–223
Teen Check-Up, 113
Telephone contact, 73, 121, 191
Therapist effects, 71–72, 238
Therapist fidelity, 220, 238
Therapists, 219–239
    accountability of, 66
    in context, 221–223
    importance of, 219–220
    parents blamed by, 155–156
    and pillars of effective interventions,
      238–239
    and question–answer process, 159
    role of peer assumed by, 155
    and service delivery systems,
      235–238
    strategy development for, 230–235
    and supervision team, 223–230
Therapist skills, 167–171
Therapist training, 214
Time-out, 130, 131, 195
Time-sampling coding, 44
Tobacco use, 205, 213
Toys, 154, 155
"Traditional black discipline," 173
Training
    ongoing, 236–238
    standards regarding, 262–263
Training procedures, 224

Traits
    assessing, 96–98
    parenting, 98–100
Trait variance, 95
Transitions, 9–10
Transtheoretical approach, 58, 111–112
Traumatic events, 149, 160
Trust, 249

Understanding, 80–81
Unstructured interview, 153

Verbal cues, 168
Verbal schemas, 45–47
Videotapes/videotaping
    of feedback during assessment, 156

humor in, 192
    in parenting interventions, 184, 185
    for therapist feedback, 225–226
Violent behavior, 46

Warmth, 72
WIC (Women, Infants, and Children),
    25
Women, hostile attitudes toward, 46
Women, Infants, and Children (WIC),
    25
Working with resistance, 220
Worrying, excessive, 39
Writing board, 121

Youth Self-Report Form, 154

ABOUT THE AUTHORS

Thomas J. Dishion, PhD, is both the director of research at the Child and Family Center and a professor of clinical psychology at the University of Oregon. He received his PhD in clinical psychology from the University of Oregon. His interests include understanding the development of antisocial behavior and substance abuse in children and adolescents and designing effective interventions and prevention programs. In particular, he and his colleagues have examined how peer and family dynamics contribute to escalations in adolescent substance use, delinquency, and violence. His intervention research focuses on the effectiveness of family-centered interventions and the negative effects of aggregating youth at high risk into intervention groups. He has published more than 90 scientific reports on these topics, a book for parents about family management, and 2 books for professionals working with troubled children and their families. Previously, he was a research scientist at the Oregon Social Learning Center.

Elizabeth A. Stormshak, PhD, is an associate professor in counseling psychology in the College of Education at the University of Oregon and is also the assistant director of the Child and Family Center. Her primary research focus is on the prevention of problem behavior in early and middle childhood, including substance use, conduct problems, and peer deviance. She has received multiple federal grants to develop and implement prevention programs relevant to both early and middle childhood. Recently, she received a grant from the National Institute on Drug Abuse to implement the Adolescent Transitions Program and Family Check-Up model with a culturally diverse group of urban families. In this project, her research focuses on how to engage families in the intervention process and enhance long-term positive outcomes for youth. Dr. Stormshak is a graduate of Pennsylvania State University, where she received her PhD in clinical psychology. She lives in Eugene, Oregon.

319